# HONEST
# POLITICS NOW

Pam & Joe,

I hope that you enjoy
the book. It was certainly
a labour of love. Mulroney's
pursual on the river continues to
make our lives a challenge!

Rob

# HONEST POLITICS NOW

## WHAT ETHICAL CONDUCT MEANS IN CANADIAN PUBLIC LIFE

EDITED BY IAN GREENE
AND DAVID P. SHUGARMAN

JAMES LORIMER & COMPANY LTD., PUBLISHERS
TORONTO

James Lorimer & Company Ltd., Publishers acknowledges the support of the Ontario Arts Council (OAC), an agency of the Government of Ontario, which in 2015-16 funded 1,676 individual artists and 1,125 organizations in 209 communities across Ontario for a total of $50.5 million. We acknowledge the support of the Canada Council for the Arts, which last year invested $153 million to bring the arts to Canadians throughout the country. This project has been made possible in part by the Government of Canada and with the support of the Ontario Media Development Corporation.

  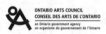 

Cover design: Tyler Cleroux
Cover image: Justin Tang/The Canadian Press

Library and Archives Canada Cataloguing in Publication

Honest politics now : what ethical conduct means in Canadian public life
/ edited by Ian Greene and David P. Shugarman.

Includes bibliographical references and index.
Issued in print and electronic formats.
ISBN 978-1-4594-1241-5 (softcover).--ISBN 978-1-4594-1242-2 (EPUB)

    1. Political ethics--Canada.  2. Political corruption--Canada.  I. Greene, Ian, editor  II. Shugarman, David P., 1943-, editor

JL86.C67H66 2017               172'.2             C2017-901366-1
                                               C2017-901367-X

James Lorimer & Company Ltd., Publishers
117 Peter Street, Suite 304
Toronto, ON, Canada
M5V 0M3
www.lorimer.ca

Printed and bound in Canada.

# Contents

PREFACE TO THE NEW EDITION
Ian Greene and David P. Shugarman     7

CHAPTER 1: ETHICS AND THE PRINCIPLES OF DEMOCRACY
David P. Shugarman, Ian Greene and Naomi Couto     15

CHAPTER 2: ETHICAL DUTIES
David P. Shugarman, Ian Greene and Naomi Couto     40

CHAPTER 3: ETHICAL PROBLEMS IN PUBLIC LIFE
Ian Greene, David P. Shugarman and Robert Shepherd     60

CHAPTER 4: CASE STUDIES: CONFLICTS OF INTEREST AND ENTITLEMENT
Ian Greene and Robert Shepherd     95

CHAPTER 5: ETHICS COMMISSIONS
Ian Stedman and Ian Greene     124

CHAPTER 6 : MONEY IN POLITICS: THE ETHICS OF ELECTION FINANCE
REGULATION AND EXPENSE CLAIMS OVERSIGHT
Lori Turnbull, Ian Greene and Robert Shepherd     154

CHAPTER 7: ETHICS OF LOBBYING AND INFLUENCE
Robert Shepherd     179

CHAPTER 8: WHISTLE-BLOWING AND ETHICAL PRACTICE
Robert Shepherd     207

CHAPTER 9: MUNICIPAL ETHICS ISSUES
Gregory Levine and Naomi Couto     237

CHAPTER 10: DIRTY HANDS, DECEPTION AND DUPLICITY
David P. Shugarman and Shaun Young     267

CHAPTER 11: WHY ETHICAL POLITICS IS ESSENTIAL
David P. Shugarman and Ian Greene     312

CONTRIBUTORS     332

ACKNOWLEDGEMENTS     334

NOTES     338

SELECTED REFERENCES     376

INDEX     384

*To our families*
*with the hope that ethical politics will become a fact of their lives*
*and to*
*every public official with integrity, and the courage to practise it.*

# PREFACE TO THE NEW EDITION
## Ian Greene and David P. Shugarman

This book presents a framework for sorting out right from wrong in politics. It doesn't claim to have all the answers. Readers will no doubt disagree at times with some of our suggested courses of action. But sustained with good will and a democratic sensibility, we Canadians can make progress. Indeed, we believe the country has already contributed more than most in terms of developing procedures that could lead to an ethical democracy. In typically Canadian fashion, however, we have done little to publicize these innovations.

The original edition of *Honest Politics* was published in 1997 with Ian Greene and David Shugarman as co-authors. By 2016, there had been so many changes in Canada's ethics regimes, and sadly, so many new ethics scandals to analyze, that Greene and Shugarman agreed to spearhead a new and updated edition — but only if they could involve younger scholars whose involvement would allow Greene and Shugarman to remain mostly retired. We are delighted to be joined by six other contributors, all of whom are as committed as we are to advancing ethical politics in Canada. Although we apply the same general framework for ethical analysis as the 1997 edition, most of the examples to which we refer are new. And although the advance of ethics regimes in our political system since 1997 is promising, the need for further reforms is just as urgent today as it was then.

This book is primarily about the ethical expectations and standards that govern the conduct of elected officials. In this respect we concentrate on the ethics of political processes and the behaviour of politicians and occasionally their top political associates and organizers. In so doing, we focus on four key areas of misconduct, each of which constitutes a betrayal of the public's trust in the integrity of government. These are conflicts of interest, undue influence, improper use of public office (involving deception, duplicity and/or the suppression of information) and what we call "dirty-handed politics." Each of these constitutes an example of abuse of trust, itself a departure from the duty to behave ethically according to the principles of democracy. As such, we view a number of actions as ethical wrongs even when they are not deemed illegal, such as making false promises or lying about one's opponents or padding expense claims. We examine both the most troubling aspects of abuses of trust, and the growth in regulations at all levels of government that are aimed at reining them in. We are convinced that a clear understanding of these subjects is necessary to ensure a commitment to democratic practices in serving the public.

Except in passing we have tried to avoid discussing ideological disputes over the content and direction of public policy. To be sure, other issues require serious attention, such as gender inequality, the treatment of Aboriginal Canadians and the ethics of public policy more generally, but we believe these issues are so important they deserve separate books.

Greene's and Shugarman's views about ethical politics have been heavily influenced by their reflections on their own past experiences in politics, which began when they were undergraduate students at the University of Alberta in the 1960s. Although they did not know each other at the time — they met as colleagues at York University in the 1980s — they both became fascinated by the relation between ethics and politics after taking political theory classes taught by Tom Pocklington, who became president of the Canadian Political Science Association when *Honest Politics* was first published in 1997.

Shugarman's introduction to active politics was knocking on doors for the Alberta NDP. In Edmonton West he campaigned on behalf of Pocklington, who was an NDP candidate for the provincial legislature. Shugarman and the future prime minister, Joe Clark, became friends while classmates in Pocklington's advanced political theory class. However, Clark failed to get Shugarman involved in Davie Fulton's bid for the leadership of the Conservative Party. As a lark, Shugarman started a new party called the Constitutionalist Party for the University of Alberta model parliament, where he campaigned against Preston Manning, then leader of the campus Social Credit Party. Both Shugarman and Manning ended up sitting on the opposition side of the House, trying to bring down the "uppity" Liberals.

When Greene entered first year at the University of Alberta in 1966, he got to know Clark through another model parliament. Under Clark's influence, Greene joined the Campus Conservatives, on whose executive he later served. He was an alternate delegate at the 1967 "dump Dief" Conservative leadership convention in Toronto, and a year later became campaign manager for Robert Thompson in Red Deer after Thompson abandoned the leadership of the Social Credit Party to join the Conservatives in time for the federal election. In the early 1970s, Greene worked as the executive assistant to a cabinet minister in Peter Lougheed's government for a year, and a few years later he worked for a time as a middle manager in Alberta Social Services. After finishing graduate school, he decided that academic research did not mix with active politics. Shugarman, however, has occasionally been involved in NDP campaigns in Toronto, though, like Greene, he is not a formal member of any political party. Lest Liberal supporters feel left out, we admit that we have both occasionally voted Liberal, and during the 2015 election, Greene volunteered as a scrutineer for the Liberals in Toronto Parkdale–High Park. At graduate school at the University of

Toronto one of us (Shugarman) even had a roommate who went on to become the leader of the Ontario Liberals and, eventually, premier (David Peterson).

We mention these things not to indulge in name-dropping but to emphasize that both of us know and understand practical politics and politicians. The analysis and recommendations in the chapters that follow don't come out of an insulated ivory tower. Without our experiences in active politics — the hope of electoral victory, the sting of defeat, the feelings of intense partisanship, the extreme pressure to make your candidate look good at all costs — it would have been difficult to analyze the relationship between ethics and politics from the perspective of participants in the political process. Our role as academics, by contrast, has given us the opportunity to reflect on these experiences and put them into a broader theoretical perspective.

Our new co-authors' range of experience and academic rigour has added breadth to this book. Each of the new co-authors has either helped to revise an original chapter or has taken the lead in writing a new one. Chapter 5 of the 1997 edition, "Undue Influence," has evolved into two new chapters on party financing and lobbyist regulation, respectively, and new chapters dealing with whistle-blowing and municipal ethics issues have been added as well. Although all eight of us were assigned a lead or revision role in one or more chapters, Greene and Shugarman retained responsibility for the direction, themes and overall coherence of the book, as well as the final editorial decisions and the overall conclusion. Both of us took responsibility for reviewing each chapter as it was drafted; however, Greene did the lion's share of detailed editing, updating and collating along the way.

Robert Shepherd is a professor at Carleton University, and is president of the Canadian Association of Programs in Public Administration. Prior to 2007, when Shepherd began his academic career, he gained extensive experience working in the federal public service. He is the lead author of the chapters on whistle-blowing and lobbyists (Chapters 7 and 8), and he played an important part in drafting revisions to Chapters 3, 4, 6 and 11. He also made helpful comments regarding Chapters 1 and 2. Ian Stedman, who at the time of writing was a PhD student at Osgoode Hall Law School at York University, had worked for more than three years in the Office of the Integrity Commissioner of Ontario and sat on the Research Ethics Board at Toronto's Hospital for Sick Children. He is the lead author of Chapter 5 (on ethics commissions) and assisted with the research on case studies for Chapter 5 (on lobbying). Lori Turnbull wrote a PhD dissertation at Dalhousie University on the Canadian approach to tackling conflict of interest issues, and is a professor at Carleton University seconded to the Government of Canada's Privy Council Office. She is the lead author of Chapter 6 (on election financing). Greg Levine has had a long career in ethics and law, including his work with the Office of the Ombudsman in British Columbia. He has been the integrity commissioner for several Ontario municipalities, and has written several books on the law of government ethics. He is the lead author of Chapter 9 (on municipal ethics). Naomi Couto is a professor of public policy and administration at York University. She does research into policing, women and the law and ethics issues in the public sector. She was of considerable assistance in updating Chapters 1 and 2, and in the drafting of Chapter 9 (on municipal ethics issues). Shaun Young has a PhD in political science, an MA in applied ethics and many years of experience in the Ontario public service, as well as in administrative and teaching roles at the University of Toronto. He worked with David Shugarman on the revisions to Chapter 10 (on dirty hands).

Chapter 1 begins with the argument that ethical politics is a requirement for democratic government. We then turn in Chapter 2 to the ethical duties that are the basis for the more specific codes of ethical conduct. Chapter 3 argues that conflicts of interest, patronage, undue influence (including some lobbying and election-financing practices) and abuse of trust are incompatible with any idea of democracy that flows from mutual respect. Chapter 4 presents case studies of conflicts of interest and other kinds of abuse of trust. Chapter 5 describes Canadian experiments in the enforcement of political ethics through conflict of interest and ethics commissioners. Chapter 6 considers money and politics and examines various attempts by federal and provincial governments, dating from the 1970s, to constrain undue influence by both publicizing and placing limits on campaign contributions and fundraisers. It also highlights the politics of expense claim abuse. Chapter 7 reviews lobbying legislation across Canada and presents several case studies about the impact of this legislation. Whistle-blowing legislation in Canada is described in Chapter 8, along with three key whistle-blowing cases. Chapter 9 considers the growing field of municipal ethics legislation, which to some extent reflects federal and provincial legislation, but is distinct because municipal systems, unlike their provincial and federal counterparts, are not parliamentary in character. In Chapter 10, we consider "dirty-handed politics" — unethical behaviour rationalized as serving the public good. Finally, in Chapter 11 we highlight some key proposals for new and/or stronger institutionalized supports for ethical conduct.

Between 1992 and 2005, a number of workshops on ethical politics were held at York University and sponsored by the York Centre for Practical Ethics (now the York Collegium for Practical Ethics, or YCPE) and York's McLaughlin College. Thanks to a grant from the Social Sciences and Humanities Research Council of Canada, the YCPE brought together leading politicians, public servants, academics and journalists to discuss ethical issues in contemporary Canadian politics in 1992 and 1994. Their insights inspired the publication of *Honest Politics* in 1997.

If there is a single factor most likely to sap the vitality of a nation, it is political corruption. It has eaten away at the people's trust on a number of occasions. Such was the case in New Brunswick in 2010, when Shawn Graham became the first premier to lose an election after only one term in office. In the 1990s, serious ethical issues caused people to lose trust in Bill Vander Zalm's government in British Columbia and Grant Devine's in Saskatchewan in the 1990s, to the point where the provincial parties they represented (Social Credit in B.C. and Progressive Conservative in Saskatchewan) are now moribund. The sponsorship scandal was a major cause of the fall of the federal Liberal government in 2006. In 2015, the Senate expenses scandal was a major factor in the defeat of the federal Conservative government. And too often, abuse of trust is also prevalent at the municipal level, as indicated by the sad saga of Toronto's former mayor, Rob Ford, who not only embarrassed the city by smoking crack cocaine during his tenure, but was nearly booted out of office by the courts in 2013 for blatantly ignoring conflict of interest rules. As well, Joe Fontana, the former mayor of London, Ontario, was handed a jail term in 2014 for breach of trust.

Many consider the notion of "ethical politics" to be an oxymoron. They want ethics in politics, but as case after case of wrongdoing is uncovered they consider this a lost cause. But however much the people may come to expect a certain level of corruption among their elected official, they don't find this acceptable. And yet we have a long way to go before our children can inherit a country in which ethical politics is as much a requirement of our democracy as are free and fair elections, judicial independence and human rights. Ethical politics will undoubtedly be a major preoccupation of the next few decades.

Ethics tends to be a controversial subject among politicians, academics and the public at large. The subject has profoundly personal overtones and is easily connected to feelings of guilt, self-righteousness, blame or outrage. We certainly are not setting ourselves up as paragons of virtue. In fact, the more we have reasoned through ethical issues, the more we have become aware of our own shortcomings — past and present. But it is better to treat these failings as opportunities for learning than as triggers for self-flagellation. Ethics is primarily about respect for people. And unless we respect the right to be wrong while working for improvements in how politics is practised, we are unlikely to make any progress towards a more honest political system.

We look forward to a time when Canadians are as adept at electing ethical politicians as they currently are at turfing out the corrupt ones they have unwittingly put in office. We also look forward to the time when universities and colleges will require the subject of ethical politics in their political science and public administration courses. We hope that this book will make a modest contribution to this end.

— Ian Greene and David P. Shugarman
Toronto and Victoria, April 2017

# CHAPTER 1
# ETHICS AND THE PRINCIPLES OF DEMOCRACY

## David P. Shugarman, Ian Greene and Naomi Couto

"A Legislative Assembly comprised of members committed
to the principles of honesty and integrity is fundamental to a
democratic society as Canadians understand that term."
— Mr. Justice Isadore Grotsky[1]

The integrity of our elected representatives depends on their following fundamental democratic principles and fulfilling their duties to their fellow citizens. It also requires well-functioning, responsive institutions, good laws, exemplary conduct by those at the top and a political culture supportive of ethical governing practices.

There are many reasons for Canadians to feel optimistic about progress being made to improve ethical governance at the municipal, provincial and federal levels. New institutions and agencies of ethics officers, clearer conflict of interest laws and guidelines, and various systems of monitoring the actions of our representatives have developed to strengthen ethical conduct. This book will provide an examination of many of these new steps, as well as arguments for their introduction and potential efficacy. These developments, however, owe much to the fact that the late twentieth and early twenty-first centuries were not good times for honest politics in Canada, as the following examples, in no particular order of shameful severity, will attest.

**Item 1:** In September 1995 Lorne McLaren, Premier Grant Devine's labour minister, was sentenced to three and a half years in jail for his part in a scheme that defrauded the people of Saskatchewan of nearly $850,000 from 1987 to 1991. The strategy, which had been approved at the highest levels of the Saskatchewan Progressive Conservative caucus, diverted funds earmarked for constituency communications expenses to numbered companies, and from there into the pockets of Conservative MLAs and cabinet ministers as a form of personal reward. Eventually, eight members of the Devine cabinet were convicted of fraud, including Eric Berntson, the former deputy premier of Saskatchewan. When, in 2001, the Supreme Court of Canada denied Berntson's appeal and upheld his conviction and one-year jail term, he resigned the Senate seat he'd been appointed to by Prime Minister Brian Mulroney back in 1990.[2]

**Item 2:** Between June 1993 and December 1994, former Prime Minister Brian Mulroney accepted envelopes stuffed with thousand dollar bills from a businessman named Karlheinz Schreiber at three secretive meetings (one in downtown Montreal, another at Mirabel Airport and a third at a New York hotel). Later, Mr. Schreiber claimed he handed over $100,000 each time; Mr. Mulroney claimed each envelope *only* contained $75,000.[3]

Mr. Schreiber was known in government circles to have been a lobbyist for arms dealers and companies manufacturing major passenger jets and helicopters. The aircraft company that he represented was the major European consortium Airbus Industrie, the same company which a few years earlier had been awarded a major contract from the Mulroney government to sell large commercial jetliners to Air Canada (at the time a government-owned airline). The Oliphant inquiry into the scandalous Mulroney-Schreiber relationship found that the funds for these payments came from commissions paid by Airbus to Mr. Schreiber for his lobbying activities. Commissioner Oliphant also emphasized that the first of the payments to Mr. Mulroney took place shortly after his resignation as prime minister but while he was still a sitting member of Parliament. Additionally and significantly, the commissioner noted that no paper records were kept of the reasons for the payments or of the amounts involved.

Furthermore, although Mr. Mulroney initially claimed that he didn't know Mr. Schreiber well and that he saw him only infrequently, it emerged from the public inquiry and subsequent newspaper reports that they had known each other for two decades and, according to Mr. Mulroney's chief of staff, met often during Mulroney's final years in office. Although Mr. Mulroney initially failed to declare his payments as income to the Canada Revenue Agency, he did so about five years after the last payment.

These already troublesome aspects of the scandal were further compounded by the fact that in 1997, almost nine years prior to the revelations of secret payments, Mr. Mulroney was awarded $2.1 million by Canada's Department of Justice, along with an apology, to settle his claim that he had been defamed by a department initiative that was leaked to the press. The department had, on behalf of the RCMP, written to Swiss authorities requesting assistance in investigating Mr. Mulroney and Mr. Schreiber allegedly engaging in fraud regarding the purchase of thirty-four Airbus jets. During the preliminary proceedings in Mr. Mulroney's defamation lawsuit, government lawyers asked him about his relationship with Mr. Schreiber after he resigned as PM. He claimed they had met only once or twice for coffee, and he never mentioned their secret meetings, or his acceptance of the covert payments. (All of this was subsequently detailed in the Oliphant inquiry.) In Commissioner Oliphant's carefully worded but nevertheless searing summation, the former prime minister's attempted rationalizations were described as incredible and "patently absurd" and his conduct deemed "inappropriate." According to the commissioner, "Mr. Mulroney's actions failed to enhance public confidence in the integrity of public office holders."[4]

After the Oliphant inquiry wrapped up,[5] Mr. Schreiber, who had dual Canadian-German citizenship, was extradited to Germany, where he was convicted of tax evasion and sentenced to six years in prison. Here in Canada, Mr. Mulroney was never charged with anything; the RCMP apparently ceased its investigations of the matter. His role, or lack thereof, in facilitating a huge contract to purchase Airbus aircraft remains a matter of speculation. This is a sad postscript to the career of a prime minister who led the charge amongst Commonwealth nations against apartheid in South Africa, and it is perhaps indicative of the fragility of ethical reasoning amongst those who possess great power.

**Item 3:** Shortly after Mr. Mulroney pocketed his third secret cash payment the Jean Chrétien-led Liberals trounced the Progressive Conservative Party in a general election. Soon thereafter, the Prime Minister's Office, reacting to the separatist Parti Québécois almost winning a referendum on independence, devised a largely secretive program to weaken support for separatism in Quebec and strengthen national unity. The program stressed the importance of Canada to Quebecers; it used advertising campaigns to remind Quebecers of federally supported institutions and programs in their province and increased funding for special community events and activities in Quebec. The plan, dubbed the Sponsorship Program, eventually became known as the sponsorship scandal, or the Adscam affair, and was the subject of a report by both Canada's Auditor General and a major public inquiry headed by Justice John Gomery.[6] These investigations revealed that the program's disbursements involved around $100 million of unaccounted for spending and serious violations of government rules and regulations, especially when it came to transparency and accountability measures. In some cases, invoices were submitted and paid, though work was never actually performed. On top of that, in an elaborate kickback scheme, portions of money paid out to various communications firms found their way back into the hands of agents charging special commission fees, portions of which ended up in the coffers of the Quebec branch of the Liberal Party of Canada. The section head in charge of government advertising within the Public Works and

Government Services Department was permitted a great deal of leeway and managed to bypass the oversight role of his seniors within the department. And early on considerable latitude was given to private ad agencies to administer much of the program. Additionally, the minister in charge of the department "became directly involved in decisions to provide funding to events and projects for partisan [party] purposes, having little to do with considerations of national unity."[7] On top of these misadventures no one at either the cabinet or senior-civil-service level would take responsibility for how and why so many things went wrong with the program management.

The fallout from the scandal was considerable. The heads of three crown corporations lost their jobs when it was found that money from their sectors was transferred inappropriately to fund program activities. As a result of RCMP investigations, several individuals were found guilty of numerous fraud charges: the man who ran the program from Public Works was sentenced to three and a half years in prison, and two owners of major communications firms with ties to the Quebec branch of the federal Liberals were sentenced to prison terms of between one and a half and two and a half years.[8] And one of the key figures accused by the Gomery inquiry of orchestrating kickback schemes, Jacques Corriveau, was convicted of defrauding the federal government of $6.5 million late in 2016.[9] In 2017 he was sentenced to four years in prison, and fined $1.4 million. (His sentence appeal will not likely be heard until 2019.)[10] One cabinet minister, Minister of Public Works and Government Services Alfonso Gagliano, was criticized by Commissioner Gomery for allowing the Sponsorship Program to operate without proper oversight. However, no senior member of government was ever taken to court. It was left to voters to punish the Liberals. They did so by refusing to re-elect the party the first chance they got.

**Item 4:** In the 2006 general election Liberal David Emerson was re-elected as a member of Parliament for the riding of Vancouver-Kingsway. Mr. Emerson had served as minister for industry during Paul

Martin's brief reign as prime minister following Jean Chrétien's resignation. However, the Conservatives, led by Steven Harper, defeated the Liberals in that year's election. This was partly a result of the sponsorship scandal and Mr. Harper's promise to bring in new measures to insure greater accountability and integrity. Two weeks later, and without serving a single day in the new parliament, Mr. Emerson stunned political observers, his own campaign team and his constituents when he announced that he was taking the role of Minister of International Trade in Prime Minister Harper's new Conservative government. After vociferously criticizing Mr. Harper and his party during the election, and soundly defeating his Conservative opponent in Vancouver-Kingsway, Mr. Emerson thumbed his nose at the voting public and jumped to the winning side, at Mr. Harper's invitation.[11]

These are glaring examples of unethical practices, what ethicists call *abuses of trust*. Once revealed, such practices weaken the public's confidence and trust in their politicians and in the functioning of their democracy.

When public officials abuse the trust that is placed in them by securing special benefits for themselves or their friends, we say they have acted unethically. In doing so they violate the principles of equality and respect — the very cornerstones of democracy. But some public officials justify unethical practices as the necessary means to achieve good results. For example, throughout the early 1970s members of the RCMP were involved in a succession of shady, duplicitous practices known as the "dirty tricks" campaign. According to the McDonald Royal Commission on the RCMP, officers were involved in break-ins, wiretapping, incidents of disinformation, illegal mail openings and scare tactics; they also spied on political parties and members of Parliament. Members of the force who testified before the Royal Commission saw nothing wrong with these actions because from their perspective they participated in these activities for the greater good of Canadians as a whole. Not a single member of the Liberal government then in power was willing to take responsibility for what happened, despite the admission of a former chief of security services in Quebec that certain illegalities, such as opening mail and theft, "were so commonplace they were no longer thought of as illegal."[12]

We call this second type of ethical misconduct "dirty-handed politics." It occurs when leaders feel embattled and regard politics as a form of warfare. Convinced that their cause is right — and their opponents' wrong — they will do or authorize to be done anything that they believe is needed. They reason that it is often necessary for representatives to "get their hands dirty" by resorting to unscrupulous tactics to pursue their version of the public good. Compared to using public office for private purposes and siphoning off public monies into private hands, dirty-handed politics is clearly a different kind of political corruption. What these corrupt practices have in common is that they violate democratic procedures and undermine democratic values.

Ethics concerns the way people *ought* to act in their relations with one another. Throughout history, humans have wrestled with tough ethical issues. Because the opportunities for human action are enormous and constantly changing, no set of ethical principles and applications can determine what ought to constitute appropriate behaviour in every situation. Reasonable people who accept the same principles can disagree about how those principles should apply. The value of an ethical approach is that it provides an opportunity to work out resolutions to difficult situations reasonably and in an environment of social co-operation. And, to the extent that there are constants underlying and informing ethical conduct, persons exercising their moral autonomy do so while respecting the rights of others.

## MUTUAL RESPECT

Democracy is founded on the principles of equality and respect for all individuals. Mutual respect involves a shared understanding and commitment among and by citizens that every person is entitled to be treated as a social being with intrinsic worth no matter her or his special attributes, standing in society or lack of the same; that all persons are, as the eighteenth-century German philosopher Immanuel Kant put it, essentially "ends in themselves" rather than conveniences or instruments for others' desires or needs.[13] It means that we expect others not to treat us as fodder, or commodities, of value only because of our usefulness to their purposes and interests; and we recognize a like obligation and disposition owed to others. It means that everyone has, and needs to be able to exercise, basic rights necessary to personal autonomy and self-expression.

Mutual respect is not to be confused with people finding each other likeable or agreeable. It is not about a mutual admiration society of clothing styles, choice of music or food, the sharing of religious preferences or agreeing on whom to vote for and why. Rather, it is about each person respecting another's equal right to make choices, to be different, including the right to be wrong come election time (even when we *know,* or think, we're right). It involves *our* acceptance of the results of voting and the other side winning, insofar as they respect our right to differ and work towards getting our side, our party, in power the next time.

Several factors have led to the ascendance of mutual respect in the world's democracies. First, the world's religions have undoubtedly played a major role. Not only do religions concern themselves with ethics, but also the ethical principles held by most religions tend to have a lot in common. Among these principles is the belief that every human being has equal worth, and therefore is equally deserving of respect. Indeed, this tenet is so pervasive that it has survived movements to quell it and has had a major impact not only on the institutional structures of religious organizations, but also on their adherents' views about democratic government. Among secular humanists who have rejected religion but still seek guiding principles around which to organize their lives and their society, there are few who would reject the "golden rule": do to others as you would have them do to you.

Second, the philosophy of liberalism also contributed to the prominence of the principle of mutual respect. Liberalism first developed in

England during the turbulent seventeenth century, when civil wars were fought between those who believed that a peaceful and orderly society would result only through a monarch with absolute authority and those who held that government must exist by the consent of "the people." The liberals' victory in the Glorious Revolution of 1688 has had a profound impact on the history of the democratic world. The philosophy of liberalism is complex and has many variants; but the essentials are that mutual respect implies government by consent of the governed, and as much individual freedom as is consistent with safeguarding the equal freedom and security of others. Liberalism broke the stranglehold that the land-owning classes had previously held over the economy, and established the sovereignty of the people in government. The ideals of liberalism powered the American Revolution and enormously influenced Canada's evolution.

But with liberalism, as with any grand philosophy, there has always been a gap between ideals and reality. Early liberalism's emphasis on equality of opportunity for material enrichment in a free-enterprise economy resulted in considerable inequalities between those successful in trade and commerce on the one hand and labourers and the unemployed on the other. Furthermore, early liberalism denied women (except royalty) and men from the lower classes (a majority of the adult male population) any voice in government. As liberalism experienced pressure from those demanding inclusion in politics and criticisms from both socialists and conservatives, it adapted itself to democratic governance and the universal franchise.

Representative democracy with a universal franchise is a relatively recent invention. Its development coincided with the increasing importance of mutual respect in the evolution of liberal ideology, as we noted earlier. But the gap between ideals and practice alluded to above explains, in part, the fact that ethical practices do not always reflect the standard of mutual respect. As the protection of human rights and the maintenance of social obligations are taken more seriously, more attention ought to be devoted to ethics in government. It has only been since the enactment of the *Charter of Rights and Freedoms* that Canadians have begun to focus strongly on ethics issues, and so naturally there is still a lot of work to do.[14] Democratic ethics concerns rights and responsibilities. A focus on the ethical misconduct of politicians examines the nature of abuses of the right to govern and derelictions of responsibilities to citizens.

## FIVE PRINCIPLES OF DEMOCRACY

There are five principles of democracy that follow from mutual respect: social equality, free and fair elections with deference to the majority, minority rights, freedom, and integrity. A familiarity with these principles provides a foundation for judging ethical behaviour in the public sphere and for resolving ethical questions in a democratic context.

### Social Equality

There is no doubt about the importance of social equality to Canada's political culture today. Although this belief does not always translate into action, and media stories about racism in police practice or sexism in the workplace are relatively frequent, the public's belief in social equality is probably at an all-time high.

The support for social equality can be traced in part to early liberalism, which advocated free and equal access to the marketplace for entrepreneurs, regardless of their social background. Although early liberals felt that social class did not constitute a legitimate reason for limiting equality, they accepted the unequal position of men without property and women in general. But the rhetoric of liberalism encouraged the lower classes to press for a broader application of equality. As Macpherson and others show, women and working-class men demanded equality in the right to vote and more equality in social and economic decision making than capitalism already provided.[15] Ultimately, this helped to transform liberal societies into liberal democracies.

The equality principle in Western political thought has been interpreted in a variety of ways. The theories of equality can be divided roughly into two categories: formal equality and social equality. Formal equality, which has two aspects, is the narrowest approach. First, it suggests that those in similar situations should all be treated the same way. For example, in 1973 the Supreme Court's decision in *Lavell* implied that as long as all Indian women in Canada are treated equally by the law, then the requirement of equality under the *Canadian Bill of Rights* is satisfied, even if Indian men receive more favourable treatment.[16] Second, formal equality emphasizes removing legal or institutional barriers to choice, but without providing the means to make choice a real possibility. Formal equality therefore grants everyone an equal right to vote and an equal right to stand for election, but it does not guarantee everyone equal access to and influence on parliamentarians between elections. And unless one has the time, experience and money, the chances of participating meaningfully as a candidate for election are slim. A simple scenario can exemplify formal legal equality and its limitations: In a society that prohibits religious, racial or sexual discrimination, everyone has the right to register at a first-class hotel. But of course that right does not mean much to those who cannot afford to stay at such a hotel. Much like the universal right to spend the night under a bridge, only some will avail themselves of the opportunity.

Theories of social equality begin with the assumptions that all humans deserve to be treated as equals and that the real-life situations of disadvantaged groups need to be considered to ensure that equality is not just a hollow promise. There are many variations on this theory, ranging from those that propose only slight adjustments to the rules of formal equality to those that advocate affirmative action programs to facilitate the formal equality of groups subject to unfair discrimination.[17]

The Supreme Court's decision in *Lavell* was vehemently attacked for its narrow approach to equality, and after the *Charter of Rights and Freedoms* came into effect, the court rejected formal in favour of social equality as a means of interpreting the *Charter*.[18] The Supreme Court's preference appears to reflect the views of many Canadians. A survey of the attitudes towards civil liberties conducted by Peter Russell and others in the late 1980s found that 72 per cent of Canadians disagreed with the statement, "Some people are better than others," and 73 per cent disagreed with the proposition that "all races are certainly not equal"; this support for equality is reflected in more recent surveys.[19] There is undoubtedly much greater support for social equality in Canada in 2017 than there was several decades earlier.

This concern with equality may be in part a response to the media coverage of the American civil rights movement and similar movements in Canada that have fought for the equal treatment for women, visible minorities, the disabled and the elderly since the Second World War. It may also reflect the emphasis that liberal ideology has placed on a broader notion of equality since the late 1800s, and which was furthered by the socialist movement in the twentieth century.[20]

Consistent with this trend, the equality clause in the *Charter of Rights and Freedoms* attempted to broaden the scope of legally enforceable equality provisions in Canada by expanding the more limited provisions contained in the 1960 *Canadian Bill of Rights*. In particular, section 15(1) of the *Charter* guarantees the "equal benefit of the law," which makes it one of the most far-reaching equality clauses of any modern bill of rights.[21]

Although there is an increased demand for and acceptance of practices that promote greater social equality, there is certainly no general consensus about how far social equality should go. Such issues as pay equity, compulsory retirement, the segregation of adolescent sporting associations according to gender, the "right to die with dignity," the equal treatment under the law of sex workers and discriminatory auto-insurance rates have sparked controversy over how social equality should be implemented. The issues of government contracts and judicial appointments could be added to this list. Should decisions be made impartially — that is, based on equal opportunity modified by merit? Or should supporters of the party in power be given preference, and if so, in which situations? Although many of our governments are led by decision makers who believe that economic efficiencies should take priority over measures to lessen social inequality, and that moves towards greater equality are sometimes "too costly,"[22] the overall trend in public expectations and attitudes seems to be an acceptance of higher levels of social equality.

With regard to gender equality, public officials have an ethical responsibility to treat women and men with equal concern and respect, but there are a number of obstacles that stand in the way of this ideal. There remains the legacy of sexism in our society. This has led not only to a tendency to pay men more than their female counterparts in the workplace, but to various forms of unequal treatment in the political arena as well: from the sometimes dearth of washrooms for female legislators and judges in many legislative buildings and court houses to a shortage of day-care facilities for parents who enter public life. The failure of too many men to accept an equitable share of the responsibility for child care has had a profound effect on many women's opportunities to join public life — both in elected and appointed positions. And masculine stereotypes of expected behaviour continue to dominate theories of political interaction, from international relations to domestic party politics. When "manly" virtues are emphasized in politics, as they are in competitive sports, women are often discouraged from participating and encouraged to remain on the sidelines.[23] However, times are slowly changing, as evidenced by the achievement of gender parity in Canada's cabinet in 2015, and occasional gender equality amongst judges in Canadian courts.[24]

Ethical politics clearly requires the full and equal participation of women in public life. However, as with debates over social or economic policy, this important and complex issue cannot be adequately addressed within the framework of this book, which focuses on the conduct of politicians and the procedures that need to be followed to avoid abuses of power.

Sexual practices become relevant to the public sphere whenever public officials attempt to use their office to obtain sexual favours, but there are hopeful signs that sexual harassment is no longer tolerated in our political institutions. For example, in November 2014, Justin Trudeau expelled two male members of his caucus for engaging in what he considered to be inappropriate and unwanted sexual advances towards female members of another caucus.[25] In 2016, Trudeau fired a male cabinet minister for allegedly carrying on an inappropriate sexual relation with a female staff member.[26] Although the facts of this latter case were still in dispute at the time of writing, there is no dispute about whether sexual harassment is ever ethically acceptable.

The greater emphasis placed on social equality during the past few decades may explain why Canadians seem more concerned than ever about not just gender-related breaches in political ethics, but a whole spectrum of issues. In the past, if ministers exercised discretionary powers to reward their friends (whether personal or political), their relatives or themselves, such practices were tolerated, though rarely applauded, as the inevitable consequences of the political process. Today, however, Canadians are less complacent about such practices.

## Free and Fair Elections with Deference to the Majority

The principle of mutual respect suggests that everyone in a particular community should have an equal opportunity to participate in the decision-making process. In small communities, a decision reached by consensus, once everyone has had a chance to be heard, makes the most sense. Such an approach has for centuries been an important part of the decision-making process in many of North America's Aboriginal communities.[27] In Canada, consensus-based decision making often occurs naturally in communities that are small enough to be governed by all their members — for example, in families, parental associations in small schools, in academic departments and in small churches, synagogues or mosques. But when disagreements cannot be resolved through discussion and compromise, a majority vote is a fair, though far from ideal, way of settling the issue. It is fair because everyone in the community has an equal right to vote; it is not ideal because the losers in a vote are sometimes treated as inferior to the winners.

Most communities are too large for consensus-based decision

making; the solution in these cases is to provide for intermittent elections to select community representatives who can then make decisions as trustees. From an ethical perspective, both the elections and the subsequent decision-making process must demonstrate mutual respect.

Deference to the majority is not as simple as "majority rule." Every effort must be made to find a broad consensus. When that is not possible, then the issue should be settled by a majority vote. But representatives must be selected fairly, and they need to be in a position to make fair decisions. Fairness means that speakers from all sides have a right to be heard, that the decision makers are not in a position to benefit personally (i.e., present no conflict of interest), that undue influence — pressure contrary to democratic principles — is not brought to bear on decision makers and that no decision violates the basic principles of democracy. This latter point means that in order to treat minority groups with equal respect, their basic entitlements in a democracy, their "rights," must be protected.

## Minority rights

Even when minorities are on the losing side of an issue, they still have the right to be treated with equal concern and respect. There is a tendency for majorities to disregard minorities in their haste to achieve their goals, and so all democracies have developed mechanisms to remind us of our philosophical commitment to respect minorities. In Canada, these safeguards are to be found in the *Canadian Charter of Rights and Freedoms*, the *Canadian Bill of Rights*, the various provincial bills of rights and the federal and provincial human rights acts. Minority rights are also reflected in parliamentary and legislative rules and conventions. The rules of debate and the practice of providing major opposition parties with official status and resources are all intended to allow the opposition a full hearing.

Human rights legislation is an attempt to list the most important ways in which all members of society, and in particular minorities and the less advantaged, deserve to be treated with equal concern and respect. For example, the *Charter of Rights* highlights fundamental freedoms (freedom of religion, expression and assembly), the democratic rights to vote and run for office, legal rights such as the right to counsel, to fundamental justice, and to an independent and impartial judge, and the right to equality without discrimination. The rights to use and to be educated in the English and French languages receive special treatment, and there are some safeguards for Aboriginal rights and for the right to move within Canada for employment purposes.

The protection of minority rights is central to ethical politics, as the principle of mutual respect invests citizens in a democracy with a duty to ensure that minorities are treated equally. The *Charter of Rights* confers a duty on all public officials — elected and appointed — to respect the rights listed in it. Failure to do so is thus a legal as well as an ethical lapse.

One of the more interesting features of the *Charter* is section 1, which places on the rights described therein only "such reasonable limits prescribed by law as can be demonstrably justified in a free and democratic society." In this way the Supreme Court has decided that a law that violates a *Charter* right can survive only if it has an important objective in a democratic context, if it sets out to achieve that objective rationally, if rights are limited as little as necessary to achieve that objective and if the law does more good than harm.[28] Public officials have an ethical duty to undertake this kind of analysis whenever they are considering a policy that might interfere with a *Charter* right. Unfortunately, there is a temptation to avoid that ethical responsibility by trying to "*Charter*-proof" a law — that is, to devise a plan to prevent a *Charter* challenge rather than take minority rights seriously.[29]

## Freedom

Mutual respect accords individuals the right to decide how to conduct their lives. Limits are placed on various freedoms only to help attain the higher goal of mutual respect. Clearly, the plethora of federal, provincial and municipal laws and regulations and the taxes we pay to support the programs authorized by these laws place important qualifications on our freedom. These qualifications fall into three general categories: negative restrictions designed to prevent harm to others (for example, the *Criminal Code*, the provincial *Highway Traffic Act* and some municipal parking bylaws); positive measures designed to promote equality of opportunity (for example, medicare, social welfare entitlements, fair-trade laws, education systems and libraries); and taxation requirements to pay for these programs.

The extent to which it is necessary to limit freedom is a difficult question, but it always boils down to a related one: How best to advance the ideal of mutual respect? Ronald Dworkin contends that in cases where claims to liberty and equality conflict, freedom must yield to equality.[30] But if freedoms are limited for other reasons — for example, for administrative convenience or to provide special benefits to some at the expense of others — then freedom is limited in an unethical fashion.

## FREEDOM OF EXPRESSION

Although citizens in a democracy enjoy many freedoms, one that is central is freedom of expression. This freedom is a good in itself, but it also promotes mutual respect. In addition, full public discussion of issues is essential for the machinery of democracy to work. According to John Stuart Mill, Jean-Jacques Rousseau and Carole Pateman, public debates about important issues help citizens to understand others' points of view and to enter into the kind of compromises necessary for democracy to function. Mill argues that an open dialogue about contentious subjects, in which no points of view are suppressed, is the most likely to lead to reasoned, enlightened policy choices.[31]

The right to freedom of expression is exercised only when Canadians permit and promote full and free public discussion of events and issues. Several major Canadian political cover-ups provide examples of the suppression of such discussion. The first is the Somalia affair. In 1993, members of the Canadian Airborne Regiment murdered a civilian whom they had captured while they were on a humanitarian mission in Somalia. Subsequently, according to testimony before the public inquiry into these events conducted by Justice Gilles Letourneau, senior officials in the Canadian Armed Forces and the Defence Department ordered the destruction of official documents that would have shed light on the circumstances surrounding the killing.[32]

The second included the suppression of information by the Canadian government and military regarding the torture of Afghans who had been detained by Canadian forces and then handed over to the Afghan military starting in 2005. This situation is analyzed in more detail in Chapter 8 under the case study of Richard Colvin. Senior Canadian officials in Afghanistan reported to officials in Ottawa that there was credible evidence that Afghan authorities, in violation of the Geneva Convention, were routinely torturing detainees handed over to them by the Canadian military. The reports were ignored, first by the government of Paul Martin in 2005, and then by the government of Stephen Harper from 2006 to 2009. In 2007, media attention resulted in government denials, but the reports of Richard Colvin, made public by the Military Police Complaints Commission (MPPC) in 2009, indicated that the evidence for torture was credible. A majority in Parliament, including Justin Trudeau, voted for an inquiry into the affair, and the government's response was to prorogue Parliament. In 2012, the MPPC issued its report, which found no specific instances of wrongdoing by Canadian forces personnel, but made recommendations, subsequently implemented, to ensure that Canadian forces take appropriate action to prevent the mistreatment of Afghans in the future. In June 2016, the Trudeau government announced that there would be no further inquiry into the issue, as the Canadian mission to Afghanistan had ended in 2014.[33] What this sad affair indicates perhaps more than anything else is that attempts to cover up ethical breaches and to suppress public discussion frequently do more political damage than owning up to such ethical lapses in the first place.

Another example of the damage done by failing to publicize official wrongdoing was the suppression by the Ontario cabinet of the true cost of cancelling two gas-fired electrical plants during the 2011 provincial election campaign. That cover-up led first to the prorogation of the legislature, and then to the resignation of Premier Dalton McGuinty and Energy Minister Chris Bentley.[34]

Finally, there is the 2013 attempted cover-up by Stephen Harper's administration of the $90,000 cheque given to Senator Mike Duffy by Chief of Staff Nigel Wright to help the senator repay certain expense claims then embarrassing the Conservative government. Again, it was the cover-up itself that eroded public trust in the government; indeed, the scandal was a major factor in the defeat of the Harper government in 2015. In the end, Duffy was exonerated while the cover-up by the Prime Minister's Office was itself condemned.[35]

Those who have intentionally tried to prevent relevant information from entering the public realm have failed to live up to their ethical responsibilities as leaders of a democracy. Such lapses can be combatted to the extent that public officials are able to develop a personal ethical position. But because most academics have neglected ethics up to now, little effort has been made to train students — and future politicians — to think through these kinds of ethical concerns.

One of the safeguards of democratic government is the principle of transparency. Save for private information like individual health or financial records, all information collected by governments should be open to the public — both because of the potential usefulness of much of this information, and to prevent corruption. Beginning in the 1980s and 1990s, the federal government, and eventually all provincial and territorial governments, enacted freedom of information and privacy laws to further the complementary ethical principles of openness and privacy.[36]

But mutual respect as applied to freedom of expression implies more than simply getting all relevant facts out into the open and then carrying on a responsible public debate. The process of public debate itself needs to demonstrate a concern for mutual respect. The Supreme Court has found that Canadian anti-hate laws represent a reasonable limit to freedom of expression, in part because messages of hate violate the fundamental principle of equal concern and respect. The rules of debate in Parliament and provincial legislatures are intended to promote an atmosphere of mutual respect. Unfortunately, this ideal is at times buried in an avalanche of political self-interest. In his annual report for 1994–95, Ontario's integrity commissioner, Gregory Evans, wrote:

> My previous experience as a judge conducting judicial
> business in a courtroom where a certain decorum is
> demanded and a sense of dignity prevails, did not prepare me
> for the raucous behaviour in the Legislature which through
> the medium of television invades private living rooms . . .
> [A former cabinet minister told me] it's just like a "game."
> I did not agree . . . Most observers would welcome some
> flashes of wit and humour, some overheated rhetoric, and
> verbal jousting, if they were not carried to the extent that it
> interfered with the business of the Assembly . . . Why provide
> a fertile field for the critics and the cynics?[37]

On November 1, 1995, Ian Greene testified before the Joint Committee of the Senate and House of Commons on a Code of Conduct, the committee charged with recommending an appropriate code of ethics for MPs and senators. Greene's main point was that ethical standards in politics are based on mutual respect. Having just witnessed a particularly stormy question period in the House of Commons, he asked how the committee members could develop a meaningful code of conduct if they could not even treat each other with respect during a debate?[38] After the hearing, a committee member who had been a teacher said she was deeply embarrassed by the example that members were setting for visiting classes. And an MP representing the former Reform Party was reminded of one of his original reasons for running for office: to bring some decorum to question period. The problem was, he said, that without participating in the vitriolic exchanges in the House, Reform did not get much television coverage. And without television coverage, their popularity ratings plummeted. This brings us to the question of the media and ethics.

In one of Canada's most famous judicial decisions, the media were described as "the breath of life for parliamentary institutions."[39] And indeed, we rely on the media to provide us with the information we need for informed public debate, and we expect political news coverage to be comprehensive, balanced, accurate and impartial.

Without an ethically attentive media, it is difficult to have ethical politics. Most outlets have codes of ethics for their journalists that stress impartiality and prohibit conflicts of interest. Although many journalists take these codes seriously, they are often written in very general language that could be interpreted in widely different ways, and they have yet to tackle some of the more difficult issues related to impartiality in the reporting of the news.

Moderate and balanced positions are often neglected by the news media in favour of more sensational coverage. This competition for readers and viewers can lead to distortions. For example, some visible minorities claim that the coverage of their communities by mainstream media organizations is biased, either because there are not enough journalists from their community, or because a media outlet may be catering to the biases of the majority.

Another problem is that the television-news format itself, which many Canadians rely on for their understanding of public affairs, has severely limited the number of ways in which most issues can be treated. Greene and Shugarman, for example, were once contacted by a national television news program to provide background on one of the conflict of interest bills introduced (though never passed) in the House during the latter years of the Mulroney government. In the end, the correspondent concluded that the issues were too complex for the forty-five seconds he had been allotted, and so he decided to treat the event as a story about the Mulroney government's "posturing."

The tendency to comment incessantly on politicians' "posturing" instead of analyzing the substance of public issues is targeted by James Fallows, a national correspondent for the *Atlantic Monthly*. He attributes this to two factors: many journalists' lack of in-depth knowledge about public issues, and their tendency to imitate the most prominent members of their profession.[40] As a result, important issues are not examined in depth, and informed public debate is increasingly rare. Moreover, politicians are often impelled to take positions that are likely to receive attention rather than ones that might be more thoughtful, nuanced or fair.

Complicating the media's role in politics is the rise of social media like Facebook and Twitter. This is a mixed blessing. Some learn more about politics through social media than they ever would have through radio, television or newspapers. But for many, social media means an exposure to a narrow and distorted version of events. Whereas traditional media had ethical limits, purveyors of hate and bigotry have a much freer hand on Facebook or Twitter. For example, in the 2016 US presidential election, social media contributed to the widespread propagation of Donald Trump's hateful, misogynistic and xenophobic rhetoric, not to mention that of his most extreme supporters. This is the antithesis of mutual respect.[41]

Although this book focuses on ethical issues that impinge directly on politicians, it should not be forgotten that politicians and the media have a symbiotic relationship; the ethical standards in one domain will always have a profound influence on the other. David Olive writes that in Washington, journalists "who condemn rampant influence-peddling . . . accept undisclosed gifts and fat speaker's fees from groups seeking to influence pending legislation. Celebrity columnists and reporters hide behind anonymous sources of dubious credibility when imparting unverifiable 'truths' . . . Dialogue is fabricated when transcripts are not at hand, in order that high-ranking officials can be depicted as profane and ridiculous."[42] Any comprehensive attempt to raise ethical standards in politics is bound to fail unless there is a concurrent reform of ethical standards in the media, including the new media. Respect for freedom is clearly an essential ingredient of mutual respect, of which freedom of expression and freedom of the media are important elements. Nevertheless, in a democracy, freedom needs to be exercised with ethical responsibilities in mind.

## Integrity

Integrity is honesty modified by concern and respect for our fellow human beings. As Stephen Carter puts it, "one cannot have integrity without being honest . . . but one can certainly be honest and yet have little integrity."[43] For example, a party could make a campaign promise to fight crime by doubling the sentences available under the *Youth Criminal Justice Act* and making them mandatory. If that party is elected and follows through with its promise, we would consider it honest. But many studies show that young offenders learn how to become better criminals in the places where they are incarcerated. If party officials were aware of these studies and admitted their credibility but ignored them in order to gain easy votes, then they would lack integrity.

So integrity is actually a complex ideal, closely related to the political problem of "dirty hands." In a dirty-hands situation, a public official knowingly does something dishonest but justifies this action as being in the public good. Although it may sometimes be necessary during wars and other emergencies for public officials to act dishonestly in order to advance the public good, dirty-handed actions are unethical in a peacetime democracy. And yet public officials may try to rationalize their dishonesty for several reasons. First, they may lack the creativity, insight and fortitude needed to resolve a difficult situation with integrity. Second, they may be influenced by the political culture in which they find themselves: If everybody does it, it's okay. Third, integrity demands courage; dirty-hands solutions are often easier, and sometimes less risky, than ethical ones.

Integrity is often an issue in election campaigns. Not infrequently, a political party will make promises, only to break them once elected. The federal Liberals' flip-flop on replacing the GST after the 1993 election is a good example.[44] In some cases, these scenarios represent dirty-handed problems: Loyalists feel so strongly that their party should be in power for the public good that they are willing to make irresponsible promises to win. In many cases, however, such promises are made on the basis of an insufficient understanding of an issue, and it is not until after the election that party loyalists, provided with comprehensive information, realize that fulfilling a particular promise would constitute bad public policy. Certainly, political parties should be held accountable for breaking promises. But integrity is sometimes better served when a party admits to this, than when it proceeds to implement a promise that it has discovered would lead to harmful results.

Another complicating factor is that few people who vote for a particular party support every single plank of that party's campaign platform. Studies of voting behaviour show that most voters base their decisions on factors other than policy, such as the personal attributes of the leader and local candidates. Very few voters are aware of more than one or two of the issues in a campaign.

The integrity of election promises is an important and difficult ethical problem. Two things lessen the likelihood of parties and candidates landing in this type of hot water. First, parties should not make promises unless the implications of those promises are thoroughly researched. Second, making such promises with integrity should be addressed by a party's code of ethics.

## CONCLUSION

In this chapter we have argued that the political institutions and practices in a democracy need to focus on the standard of mutual respect. The commitment to this standard implies social equality, deference to the majority through free and fair elections, concern for minority rights, respect for freedom, and the pursuit of integrity in public life. Democracy cannot function without representative institutions that protect and promote both human rights and ethical political practices.

An ethical approach to democratic politics is one where political actors are expected to make principled decisions based on mutual respect. If they put personal gain or the interests of political friends ahead of the public interest, they have acted unethically by abusing the trust placed in them. Even if they behave dishonestly while believing their behaviour is in the public interest, there is an ethical lapse, at least in peacetime.

In the next chapter we show how mutual respect and the general principles of democracy are related to more specific ethical duties and the legal principles applicable to public administration.

# CHAPTER 2
# ETHICAL DUTIES

## David P. Shugarman, Ian Greene and Naomi Couto

"Canadians . . . are entitled to expect their politicians to
conserve and enhance public confidence and trust in the
integrity, objectivity, and impartiality of government."
— Oliphant Commission, 2010[1]

The five key principles of democracy stemming from mutual respect —
social equality, free and fair elections with deference to the majority,
minority rights, freedom, and integrity — imply certain ethical duties
on the part of public officials. First, since they are entrusted with representing the best interests of their fellow citizens, they have a responsibility
to safeguard that trust by not abusing it. Second, they have a responsibility to act as impartially as possible when carrying out programs established by law. And third, they have a responsibility to account for their
activities and decisions.

## TRUSTEES OF THE PUBLIC INTEREST

As trustees of the public interest, all public officials, whether elected
or appointed, have a duty to act on behalf of the public interest.[2] The
ethical duties of one set of public officials — legislators — are further
complicated by the fact that they also have obligations to their constituents and to their party. Furthermore, politicians and those they
represent need to acknowledge that there is seldom a clear consensus
as to what, precisely, the public interest is. What is clear, by contrast, is

that politicians are expected to deal with these questions, and whatever tensions might arise as a result, with integrity.

A relationship based on trust requires a shared understanding on the part of both electors and elected that the latter will respect their fellow citizens, serve the best interests of the majority without neglecting or violating the rights of minority groups or individuals, abide by the rule of law, avoid nepotism and clientelism and be conscientiously resist undue influence. The trust conveyed in a democracy is not a form of paternalism — trust us because we know what's best for you even if you can't follow our superior wisdom — but rather an exemplification and corollary of mutual respect: leaders' commitments meeting electors' expectations that responsibly attending to the public interest involves doing so transparently and accountably.

As we saw in Chapter 1, illegally using public funds for personal purposes; accepting hundreds of thousands of dollars in secret from a shady lobbyist; betraying voters by joining the cabinet of a prime minister you spent weeks campaigning against; and refusing to take responsibility for how seriously mismanaged and riddled with corruption a secretive government program that you spearheaded became — these are all examples of public officials abusing the trust placed in them by the electorate, whether or not these actions resulted in legal sanctions. Such practices have the effect of undermining the fundamental principles of democracy.

## IMPARTIALITY

For our purposes, impartiality means a lack of bias on the part of a public organization in its decision-making process. An impartial procedure is one where all parties to an issue have an opportunity to present their perspectives and their views are considered in a fashion that is as free from bias as possible. Impartiality is a corollary of the basic principle of mutual respect, and it is implied by each of the five principles of democracy. While the right of those charged with offences to impartial treatment is essentially what the legal rights sections of the *Charter* are about, the *Charter* represents the "entitlement" side of democracy.

On the responsibility side, citizens, and in particular those entrusted with public office, have ethical duties to treat others impartially as well.

In 1996 an investigating committee of the Canadian Judicial Council recommended that Quebec Superior Court Justice Jean Bienvenue be removed for remarking, during a sentencing procedure, that women could "sink to depths to which even the vilest man could not" and that the Nazis killed Jews "in the gas chambers, without suffering."[3] The committee concluded that Bienvenue had failed to uphold the standards of impartiality expected of him, and he resigned as a result. In 2009, the same council recommended the removal of Ontario Superior Court Justice Paul Cosgrove for failing to uphold judicial impartiality during a 1999 murder trial. The council described his misconduct — that during the trial he sided consistently with the defence — as "pervasive."[4] Cosgrove also resigned. In 2016, the council conducted an inquiry into the conduct of Federal Court Justice Robin Camp at a sexual assault trial he had presided over in 2014 when he was a judge with the Provincial Court of Alberta. Camp admitted that during the trial he had asked the victim why she "couldn't just keep [her] knees together," and that he made other sexist comments that constituted judicial bias.[5] He later apologized and undertook counseling. Though he subsequently claimed that he had overcome his bias, the council nevertheless recommended Camp's removal, and Camp resigned.[6]

Although the duty to be impartial is often associated with law, it also applies more broadly, though in different ways, to public officials. While politicians do not have a duty to be impartial when, say, outlining their party platforms (though they do have a responsibility to do so honestly), cabinet ministers have a duty to act impartially when administering the law, and MPs have a duty to represent their constituency impartially and not promote the interests of just a few select constituents. In the Pearson Airport affair of 1993–96, members of both sides of the Senate violated the duty of impartiality when they produced a biased report that they then tried to pass off as impartial.[7]

Perhaps the greatest threat to the impartiality principle is patronage, the practice by some governments of providing special favours to

their partisan supporters in the selection of appointments or the awarding of contracts. Patronage became rampant in the United Kingdom
and Canada after the introduction of cabinet government two centuries
ago, and in the United States after the War of Independence. The practice provided an opportunity for those who had been powerless to take
advantage of the potential spoils of office at the expense of those outside
the party in power. Though patronage declined in Britain and the United
States during the late nineteenth and early twentieth centuries, the habit
continues to die a slow death in some parts of Canada. It has remained
a factor in provincial judicial appointments in the three Maritime provinces after it was reduced or abolished in Western Canada in the 1970s,
and it was an important component in federal judicial appointments at
the trial-court level during the Mulroney period.[8] Although the federal
Liberals took some steps towards reducing patronage in federal judicial
appointments after 1993, especially during Paul Martin's short term as
prime minister in 2005,[9] the Harper government did its best to revert to
appointing judges sympathetic to its ideological cause.[10] Since its election
in 2015, the Trudeau government appears to be moving towards a system
of non-partisan appointments, which we applaud. Likewise, the constitu-
tions of some Caribbean countries require a non-partisan, merit-based
process for judicial appointments — in part in reaction to the problems
with the Canadian system. We in Canada can do much better.

Patronage still plays an important role in all Canadian jurisdictions
regarding appointments to tribunals and boards, and the awarding of
some contracts. One of the worst abuses concerns lucrative government
advertising and public-relations contracts, which often go to firms with
the requisite political connections. In addition, there are the thousands
of "order-in-council" appointments to supposedly independent boards
and commissions. Both at the provincial and federal levels, party supporters therefore often end up filling these positions regardless of their
qualifications as per the cherished political tradition.

Patronage is so ingrained in Canada's political culture that it will
take extraordinarily strong political will and careful planning to elimi-

nate it altogether. With very few exceptions, such as the selection of the political staff in a minister's office, patronage should instead yield to the criterion of impartiality.

## ACCOUNTABILITY AND RESPONSIBILITY

Accountability means demonstrating that the expectations of public office are being met and that one's responsibilities have been carried out. But the most appropriate methods of accountability will vary from one situation to another, as Kernaghan and Langford have illustrated.[11] For instance, line accountability through a hierarchical chain of authority has been used effectively in most civil-service organizations across Canada. At the cabinet level, ministerial responsibility as a means of maintaining accountability has long been meshed with the clear understanding that the prime minister, as the so-called first among equals, is where the "buck stops" when it comes to establishing both ultimate responsibility and accountability in our system of government. For judges, however, line accountability would violate judicial independence; accountability must therefore be achieved through measures like appointment and promotion procedures, the moral suasion of the chief judges, judicial councils, courts advisory committees, continuing education, annual reports and, of course, the delivery of reasoned public judgments.

Elected officials are accountable to their constituents at election time, and sometimes beyond that in jurisdictions like British Columbia, where recall legislation is in place. In the parliamentary system, the principles of responsible government provide a mechanism for continuous accountability. Responsible government is a tradition, or convention, that has long been a part of the "unwritten" constitution. (Canada's constitution is composed of written parts like the *Charter of Rights and Freedoms*, judicial decisions about constitutional interpretation, and unwritten conventions.) Responsible government has three aspects: ministerial responsibility, cabinet solidarity and the rule that the cabinet can exercise power only so long as it maintains majority support in the legislature. To maintain that support, members of the government are required to explain to their fellow parliamentarians how they have discharged their responsibilities, i.e. they must be accountable.

All three aspects of responsible government have ethical overtones. If a cabinet loses the support of the legislature in a vote of confidence but does not resign, it has behaved unethically as well as unconstitutionally, and it faces dismissal by the governor general or lieutenant governor, as well as the likelihood of electoral defeat. Ministerial responsibility means that cabinet ministers must explain the actions of officials in their departments (especially during question period), and they must resign if a serious administrative error has occurred under their watch. Because such accountability is required of ministers, public servants can remain anonymous and are not singled out for public blame. The purpose of such anonymity is to encourage both impartiality in public administration as well as loyalty to the minister. If ministers avoid responsibility, as the prime minister and the Minister of Public Works did during the sponsorship scandal, or if ministers blame public servants instead of shouldering the responsibility themselves, as Defence Minister Peter MacKay did in 2009 when he blamed long-time public servant Richard Colvin for covering up the torture of Afghan detainees (more on this in Chapter 8), they have failed to act with integrity.

Cabinet solidarity means that the cabinet is collectively responsible for policy decisions. A minister who disagrees with any policy position adopted by the cabinet must resign. This was the case with former Alberta Associate Minister for Energy Donna Kennedy-Glans, who in 2014 said "the promised reforms by Redford were dying on the vine."[12] Cabinet solidarity is intended to ensure that ministers will thoroughly debate all policies before they are agreed upon, and it marks a recognition that their personal political futures are intimately connected with that of the cabinet. To act with integrity, ministers must either do their best to explain cabinet policies to the public or resign.

## LEGAL PRINCIPLES

For the principle of mutual respect to inform the political process, ethical supports must be developed to facilitate its practice. These supports can take different forms — for example, constitutional conventions and traditions, rules of debate, and legislated or non-legislated codes of ethics.

Each of these reflects the general principles considered in Chapter 1 and the duties noted above. However, two important legal principles — the rule of law and the duty of fairness — help us to apply these general principles and duties. Though the legal principles help to bring the general principles down to earth, they are not enough by themselves to promote ethical politics. They must be buttressed and supplemented by ethical supports like conflict of interest rules.

### The Rule of Law

The rule of law reinforces the practice of mutual respect throughout Canadian society. In 1985, the Supreme Court described two aspects of the rule of law: a civilized community governed by law rather than by the arbitrary decisions of public officials, and laws that apply to public officials and institutions no differently than they apply to private individuals.[13] In other words, a legal framework is provided for social co-operation, and everyone's conduct is subject to non-arbitrary regulation.[14] If a public official attempts to exercise authority that is not sanctioned by law, such action is known as an abuse of power.[15] Public officials may exercise only the authority given to them by the laws approved by representative legislatures and applied even-handedly to everyone. The rule of law emphasizes equality, in that everyone has the opportunity to participate in the making of laws by voting or running for office. Furthermore, the equal application of the law helps protect minority rights.

Important as these principles have been to the unwritten part of Canada's constitution since 1867, it wasn't until the proclamation of the *Charter of Rights and Freedoms* in 1982 that our constitution effectively associated the rule of law with democracy. The *Charter*'s preamble recognizes the rule of law as one of Canada's founding principles. Furthermore, it makes clear that any deviations from the equal-application principle, such as restricting the right to vote to those over eighteen, or prohibiting those without a driver's licence from operating motor vehicles, must not only be clearly spelled out in law, but also shown to be reasonable in a free and democratic society.[16]

John Locke, liberalism's most prominent early supporter, argued in 1690 that a reasonable government would exercise power not through extemporary arbitrary decrees, but "by promulgated standing laws, and known authorized judges . . . not to be varied in particular cases, but [to uphold] one rule for rich and poor, for the favorite at court, and the countryman at plough."[17]

Locke argued that the rule of law is meaningless unless the law is applied impartially. The executive branch of government — the cabinet and the public service — is responsible for carrying out programs approved by the legislature, and the judicial branch is responsible for settling disputes over how the law is to be applied and interpreted. Locke stressed the importance of an impartial application of the law by the executive and judicial branches in order to protect the supremacy of laws approved by elected legislatures. He argued that any activity involving the application of law requires impartiality, and thus, unbiased judges and administrators.

More than three hundred years later, some progress has been made towards the achievement of Locke's prescription for impartiality in liberal societies, but more so in the judiciary than in the executive branch of government. Ironically, the slower progress in the latter can be attributed, in part, to the advent of responsible government in countries like Canada, which have adopted parliamentary institutions. This means that the cabinet must be selected from the party with the greatest number of seats and it must maintain the support of a majority of the legislature to stay in power.

Responsible government came about in the United Kingdom around the middle of the eighteenth century. In a sense, it represented a step backwards for the principle of impartiality because it established the notion that the cabinet would necessarily be partisan. In this way, argues David Smith, political parties gained more opportunities to reward their supporters and allow them to use public office to achieve personal goals.[18]

At the same time, however, the judiciary was becoming more independent from the rest of government, and the principle of judicial impartiality was becoming more entrenched. The eighteenth-century French political scientist, Baron de Montesquieu, noted these developments and described the United Kingdom somewhat misleadingly as having three distinct branches of government — legislative, executive and judiciary, each a check on the other.

Montesquieu's observations were influential insofar as impartiality came to be associated primarily with the judicial branch of government. But the common-law duty of fairness serves to remind us that the executive branch also has an ethical responsibility to generate impartial decisions about how the law is to be implemented.

## Fairness

The duty of fairness is a common-law rule that obliges all public officials, including cabinet ministers, to act impartially when making administrative decisions. It was developed by the Supreme Court beginning in 1979 as an elaboration of the principle of the rule of law.[19]

The duty of fairness is based on the older common-law principle of natural justice, which holds that those coming before a judicial or administrative tribunal must be given a fair and impartial hearing, and opposing litigants must have the opportunity to explain their views fully. Natural justice is sometimes referred to as fundamental justice, and section 7 of the *Canadian Charter of Rights and Freedoms* states that the rights of Canadians to life, liberty, and security of the person cannot be interfered with "except in accordance with the principles of fundamental justice."[20]

According to the common law, judges and members of administrative tribunals must fulfill the following three criteria in order to be considered impartial. They cannot be in a position to gain financially from one of their decisions; they cannot be in a position to favour people who are or were closely associated with them; and if they have previously expressed views that indicate that they cannot reasonably be expected to apply a particular law even-handedly, they should disqualify (recuse) themselves.

David P. Jones and Anne de Villars describe these criteria as the "rule against bias." And indeed, at one time or another most Canadian judges have disqualified themselves from hearing a particular case because they feared that they might appear biased to one of the litigants before them.[21]

According to the Supreme Court's interpretation of the duty of fairness, all public officials who make decisions about the application of the law must be impartial, and the criteria outlined above also apply to administrators to whatever extent is reasonable. The judiciary needs to determine what is reasonable on a case-by-case basis. The duty of fairness applies to cabinet ministers when they act as administrators of the law, but not when they act as legislators and policy-makers.[22]

The courts have applied the duty of fairness to public officials' decisions in a number of cases since 1979, but very few have involved cabinet decisions, as these are rarely challenged in court. One of the few cases involving ministers of the Crown was a 1981 decision in which the Supreme Court of British Columbia reviewed a cabinet decision that had overturned the decision of a provincial licensing commission.[23]

It is useful to consider how the duty of fairness applies, in theory, to public officials. The first aspect of the rule against bias — not being in a position to gain financially from a public office — is clearly relevant to all administrative decision making by cabinet ministers and other public officials. This principle is reflected in the conflict of interest rules covering cabinet ministers, other elected officials and public servants in general. For example, Bill Vander Zalm, the premier of British Columbia in 1990, was found by an independent investigation to have been in situations where he could have used his office for personal financial gain; this meant that he was guilty of violating conflict of interest rules. He paid the ultimate political penalty and resigned from office.

The second aspect of the rule against bias is the prohibition against providing favours to friends and former associates. According to J.O. Wilson, this means that judges must disqualify themselves from making decisions in cases that involve family members, friends and former business associates.[24] In the case of cabinet ministers and public servants, this implies that they should refrain from making any administrative decisions that could result in special privileges for their family members, business and professional associates and friends. For example, Richard Le Hir, who was a cabinet minister in the 1995 Parti Québécois government, was forced to resign because the process he had approved for hiring persons to conduct studies on sovereignty was not impartial and resulted in many of the contracts being handed out to friends and associates of the top bureaucrats in Le Hir's office.

Because many of a cabinet minister's friends and allies are members of the same political party, it makes sense that a minister should refrain from making administrative decisions that might benefit them. Unfortunately, some cabinet ministers don't see it this way, perhaps because of a misunderstanding of the role of ethical principles in democracy. However, the most principled ministers do try to avoid favouring friends and party members.

The third aspect of the rule against bias — disqualification for making biased statements — applies straightforwardly to non-elected public officials, but presents some difficulties for cabinet ministers. In the parliamentary system, cabinet ministers wear two hats: They are legislators when working on changes to laws and regulations, and administrators when supervising their departments and making administrative decisions under the law. They are elected as legislators in part because of their positions on various issues, which are anything but impartial. It therefore requires great skill for cabinet ministers to respect the rule of law when undertaking their ministerial duties, and at the same time to be actively involved in changing the law as legislators. This difficulty is illustrated in Chapter 4 by the case of Diane Finley, who used her ministerial powers to the advantage of a Conservative Party favourite.

The cabinet has a dual purpose: to administer existing programs established by law, and to attempt, through amending the law, to change these programs or to create new ones that reflect the party's platform. This dual role — and the failure of our political system to resolve the conflicting expectations it creates — has left cabinet ministers unsure of how impartial they ought to be in particular situations. This lack of clarity helps to explain why patronage, conflicts of interest, undue influence and abuses of power remain in a country that supposedly respects the rule of law.

## THE ARGUMENTS AGAINST AN ETHICS-BASED APPROACH

To some readers, our suggested approach to ethical politics may seem so straightforward as to be self-evident. But this is likely the case only with readers for whom the principle of mutual respect is important. It isn't a priority for everyone, though, and whenever an ethics-based approach to politics is discussed, certain familiar criticisms inevitably come up.

The argument we hear most frequently goes something like this: "Most politicians are corrupt" or, more sympathetically, "are forced by the system to act in corrupt ways even if they begin with honest intentions." This rather cynical view suggests that, by its very nature, power provides a rationale for unethical politics.[25]

And yet from our perspective, this view is insupportable. When clear ethical standards are set, the evidence suggests that the majority of elected officials in Canada do behave ethically. In 1991, a former British Columbia ethics commissioner, Ted Hughes, remarked that "my experience with the seventy-five current members of the B.C. Legislature . . . is that today we don't have a rogue amongst them. If that's so, I think that augurs well for the future because I'm satisfied that they all want to do the right thing and they've now got, with [ethics] legislation, the assistance to make that possible."[26]

Prior to the ethics reforms that began in the late 1980s with the creation of conflict of interest commissioners and lobbyist registries, the major problems had to do with the fact that standards for ethical behaviour were either non-existent or unclear. Prior to the 1990 enactment of conflict of interest legislation in B.C. and Hughes's appointment as ethics commissioner, there had been seven major conflict of interest scandals in five years. After 1990, there have been only two substantiated incidents up to 2015,[27] which is a good indication that the new system is working.

Another argument for dismissing an ethics-based approach goes like this: Because there is no absolute proof that mutual respect is better than any other basic value, politics is really just a game of wits. This outlook is supported by some of the more radical theories of skepticism and, to some extent, by contemporary postmodernism. And while it is true that in both science and philosophy there are no absolute proofs of anything, including our own existence, we nevertheless believe there is overwhelming evidence that democratic government based on mutual respect is more satisfactory than any other form of government.

John Rawls has argued that if we could imagine a group of reasonable persons suddenly cut off from the rest of society, such persons would invent a government based on mutual respect because this principle would result in all of the individuals involved being better off than in any other possible system where equality, liberty and justice are valued.[28] Another similar approach is the idea that the principle of mutual respect is related to individual rights. From this perspective, individual rights are treated as "natural" in the sense that persons, by virtue of their humanity, have certain entitlements that are independent of any political agreements or historical arrangements. These include the right to be treated as an equal, the right to have one's autonomy respected and the right to develop one's uniquely human attributes in association with others. Each of these are fundamental to any moral order.

And for those who find comparative evidence more convincing than theory, since 1989 the United Nations has rated all countries in the world according to a "human development index," which takes into account certain indicators of quality of life such as health, education and income. Democracies that value mutual respect are consistently at the top of the index (Canada, for instance, has held the top spot four times), while corrupt dictatorships tend to be near the bottom.[29]

In our experience, most politicians who engage in unethical behaviour are opportunists who simply take advantage of the situation without thinking about it very much. For example, George Hees, a member of Parliament for thirty-seven years, a former president of the Progressive Conservative Party, head of the Montreal Stock Exchange and a cabinet minister in both the Diefenbaker and Mulroney governments, admitted the following to a reporter: "You ask any member why they're here and they'll tell you it's to serve the people. That's bull! . . . They're here because of why we're all here. Because we're arrogant and full of ourselves, vain and ambitious . . . I'll at least admit it."[30]

Holders of such opinions often believe that what they do is acceptable because competitive politics is about ego gratification, the reach for personal advantage and the dispensing of favours. From their perspective, undue influence and conflicts of interest aren't really problems, since everyone is entitled to as much influence and advantage as he or she can grasp. The trouble with opportunism and egoism is that in a world filled with egoists and opportunists, eventually 'everyone is victimized by someone else.'

## MAKING ETHICAL JUDGMENTS

When a public official is faced with a troubling ethical issue, he or she should first consider whether the situation is covered by the law. A reflection of the public will, the law should be considered binding in nearly every case.

There are two exceptions, however. First, a law might violate the *Charter of Rights* or another part of the Constitution, and in such a case the public official should seek advice from legal counsel in the government department that he or she works in. Second, public officials sometimes feel strongly that the law itself violates a higher moral principle. These circumstances are often exceedingly complex, as Kernaghan and Langford demonstrate, and public officials should be very cautious about substituting their own judgment for that of the legislature.[31] However, situations do occasionally arise where there is a legitimate conflict between an official's ethical principles and the law. Fortunately, some government agencies now have ethics counsellors who can advise in such a situation. For example, a police officer opposed to abortion may object to an assignment to protect an abortion clinic, in which case an ethics counsellor may support a reassignment request. Elected officials, of course, seldom face such dilemmas, as they are more concerned with the making of the law than its implementation.

Cabinet ministers, however, might have ethical qualms about the laws they are supposed to administer, and they have an ethical duty to raise such issues with their cabinet colleagues. For example, in 2012 the Harper cabinet passed two orders-in-council that cut off medical coverage to many refugee claimants, including those whose claims had been denied but whose home countries were deemed dangerous, and those from "designated countries" not considered refugee-producing states by the Canadian government. This draconian policy was challenged in federal court by a group known as Canadian Doctors for Refugee Care. In striking down the orders-in-council, the trial judge, Justice Mactavish, wrote that

> The effect of these changes is to deny funding for life-
> saving medications such as insulin and cardiac drugs to
> impoverished refugee claimants from war-torn countries
> such as Afghanistan and Iraq . . . [They also] deny funding for
> basic pre-natal, obstetrical and pediatric care to women and
> children seeking the protection of Canada from "Designated
> Countries of Origin" such as Mexico and Hungary . . . [and]
> any medical care whatsoever to individuals seeking refuge
> in Canada who are only entitled to a Pre-removal Risk
> Assessment, even if they suffer from a health condition that
> poses a risk to the public health and safety of Canadians."[32]

The purpose of the 2012 cabinet orders, according to Justice Mac-tavish, was to save costs by discouraging refugee claimants from seeking asylum in Canada.[33] The Harper government responded to Justice Mactavish's decision by filing an appeal, but the case had yet to be heard when the Trudeau Liberals were elected in October 2015. One of the new cabinet's first dilemmas was to consider the ethical implications of upholding the 2012 cabinet order, and cabinet decided it was ethically repugnant. The cabinet directed that the appeal be dropped, and the funding of refugee health care be restored.[34]

The most common ethical concerns that elected officials face, however, are ones on which the law is silent. For example, as we pointed out above, Canadian law was until the eighties and nineties almost entirely mute on how elected officials should deal with conflicts of interest or the undue influence of lobbyists.[35] Indeed, some gaps remain in the federal and provincial legislation surrounding both issues, (as noted in Chapters 5 and 7). There are also weaknesses in the laws regulating party contributions at some levels. In cases that fall into these legal lacunae, public officials must go through a process of ethical reasoning to reach a satisfactory ethical solution.

On the surface, this seems simple: You take the situation in question and apply to it the principle of mutual respect and each of the five principles of democracy that follow from it. Greene and Shugarman know of a candidate who contested the leadership of a provincial party during the 1970s. He withdrew from the race prior to the convention — even when many thought he would win — because he objected to the conditions set by those funding his bid. We do not know the details of these conditions, but for the purposes of this example let us speculate that the prominent political family that funded the leadership candidate expected him to appoint some of its members to patronage positions and to arrange for some hefty provincial advertising contracts to be awarded to family businesses. The candidate's ethical reasoning process might run as follows:

- The conditions of the deal will not allow me to make decisions based on equal concern and respect, but will force me to show special consideration to the funders.

- The deal violates the principle of social equality because it will result in increased wealth and privilege for a family already considerably privileged.

- The family is not seeking to advance the welfare of the majority, but rather its own special interests, and it certainly does not form part of a disadvantaged minority.

- The principle of freedom in this instance does not seem to be directly relevant to the decision.

- It would be difficult for me to act with integrity were I to become premier and reward my funders as anticipated because I would not be able to announce the real reason behind the patronage appointments or contracts.

- For all these reasons, it would be unethical to accept funding for my leadership bid with these particular conditions attached. Unless other, more ethical funding becomes available, I must withdraw from the leadership race.

In our example, this process leads to a clear solution. But there are other situations where an ethical decision would be far more difficult. What if, in the above example, the wealthy family did not demand favours for itself, but rather a commitment to cut taxes and to support bilingualism? The reasoning process would be the same, but the result might be different depending on the candidate's evaluation of the impact of each relevant principle.

Let us take another example. Suppose a federal MP is deciding whether in a free vote to support special legislation to enable the construction of a toxic waste disposal plant in an adjacent constituency. The majority in the adjacent riding support the plan because of the economic benefits it will bring to the region, but a substantial minority — those living in close proximity to the proposed construction site — oppose the idea even though scientific studies indicate that the risk to health, at least in the short run, would be minimal. The MP's constituents do not have opinions as strong as those of the adjacent riding, but a slight majority favours the plan because toxic waste now being stored in their area could be eliminated. The ethical policy choice is not clear. None of the principles of democracy provide direct guidance, and the dilemma may well boil down to a choice between deference to the majority and minority rights.

In this case, reference to the more elaborate theories of consequentialism and intentionalism might be helpful. Consequentialist theorists, such as utilitarians, stress results over process. Utilitarianism is a variant of liberalism popularized by the English philosopher John Stuart Mill more than a century and a half ago. It adopts a goal-oriented approach to ethical propriety whose chief tenet is the principle that individuals and institutions ought to strive for the greatest happiness for the greatest number. A utilitarian "holds that actions are right in proportion as they tend to promote happiness, wrong as they tend to produce the reverse of happiness."[36] Viewed in this way, the object of public policy is to increase the net benefits that are accruable to the greatest number of people.

Intentionalist theorists emphasize the importance of always acting in a manner that makes it a duty to a) conduct oneself in ways that everyone else could and would adopt as rightful, and b) treat all others as ends in themselves, rather than as means to achieve particular goals. The will to do one's duty thus takes priority over a consideration of the results of one's actions or decisions. Both approaches are consistent with the principle of mutual respect, and in most day-to-day situations a consequentialist and an intentionalist would agree on what constitutes an ethical course of action in politics. There are some difficult, though relatively rare, situations where they would disagree, as the case of the proposed toxic waste plant illustrates. A consequentialist MP, thinking of the overall benefits to the community, would likely support the plant, while an intentional-ist, placing a greater emphasis on the welfare of those living close to the plant, would probably oppose it. It should be stated here that though we are acutely aware of the old adage that says the road to hell is paved with good intentions, where the two approaches conflict, Greene's and Shugarman's preference would be toward intentionalism. We prefer intentionalism because its stresses the individual worth of all people, a consideration that seems more in accord with mutual respect.

Now, let us make our example even more difficult by hypothesizing that the MP's sister-in-law had a financial stake in the proposed toxic waste plant. Would this relationship affect the MP's impartiality seriously enough to dis-qualify him or her from voting? (More details would be needed to answer that question properly.) Moreover, does the duty to act as a trustee of the public interest apply to the MP's constituents only, or to other Canadians as well? The MP's answer would depend on his or her own thinking about the nature of mutual respect. What is important from an ethics perspective is that the MP has applied the relevant ethical principles to the best of his or her ability in deciding what to do, and can therefore provide an ethical defence of his or her choice if called upon to do so.

In the case studies mentioned in this book, we will apply the kind of ethical analysis described above. In some cases, ethical judgments seem straightforward and we do not hesitate to present our conclusions. In other cases, the ethical course of action is not so clear-cut, and we defer to the judgments of our readers.

## ETHICS SUPPORTS

A number of mechanisms have already been developed to promote ethics in Canadian politics. They include conflict of interest legislation and codes of conduct, lobbyists' registration legislation, party financing laws, independent conflict of interest commissioners, "wrongdoing" commissioners and legislation to protect whistle-blowers, election finance legislation, election commissioners and regimes to review expense claims. All of these supports will be examined in the chapters to come. Other mechanisms, such as auditors general, internal audit procedures, information and privacy legislation and the institution of ombudsmen in some jurisdictions, though important, have been examined extensively by others.

Figure 1: Principles and Duties in a Democracy, and Some Ethics Supports

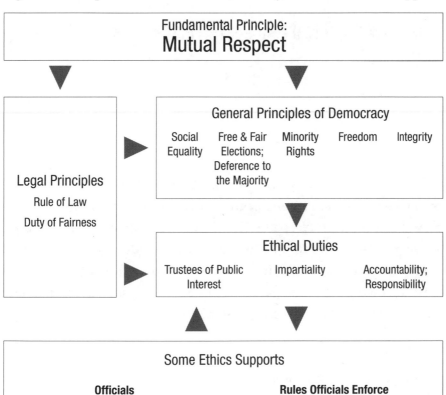

# CHAPTER 3
# ETHICAL PROBLEMS IN PUBLIC LIFE

## Ian Greene, David P. Shugarman and Robert Shepherd

In this chapter we draw attention to serious ethical problems in the public sector that are amenable to control through checks like whistle-blowing, or supports like better legislation and enforcement procedures. These problems have to do with patronage and ideological preference, conflicts of interest, undue influence related to improper lobbying and party-financing activities and abuses of authority, such as wrongdoing and entitlement when filing expense claims.

## PATRONAGE

Patronage refers to the government's power to provide rewards to friends and supporters, particularly those making large financial contributions to the party in power. Patronage's established role in the parliamentary system is an unintended side effect of the development of responsible government. As the party with the majority or plurality of seats in the House of Commons wrestled control of the cabinet away from the monarch in the United Kingdom in the 1700s, and in Canada the 1800s, governments realized that they could use their appointment and decision-making powers to reward supporters, and thus encourage their continued support. The obvious conflict between patronage and the rule of law was simply accepted as one of the many ways in which people paid lip service to a particular ethical principle but in practice did something entirely different.

In the early 1900s, the German social scientist Max Weber adapted the term *bureaucracy* to describe an ideal organization that maximizes efficiency, effectiveness and fairness. The "bureaucratic revolution" that started in Canada in the 1920s, which was in part an attempt to reform the public service along the lines recommended by Weber, sought to restructure a bloated and inefficient public service. It came about in response to several forces: the need for a more effective delivery of postwar programs; public pressure to spend tax dollars more efficiently; and the extension of the democratic franchise to include the poor and women.[1] Grassroots political movements, such as farmers' organizations, promoted the merit system for public service appointments because they believed the traditional patronage system worked primarily for the benefit of the rich. Reg Whitaker argues that big business also endorsed the merit system out of concern that the newly enfranchised lower classes would use the patronage lever to hire and promote their friends.[2] For a few decades after these major reforms, bureaucracies proved their worth through the greatly improved efficiency and fairness of the public service, and the bureaucratic model was widely copied in the private sector. But in the second half of the twentieth century, many bureaucracies themselves became stale and inefficient, leading to the recent movement to reinvent government again.[3]

It is important to understand how the original bureaucratic revolution led to higher ethical standards in the public sector. According to Weber, the two basic principles of a bureaucracy are:

- Hiring according to merit instead of social class or privilege. This led to the establishment of federal and provincial public service commissions in an attempt to replace the hiring of public servants based on patronage with a system based on merit.

- Legally defined relationships between managers and their employees — i.e., job descriptions — to ensure managers do not abuse their power, employees' performances are measured fairly and workers are promoted or demoted according to objective criteria.[4]

Ideally, hiring and promotion in bureaucracies are conducted according to merit. Services are provided impersonally, impartially and equitably according to rules applicable to both "the favorite at court, and the countryman at plough,"[5] and not according to privileges stemming from patronage or social class.

When these reforms began, they affected primarily the lower echelons of the public service; at the cabinet level, ministers resisted giving up the perks of public office. Federal and provincial cabinets maintained partisan control over the distribution of the "spoils" from economic development programs, over contracts for some lawyers and other professionals and discretionary appointments such as judgeships and positions on agency boards.

According to Whitaker, this meant that the benefits of patronage remained available "almost exclusively to people with professional or business qualifications."[6] This is still true in the first part of the new millennium, as evidenced by appointments to high-ranking federal and provincial positions like Guy Giorno and Nigel Wright, both of whom were prominent actors in the private sector before they became chiefs of staff at the provincial and federal levels, respectively. There has also been an increase in the number of prominent business people appointed to senior bureaucratic positions, supposedly to bring a corporate sensibility to bear on government decision making.

Those in permanent public service positions are expected to apply the law impartially and to provide services to all members of the public equally. However, Canadian cabinet ministers have inherited a confusing array of expectations regarding impartiality. With respect to their responsibilities in the day-to-day activities of their departments, they have a duty to act impartially. Yet in those discretionary areas that escaped the reforms of the bureaucratic revolution, partisanship is not only accepted, but often expected.

For example, during the 2015 election campaign the quality of some of Prime Minister Stephen Harper's Senate patronage appointments came into question. Before the election two Harper-appointed senators, Mike Duffy and Patrick Brazeau, were charged by the RCMP with fraud for allegedly falsifying their expense claims, and Brazeau pled guilty to criminal charges regarding assault and cocaine.[7] Although Duffy was acquitted and the expenses charges against Brazeau were dropped, these episodes led to public disgust at the use of patronage in the Senate. Some previous Liberal appointments — in particular Senator Raymond Lavigne, a former Liberal MP appointed to the Senate by Jean Chrétien in 2002 — were subjected to similar criticism. Lavigne was convicted of breach of trust and defrauding the Senate, and served a six-month jail sentence in 2013.[8] Justin Trudeau's promise to replace the patronage system with one based on merit is a welcome development. But the fact that it took so many years to get to this stage indicates that patronage is a resilient force in the Canadian political landscape.

A similar issue came to the fore during the 1984 federal election campaign. In his last month as prime minister, Pierre Trudeau made 172 patronage appointments.[9] On the day the election was called, John Turner, the new Liberal leader, announced the appointment of seventeen Liberal MPs to patronage positions — in the Senate, the judiciary and the diplomatic corps.[10] During the election, Brian Mulroney loudly criticized the Liberals for this "shocking vulgarity," and he promised to clean things up.[11] And yet immediately after becoming prime minister, Mulroney established an even more robust system for filling order-in-council positions with loyal party supporters.

One of the planks in the Liberal platform in 1993 was to reduce the number of partisan appointments and to ensure government appointees would be competent. To some extent this happened, as will be discussed below. However, patronage appointments returned with a vengeance under Harper, who filled order-in-council appointments with ideological allies and party donors.[12]

In an effort to distance herself from the organized patronage of the Mulroney government, so thoroughly documented by both Jeffrey Simpson and Stevie Cameron,[13] Prime Minister Kim Campbell advertised in the *Canada Gazette* for qualified applicants for many order-in-council positions. Campbell lost the 1993 general election before it was possible to make appointments under the new system, but the Chrétien government used the Campbell system to make its first batch of appointments in 1993 and 1994. The government took credit for beginning the hard process of replacing patronage appointments with merit-based ones. It wasn't long, though, before the Liberal government started committing the same sins as occurred in the Mulroney period. Although a number of merit-based appointments were made as per Campbell's example, a parallel system of patronage appointments still operated, although Penny Collenette, Chrétien's appointments secretary, tried to ensure that these officials were at least qualified for their jobs.[14]

Mulroney's appointments secretary has admitted that the prime minister's patronage appointments "in some cases [represented] reward over competence."[15] One poignant example was the use of the Convention Refugee Determination Division (CRDD) of the Immigration and Refugee Board to reward Conservative party faithful. A 1991 study by the Law Reform Commission of Canada found that most of Mulroney's appointments to the CRDD "came to the job with little or no training in law or procedure.[16] The CRDD was not infrequently called on to make life-and-death decisions regarding refugee claimants; the presence of the prime minister's "functionally illiterate"[17] friends certainly did not result in enlightened decision making. Under Chrétien, the system of advertising in the *Canada Gazette* led to higher-quality appointees to the CRDD, although a disproportionate number had Liberal Party connections. With patronage ingrained in the Canadian political system since 1867, it takes courage and ethical leadership to bring about change. For example, because John Savage, premier of Nova Scotia from 1993 to 1997, abolished a large part of the patronage system in that province, many in his own party turned against him, claiming that it was "their turn at the trough."[18]

Under Stephen Harper, blatant patronage once again became the norm, with more than seventy patronage appointments made over two days in June, 2015.[19] Indeed, in one of the most distasteful uses of patronage in modern Canadian history, Harper made more than thirty appointments whose terms were not scheduled to begin until *after* the 2015 election.[20]

The practice of rewarding lawyers faithful to the governing party by appointing them as federal "legal agents" was another serious problem. Many of these agents ended up acting as federal Crown attorneys in narcotics prosecutions. Whenever the government changed, however, nearly all of these appointees were fired and replaced by agents loyal to its successor. According to Tu Thanh Ha, during the 1994–95 fiscal year, "Ottawa handed out nearly $45 million to 600 legal agents."[21] In the 1980s, interviews with key personnel in the Ontario court system revealed widespread concern about the harm to the justice system caused by abuse of these prerogatives, and yet many lawyers were untroubled; to them, it was simply a natural and harmless part of Canadian politics since few non-lawyers knew what was going on. Indeed, many of those without such contracts expected that they would get their turn once the party they supported was in power.[22]

Minister of Justice Allan Rock tried to reform this system when he entered the cabinet in the fall of 1993, but it was reported that he met a wall of resistance from Liberal lawyers, especially those from small-town Canada, who had been expecting their rewards. The best he could do was reduce the overall number of federal legal agent positions available, and ensure that those who received the remaining plum appointment were at least minimally qualified. As well, instead of firing all of the Tory-appointed agents, some of the better-qualified lawyers from the previous regime were kept on.[23]

A change made by the Harper government was to reform the system by creating the Public Prosecution Service of Canada (PPSC) in 2006. Part of the rationale for this move was to address the problems resulting from the patronage system, and replace it with a more merit-based system.[24] A merit-based, competitive process for offering five-year contracts to part-time legal agents has been in place since 2010 according to officials in the PPSC. But from our perspective, it is unfortunate that the federal government did not go one step further and abolish the system of federal prosecutors altogether. After all, the federal prosecution service was set up partly to dispense government patronage rather than to truly improve the justice system, and the bifurcated system of prosecutors continues to contribute to unnecessary delays in the criminal justice system.

## Ideological Preference

Another potential departure from merit-based appointments is ideological preference, which refers to a government's tendency to appoint ideological supporters to positions of influence, regardless of whether they were party members or financial supporters. We argue that the more a given position involves the impartial application of the law, the less ideological preference should play a part in the appointments process. In instances where such appointments involve policy development or the implementation of the government's platform, ideological preference can legitimately play a role. In other words, appointments to the judiciary or administrative tribunals should be based primarily on merit, while ideological preference can play a role in the appointment of ministerial aides, for example, or members of the Prime Minister's Office or the appointment of deputy ministers who will implement the government's priorities in key policy areas — so long as they are competent.[25]

Pierre Trudeau initiated a tradition of non-partisan, merit-based appointments to the Supreme Court of Canada, although given the ability to choose from several well-qualified potential Supreme Court appointees, there is no doubt that he and subsequent prime ministers have made choices based to some extent on ideology. However, Prime Minister Harper's attempt to appoint Marc Nadon to the Supreme Court in 2013 represented an excessive use of ideological preference.

Harper appointed Nadon, a semi-retired Federal Court of Appeal judge, to fill one of three Quebec positions on the Supreme Court. A number of Quebec judges and lawyers were arguably more qualified than Nadon, but some of Nadon's decisions on the Federal Court indicated that he might be more sympathetic to the Harper government's law-and-order agenda.[26] Nevertheless, Nadon's appointment was challenged as unconstitutional by Toronto lawyer Rocco Galati, not on grounds of merit, but rather because he lacked the requisite credentials in Quebec civil law. Galati's litigation succeeded, much to the approval of those who have long advocated a less partisan system of Supreme Court selections. In 2014, in a six-to-one decision that included two Quebec judges, the Supreme Court ruled that the appointment was indeed unconstitutional.[27]

In 2016, the Justin Trudeau government appointed former conservative Prime Minister Kim Campbell to head a non-partisan committee to draw up a short list of candidates to fill a Supreme Court vacancy. Any Canadian lawyer with ten years' experience could apply for the position. From the list drawn up by Campbell's committee, Trudeau selected Malcolm Rowe of Newfoundland, and then organized two sets of public hearings about the appointment. In the first, the government explained to MPs the rationale behind the choice, and in the second, Rowe himself was subjected to questioning from MPs in front of an audience at the University of Ottawa.[28] This is a step forward in terms of reducing the ideological influence over federal appointments.

Beginning with Pierre Trudeau, there have been three different kinds of advisory systems to help ensure appropriate judicial appointments to Canada's superior courts, but the first two served merely to limit the worst aspects of traditional patronage and ideological preference.[29] In 2016, the government of Justin Trudeau established a new system of advisory committees for federal judicial appointments below the Supreme Court level. Government-appointed representatives constitute a minority on these committees, and anyone can apply to sit on them. This could well serve to eliminate both traditional patronage and severely curtail ideo-logical preference in federal judicial appointments.[30]

Members of most administrative tribunals do not have security of tenure. At both the federal and provincial levels, they are appointed for term positions, usually ranging from one to five years. But in 1996, Ontario Premier Mike Harris removed three members of the Ontario Labour Relations Board in the middle of their terms. That action ended up before the Ontario Court of Appeal, which found the government's action invalid.[31] In 1997, the Harris government began to appoint members of the Ontario Labour Relations Board and members of other administrative tribunals "at pleasure." In other words, the government could fire them at any time for any reason. This was an alarming attack on the impartiality principle.[32] Not only can patronage or ideological preference interfere with the quality of appointments, it can also have an effect on appointees' impartiality toward the end of their terms. When the party in power changes at either the federal or provincial level, some of the former government's appointees are kept on at the tribunals to provide continuity. Members no doubt feel pressure to please their new political masters in order to be reappointed. Such actions jeopardize the principle of impartiality.

In 2013, Ron Ellis, a veteran of administrative law in Ontario, penned *Unjust by Design*, a harsh indictment of the impact of patronage appointments to administrative tribunals in Canada, both provincially and federally.[33] However, in 2015, changes began to occur at the federal level. The Justin Trudeau government advertised tribunal and other prominent positions in the *Canada Gazette*. The idea was that these appointments should be free of politics, seen to be merit-based and subject to greater parliamentary scrutiny. The addition of a separate independent appointments commission in the Senate is also seen as a way to ensure senators are selected according to merit. Although some of this was a response to crises at the federal level, they nonetheless help to repair the perception that prime ministers can reward their friends with high-profile positions.

## Observations

Our political system has not yet worked out an acceptable division between positions that can justifiably be held by loyal party supporters or ideological sympathizers, and those that should be awarded on the basis of an impartial assessment. Very few would object to ministers hiring loyal party supporters to work as ministerial assistants, although some ministers, federal and provincial, disregard party affiliation even when making such appointments. Also, while there is clearly no justification for patronage in judicial appointments or appointments to administrative tribunals, a background in party politics should not be considered a liability, and in some situations appointees' policy orientations can be a relevant criterion for selection. But what about other order-in-council appointments? At the federal level, there are over twenty-five hundred order-in-council positions. These include appointments to the boards of Canadian National Railways, Petro-Canada, the Bank of Canada and the CBC, as well as the Immigration and Refugee Board, various port commissions, the Canada Pension Commission, the RCMP Review Board, the Environmental Assessment Board, the National Parole Board, provincial lieutenant-governorships, provincial superior and appellate court judgeships, the Federal Court and the Supreme Court of Canada.

Our view is that merit must be the sole criterion for all order-in-council appointments. Political officials often argue that few will work for a political party unless they are rewarded after an election. However, this assumes that all public service is based on self-interest rather than a sense of civic responsibility or social justice.[34] By eliminating ethically dubious incentives, political parties might open themselves up to more support from ordinary people. It takes tens of thousands more loyal party workers to win an election than there are available patronage positions. The lure of such positions might do more to increase party disaffection than to build support and cohesion, since the spoils could be seen to go to the least ethically minded party supporters.

Granted, making appointments according to merit is not a simple procedure. Criteria for a particular position should be set out clearly, and a system established for matching candidates' qualifications to these criteria as objectively as possible. Of course, bias can still affect the evaluation process. Even if a candidate's political leanings are ruled out, other equally objectionable selection criteria could come to the fore in a supposedly merit-based system. For example, some ostensibly impartial criteria for appointing judges have been criticized for placing too much emphasis on candidates' records of service to a bar association or law society and too little on non-legal community service and diversity.[35] Better ways need to be found to minimize the influence of irrelevant factors in making merit-based appointments.

The original bureaucratic revolution did not succeed in eliminating patronage at the upper levels of our political system. Yet patronage might be closer to its last breath as a result of the wave of reforms to the selection process currently observed federally, and in many provincial capitals.

## CONFLICTS OF INTEREST

In the literature on politics, business and law, conflicts of interest are ascribed two different meanings. One concerns conflicts between public and private interests, and this is the meaning we focus on in our ethics analysis. The other, more general notion involves disagreements about what the public interest is and how it should be served. This more general concept we will refer to as a conflict of values.

Simply put, a conflict of values is a conflict over principles and beliefs. This can occur, for example, between working people and wealthy shareholders over a company's occupational health-and-safety policy, between capitalists and socialists over the regulation of business or between smokers and non-smokers over the regulation of public places. Though conflicts of values should be resolved in a fair and orderly manner, the democratic methods for dealing with such conflicts become corrupted when one side unfairly advances its own cause or subverts the legitimate activities of its opponents.

In the public sector, a conflict of interest occurs when an elected or appointed public official attempts to promote a private interest, for him- or herself or for some other person(s), that results, or appears to result, in interference in the impartial discharge of one's duties or a gain or advantage by virtue of his or her position.[36] Conflicts of interest are therefore unacceptable in a society that values impartiality, fairness and integrity. Equally important is the fact that public officials who use their positions to provide special benefits to themselves, their families, or their political friends, undermine the legitimacy of the institutions they purport to serve. If such conflicts are allowed to persist, citizens will see few reasons to support public institutions or to respect the work of the officials who occupy them. Where there is a conflict between public and private interests, the public should always prevail.

But these ideas are based on general principles, and it is challenging to reach a consensus about how they should be applied to certain vexing cases. That is where the rules of ethical politics come into play. The various ethics rules represent an effort to reconcile general principles with society's expectations about the appropriate behaviour of public officials.

## Rules Governing Conflicts of Interest

There is a four-tier hierarchy of conflict of interest violations in Canada. At the top are conflicts of interest that lead to financial benefit. Rules in the *Criminal Code* prescribe prison terms, but unlike in France, where penalties are outlined in the civil law, relatively few public officials are prosecuted for benefitting from a conflict of interest. This is likely a result of two combined factors: the relatively high ethical standards of most public officials and the difficulty of obtaining sufficient evidence against the few who commit violations.

Next are conflicts that do not result in financial benefit. For example, public officials may find themselves in violation of whatever conflict of interest code or legislation they are subject to without actually benefitting from it. If someone could benefit unfairly from their public office (say, by being in a position to award contracts to companies in which they or an associate has an interest), then that person has a duty to remove him- or herself from that situation. This official could sell certain assets, for example, or delegate decision making to someone who would not have a conflict of interest. If they fail to take such steps, then they are guilty of what is known as a *real* conflict of interest, even if they do not receive any benefits.

Then there are *apparent* conflicts of interest. Even if all the rules are complied with, most conflict of interest codes state that public officials, in addition to acting impartially, have a responsibility to *show* the public that they are acting impartially. For example, the *Conflict of Interest Code for Members of the House of Commons*, which covers cabinet ministers and some other public officials, says that "public office holders have an obligation to [act in a manner] that will bear the closest public scrutiny, an obligation that is not fully discharged by simply acting within the law."[37] In other words, public officials have a duty to avoid situations in which a well-informed observer might reasonably believe a public official to be in a conflict of interest, even if such behavior is, technically speaking, not covered by the rules.

Finally, we have situations in which conflict of interest codes are violated without a real or apparent conflict of interest having occurred. For example, most public officials are required to make confidential or public disclosures of so-called non-personal assets and liabilities. Non-personal assets comprise investments other than one's home, cottage or car. These disclosures enable ethics counsellors to provide specific advice about how to avoid conflicts of interest. Failure to make a full disclosure is a breach of the rules, even if the assets and liabilities themselves do not or would not result in a conflict of interest.

Consistent with this analysis, Mr. Justice William Parker, who presided over the inquiry into the conflict of interest allegations against Sinclair Stevens in 1986–87, defined a real conflict of interest as "a situation in which a minister of the Crown has knowledge of an economic interest that is sufficient to influence the exercise of his or her public duties and responsibilities." A *potential* conflict of interest exists when a minister "finds himself or herself in a situation in which the existence of some private economic interest could influence the exercise of his or her public duties or responsibilities . . . provided that he or she has not yet exercised such duty or responsibility."[38] A potential conflict becomes a real conflict where a minister fails to dispose of relevant assets or withdraw from certain public duties or decisions.

Parker's analysis was the best up to 1987. However, by 2017, in addition to conflicts of interest involving potential financial gain, the concept has broadened in most codes to include other situations that may result in public officials granting favours for family members, friends or party supporters. Clearly, the potential for financial gain is not the only incentive that may tempt a public official to act in a self-interested fashion.

## Unwritten Conflict of Interest Rules

Until the 1960s, there was little appetite for written conflict of interest codes for elected officials in Canada. Federal and provincial governments followed the approach inherited from the British: "reliance on unwritten rules and customs to avoid conflict of interest" by cabinet ministers.[39] This is not to say that written rules didn't exist. The *Criminal Code* has always prohibited the bribery of public officials and the granting of benefits by ministers in return for explicit favours. In addition, the statutes governing Parliament and the provincial legislatures, the standing orders of the House of Commons and provincial legislatures and the federal and provincial elections acts all deal to some extent with conflict of interest.

However, most of these provisions are designed to provide penalties if an offence can be proven in which a public official benefits from the exercise of his or her duties while in public office (the highest tier of the conflict of interest hierarchy), or occasionally when ministers could potentially benefit from public office and don't take remedial action (the second-highest tier). Only in the last thirty years have unwritten codes of conduct been replaced by specific rules prohibiting ministers and senior public from continuing involvement in any situations in which they could potentially derive personal benefit from public office. Such codes are now accepted in most Canadian jurisdictions, where they have pro-liferated at the departmental and ministry levels to include senior and junior public servants.

It is curious that the shift to written rules did not occur earlier. Ken-neth Kernaghan suggests two reasons for the advent of codification: greater media attention to conflict of interest stories, the fallout from the Watergate affair in the United States that forced debate and action and "a gradual but substantial modification in the public's view of what standards of conduct are appropriate for government officials."[40] Public standards may also have changed because of the increased demand for social equality. Conflicts of interest are frowned upon not only because MPs and ministers might take advantage of their office for personal gain, but also because they might receive advantages, or distribute such advantages to their friends and party colleagues, on a basis not equally available to all citizens.

## Federal Conflict of Interest Rules

In the federal sphere, written guidelines for cabinet ministers first appeared in 1964. That year, Prime Minister Lester B. Pearson dis-tributed a letter to his ministers regarding cabinet ethics in response to public concern about political corruption. The letter stressed that formal adherence to the law is not enough; ministers "must act in a manner so scrupulous that it will bear the closest public scrutiny."[41] It warned in general terms against having a financial interest that might appear to interfere with official duties and the use of privileged infor-mation for personal gain. The ambiguity of the letter illustrates how little thought had previously been given by Canadian ministers about the nature of cabinet conflicts of interest.

No major changes were made to Pearson's guidelines until early 1973, when public concern was aroused by several conflicts of interest allega-tions involving cabinet ministers. As a result, Allan MacEachen, president of the Treasury Board of Canada, produced a green paper containing draft legislation aimed at preventing conflicts of interest among MPs (including cabinet ministers) and senators. According to MacEachen, all public office holders are trustees of the public interest, and if they allow their private interests to take precedence, a conflict has occurred. The recommendations focused on preventing situations in which members could derive a personal financial gain from public office.

But the legislation that MacEachen recommended never material-ized. Instead, Prime Minister Pierre Trudeau sent a letter to all min-isters, which contained more specific conflict of interest guidelines reflecting some of MacEachen's recommendations. They provided for the disclosure of non-personal assets and the choice of either selling assets that could possibly lead to a conflict of interest or placing them in a blind trust. In 1974, the Office of Assistant Deputy Registrar Gen-eral (ADRG) was created to process the compliance documentation for ministers and other public officials covered by the guidelines. When Joe Clark became prime minister in 1979, he broadened the guidelines to apply to spouses and dependent children of ministers, thus closing some potential loopholes. In addition, he made the guidelines public for the first time. The application of the guidelines to spouses proved to be controversial, as some felt that this provision violated their privacy. Once back in office in 1980, Pierre Trudeau removed the applicability of the guidelines to spouses.

In 1983, former federal cabinet minister Allistair Gillespie was accused of having profited from dealings with his old department soon after leaving public life. The scandal precipitated the creation of a task force on ethical conduct co-chaired by Michael Starr and Mitchell Sharp, former cabinet ministers from Conservative and Liberal governments, respectively. The task force presented the most thorough analysis of the conflict of interest problem in Canada up to that point. Their report stated clearly that conflict of interest rules are intended to promote impartial decision making and equality of treatment. It envisioned a legislated code of ethical conduct that would apply to practically all public officials. The statute would also create an Office of Public Sector Ethics to aid in enforcing and interpreting the code. The Mulroney government chose not to implement these recommendations, however. Instead, in response to widespread claims that his government was prone to corruption, Mulroney produced a non-legislated conflict of interest code, which was somewhat more detailed than Trudeau's.

Both Trudeau's and Mulroney's guidelines contained rules concerning the handling of assets to prevent personal profit from use of public office, and the granting of special favours to friends and associates. Neither document, however, actually defined a conflict of interest. This omission illustrates the fact that rules have often been instituted hastily in response to public scandals, rather than in a conscious effort to safeguard the rule of law, social equality and ministerial impartiality. However, both sets of guidelines at least acknowledge the impartiality principle. The covering letter that accompanied Trudeau's guidelines in 1980 pointed to the goal of "fulfilling one's official responsibilities in an objective and disinterested manner." The Mulroney guidelines contained nine guiding "principles," the first of which was the need for "objectivity and impartiality of government."[42]

In the two-year period after these guidelines came into effect in January 1986, the federal government suffered through no fewer than fourteen conflict of interest incidents involving ministers or their aides.[43] The most publicized of these was the Sinclair Stevens affair. Stevens had been accused of numerous violations of the conflict code, in particular his continued management of his companies, which had been placed in a blind trust and for which his wife continued to act as solicitor. These allegations resulted in a judicial inquiry conducted by Mr. Justice William Parker, Chief Justice of the High Court of Ontario. After finding that Stevens had been in violation of the federal conflict code on several occasions (a conclusion later set aside in judicial review),[44] Parker recommended federal conflict of interest legislation, which would apply to spouses as well as to ministers. Like the Starr-Sharp report, Parker recommended the establishment of an independent ethics office to advise individual ministers and their families.

In an attempt to regain public confidence, in 1987 the Mulroney government tightened up the rules surrounding blind trusts and required ministers' spouses and dependents to disclose their assets in confidence to the ADRG. And in February 1988 the Mulroney government introduced conflict of interest legislation that would have covered the cabinet, members of Parliament and the Senate. It would have established an independent ethics commission. However, the proposed bill would have set lower standards for conflicts of interest involving party patronage. Gifts and loans received by MPs from political parties would not have to be reported to the commission. This was probably intended to reflect the position that there is nothing wrong with political parties doing favours for their elected members. However, the exemption left open the possibility that public office favours might be granted in return for donations to parties that might be earmarked, for example, to supplement the leader's salary, and such situations would be outside of the powers of the commission to review.

Because some in the Conservative Party thought the proposed legislation was too strict, while others thought it contained too many loopholes, the bill was put on the back burner and was never enacted. It was reintroduced in essentially the same form during Mulroney's second mandate, and suffered the same fate. According to Stevie Cameron, the prevention of conflicts of interest involving the government was simply not a priority for the Mulroney regime.[45] As a result, conflict of interest allegations continued to dog the government. They were a major factor in its overwhelming defeat at the hands of the Chrétien Liberals in the 1993 election.

The Liberal Party's platform for that year, contained in the well-publicized "Red Book," devoted one of eight chapters to "governing with integrity."[46] It promised the appointment of an independent ethics counsellor primarily to oversee the activities of lobbyists, but it left open the possibility that this official might play a broader role, including supervising the prevention of conflicts of interest. It also promised the development of a code of conduct for cabinet ministers, MPs and senators.

The Chrétien government moved slowly towards these goals. In 1994, the title of the ADRG was changed to Ethics Counsellor, and

Howard Wilson became the first to hold this office. Wilson helped to update the conflict of interest code covering cabinet ministers and other public officials, which became effective in June 1994. It was similar to the Mulroney code, but clearer. The ethics counsellor had a higher status than the ADRG, but still lacked the independence promised by the Liberals in 1993. A Special Joint Committee of the House and the Senate began meeting in September 1997 to develop the new code, but not much happened until the government's need to react to the sponsorship scandal resulted in real action. In 2003, the Chrétien government introduced legislation to create an independent conflict of interest commissioner for both the House of Commons and the Senate. The bill was turned back at the Senate because as an independent chamber, senators demanded a separate commissioner. In 2004, the legislation was re-introduced but changed to provide separate commissioners for each house.[47] The commissioner for the House of Commons was entitled the ethics commissioner, and Senate's was named the Senate ethics officer. *Bill C-4, An Act to Amend the Parliament of Canada Act (Ethics Commissioner and Senate Ethics Officer) and other Acts in consequence* received royal assent on March 31, 2004. A code of conduct for MPs and another similar one for senators were created and adopted by their respective houses in 2005. In addition to having jurisdiction over MPs, the ethics commissioner was also put in charge of administering the *Conflict of Interest and Post-Employment Code for Public Office Holders* (better known as "The Prime Minister's Code") that covered more than two thousand senior federal public officials known as public office holders. In 2006, the Harper government enacted legislation that changed the name of the Ethics Commissioner to the conflict of interest and ethics commissioner, and elevated the status of the Prime Minister's Code by replacing it with the *Conflict of Interest Act*. (Subsequent developments are discussed in Chapter 5.)

The overlap between the conflict of interest rules applicable to federal legislators, and those for the federal public service, is noteworthy. At the same time that ethics regimes were being created to address matters related to ethics for legislators, Jocelyne Bourgon, then Clerk of the Privy Council, established nine task forces in 1995, each led by deputy ministers, to address various issues that had surfaced as a result of the Chrétien government's 1994 Program Review. One of those task forces focused on the values and ethics of the public service.[48] It was led by John Tait, the former Deputy Minister of Justice, who was later appointed a principal advisor to the Privy Council Office. Tait designed the task force that applied a "bottom-up" approach to study a range of problems and challenges facing the public service, and ultimately to identify the core values of the public service. The task force's work resulted in a "statement of principles" for the Public Service of Canada. Tait's report later became the basis for the both the Prime Minister's Code, which was superseded by the *Conflict of Interest Act* (which applies to cabinet ministers and more than two thousand public office holders), and the values and ethics code for the public service. The "Tait Report" remains the main source document for guiding matters of ethics, including issues of conflict of interest for public servants.[49]

As of 2017, the conflict of interest prevention regime for the House of Commons, the Senate and other senior public offices is much better than it was several decades ago, though it is not perfect. Most of the time, democracy grows in short bounds, not great leaps.

## Provincial Conflict of Interest Rules

The provincial experience has run parallel with federal developments. As noted in Chapter 5, the provincial premiers began to draft guidelines for their ministers in the early 1970s in response to public concern about conflicts of interest, often in reaction to scandals. These documents frequently evolved into legislation, which usually applied to cabinet ministers as well as to other members of provincial legislative assemblies. All the provinces and territories now rely primarily on legislation and independent commissioners to prevent conflicts of interest amongst legislators. (For more on this see Chapter 5.)

## Summary of the Development of Conflict of Interest Rules

At both the federal and provincial levels, it was often the case that written guidelines responded to various crises of confidence in the government resulting from public outrage about cabinet ministers using their positions for personal gain. At first, conflict of interest rules usually attempted simply to prevent personal financial gain from public office. But the rules gradually began to increase in scope to include the granting of favours to friends and associates.

The most common response to conflict of interest scandals has been to make the rules ever more complex and to move from informal guidelines to legislation. This is consistent with current federal efforts to tighten ethics rules to hold individuals to account for the ethical dimensions of specific decisions and actions rather than observe some universal duty to behave ethically.[50] When legislation was drafted it applied to both ministers and other legislators, sometimes with little recognition that the appropriate standards of impartiality for cabinet ministers should be higher. Moreover, although most of today's conflict of interest rules pay homage to the principle of "ministerial impartiality," this concept is rarely defined with any clarity. In short, conflict of interest rules for Canadian ministers and elected members have come about more as incremental adjustments to political crises than as carefully reasoned responses to basic principles of the political system.

## UNDUE INFLUENCE

Undue influence is the use of privileges or connections not available to the general public to affect policy-making. In other words, it is the attempt to manipulate public policy in violation of citizens' right to be treated as equals in the design and implementation of public policy. Undue influence is unacceptable in a democratic society for the same reasons that conflicts of interest are: it disregards the principle of equality and allows the policy process to be used for special interests.

Both electoral and lobbying processes are particularly vulnerable to undue influence. Elections can be corrupted if someone donates money to a candidate or a party in return for a favour, such as a contract, job or change in policy that provides an advantage to a particular economic interest. As British Columbia's ethics commissioner noted in his 1993–94 *Annual Report*, "campaign contributions and assistance, whether financial or otherwise," can in some circumstances lead to a conflict of interest if an elected member makes a decision affecting the contributor.[51] Although lobbyists can serve a useful public function by providing valuable policy information in a timely manner, they can also corrupt the policy-making process by arranging for political donations in return for favours, or by offering unfair incentives to public officials such as lucrative job prospects in the private sector, exotic vacations or even numbered bank accounts in Switzerland.

## Election Financing

The first attempt to control election financing in Canada dates from 1874. Prior to that time, only things like giving money to a party in return for favour, or bribing an elector with a promise of alcohol, were considered illegal.

Legislation specifically regulating party financing first came about in 1874 as a result of the Pacific scandal, according to W.T. Stanbury.[52] Prime Minister John A. Macdonald had accepted very generous campaign contributions from the financial backers of the Canadian Pacific Railway. At the same time, the railway received generous contracts and subsidies from Macdonald's Conservative government. What appeared to be an obvious connection between campaign contributions and government favour was an important factor in the defeat of Macdonald's government in the 1874 election.

One of the first actions taken by Alexander Mackenzie's Liberal government after winning the election was to have Parliament enact the *Dominion Elections Act*, which provided for the registration of political parties, required candidates to appoint official agents to receive campaign contributions and required statements of the candidates' finances to be published within two months of an election.

No major changes were made to this legislation until it was replaced by the *Election Expenses Act* of 1974. The new legislation was brought about by the realization that the cost of fighting elections was continuing to escalate, and that without reasonable limits placed on campaign spending, elections would be determined primarily by whoever could raise the most money.

The 1974 law continued the registration and agency system for parties and candidates established a century before, but it tightened up some loopholes that had previously made it possible for candidates to avoid the rules. As well, it limited campaign expenditures on media advertising to $0.10 per elector and, in order to ensure compliance, required "third parties" (public interest groups) to advertise under the umbrella of a registered party. Candidate spending limits were set at $1.00 per elector for the first 15,000 registered voters, plus $0.50 for the next 10,000 and $0.25 for each elector over 25,000. Candidates who received at least 15 per cent of the votes cast would receive reimbursement for some of their election expenses. Radio and television stations were required to accept up to 6.5 hours of prime-time paid advertising from registered parties according to a formula deemed to be fair to each registered party, and they were required to apply the same rules to all candidates wanting to buy advertising time. Registered parties were required to disclose all their revenues and expenditures on an annual basis; the public disclosure would include the names of all donors giving more than $100. Donations and expenditures during election periods had to be reported separately by both candidates and parties. Tax credits were provided for individuals and corporations making donations to parties and candidates; the maximum tax credit that could be claimed was $500 for a donation of $1,150. However, no limits were set on the total amounts of individual donations.[53]

During the 1984 election campaign, a right-wing lobby group, the National Citizens' Coalition, challenged the restrictions on third-party advertising under the *Charter of Rights* and won. The eventual result was the establishment of the Royal Commission on Electoral Reform and Party Financing in 1989 to review the entire field of election financing.

The commission's report, which comprised twenty volumes including research studies, provided the most in-depth review of the electoral system in Canada's history. In 1991, the commission recommended changes that would make the system more transparent, but no major changes were suggested in terms of the direction of the *Election Expenses Act*. A relaxation of the restrictions on third-party advertising was recommended so that this provision would comply with the *Charter*, and these changes were accepted by Parliament. Restrictions on third-party advertising are important. If they are not in place, election spending limits cannot be effectively enforced. Elections would then be open to manipulation by large financiers even more than they already are, and this would have serious implications for the democratic principle of equal concern and respect.

One of the more controversial issues dealt with by the royal commission was the question of limits on individual campaign contributions, but in spite of evidence produced for the commission that limiting annual contributions would help to reduce undue influence, in the end the commission did not recommend setting limits, and consequently the Mulroney government took no action. The purpose of setting limits is to keep individual contributions low enough to be ineffective as bribes, making the exchange of political favours for campaign contributions unlikely. Ontario and Quebec had at times set strict limits on annual contributions from single sources at both the provincial and the municipal levels. In 1997, a non-election year, these limits were $750 in Ontario and $3,000 in Quebec (allowable amounts double during a campaign period). As well, Quebec prohibited donations from corporations and unions; only individual donations were allowed. The Progressive Conservative government of Mike Harris, elected in Ontario in 1995, eventually raised these limits tenfold. After the Dalton McGuinty Liberals were elected in 2003, they left the increased limits in place, as it made fundraising easier for them. In 2016, the Liberal government of Kathleen Wynne, under intense pressure from the media and the Opposition to reduce undue influence on election financing, substantially reduced contribution limits, as we note in Chapter 6.

However, in the wake of the sponsorship scandal, the Chrétien government brought in legislation to place strict limits on federal contributions in 2003, which were enhanced by the Harper government in 2006. The result is that all three major federal parties have had to reach out to their supporters for small financial contributions with much greater effort. Each has been relatively successful in doing so, which we think is better for democracy than relying on fewer, richer supporters.

Without limits on campaign contributions, benefits that donors receive through discretionary government decisions become suspect. The following examples come from a study conducted by Ian Greene for the 1991 Royal Commission on Electoral Reform and Party Financing:

- David Lam and his wife gave $17,000 to the PC Canada Fund in 1988; Mr. Lam was appointed lieutenant governor of British Columbia by the Progressive Conservative prime minister.[54]

- Two companies that donated $33,000 to the Ontario Liberal Party received a $5 million paving contract from the Liberal government. Companies that did not donate either got no contracts, or only small ones.[55]

- Don Cormie, head of the Principal Group, gave $20,000 to Don Getty's campaign for the leadership of the provincial Progressive Conservative Party in 1985. The Code inquiry was eventually established to investigate the failure of the Principal Group and losses to investors. Alberta's Conservative government was criticized by the inquiry for failing to take appropriate action against the subsidiaries of the Principal Group prior to the company's bankruptcy.[56]

- The Swiss arms manufacturer Oerlikon contributed $3,000 to the federal Progressive Conservatives in 1986; it received $678 million in federal contracts. Diedra Clayton of Oerlikon said that the company was led to believe that firms receiving government contracts in Canada were expected to make donations to the political party in office. She said that the company was approached by the Progressive Conservative Party spokesperson, whom she told, "If others do it, then we will do it too."[57]

- *Le Devoir* discovered that fifty-four companies hired by a federal Crown corporation responsible for the Old Port project in Quebec City donated more than $140,000 to the Liberal Party, which controlled the federal government until 1984. The federal funding for the project amounted to $155 million over five years; $90 million was spent without any control by Parliament. Each of the companies donated an average of just over $1,000 during each of three years.[58]

In 2017, British Columbia remained one of the few provinces with minimal constraints on political donations. This vulnerability made it worthwhile for the *Globe and Mail* to research the possible connection between donations and political favours. The paper reported the following:

- Two in-house lobbyists for a liquefied natural-gas plant donated $69,500 to the governing Liberal party in B.C. over the three years prior to 2017. During that time, the company's environmental assessments passed, and it negotiated "a controversial subsidy on electricity rates from the province and other tax breaks."[59]

- Between 2011 and 2016, the B.C. car dealer's group donated "more than half a million dollars"[60] to the B.C. Liberal Party. A former B.C. Solicitor General reported that the Association tried to pressured him to fire the chair of a "government-backed consumer protection agency, because he was taking the industry to task for misleading advertising."[61]

- "The *Globe* investigation found lobbyists and others have been donating multiple times in their own name, while being reimbursed by companies they represent. This practice is a clear breach of one of the few rules that do exist when it comes to campaign donations . . . The lobbyists often make the contributions in the form of buying tables at party fundraisers. It is, quite simply, the cost of doing business in B.C. where the governing Liberals raked in $12-million in fundraising dollars last year alone. No wonder they have refused to change the fundraising laws to bring the province in line with other jurisdictions not only in Canada but around the world."[62]

As Greene writes, "there is no proven relation between the favour and the donation — the problem is that the close proximity of the two events raises the question of whether there might be a connection."[63] And indeed, these kinds of stories do little to assure Canadians that there is no relation between campaign donations and political favours. Perhaps for this reason, the federal government and six provinces have placed limits on annual donations to political parties; only B.C., Saskatchewan, Newfoundland and PEI had no limits as of 2017. Why are there holdouts? As Gary Mason commented, "the practice of allowing the rich and powerful to have an outsized role in the outcome of elections in B.C. is simply not an issue that is top of mind with most voters."[64] Change will come only when voters demand it.

The solution to undue influence in party financing is simple: annual donations from single sources, including donations at fundraisers, should be limited to somewhere between $500 and $3,000, as is the case now in Ontario, Quebec, Manitoba and for federal parties. (Alberta, Nova Scotia and New Brunswick had set contribution limits at $4,000, $5,000 and $6,000 respectively, which from our perspective is still too high, but better than no limits at all.) As well, as of 2017, the Ontario legislature prohibited members of the legislature, as well as staff in the premier's office, chiefs of staff of cabinet ministers and employees of political parties, from attending fundraising events so as to prevent allegations of "cash for access."[65] Some party bagmen will undoubtedly complain that such a rule would hamstring party finances. However, if a party cannot attract a large number of small individual donors, especially given the very generous donor tax credits, it cannot claim to be representative of any significant group in society.

But limits to campaign contributions will resolve only part of the problem. Even in a jurisdiction with strict individual contribution limits, those intent on circumventing the rules will find a way to do so, although not always with impunity. In addition, the basic principles of political ethics need a firm foundation in the political parties and candidates. The development of codes of ethics by political parties, as well as extensive public education programs offered by electoral commissions or ethics commissioners, would help in this regard.

## Lobbyists

In contrast to the rules governing elections and party financing, the regulation of lobbyists only began in 1988 at the federal level; similar regulations have been proclaimed in eight of ten provinces, with legislation still pending in New Brunswick.

Ethics in lobbying is concerned with the moral obligation of lobbyists, regulators, and persons being lobbied, to respect the public's right to be informed of attempts to influence policy decisions, legislation, rules, procurement, contracts and other public decisions. (The term "lobbying" dates back centuries in the Parliamentary tradition.

Constituents would meet their MPs in the lobbies of the Parliament buildings to request assistance.) Since the 1970s, the proliferation of professional lobbying firms in Ottawa, or "hired guns," has caused concern about the potential for undue influence, especially among opposition MPs, regardless of party. Although the lobbying of elected members has always been an important part of democratic politics, a significant increase in the number of lobbyists in the 1980s was something new. In September 1985, Brian Mulroney announced a consultation process to establish a new registration policy for lobbyists. Some claim that Mulroney was forced into this position by the activities of lobbyist Frank Graves, whose intervention on behalf of east coast fishermen hoping to secure fishing licences went directly to the prime minister and then became public, embarrassing the PM.[66] Around the same time, the interventions of Mulroney's friend, the lobbyist Frank Moores, raised many concerns about undue influence.[67] As noted in Chapter 7, Moores was a lobbyist for Airbus Industrie at the same time that he was appointed by Mulroney to the board of Air Canada, then a Crown corporation. Such activities led to the enactment of the *Lobbyists Registration Act* in 1989.[68]

Since then, lobbying practices in Canada have advanced due mainly to technology, but also because the stakes in policy-making, procurement and influence are that much higher. As shown in Chapter 7, shifts in government thinking on matters like clean energy, pipelines, Indigenous land claims, infrastructure development and public construction projects, the contracting out of various public services and rules that privilege some economic activities over others like tobacco, raise the stakes significantly for market decisions and government intervention in these areas. The creation of federal, provincial and municipal lobbying registrars and commissioners is evidence of the increasing significance and importance placed on access to governmental decision makers. Technology, of course, can both make access more efficient and transparency more difficult, as evidenced by US presidential candidate Hilary Clinton, and the approximately thirty thousand emails that she sent over a private server rather than the government account she was given as secretary of state. Transparency means there is always the possibility that one's performance or actions will be monitored, and that one will be held to account for them. It is human nature to want to avoid this. But, for public officials there is a much higher expectation of a duty of care. Likewise, lobbyists have a public obligation to make the degree of their influence known, especially when that influence can translate into benefit for some over others.

Locally, a notable advance in lobby legislation has been observed with many Canadian municipalities either creating lobbyist registries or lobbying officers responsible for ensuring integrity in lobbying practices. Toronto and Ottawa have each created lobbyist registrar offices within their accountability structures for this purpose, and these have now been followed by many other municipalities, including Brampton and London, and similar municipal measures have been mandated in Quebec and Newfoundland under provincial regimes. Several cities, including Vancouver, have been contemplating the creation of a registry to document who is attempting to influence city councillors and mayors. As more services and procurement decisions are downloaded to municipalities, the stakes are higher than ever. The next challenge will be to harmonize the rules so as not to complicate the rights of citizens and organizations to communicate with elected officials.

## OTHER ABUSE OF AUTHORITY ISSUES

### Expense claims

Although complaints about lavish expense claims are a staple of politics, they reached such a crescendo in Ontario in 2009 that the Liberal provincial government felt forced to take action. Premier McGuinty "announced new rules to keep a closer eye on the expenses of approximately 300 top executives at twenty-two of Ontario's 615 arm's-length agencies, boards and commissions by having them approved by the province's integrity commissioner."[69] The *Public Sector Expenses Review Act* was enacted late in 2009, and it tasked the Office of the Integrity Commissioner with reviewing the expense claims of not only the top executives of the twenty-two agencies noted above, but of cabinet ministers, parliamentary assistants and leaders of the Opposition and their staff. The reviews take place after the expense claims have been submitted: The Office of the Integrity Commissioner reviews for compliance with the rules, and directs the repayment of funds claimed in violation of the rules. After this vetting, the expense claims are made public on the agencies' websites. The goal is not only to ensure that expense rules are complied with, but to encourage claimants to consider the public interest when claiming expenses, as they will be publicly posted. This practice has proved so effective that the integrity commissioner may conduct periodic reviews of posted expenses for all provincial agencies, boards and commissions.[70] In effect, as of 2014 the commissioner may review not only the expenses of the top twenty-two arm's-length agencies, but any agency within the purview of the Ontario government.

The 2013–16 Senate expenses scandal also drew the public's attention to potentially excessive expense claims. (This case is discussed in detail in Chapter 6.) The Trudeau government has opted to appoint non-partisan, independent senators in an attempt to recreate what the Senate was intended to be in 1867. The government has also brought the definition of what constitutes provincial residency for Senators in line with what most of us would consider reasonable. We applaud these changes. However, the Senate itself needs to reform its expense rules and procedures if it is to regain credibility.[71] The model set by the Ontario integrity commissioner might serve as an example.

In the summer of 2016, Health Minister Jane Philpott came under fire for charging nearly $2,000 on each of two separate days for a limousine in the Greater Toronto Area when other taxi companies could have done the work for less. The limousine company was owned by one of Philpott's supporters. The federal ethics commissioner investigated and found no violation of the conflict of interest rules, as the cost of the limousine was average, and there was no evidence of favouritism.[72] Nevertheless, Philpott personally covered the limousine charges,[73] and the incident produced many headlines — rivalling Conservative cabinet minister Bev Oda's expense claim for a $16 glass of orange juice[74] — indicating just how careful politicians need to be about their travel expense claims.

This is certainly true for ministerial staff as well. For example, in the fall of 2016 it was revealed that two of Prime Minister Justin Trudeau's top aides, Gerald Butts and Katie Telford, submitted moving expense claims of $126,669 and $80,382, respectively, for moving from Toronto to Ottawa in 2015. These amounts "included $20,799.10 and $23,373.71, respectively, for the 'personalized cash payout,' along with a further $20,819 in a land transfer tax for Mr. Butts."[75] Both Butts and Telford subsequently paid back these latter amounts, writing in a Facebook post, "We take full responsibility for this having happened and because of that we are sorry. We've learned a lot of lessons over the past few days, and we commit to continuing to improve transparency in the future. The Prime Minister has asked the Secretary of the Treasury Board to create a new policy to govern relocation expenses across government."[76]

Of course, most travel arrangements for cabinet ministers, MPs and senators are made by their staff, many of whom are young and lacking in ethics education. But politicians need to ensure that their staff understand these rules and principles. Staff take cues from their superiors; if their superiors exhibit an attitude of entitlement, staff are likely to follow. Take for example David Dingwall, President and CEO of the Royal Canadian Mint, who caused a debacle in the fall of 2005 when he appeared before a parliamentary committee arguing for a severance package after he was forced to resign for making inappropriate expense claims. As he put it, "I'm entitled to my entitlements." Or, recall the case of Ted Weatherill, who was fired from the Labour Relations Board in 1998 over a "bloated expense account," including a $700 lunch in Paris. Politicians and senior officials must assume responsibility for the actions of themselves and their staff. However, a culture of entitlement still predominates in the minds of some officials in high offices.

## Whistle-blowing and Public Disclosure

Since the 1970s, governments around the world have been wrestling with the issue of how to persuade honest public servants who observe corruption and wrongdoing in their workplaces to come forth with complaints. Such people are known as "whistle-blowers," after the term coined by US author, political activist and five-time presidential candidate Ralph Nader in the 1970s. For decades, Nader challenged governments to be more open and accountable. His coinage has come to mean "One who reveals wrongdoing within an organization to the public or to those in positions of authority," and in fact he regarded whistle-blowing as akin to a referee using a whistle to call an illegal play, as opposed to snitching or informing on others.

It is now widely accepted that whistle-blowing encourages duty-bound public servants to report improper behaviours, illegal or illegitimate practices or other inappropriate activities to their superiors. It encourages a speak-up culture that provides a foil against unbridled loyalty to public office holders.

Although many senior public officials see the benefits of whistle-blowing, the default in many institutions is to "shoot the messenger." Myths have developed that whistle-blowers are not team players, are disloyal or have mental health issues. These stereotypes have been repeatedly disproved; in almost all cases whistle-blowers are people who feel compelled to do the right thing. The challenge is to create a regime and an organizational culture that encourages individuals to speak up when they observe wrongdoing, and to protect them from reprisal if they do. Systems must be created that provide the means to come forward anonymously, and with confidence that complaints will be addressed fairly. It has been proven that such measures increase morale and strengthen the perception that wrongdoing will not be tolerated. Creating the means to blow the whistle within organizations is now regarded as a positive addition to the ethics regime as it reinforces the Jeremy Bentham adage that people and institutions will always behave better if they know they are being monitored.

The federal government, along with several provincial governments, have enacted whistle-blowing legislation that is designed to meet these challenges, and which aims to balance the need for a speak-up culture with organizational loyalty. These legislative innovations are reviewed in Chapter 8. The accompanying case studies provide some insight not only into the circumstances that compel some individuals to blow the whistle, but what can happen in institutions when the means to come forward are not available.

## CONCLUSION

Rules to ensure ethical behaviour are intended to promote the basic principle of mutual respect. Mutual respect demands impartiality in applying the law. In government programs that have adopted sound practices of public administration (clear rules for management-employee relations, the merit principle, equality and fairness in providing services), ministers, if called upon to make administrative decisions, are expected to act impartially and fairly. But some of the upper levels of government escaped the original "bureaucratic revolution," and political patronage and favouritism remain important ethical problems.

As a result, movements towards higher ethical standards have not advanced consistently. The actions by the Harris government in Ontario in the 1990s to reintroduce old fashioned patronage into the administrative tribunal system, and the Harper government's attempt between 2011 and 2015 to introduce more ideological appointments into the federal judiciary, ought to be a wake-up call to those who think that advances in ethical politics cannot be rolled back.

It is also the case that conflict of interest, undue influence and personal gain remain a problem. In 2016 alone, we saw federal ministers come under fire for attending pay-for-access fundraisers; a prime minister use public funds to pay his children's nannies through the Foreign Workers Program even though he had campaigned vehemently against it; a former Quebec deputy premier arrested for corruption, fraud and bribery; senior public officials in British Columbia charged with breach of trust in a vote-getting scandal; and senior officials in Ontario charged after deleting files related to the gas plants scandal. There is no shortage of wrongdoing in Canada, despite our claims of moral superiority.

There is no single solution to these ethical problems. But rectifying the lack of understanding or commitment to the importance of fair procedures or rules among Canadians would be an important step. Until recently, practical ethics received almost no attention in the elementary and high school system, and it fared only slightly better in colleges and universities. Furthermore, the bad habits of the past create a "hangover effect," and the negative behaviour of politicians sometimes discourages honest people from running for elected office, while encouraging those who seek primarily personal enrichment.

Yet compared with the situation in Canada a century ago, even thirty years ago, we have seen a net gain. It takes centuries to build a civil society, and the modern concern with fairness developed only relatively recently. A challenge for our contemporary bureaucracy is Canada's aging population, and public servants who are likely to become much younger as individuals advance through the ranks much more quickly. It is more important than ever to emphasize sound ethics in institutions that will guide behaviours.

Some of the successes and failures of the current systems and rules governing conflicts of interest, undue influence and other abuses of trust can be assessed through an analysis of some recent cases. The next chapter presents case studies of conflict of interest scandals as well as some examples of abuse of trust through entitlement.

# CHAPTER 4
# CASE STUDIES: CONFLICTS OF INTEREST AND ENTITLEMENT

## Ian Greene and Robert Shepherd

The need for rules and procedures to prevent abuse of trust becomes painfully clear when we take a closer look at some of the ethics scandals of recent years. These cases are presented under the headings of conflicts of interest and entitlement.

## CONFLICTS OF INTEREST

The conflict of interest cases reviewed in this chapter are organized according to the hierarchy of wrongs presented in Chapter 3. The most serious wrong is the *Criminal Code* offence of *fraud*, that of receiving a financial benefit in return for a public office favour, as illustrated by the cases of Robert Poirier (2015) and Jacques Corriveau (2016).

The next level of conflict is what Mr. Justice William Parker, in the Sinclair Stevens inquiry report, called a *real* conflict of interest, that of knowingly being in a position to benefit personally from public office and continuing in that situation even if no personal benefits result. The Shawn Graham (2012) and Diane Finley (2015) cases provide examples of this kind of conflict.

The third level is an *apparent conflict of interest.* In this situation, a reasonable perception exists that the performance of a public official's official duties is affected by his or her private interest. For this, we will consider the controversy surrounding former Alberta Premier Alison Redford, who was in office from 2011 to 2014.

The fourth level of conflict is a violation of the rules designed to prevent conflicts of interest, although not being in a real conflict of interest. There is nothing inherently wrong with being in a potential conflict of interest. But this may become *real* conflict of interest, which is unacceptable, unless the decision maker takes appropriate action to remove him- or herself from that conflict. A conflict of interest code can be thought of as an instrument to prevent potential conflicts of interest from becoming real ones, such as when it mandates the timely disclosure of assets. Helena Geurgis, Conservative MP from 2004 to 2011, and Christian Paradis, Minister of Public Works in 2009, provide our case studies here.

Finally, we look at how conflicts of interest can extend beyond mere financial transactions. Michael Bonner, a senior policy advisor to Employment Minister Jason Kenney in 2013, was found to have violated the conflict of interest rules for accepting free tickets to events from lobbyists.

To set the stage for the case studies, it is important to consider the most important study of the concept of conflict of interest conducted in the twentieth century: the Sinclair Stevens inquiry.

## Sinclair Stevens and York Centre

In April 1986, the *Globe and Mail* published a series of articles alleging that the federal industry minister, Sinclair Stevens, had used his public office to further his personal business interests. The allegations kept coming until mid-May, when Stevens resigned, and Mr. Justice William Parker, Chief Justice of the High Court of Ontario, was tasked with looking into the alleged conflicts of interest. Parker conducted much of his inquiry in public, and the hearings on cable television attracted one of the largest audiences Canada's parliamentary channel had ever seen. The coverage brought the issue of conflicts of interest in Parliament to many Canadians' attention.

Parker found that Stevens had been in a real conflict of interest position on at least fourteen occasions.[1] However, in 2004, Stevens succeeded in having Parker's conclusions set aside in a judicial review, where they were "declared to have no force or effect." Remarkably, the Mulroney cabinet's conflict of interest code contained no definition of what constituted a conflict of interest. Cabinet ministers were required to avoid conflicts, of course, but it was assumed that the ministers knew what constituted them. Parker applied the common law definition of conflict of interest, but in the judicial review, the judge considered that this approach was a violation of Stevens's right to procedural fairness, in that he was being held to a standard of which he was unaware.[2] This episode indicated that the state of thinking about conflicts of interest in Canadian politics was not highly developed in the 1980s.

Nevertheless, Parker's analysis of the nature of conflicts of interest was seminal.[3] His report was the most thorough investigation into this topic ever undertaken in Canada up to that point, and it was arguably one of the most important catalysts for the development of procedures to prevent conflicts of interest in Parliament and the provincial legislatures.

As noted in Chapter 3, Parker defined the difference between a *real* and a *potential* conflict of interest, a distinction used for analytical purposes in this chapter. As for his recommendations, his first was the full and confidential disclose of cabinet ministers' financial situation to an independent advisor. At that time, the federal advisor was known as the Assistant Deputy Registrar General (ADRG).[4] To protect members' privacy, Parker wrote that there was no need for elected members to disclose personal assets "such as place of residence, household goods and personal effects, automobiles, cash and saving deposits, RRSPs, and so forth." However, "all other financial interests — all sources of income, assets, liabilities, holdings and transactions in real or personal property — would have to be disclosed in a financial disclosure statement that would be filed in the Public Registry and made available to the media and other interested citizens."[5] Variations of Parker's recommendation have been implemented in all jurisdictions with a conflict of interest commissioner.

Second, Parker recommended the abolition of the blind trust as a means of preventing conflicts of interest involving family assets, unless the trust is truly blind: a recommendation that has been overlooked in some jurisdictions. Third, he recommended that the conflict of interest code be simplified, and most importantly that it contain a clear definition of a real conflict of interest.[6] Fourth, he recommended that the conflict of interest guidelines apply to ministers' spouses, which is now generally the case across the country. Fifth, he advised that the office of the independent advisor should "have a clearer mandate, broader powers, and a higher profile," and "should be able to make rulings and have the power and resources to investigate possible conflicts and to hold independent inquiries when necessary."[7] This recommendation has been implemented in federal, provincial and territorial jurisdictions across the country, starting in Ontario in 1988.

Parker also outlined three methods of avoiding a real conflict of interest: divestment, disclosure and recusal. In Parker's view, because blind trusts frequently fail, and because forcing members to sell non-personal assets is often unfair, and might even discourage good people from running for elected office, the emphasis should shift to broad public disclosure. The premise is that a "healthy measure of public vigilance," made possible through public disclosure, will eventually result in greater confidence in the integrity of elected officials, as long as they avoid conflicts of interest.[8] Ministers should therefore be required to sell assets only when these assets would be likely to place them in a potential conflict of interest so frequently as to seriously interfere with their ability to perform public duties. With the emphasis on disclosure rather than divestment, however, cabinet ministers would in some instances find themselves in potential conflicts, in which cases they would have to recuse themselves.[9]

## Fraud

Fraud is defined in section 380 of Canada's *Criminal Code* as follows: "Everyone who, by deceit, falsehood or other fraudulent means . . . defrauds the public or any person . . . of any property, money or valuable security or any service."[10] If the fraud exceeds $5,000, the penalty could be up to fourteen years in prison. If less, the maximum penalty is two years.

Because the definition is so broad, only some frauds are the result of a conflict of interest; indeed, these types of convictions are relatively rare. This is due in part to the fact that it is often difficult to prove beyond a reasonable doubt that fraud has occurred. After all, fraudsters rarely keep records that could be used in court.

### ROBERT POIRIER, FORMER MAYOR OF BOISBRIAND

Thanks to the efforts of investigative reporters, there was an increased number of reports into collusion between leading municipal politicians, construction firms and the mafia in Quebec in the first decade of the millennium. As a result, in 2011 the provincial government created an anti-corruption unit, UPAC.[11] UPAC was composed of experienced police officers and prosecutors.[12] Its first important achievement was the successful prosecution of Robert Poirier, the former mayor of Boisbriand (a city about forty kilometres north of Montreal), for fraud and corruption.

Poirier had been the chief organizer of a group of city councillors and bureaucrats that fixed construction contracts in proportion to the amount of money that construction firms gave to his municipal political party. He was arrested in 2011, convicted in 2015 and in 2016 was sentenced to eighteen months in prison, followed by three years of parole.[13] A major reason for the conviction was that UPAC had persuaded Lino Zambito, former vice-president of the Quebec construction firm Infrabec, to admit his role in the collusion scheme and testify as a witness for the crown. His explosive testimony led to the creation of the Commission of Inquiry on the Awarding and

Management of Public Contracts in the Construction Industry, better known as the Charbonneau commission, where Zambito became the star witness.[14] The commission reported in November 2015 that it found widespread corruption in Quebec's construction industry, aided and abetted by dishonest politicians and public servants. The report made sixty recommendations, including strengthening support for whistle-blowers.[15]

As a result of the investigations by UPAC and the testimonies at the Charbonneau commission, approximately three dozen other people were charged with fraud and sundry offences, including Gilles Vaillancourt, former mayor of Laval, and Michael Appelbaum, former mayor of Montreal. Their preliminary inquiries were held in 2015, and after being committed to trial, Vaillancourt and thirty-three others elected for trial by judge and jury, while Applebaum elected for a trial by judge alone. In 2017, Applebaum was found guilty on eight counts of fraud corruption and sentenced to a year in jail and two years' probation.[16] The other trials will likely take place in 2017 or 2018.[17]

In 2015, Lino Zambito pleaded guilty to fraud and conspiracy charges, for which he could have faced up to ten years in prison. However, taking into account Zambito's confession and his honesty at the Charbonneau commission, both the Crown and Zambito's lawyer recommended a sentence of two years less a day to be served in the community, plus 240 hours of community service, plus probation for three years.[18] The judge accepted the recommendation.

## JACQUES CORRIVEAU AND THE SPONSORSHIP SCANDAL

In the 1980s and 1990s, Jacques Corriveau was active in the back rooms of the Quebec wing of the federal Liberal Party. In the 1980s, he was its vice-president, as well as the vice-president (francophone) of the federal Liberals. He worked hard on his close friend Jean Chrétien's leadership campaign in 1990. He continued to have a great deal of influence over the party and the Prime Minister's Office in the late 1990s and early 2000s, regardless of "whether or not he still occupied an official position within the Party."[19] In his report, Justice John Gomery identified Corriveau as a central figure in the sponsorship scandal.

The Sponsorship Program was first approved by the federal cabinet in 1994. At the time, it was a small program designed to sponsor events with advertising by the Canadian government anywhere in the country. However, after the 1995 Quebec referendum, in which the sovereignty option was narrowly defeated, the program was substantially ramped up. Between 1994 and 2003, $332 million was spent on sponsorship programs, $147 million of which went to fees and commissions charged by advertising and communications firms.[20] After 1995, the program was administered outside of the usual oversight mechanisms that could have prevented fraud and corruption, with funds distributed through advertising and communications agencies that charged significant commissions. During its first few years the program was led by Charles Guité, the Executive Director of the Communication Coordination Services Branch in the Public Works Department, who retired in 1999. Guité's approval of sponsorships was initially directed by the prime minister's principal secretary, and later by Minister of Public Works Alfonso Gagliano. Beginning in 1999 and 2000, media reports based on information from access to information requests indicated that large amounts of money had been spent on sponsorship projects for which little if any work was completed. Subsequently, two reports by the auditor general indicated that substantial amounts of money from the sponsorship program could not be properly accounted for. In 2002, Prime Minister Chrétien appointed Ralph Goodale as Minister of Public Works, and directed him to "find out what is the problem and fix it."[21] Goodale realized that the program was in such deep trouble that he suspended it, although it was later resumed without using the advertising and communications agencies as intermediaries. In December 2003, when Paul Martin became prime minister, his cabinet's first action was to cancel the Sponsorship Program.[22] In early 2004, under huge public pressure, the Paul Martin cabinet established a commission of inquiry into the Sponsorship Program, under the direction of Justice John Gomery.[23]

While the Sponsorship Program operated, Mr. Corriveau was the owner of PluriDesign Canada Inc., a graphic design business. In 1994 or 1995, the executive assistant to the Minister of Public Works introduced Corriveau to Charles Guité, and told Guité to "look after him" (Corriveau), and that Corriveau was a good friend of the prime minister.[24] (In 2006, Guité was convicted of fraud for his role in the Sponsorship Program, and sentenced to three and a half years in jail.)[25] PluriDesign handled many parts of the advertising program for the Liberal Party's Quebec wing. For example, in 1997, it contracted with the Liberal Party for the production of $900,000 worth of posters and campaign materials.[26]

At the inquiry, Justice Gomery found Corriveau to be an unreliable witness. He often contradicted himself, and claimed to have forgotten much of what transpired regarding his involvement in the Sponsorship Program. He claimed his memory had been affected by anesthesia used during an operation in 2004. However, he never produced medical evidence for this claim. Gomery stated that Corriveau's "motivation to attempt to hide the facts and to mislead the Commission became apparent as the evidence unfolded; he was the central figure in an elaborate kickback scheme by which he enriched himself personally and provided funds and benefits to the LPCQ."[27]

Gomery concluded that between 1994 and 2003, Corriveau had charged approximately $6 million in fees and commissions "for no consideration other than Mr. Corriveau's political influence."[28] Gomery found that there were agreements between Corriveau and the advertising and communications firms for which he arranged sponsorship contracts that commissions amounting to "17.65% of the amounts received" would be paid to Corriveau.[29] These fees and commissions were disguised as services. This finding left Gomey "with no alternative but to conclude that Mr. Corriveau was at the heart of an elaborate kickback scheme."[30]

After the release of the Gomery report, the RCMP initiated its own investigation into Corriveau. The investigation lasted six years, due in part to the difficulty that the prosecution had in obtaining confidential documents.[31] It took another two and a half years to decide whether to lay fraud charges; they were finally laid in December 2013. In late 2016, Corriveau was tried by a jury. The Crown alleged that he received $6 million in cheques for services never rendered, and another $1 million in cash. The jury found him guilty of three counts of fraud,[32] and he was sentenced to four years in jail plus a fine of $1.4 million.[33] He was eighty-three years old at the time of his conviction.

Corriveau used his connections with the Liberal Party, his friendship with the prime minister and his connection with Charles Guité to direct contracts from the Sponsorship Program to his firm, along with other advertising and communications firms, in return for illegal commissions, or kickbacks. Although he did not occupy a public office, he took advantage of his connections with those who did to enrich himself and to provide illegal donations to the Liberal Party.[34]

There are only a few other examples in recent Canadian history of politicians having been convicted for fraud or influence-peddling related to conflicts of interest, although that may change after the trials related to corruption in the Quebec construction industry. Conservative Senator Eric Berntson was convicted of fraud in 1999 for his role in the Saskatchewan communications allowance scandal (described in Chapter 1),[35] and in 1998 Conservative Senator Michel Cogger was convicted of influence-peddling for accepting kickbacks in return for arranging government contracts.[36] Conservative MP Michel Gravel pleaded guilty to charges of bribery and corruption in 1988 for helping to arrange the leasing of federal government office space in return for kickbacks.[37] In 1986, Conservative Party organizer Pierre Blouin pleaded guilty to influence-peddling.[38] In 1982 and 1983, three fundraisers for the Nova Scotia Liberal Party, J.G. Simpson, Charles MacFadden and Senator Irvine Barrow, were convicted of influence-peddling.[39] As well, in 2016, former Quebec Deputy Premier Nathalie Normandeau, along with six co-accused, were arrested by UPAC and charged with offences related to illegal campaign financing and fraud related to a contract for a water treatment plant. At the time of writing, the trial had not begun.[40]

The relatively small number of examples of fraud resulting from conflicts of interest suggests four things. First, fraud may not be as widespread a problem in our political system as real conflicts of interest. Second, it is often difficult to obtain a criminal standard of proof in fraud cases. How does a prosecutor prove the connection between a donation to a political party and a government contract unless the agreement is recorded, which rarely happens, or unless a contractor, such as Lino Zambito, is willing to risk a tarnished reputation by testifying? Political contributions and government contracts may not necessarily be directly related. Third, according to Stevie Cameron, police and prosecutors are reluctant to investigate political corruption, and to carry the investigations through to prosecution. These investigations are extremely expensive and time-consuming, and they may backfire on the investigating authorities, as illustrated by the Mike Duffy case in Chapter 6. Cameron's study of corruption in the Mulroney government, *On the Take*, describes a number of police investigations that were eventually abandoned, either because of budgetary constraints or from fear of the fallout from a successful prosecution. Finally, more effective whistle-blowing legislation may result in a greater number of successful prosecutions for fraud. However, this would require government commitment to more effective disclosure systems, and a willingness to protect employees from reprisals.

## Real Conflicts of Interest

A real conflict of interest occurs when someone is in a situation in which they could use their public position for personal gain or to grant favours and does not remove him- or herself from that situation, *even if no personal benefit ultimately results.*

### DIANE FINLEY

In May 2012, a number of media reports suggested that Diane Finley, federal Minister of Human Resources and Skills Development in the Harper government, had given preferential treatment to the Markham

Centre for Skills and Independence proposal for funding under the federal Enabling Accessibility Fund in 2011. Federal Conflict of Interest and Ethics Commissioner Mary Dawson investigated the allegations once she was made aware of them in the media.

The Markham proposal was one of 167 that progressed through the initial screening conducted by the department in 2011, but it received a low eligibility score. There was only enough funding in the budget to support a handful of the top proposals. And yet at the urging of cabinet colleague John Baird, along with personnel in the Prime Minister's Office, Finley nonetheless asked for the Markham proposal to be recommended for funding.

In March 2015, Ms. Dawson issued her report. It found that Ms. Finley had been in a conflict of interest under subsection 6(1) of the *Conflict of Interest Act*, which "prohibits public office holders from making decisions if they know or reasonably should know that, in making this decision, they would be in a conflict of interest."[41]

Dawson also "found that the Markham proposal clearly received preferential treatment, as the backers of the Markham Centre were allowed to provide additional information to supplement the original proposal, something no other applicants were permitted to do. As well, the proposal was the only one given a last-minute external evaluation at Ms. Finley's request. It is noteworthy that the funding for the Markham project was later withdrawn, because established timelines could not be met and significant cost increases had resulted from building deficiencies."[42]

Despite this investigation, it remains unclear why this particular proposal was given preferential treatment, but it can be inferred from the investigation's report that Minister Baird "had close ties with Rabbi Mendelsohn," one of the backers of the proposal, and that he had "made representations to Ms. Finley in support of the Markham proposal."[43] It is clear from Dawson's report that the proposal had been discussed with members of the cabinet, including Minister of the Environment Peter Kent and Chief of Staff Nigel Wright, which means the prime minister was likely aware of the proposal as well.[44] That such discussions were taking place at this level also raises questions about the fairness of the adjudication and decision-making process, as clearly not all proposals were afforded similar attention by cabinet.

Dawson wrote that Finley should have known that by giving preferential treatment to the Markham proposal she was furthering the private interests of the group that had submitted it. It makes no difference that the funds for the proposal were later withdrawn.

## SHAWN GRAHAM

The former premier of New Brunswick, Shawn Graham, was on his way to a stellar political career after his Liberal Party won the provincial election in 2006. But in 2010 he became the first premier in the province's history to lead his government to defeat after only one term in office, and the first politician to be found in a conflict of interest since the province's *Members' Conflict of Interest Act* was enacted in 1999. The son of long-serving provincial Liberal politician Alan Graham, Shawn Graham was first elected as a Member of the Legislative Assembly for Kent-Russell in 1998, upon his father's retirement. Mr. Graham became leader of the New Brunswick Liberal Party in 2002, leading it to victory in 2006.

On March 26, 2009, members of the Liberal cabinet, including Premier Graham, approved a $50 million loan to Atcon Holdings despite knowledge that numerous smaller loans to Atcon and its related companies remained unpaid. In addition, at the time of the loan, New Brunswick was on the hook for a $13.4 million loan guarantee to the Northwest Territories for an Atcon project that would soon be revealed to be in default. The government agency responsible for providing business loans, Business New Brunswick (BNB), had reviewed the application and rejected it at three different stages as too risky. But after these processes had run their course, BNB was directed by cabinet to provide the loan.

Within months, bankruptcy proceedings had been filed against Atcon and some of its subsidiaries, and the government was forced to pay out its guarantee to the Northwest Territories. At the time of the decision, Atcon companies were important employers in the Miramichi region of New Brunswick, which had been hard hit by unemployment. Graham later attributed the approval of the loan to his government's focus on job retention at all costs.[45]

On its own, the loan to Atcon might have been considered at best poor politics, at worst a faulty financial risk management, a sort of abject lesson in the perils of government assistance to private-sector firms. However, a complaint launched by Progressive Conservative MLA Claude Williams on April 7, 2010 alleged that Premier Graham's father, Alan, was a director of Vanerply, a Swedish company wholly owned by Atcon. Further, he alleged that Alan Graham was a paid business consultant to Vanerply and other Atcon companies. It therefore appeared that Premier Graham, by participating in the cabinet decision to extend financing to Atcon, had placed himself in a conflict of interest to the extent that his actions "provided opportunity to further the member's private interest or to further another person's private interest."[46] Partly as a result of these allegations, in the September 2010 provincial election, Graham's party was defeated resoundingly by the Progressive Conservative Party.

A comprehensive, ten-month inquiry into these allegations was conducted by the Honourable Patrick Ryan between December 2010 and September 2011. Final documents were reviewed in December 2012. In 2013, the investigation found that the premier had indeed contravened the *Conflict of Interest Act*.[47] Graham resigned as Liberal leader after the election, but retained his seat in the legislature until Ryan issued his report. He was reprimanded by the commissioner and fined $3,500 before resigning his seat.

In his report, Commissioner Ryan was highly critical of both senior civil servants and politicians and pointed out multiple irregularities, failures of checks and balances and outright obstruction. Senior civil servants had attempted to obstruct the inquiry by refusing to provide documents and details on the due diligence performed when analyzing the Atcon loan request, arguing that the Crown was not bound by the *Conflict of Interest Act*.[47] One person, the deputy minister responsible for BNB, was found to have knowingly misled the inquiry regarding financial exposure of the province on a $13 million loan guarantee for Atcon in 2008 in which the province ultimately had to cover the loan.[47] Standard loan consideration procedures had not been followed by BNB staff, multiple recommendations to reject the loan had been ignored by cabinet and the responsible BNB financial officer had failed to flag Alan Graham's involvement with the company.[47] Commissioner Ryan commented on the timing of Alan Graham's exit from his duties with Vanerply, noting that it was far from straightforward. Graham maintained that he was unaware of his father's continuing involvement with Vanerply and Atcon, a fact that was not disputed by the commissioner.[47]

Instead, the conflict of interest accusations revolved around the question of "whether the evidence establishes that the Premier reasonably should have known that the decisions . . . gave rise to an opportunity to further the private business and financial interests of his father, Alan Graham."[48] Although it was concluded that the primary motivation for the loan was to save jobs in a disadvantaged area of the province and that "the loan guarantees might have happened with or without the Premier,"[49] Ryan found that the premier had a "duty of due diligence" to verify whether his father was still involved[50] and that the test must be whether he "reasonably should know."[51] The commissioner found that Shawn Graham had not been "willfully blind" but that his "dereliction amount[ed] to a high level of blindness approaching indifference."[52] He also found that a non-trivial breach of section 4 of the *Act* had been committed. Because such a serious breach had been committed by a member of the cabinet, the commissioner recommended that both a reprimand and a fine be levied.

Graham is not the only provincial leader to lose his job because of a real conflict of interest. In 1991, Commissioner Ted Hughes, British Columbia's conflict of interest commissioner, found that B.C. Premier Bill Vander Zalm had used his public office for private gain. Vander

Zalm resigned, and his Social Credit Party was wiped off the political map in the subsequent provincial election.[53]

## Apparent Conflicts of Interest

The idea of an *apparent* conflict of interest was considered by Mr. Justice William Parker in his report on Sinclair Stevens. The federal conflict of interest guidelines that applied to Stevens required public office holders to avoid apparent conflicts of interest, but the concept was not clearly defined in the guidelines. Parker concluded that "an apparent conflict of interest exists when there is a reasonable apprehension, which reasonably well-informed persons could properly have, that a conflict of interest exists."[54] In a *real* conflict of interest situation, as we have seen, a public official is, or ought to be, aware of private interests that could be affected by how he or she conducts public business. But in an apparent conflict, "no such actual knowledge is necessary . . . [although] the perception must be reasonable, fair, and objective . . . [but not necessarily] based on a complete understanding of *all* the facts."[55] In other words, public officials must not only avoid mixing their public duties with their private interests; they must also take the appropriate steps to prevent the *appearance* of such mixing.

Whether this concept is sufficiently clear to be covered by conflict of interest legislation is an important question. Ontario's first conflict of interest commissioner, Gregory Evans, considered the concept too vague to be useful, while in B.C., Ted Hughes expressed the opinion that public expectations require elected officials to avoid apparent conflicts. In 1992, an amendment to the conflict of interest legislation in that province prohibited MLAs from engaging in official duties "if the Member has a conflict of interest or an apparent conflict of interest."[56] In 1993, Hughes ruled that Robin Blencoe, Minister of Municipal Affairs in the NDP government at the time, would be in an apparent conflict of interest were he to make a ministerial decision about a large housing development that affected two of his very active campaign supporters, even though Blencoe would not have benefited financially from such a decision. In his decision, Hughes stated that a "private interest" could include something other than financial gain. "Campaign contributions and assistance, whether financial or otherwise, can, in my opinion, in some circumstances, be a private interest." Therefore, elected members must take care to ensure that they avoid situations where they can "confer an advantage or a benefit" on those who made significant campaign contributions, "financial or otherwise."[57] He concluded that a "reasonably well-informed person" familiar with these facts would conclude that Blencoe was guilty of an apparent conflict of interest if he were to make a ministerial decision about whether to approve the housing project.[58] In the end, Blencoe recused himself from having to make a decision in this case, and the cabinet appointed another minister to handle the file.[59]

Although at the time some might have thought that Hughes was extending the scope of apparent conflict of interest too far, his approach is now conventional wisdom. For example, in 2015 the Treasury Board of Canada revised its interpretation of apparent conflicts of interest to read as follows:

> An apparent conflict of interest exists when there is a reasonable apprehension, which reasonably well-informed persons could properly have, that a conflict of interest exists . . . A perceived or apparent conflict of interest can exist where it could be perceived, or appears, that a public official's private interests could improperly influence the performance of their duties — whether or not this is in fact the case . . . These definitions make clear that the appearance of conflict of interest *in the eyes of members of the public* is the distinguishing feature from the other types of conflict of interest.[60]

The guidelines also emphasized that conflicts of interest, whether real, potential or apparent, are not always easily determined, and that when in doubt, public servants should consult with senior officials to assist with determining the proper course of action.

Since the publication of *Honest Politics* in 1997, it has become widely accepted that involvement in an apparent conflict of interest, and the failure to take appropriate remedial measures, is as serious as being in a real conflict of interest.

In the case of British Columbia and the federal Treasury Board Secretariat, apparent conflicts of interest are prohibited by the formal rules. In other situations, though such infractions may not be included in legislation or codes of conduct, they are nevertheless subject to the court of public opinion. An example is the scandal that arose when Alison Redford, the former Premier of Alberta, was accused of inappropriate involvement in the choice of a law firm to handle the Alberta government's litigation against tobacco firms.

## ALISON REDFORD AND THE PUBLIC'S JUDGMENT ON AN APPARENT CONFLICT

First elected to the provincial legislature in 2008, Redford had a short, tumultuous time in provincial politics, rising quickly and falling just as fast. As a rookie MLA, she was appointed Justice Minister and attorney general in the Progressive Conservative government of Ed Stelmach, before resigning in early 2011 to run for the leadership of the Alberta Progressive Conservatives. She won on a progressive platform, replacing Mr. Stelmach as premier and validating her position with a victory in the April 2012 general election.

Before her foray into Alberta politics, Ms. Redford had enjoyed a distinguished career as a human rights lawyer and technical advisor in some of the most conflict-ridden countries in the world. She worked with South African leader Nelson Mandela in the fight against apartheid, and for the United Nations, administering Afghanistan's first democratic elections in 2005. In the 1980s she had been a senior policy advisor to the federal Progressive Conservative government of Brian Mulroney. In Alberta, however, controversy dogged the new premier almost from the beginning.

In 2012, serious concerns were raised by opposition party leaders about Ms. Redford's role in the selection of the legal consortium of International Tobacco Recovery Lawyers (ITRL) to represent the

Alberta government in a planned $10 billion lawsuit against Big Tobacco. At issue was consortium member JSS Barristers of Calgary, whose partners included Robert Hawkes, Ms. Redford's ex-husband and one-time political advisor. When it was revealed that Ms. Redford had personally made the final choice, Raj Sherman, leader of the Alberta Liberal Party, and Danielle Smith, leader of the Alberta Wildrose Party, each wrote to the provincial ethics commissioner in late 2012 to request an investigation.

In January 2013, Commissioner Neil Wilkinson opened his inquiry, which sought to determine whether Ms. Redford had engaged in "improper use of her office to further the private interest of her ex-husband, Robert Hawkes, or the private interest of the law firm in which he is a partner, JSS Barristers."[61]

In the course of his investigation, Mr. Wilkinson encountered significant bureaucratic barriers to interviewing potential witnesses and reviewing pertinent documents. For example, access to a critical briefing note analyzing the credentials of the three legal consortiums vying for the tobacco litigation retainer was denied on the basis of legal privilege. At the time, the Alberta ethics commissioner, unlike his counterparts in other jurisdictions like New Brunswick, was not authorized to access privileged information.

A compromise was eventually struck in which a mutually acceptable third party, in this case a retired judge, was permitted to view the briefing note, although he was restricted to asking just five pre-determined questions. Additionally, the commissioner was not able to interview potential witnesses in person; instead he was required to submit questions in writing, restricting his ability to follow up on any potential lines of questioning. Of nine witnesses, only one, Ms. Redford, was interviewed in person.

In his December 2013 report, Mr. Wilkinson concluded that Ms. Redford had not breached the relevant sections of the *Act*. He determined that Mr. Hawkes did not fit the definition of a person "directly associated with" Ms. Redford, which the *Act* narrowly defines as a parent, spouse or minor child.[62] He also found no evidence that Ms. Redford had provided confidential or privileged information to either JSS Barristers or Robert Hawkes.

In March 2014, following another scandal related to Redford's expense claims and other issues of entitlement described later in this chapter, Redford resigned as premier. Even though the ethics commissioner had exonerated Redford based on his interpretation of the wording of the *Alberta Conflict of Interest Act*, media commentary and public opinion seemed to take the position that Redford had nevertheless been in an apparent conflict of interest situation.[63]

It is noteworthy that Redford's exoneration by the ethics commissioner did not lay the allegations to rest. In November 2015, *CBC News* in Edmonton received leaked documents indicating that of the three legal consortiums under consideration, ITRL had been ranked the lowest, and that a draft briefing note containing this information had been revised following review by Minister Redford's executive assistant.[64] The new NDP government of Rachel Notley moved quickly to engage retired Supreme Court Justice Frank Iacobucci to review the original conflict of interest investigation. His report, tabled on March 30, 2016, found that Neil Wilkinson did not have access to the information necessary to properly determine whether a conflict of interest violation had occurred.[65] He recommended that the case be reconsidered.[66]

Premier Notley referred the report for consideration to Mr. Wilkinson's successor as ethics commissioner, retired judge Marguerite Trussler. In turn, Ms. Trussler, claiming a perceived conflict of interest on her part, asked British Columbia's ethics commissioner, Paul Fraser, to independently determine whether the investigation should be reopened.[67] In August 2016, the B.C. commissioner concluded that enough new evidence existed to warrant a new inquiry, and so Ms. Trussler asked Mr. Fraser to conduct the inquiry. Fraser's investigation was much more in-depth than Wilkinson's had been, and in 2017, he released a ruling which cleared Redford again. He found that Redford and Hawkes "weren't close," and that Redford had "no direct involvement in designing the selection process."[68]

Although the evidence shows that Redford was not in a real conflict of interest situation according to the rules, the fact that her former husband was a partner in the law firm that was selected results in an apparent conflict. Had she realized the ramifications, she may well have recused herself from the decision-making situation.

Another former Alberta premier, Ralph Klein, became embroiled in an apparent conflict of interest situation between 1993 and 1995 after his wife accepted shares presented to her by a lobbyist at below market value, and for which she did not have to pay for until sold. Although the ethics commissioner exonerated Klein, he did not fare as well in the court of public opinion. Nevertheless, Klein's public apology, and the donation of the proceeds from the sale of the shares to charity, made it possible for him to carry on as premier until 2006.[69]

## Violations of Conflict of Interest Codes

Conflict of interest rules ordinarily require elected officials to disclose their sources of income, their assets, and their liabilities to the commissioner. This disclosure is usually confidential, and the purpose is to enable an ethics counsellor to advise as to whether each particular source of income, asset or liability might result in a conflict between the private interests of the official and his or her public duties. In some jurisdictions, the commissioner has the power to disclose publicly the sources of income, assets and liabilities that might, in some situations, lead to a conflict of interest unless the member takes appropriate action.

The failure to disclose all relevant income, assets or liabilities results in a fourth-level conflict of interest violation, even if a conflict of interest would not have occurred had they been properly disclosed.

### HELENA GEURGIS

Conservative MP for Simcoe-Grey Helena Geurgis was found in violation of the federal conflict of interest rules in 2010 when she failed to report a new liability, a mortgage of $890,000 that she had signed within the specified time limit.[70] She was fined $100 by the conflict of interest and ethics commissioner.

In 2011, Geurgis was found to have violated the federal conflict of interest rules in 2009 by writing a letter to municipal politicians in her riding in support of a waste management proposal that her husband, former Conservative MP Rahim Jaffer, might have eventually benefited from.[71] Jaffer had a consulting firm in the riding that Geurgis represented, and he was establishing a business relationship with Jim Wright, who was in the green-technology business. She was in violation of the rules because she had used her position to help further the interests of a family member. While neither of these situations resulted in a financial benefit, Geurgis had nonetheless violated conflict of interest rules.

## CHRISTIAN PARADIS

Conflict of interest rules can also be broken by someone even if they themselves are not involved in a real, apparent or potential conflict of interest. This is done by helping friends or colleagues obtain privileged access to government decision makers.

In 2009, Christian Paradis was Minister of Public Works in Stephen Harper's cabinet. Rahim Jaffer, a former colleague, approached Paradis to ask for assistance. Jaffer was then a director in the Green Power Generation company, and the firm had a multi-million-dollar proposal to install solar panels on buildings owned by the federal government. Jaffer asked Paradis to help set up meetings with public works officials who were in a position to make recommendations.[72] Paradis complied, and asked one of his assistants to help arrange the meetings.[73] Incidentally, Jaffer was not registered as a lobbyist at the time, which put him in violation of the *Lobbying Act* (detailed in Chapter 7).

In 2010, an opposition MP wrote to the conflict of interest and ethics commissioner alleging that by helping Jaffer to arrange meetings with public works officials, Paradis had violated the *Conflict of Interest Act*. Commissioner Mary Dawson, after a detailed investigation, reported in 2012 that Paradis had violated two sections of the *Act*. First, he had arranged preferential access for his former colleague. Second, the *Conflict of Interest Act* states that a public official may not "*improperly* further the private interests of another person," a rule that Paradis was found to have violated. Though Paradis had not put himself in a position to benefit financially, he violated the *Act* by showing preferential treatment to someone else, thus violating the impartiality principle discussed in Chapter 2. Mary Dawson further commented that:

> In the case of Mr. Paradis, I believe that his inclination to arrange a meeting for his former caucus colleague, while inappropriate, is easy to understand: it is natural to want to help someone one knows. Nonetheless, I have found that granting access to decision-makers or those who may influence them is captured by the *Act*'s prohibition against providing preferential treatment. Ministers are in a position of power and have a special responsibility to ensure that that power is exercised fairly and in a way that is open to all Canadians.[74]

## Broadening the Scope of Conflicts of Interest

### MICHAEL BONNER AND FREE TICKETS TO EVENTS

In early 2013, Jason Kenney, then Minister of Employment, hired Michael Bonner, who had been out of the country for ten years, as a senior policy advisor. Bonner later claimed that he was not familiar with the rules contained in the *Conflict of Interest Act.*

In November 2013, the ethics commissioner received an email from a member of the public alleging that Mr. Bonner had accepted free tickets to events from corporations that were lobbying Mr. Kenney's department. Shortly afterwards, she received a referral from the Public Sector Integrity Commissioner (the commissioner in charge of protecting whistle-blowers) with the same allegations. The commissioner conducted a thorough examination, and concluded the Bonner had violated the *Conflict of Interest Act* by accepting the tickets.[75]

The three events in question were the National Arts Centre gala, with two tickets worth $390 in total provided by Vale Canada Ltd.; the Aerospace Industries Association of Canada annual reception and dinner, with a nominal fee $70 plus tax covered by Aerospace Industries, and the alumni dinner for the Parliamentary Internship Program, at a cost of $125, with a ticket provided by the Forest Products Association of Canada. After the ethics commissioner began to investigate the allegations, Mr. Bonner repaid the cost of the events to the three associations.[76]

Ms. Dawson's investigation confirmed that all three corporations were indeed lobbying Mr. Kenney's department, and that in the cases of Vale and Aerospace Industries, their spokespersons had discussed projects that they wanted to advance with Mr. Bonner at the events; for its part, Forest Products simply wanted to "fill seats" at its event.[77] Dawson concluded that Mr. Bonner had violated section 11 of the *Conflict of Interest Act*, "which prohibits a public office holder from accepting any gift that might reasonably be seen to have been given to influence the public office holder in the exercise of an official power, duty or function."[78] Bonner should have realized that the free tickets were from corporations lobbying his department, and that they "might reasonably be seen to have been given to influence" Mr. Bonner. In the case of Forest Products, what is important is that the gift was from a lobbyist seeking to influence his department, not whether lobbying actually occurred at the event.

At first, Mr. Bonner claimed that he had done nothing wrong. He argued that "the invitations were to standard Ottawa social events," and added it was "commonplace that guests, including public office holders, be invited to attend."[79] Further, as he had written to the commissioner during her investigation, "the events in question were all part of the 'Ottawa Scene' and appeared to him to be the type that he should be attending in terms of the outreach he was supposed to be doing."[80] After Dawson issued her report, Bonner admitted that he had not been familiar with the conflict of interest rules, and that he should have contacted the commissioner's office for advice before accepting the tickets.[81]

This case provides one example of how the very idea of a conflict of interest has broadened in recent years. Bonner had told the commissioner that accepting free tickets to attend events was just part of the "Ottawa scene." Indeed, this may have been the case a decade earlier before he temporarily left Canada. But as students and observers of public ethics think about the importance of principles like equality and impartiality, it makes sense that public officials would avoid situations in which they might be beholden to a lobbyist for receiving gifts not generally available to members of the public.

## Concluding Thoughts about Conflicts of Interest

Conflicts of interest vary in their degrees of severity. The Poirier and Corriveau cases are rare examples of criminal convictions for public officials. The Finley and Graham cases illustrate real conflict of interest situations, while Alison Redford's situation provides an example of an unofficial apparent conflict of interest, and from our perspective, it lends support to those who favour the toughening-up of ethics legislation. The Geurgis and Paradis examples show how the rules designed to prevent conflicts of interest can be broken even if real conflicts of interest have not occurred. The Bonner case demonstrates how our thinking about conflicts of interest broadens as we consider the ethical principles that inform them.

The Finley, Geurgis, Graham, Paradis and Bonner cases underline the importance of having independent officials always available to conduct inquiries into allegations of conflict of interest. Without a method of setting the record straight expeditiously, allegations could remain unresolved, or a cloud of suspicion may continue to hang over alleged rule breakers, thus nurturing the cynicism with which many citizens regard politicians. But in addition to independence, it would be useful for the person conducting the inquiry to have confidence in their ability to make difficult calls, as Commissioner Ryan did in the Graham case, or Commissioner Dawson did in the Finley, Geurgis, Paradis and Bonner cases. It is important for the investigating official to have a background in law or investigative procedures. The legislative committees selecting ethics commissioners should thus give careful consideration to candidates' backgrounds. A retired judge, or a lawyer with years of experience related to administrative law, is in our view likely to be more effective than someone without the confidence and training that one gains from a career in law.

# ENTITLEMENT

The case of the Saskatchewan communications claims scandal (summarized at the beginning of Chapter 1) is an excellent example of public officials abusing the trust placed in them. Raymond Lavigne, Alison Redford and Joe Fontana provide further examples of this type of entitlement.

## THE LAVIGNE AFFAIR

Raymond Lavigne ran as a Liberal candidate in Quebec in 1988, was defeated, but won in the 1993 election. He was re-elected in 1997 and 2000. He resigned his seat in 2002 so that it could be contested in a by-election by one of his party's star candidates. His reward was a Senate appointment from Prime Minister Jean Chrétien.

In 2011, Lavigne was convicted of fraud for having submitted more than $10,000 worth of false travel-expense claims. It turned out that fifty-four trips were made by one of Lavigne's staff between Montreal and Ottawa. Lavigne charged the Senate for the full amount of the mileage ($217 per trip), gave a fraction of the reimbursement to the staffer ($50 per trip) and pocketed the rest. On some of these trips, Lavigne wasn't even a passenger. As well, Lavigne arranged for one of his Senate staff to cut down trees on a property he owned near Ottawa.[82] The judge ruled that "Lavigne's sole motive was to save himself some money for the job."[83] Lavigne was sentenced to six months in jail followed by six months of house arrest. He unsuccessfully appealed the sentence. He also lost his bid for early parole in 2013. In refusing Lavigne's application, the Ontario Parole Board wrote:

> The Board believes that you seriously violated public trust
> by your fraudulent actions . . . You expressed little remorse
> and you accepted little responsibility for your criminal
> behaviour . . . [Because of] your repeated denial of any
> criminal wrongdoing, along with [the lack of] . . . confirmed
> community rehabilitative component to your release plan,
> you are not seen as a manageable risk in the community and
> parole is denied.[84]

But Lavigne didn't just fudge his expense claims, or get his office staff to do personal work. When these allegations first surfaced in 2006, Lavigne was expelled from the Liberal caucus, and after being charged in 2007, he was barred from the Senate. However, for nearly four years, he continued to collect his salary of $132,000, plus benefits. When he finally resigned from the Senate, following his conviction in 2011, he began to receive a lifetime annual pension of up to $79,000.[85]

Those, like Lavigne, who receive patronage appointments are likely to think that they deserve their entitlements as a thanks for the work they have done for their party. Lavigne may have felt particularly entitled after resigning his seat so that one of the prime minister's favourites could contest it. Apparently, he continued to harbour his sense of entitlement at his parole hearing in 2013. If there was ever a good reason to end patronage appointments to the Senate, Lavigne provides one.

## ALISON REDFORD

The Alison Redford case is another example of entitlement. Indeed, it seems the conflict of interest scandal described earlier was only the beginning of Redford's difficulties. In early 2014, the media published stories accusing her of lavish spending, including the use of government aircraft for personal reasons when commercial aircraft would have sufficed. Namely, she spent $45,000 on "first-class air tickets and a government plane" to attend the funeral of Nelson Mandela in South Africa. At first she refused to reimburse any of these funds, but under pressure from her caucus she later relented.[86] Such actions were in contrast to her domestic policies, which saw her "cut spending to below the levels of inflation plus population, and strong-armed teachers and doctors into taking wage freezes. She slashed post-secondary budgets."[87] This contrast between public policy and personal entitlement led one cabinet minister to resign, and ten backbenchers threatened to leave the caucus. Finally, on March 19, 2014, Redford announced her resignation.

Her problems worsened when, a week later, the media reported that towards the end of 2012 Redford had tried to arrange for the renovation of a top-floor office in a provincial government building for her and her daughter.[88] These plans were abandoned some time before December 2013, but they nevertheless indicate that Redford was increasingly abusing the public's trust. Redford's successor, Jim Prentice, led the Progressive Party to a resounding defeat on May 5, 2015, bringing to an end the party's forty-four years in power. The election was won by the New Democrats, who capitalized on the taint of entitlement left behind by Redford.

## JOE FONTANA

Joe Fontana, a career politician from London, Ontario, with a previously unblemished of municipal and federal service, was found guilty of fraud and breach of trust in June 2014. He was a Liberal MP from 1988 to 2006, and a cabinet minister in the Paul Martin government from 2004 to 2006. He later served as mayor of London from 2010 to 2014.

In November 2012, the RCMP charged Mr. Fontana with fraud, breach of trust by a public official and falsifying documents. The charges were related to a $1,700 payment made to the Marconi Club in London. Mr. Fontana had submitted an invoice for reimbursement to the federal government in early 2005, ostensibly for a deposit made to the Marconi Club for a political reception that never occurred.

It was subsequently proven in court that the Marconi Club had never issued an invoice for the political reception, and that the payment was used to cover a portion of the cost of Mr. Fontana's son's wedding reception, held in June 2005. Fontana admitted that he had heavily doctored a contract for his son's reception to make it appear as a political event. Using an eraser and whiteout, Mr. Fontana changed the signature on the invoice, the date and the event description. He also wrote the word "original" at the top of the existing contract and added a yellow sticky note with the notation "miscellaneous constituent reception," before submitting it to his legislative staff for reimbursement.[89]

Although the judicial penalty — four months of house arrest, eighteen months of probation, a $1,000 victim surcharge and restitution of $1,700 to the Government of Canada — was largely symbolic, Fontana did pay a heavy political price. In addition to loss of reputation (he garnered a "Teddy Waste Award" from the Canadian Taxpayers Federation in 2015), Mr. Fontana was forced to resign his position as the head of the London Police Services Board. He also resigned his position as mayor upon conviction in June 2014.[90]

Fontana has never accepted blame for his actions; he calls himself an honest man who made a "stupid mistake," and he maintains that he was just trying to do the right thing.[91] But at Fontana's sentencing on July 15, 2014, Superior Court Justice Bruce Thomas referred to both the seriousness of the offence and its incomprehensibility, noting that personal gain appeared to be the only possible explanation for Mr. Fontana's actions. He also noted that the abuse of authority was more serious than the actual amount of money involved, and that its ripple effect stretches further and lasts longer because of Mr. Fontana's position of public trust. Commenting that he was "perplexed as to why a man of such accomplishments might choose to take these actions for $1,700," Justice Thomas went on to say that "the reasons confound me. Perhaps it is simply because he could."[92]

Justice Thomas makes a good point. According to Philip Slayton, author of Lawyers Gone Bad, legal professionals who defraud their clients may do so simply because they think they can get away with it. Most do not need the money. This mentality may also help to explain the shameful financial transactions between Karlheinz Schreiber and Prime Minister Mulroney (discussed in Chapter 1).[93]

## CONCLUSIONS

Abuse of trust can take many forms, but in Canada, taking advantage of a conflict of interest has been one of the most common. The Poirier and Corriveau cases illustrate how taking advantage of a conflict of interest can result in conviction for fraud and a jail term. Involvement in a real conflict of interest, even if no criminal charges result, can lead to the end of one's political career, as the Shawn Graham case showed. However, being in an apparent conflict of interest and continuing in that situation is often judged, in the court of public opinion, as offensive as being in a real conflict of interest, as shown by the Redford case. Even breaking the rules established to prevent real or apparent conflicts of interest can result in embarrassment, as we have seen from the Geurgis and Paradis files. As the next chapter will demonstrate, the implementation of what Jean Fournier labels the "Canadian model" for preventing conflicts of interest, including robust rules against conflicts of interest and independent conflict of interest commissioners, has helped to reduce the incidence of breaches of this nature.[94]

As such rules have tightened, however, some of those seeking to enrich themselves through public office have explored other means of abusing the public's trust, for example by taking unfair advantage of public office perks. It would be a mistake to fight corruption in politics by focusing exclusively on conflicts of interest, though not ensuring a robust regime to prevent conflicts of interest would be equally misguided. The next chapter reviews Canada's federal and provincial mechanisms to prevent conflicts of interest.

# CHAPTER 5
# ETHICS COMMISSIONS
## Ian Stedman and Ian Greene

Our representative democratic system in Canada values the diversity of our country's citizenry. Citizens are encouraged to stand for election in our legislatures to give voice to the many others who may espouse similar values. This is an integral part of Canada's identity, but it also brings with it several challenges, including that of ensuring that those who hold public office understand what it means to behave ethically. History has shown us that on rare occasion parliamentarians might use their public office to unfairly benefit themselves or their family and friends. As noted in the previous chapters, this improper personal benefit is called a conflict of interest. This chapter will look closely at the regimes that have emerged in Canada's provinces and territories, as well as in Parliament, to prevent elected officials from becoming embroiled in conflicts of interest. We will examine how the rules have evolved into laws administered by ethics commissioners and we will explore how they have expanded under the commissioner model to more broadly promote the ethical conduct of parliamentarians.

Historically, conflict of interest rules have taken three forms in Canada: 1) party leaders have issued guidelines or codes of conduct applicable only to their own caucus members; 2) provincial, territorial and federal parliaments have passed legislation that is applicable to all parliamentarians; and 3) unwritten rules have emerged from the customs and conventions accepted by parliamentarians. Though Canadian parliamentarians have occasionally found themselves in conflicts of interest throughout our history, it was not until 1973 that the first legislation was actually enacted in Newfoundland.[1] Relatively comprehensive laws are now in place in every Canadian jurisdiction, although it has proven difficult for legislators to anticipate every possible ethical transgression, and the legislation has therefore not always been clear or useful. As a result, though some elected officials have committed ethical lapses because they *chose* to ignore the rules, such transgressions are more commonly a result of politicians' ignorance of what the rules actually require.

To address this kind of confusion, Ontario passed legislation in 1988 creating an independent officer of its legislature who would be responsible for the administration of conflict of interest laws.[2] This independent commissioner would serve as an advisor whom all members could trust and turn to for answers about conflicts of interest. Other legislatures across Canada have monitored Ontario's experiment, and, in a demonstration of the flexibility of Canadian federalism, have all passed similar legislation. Several jurisdictions have even expanded the scope of their commissioner's jurisdiction beyond mere conflicts of interest to encompass more general ethical matters. Those jurisdictions now refer to their officers as "ethics commissioners" or "integrity commissioners." Although the various commissioners have different titles, we will refer to them simply as "ethics commissioners."

Although not all ethics commissioners are independent officers of their legislatures, they are all tasked with providing advice to elected members about what the applicable conflict of interest and ethics rules are and how compliance with those rules can be achieved. Ethics commissioners take complaints about the conduct of members and they have the power to investigate violations of the rules and to report back to their respective legislatures with recommendations, including possible punishments for members who have violated those rules.

These ethics commissioners now have a key role in the maintenance of Canada's transparency and accountability infrastructure. It is therefore worth taking a closer look at the ways in which these offices have been established and the variety of duties that have been assigned to them throughout Canada. Our review will begin by looking at the important historical role that Ontario has played in shaping these regimes. We will then look closely at each provincial and territorial office, before ending by looking at the Conflict of Interest and Ethics Commissioner and the Senate Ethics Officer, who have jurisdiction over the members of Canada's House of Commons and Senate, respectively.

## ONTARIO

Conflicts of interest in Ontario came to the surface well before legislation was passed in 1988. In the late 1950s, several members of Premier David Frost's cabinet were forced to resign after it came to light that they had improperly benefitted from investments in the Northern Ontario Natural Gas (NONG) company.[3] The NONG scandal, which also implicated several municipal politicians, inspired the passing of Ontario's first *Municipal Act* in 1960,[4] which prohibited councillors from having an interest in a contract with a municipal corporation or local government board. Despite the cabinet resignations, however, no similar provincial legislation was passed at that time.

The *Municipal Act*'s ability to prevent conflicts of interest was periodically tested as scandals continued to befall municipal politicians across Ontario. The *Act* had already undergone several amendments by 1967, when an alderman in London, Ontario, was forced to vacate his seat after signing a contract with the city on behalf of a public service union in which he also held a position.[5] In direct response to this scandal, Premier John P. Robarts called for the Minister of Municipal Affairs to form a committee to look into the inadequacies of municipal conflict of interest legislation. The committee's report was finalized in December of 1968.[6] It contained many recommendations that remained unaddressed by the time five new high-profile scandals broke in 1970.[7] It was then that work began to address the committee's report, and Ontario passed its first dedicated *Municipal Conflict of Interest Act* in 1972.[8]

With the public's attention focused on municipal conflicts of interest and the government's new legislation, another scandal emerged in 1972, this time at the provincial level. The attorney general of Ontario had purchased land in Pickering, Ontario, on speculation. As a member of cabinet, he would have known that the site was being considered for a future airport.[9] To make matters even worse for Premier Bill Davis, his Minister of Municipal Affairs also made the mistake of intentionally approving the development of a subdivision in Chatham on land that he held an ownership interest in.[10]

When the *Municipal Conflict of Interest Act* was passed in 1972, Premier Davis was criticized for not taking similar action at the provincial level.[11] Davis responded to the mounting criticism with a statement in the legislature on September 14, 1972 that established conflict of interest guidelines for members of his cabinet.[12] These guidelines were clearly a reaction to the recent scandals, and they also marked the beginning of the codification of provincial conflict of interest rules in Ontario.

Davis's guidelines contained the following provisions:

- Members of cabinet had to make disclosures to the Clerk of the Assembly, who would then publicly report all land owned by each member — or his or her spouse or dependents — that was not for primarily residential or recreational use (the further acquisition of land for anything other than recreational or residential use was prohibited).[13]

- Ministers had to recuse themselves from matters in which they may have a personal beneficial interest.[14]

- Ministers or their family members were prohibited from having an interest in a private company that was contractually involved with the Government of Ontario.[15]

- Any pre-existing interests in public corporations held by ministers had to be divested or put into a trust over which the minister was to exercise no control or influence.[16]

- Ministers were required to refrain from day-to-day participation in outside business or professional activities.[17]

Despite applying only to members of the cabinet, these guidelines seemed to adequately address the public's desire for greater accountability at the provincial level.

When David Peterson succeeded Davis as premier, he adopted his predecessor's as yet untested guidelines with minimal change.[18] Peterson's Liberal government then ran into two major conflict of interest scandals in 1986. The first took place when it was discovered that Minister Elinor Caplan's husband, Wilfred Caplan, was an officer of a company that had negotiated $3 million in provincial financing. Peterson's guidelines prohibited spouses of cabinet ministers from having an interest in companies contracting with the government, and the issue was referred to the legislature's Standing Committee on Public Accounts for investigation.

That September the committee reported that the Caplans had clearly violated conflict of interest guidelines.[19] In addition, the committee suggested that Wilfred Caplan's $3 million financing application "may have been one of the factors that weighed upon" departmental officials when they were considering the application. The committee found no evidence that the Caplans had attempted to use their influence for personal benefit, but it expressed concern that public officials might have wanted to impress the cabinet by looking favourably upon Wilfred Caplan's application. This factor put the Caplans into a real conflict of interest situation.

The committee concluded that the best way to prevent these kinds of oversights in the future would be to create legislation to be interpreted and enforced by a "non-partisan and independent advisor." The political storm surrounding the Caplan affair blew over quickly, however. This recommendation might have gone unheeded had it not been for a series of new conflicts of interest.

First, René Fontaine, who was the Minister of Northern Development and Mines under Premier Peterson, was accused by the Opposition of failing to disclose all his holdings in forest companies, as provincial guidelines required. This matter was investigated by the Standing Committee on the Legislative Assembly, which reported back to the legislature around the same time the Caplan report was released. The committee concluded that Fontaine had breached the premier's guidelines "in three major respects" when he neglected to disclose all his holdings in three forest companies, "and in many minor respects" when he failed to withdraw from potential conflicts of interest regarding government decisions about his companies.[20] The premier was also blamed for failing to ensure that his ministers complied with the guidelines.

With two of his ministers under investigation, and rumours of other scandals circulating, Peterson was compelled to take action to limit further political damage. He enlisted John Black Aird, the former Lieutenant Governor of Ontario, to review cabinet members' compliance with the guidelines and to recommend improvements to the rules. Aird reported back to the premier in the fall,[21] and just like the Caplan committee had, recommended the establishment of clear legislation and an independent conflict of interest commissioner. He found that fifteen of twenty-one members of the cabinet, including Peterson himself, had breached the premier's guidelines in one way or another because the guidelines were too vague or poorly worded.

Aird recommended legislation that emphasized full public disclosure of non-personal assets (which would include everything except the member's home, cottage, automobile, bank savings and pension plans), combined with recusal from potential conflicts, rather than the divestment or selling of assets. As he noted in his report, "my fundamental assumption has been that full public disclosure of all economic interests and relationships is the strongest weapon in the arsenal of any conflict of interest regime . . . If a Minister is prepared to make full and continuous disclosure, then he or she ought not to be required to divest himself or herself of a single asset."[22]

Noting the mutual financial obligations that contemporary family law placed on married couples, Aird also said that the disclosure rules should apply not only to members of the cabinet, but also to their spouses. Furthermore, an independent commissioner could provide consistent interpretations of the conflict rules by having personal meetings with each member of cabinet prior to their taking office. Providing the new conflict of interest official with the powers of a commissioner under the *Public Inquiries Act* would ensure the impartial investigation of alleged breaches of the legislation. Raising the status of the rules from mere guidelines to legislation would also make it possible for the legislature to apply actual sanctions against ministers who violated them. Enforcement under existing guidelines had simply been at the premier's discretion.

The Peterson government accepted all of this advice when sponsoring the *Members' Conflict of Interest Act* in 1987. In fact, the government went beyond Aird's recommendations and drafted the legislation so as to apply to every member of the assembly, rather than only to cabinet ministers.[23] After all, MPPs who were not ministers could also find themselves in conflict of interest situations. Although not as high-profile as situations involving ministers, members' conflicts of interest, if left unchecked, could continue to erode public confidence in government.

As per Aird's recommendations, The *Members' Conflict of Interest Act*[24] also applied to the spouses and minor children of members of provincial parliament[25] and included the following key components:

- A formal definition of what constitutes a "conflict of interest."

- Rules against members using insider information to further their own private interests.

- Rules against members using their office in order to influence or seek to influence another person in a manner that could further the member's private interest.

- Rules governing gifts and when they need to be reported and publicly disclosed; the procedures to be followed if members have reasonable grounds to believe an official duty might lead to a conflict of interest; what private interests must be disclosed by members (and their spouses and children) and when that disclosure must take place; what information disclosed should be made public by the commissioner; what assets must be placed in trust by ministers and when; what particular investments ministers may hold, and what business activities they may participate in; and how current members of the cabinet must treat former members with respect to the awarding or approval of contracts, benefits or grants.

- The requirement that every member must meet with the commissioner after filing a disclosure statement.

- A provision allowing the commissioner to provide an opinion to members about whether their conduct conforms with their obligations under the Act, and allowing a member to refer a question to the commissioner with respect to another member's compliance.

- The commissioner's right to conduct a public inquiry under the *Public Inquiries Act*, and the requirement to file an annual report that includes an anonymous summary of advice given throughout the past year.

- A mechanism whereby the commissioner can be removed from his or her office if there is clear cause for removal.

The *Act* also provided for the appointment of an independent commissioner for a renewable five-year term. The commissioner's appointment was to be voted on by the legislature and he or she would continue to hold office unless there was cause for removal.[26] Ontario's first permanent conflict of interest commissioner was the Honourable Gregory Evans, former Chief Justice of the High Court of Ontario.[27] Commissioner Evans's title was changed to "integrity commissioner" in 1994 when the legislation expanded and was renamed the *Members' Integrity Act*[28] under the stewardship of the Bob Rae government.

As a member of the Opposition, NDP leader Bob Rae had been critical of the Liberals' conflict of interest legislation, claiming it did not go far enough. In particular, he was concerned that the public disclosure of assets, combined with recusal from potential conflicts, was inadequate.[29] After becoming premier in the fall of 1990, Rae issued supplementary guidelines for members of his cabinet and their parliamentary assistants that required them to dispose of "any asset, liability, or financial interest which causes or could appear to cause a conflict of interest; and all business interests."[30] In stark contrast, the 1988 *Act* had allowed ministers and their parliamentary assistants to keep such assets as long as they were publicly disclosed. Premier Rae's guidelines also prohibited cabinet ministers and parliamentary assistants from violating judicial independence by contacting a judge or interfering with the due process of the law in their contacts with administrative tribunals, prosecutors or the police. Journalist Thomas Walkom would later describe these supplementary guidelines as "the toughest conflict of interest guidelines in the province's history."[31]

Premier Rae's guidelines were criticized in the legislature on December 19, 1990, for being overly harsh.[32] It was perhaps in response to this criticism that a member of Rae's cabinet moved the next day to have the Standing Committee on Administration of Justice "review and make recommendations with respect to the guidelines governing conflict of interest."[33] The standing committee's report was tabled in the legislature in September 1991.[34] The report included strong dissents from the committee's Liberal and PC members, but ultimately recommended that the guidelines be adopted and added to the legislation that was already in place.[35]

But the committee's recommendations were not taken up and the premier's resolve was subsequently tested when the Minister of Housing, Evelyn Gigantes, allegedly violated them in June 1994 by attempting to mediate a dispute between board members at a non-profit housing centre in her riding. One board member had commenced proceedings against another under the *Provincial Offences Act*,[36] and the allegation was that Minister Gigantes had encouraged the latter to urge the prosecutor to withdraw the charges.[37] The minister's actions would potentially violate provisions 4 and 5 of the premier's guidelines, which held that "ministers shall at all times act in a manner that will bear the closest public scrutiny"[38] and "shall perform the duties of office and arrange their affairs in such a manner as to maintain public confidence and trust in the integrity of the government."[39] Moreover, the committee also considered two provisions that prohibited ministers from communicating with the judiciary and another that prohibited ministers from communicating with tribunals or other ministries concerning ongoing matters.[40]

The committee concluded that Minister Gigantes had not violated the guidelines by attempting to interfere with the judicial process, but that she had violated sections 4 and 5.[41] These were flexible provisions that were open to interpretation. Minister Gigantes resigned her position, but continued to assert that she had done nothing wrong.[42] A general election was called soon thereafter.

Before the election took place, the political parties worked together to achieve a consensus on amendments that could be made to the *Members' Conflict of Interest Act*,[43] including changing its name to the *Members' Integrity Act, 1994*. The result was *Bill 209*,[44] which passed all three readings on December 8, 1994,[45] receiving royal assent the very next day.[46] The legislature was dissolved on December 9, 1994, and would not sit again until a new government was elected on June 6, 1995. On October 6, 1995, the new *Act* was proclaimed[47] and the old legislation was replaced.

According to Commissioner Evans, "integrity" was substituted for "conflict of interest" because the former represents a concept of ethics that goes beyond purely financial matters. The new *Act* included a pre-amble that outlined the values upon which the legislation is based,[48] and it expanded the commissioner's jurisdiction to include the undefined concept of "Ontario parliamentary convention."[49] The preamble incorporated sections 4 and 5 of Premier Rae's guidelines. "Ontario parliamentary convention" has since been interpreted to encompass the rules prohibiting ministers from communicating with the judiciary or with tribunals about ongoing matters.

The inclusion of Ontario parliamentary convention in the legislation broadened the commissioner's jurisdiction to include more than mere conflicts of interest, again marking a first in Canada. In his report on the first complaint made under the new legislation, Commissioner Evans explained that "parliamentary conventions usually evolve over a period of time. When certain situations continue to arise and the legislators reach a consensus as to their disposition, they are then classified as convention and serve as precedents which may be adopted to determine future cases of a similar nature."[50] Because there was no definition in the legislation itself, the commissioner's report signalled that parliamentarians would be held to standards of behaviour that were accepted by the legislature, but that were not explicitly included in the provisions of the *Members' Integrity Act*.

Since 1994, the commissioner's jurisdiction has expanded to include the administration of government accountability rules in five other areas:

- Ontario's lobbyist registry.[51]

- Reviewing the travel, meal and hospitality expenses of cabinet ministers, parliamentary assistants, leaders of the Opposition and their staff.[52]

- Reviewing the travel, meal and hospitality expenses for senior executives, appointees and the top five employee expense claimants at Ontario's agencies, boards and commissions.[53]

- Receiving and dealing with allegations of wrongdoing from Ontario public servants and former public servants who work, or have worked, in ministries and public bodies.[54]

- Administering the conflict of interest rules that apply to ministers' staff.[55]

As will be discussed below, it is becoming common for ethics commissioners to be given more expansive duties. There may in fact be certain advantages to having various accountability regimes administered by a single office, as information received under one mandate can inform the work undertaken under another. For example, a ministers' staff member may report to the integrity commissioner that he or she attended a lunch with the minister and that it was paid for by a third party who was also in attendance. Not only is that person required to file a form to disclose that a gift or benefit was received, but the integrity commissioner would then be alerted to the fact that the minister may also have received a gift or benefit. The commissioner may then choose to make inquiries of the minister and, if necessary, offer that minister guidance on filing the relevant form. Similarly, the integrity commissioner may choose to search the lobbyist registry for the third party who paid for the meals and make inquiries in his or her capacity as the lobbyist registrar.

Every jurisdiction in Canada, including the House of Commons and the Senate, has modeled its rules after Ontario's legislation. Unfortunately, though, legislation of this sort is sometimes passed in haste when public pressure mounts,[56] and little thought seems to be given to ways in which the status quo can be improved. As the following list shows, some Canadian jurisdictions have legislation in place that is clearly out of date, and which therefore might be difficult for engaged citizens to take seriously.

## BRITISH COLUMBIA

British Columbia became the second province to create an independent ethics commissioner after Premier Bill Vander Zalm's Social Credit government was rocked by seven conflict of interest scandals involving cabinet ministers in the late 1980s.[57] The most serious of these implicated the premier himself. In September of 1990, the B.C. legislature enacted the *Members' Conflict of Interest Act.*[58] This legislation was copied, in most respects, from the Ontario legislation. The Honourable E.N. (Ted) Hughes became the interim commissioner in October 1990, and in May 1991 he was appointment to a five-year term as the province's first permanent commissioner.

There are a few important differences in current legislation between Ontario and B.C. First, the B.C. commissioner's jurisdiction is expanded to include *apparent* conflicts of interest.[59] This move was rather controversial because some wondered whether it would make the commissioner's job imprecise and significantly more difficult.[60] However, Commissioner Hughes and his successors have opined that having jurisdiction over apparent conflicts has not actually proven to be problematic.[61]

A second major difference is that the B.C. commissioner can receive complaints (also called "requests for an opinion") from the public about members of the legislature.[62] Ontario's integrity commissioner has unfortunately not been granted this same jurisdiction, despite the fact that Ontario's legislation has been amended several times since B.C.'s was first passed. Ontario's commissioner can only accept complaints or requests for an opinion from a member of provincial parliament or from the executive council.

The final major difference is that B.C.'s legislation has not been amended to include ethical considerations beyond conflicts of interest.

Interestingly, B.C.'s commissioner published two reports in 2012[63] wherein he proposed amendments to the *Conflict of Interest Act*. The Select Standing Committee on Parliamentary Reform, Ethical Conduct, Standing Orders, and Private Bills agreed with many of those recommendations,[64] but changes to the *Act* are still forthcoming.

## ALBERTA

Alberta enacted its legislation in 1991[65] after an independent review panel issued a report about allegations that were made against Premier Don Getty and another Alberta cabinet minister.[66] An ethics commissioner was not appointed until 1992, however, and the *Act* did not come into full operation until March 1993.

The *Conflicts of Interest Act* is again similar in content to the legislation enacted elsewhere in Canada. The ethics commissioner has jurisdiction over members of the legislative assembly, staff within the premier's and ministers' offices and, in limited circumstances, designated employees and senior officials (including those employed in some agencies, boards and commissions) under the *Code of Conduct and Ethics for the Public Service of Alberta*.[67] Furthermore, Alberta's legislative assembly passed the *Lobbyists Act* in 2007,[68] which added lobbyist registration to the ethics commissioner's duties. However, the ethics commissioner has the right to delegate lobbyist registrar duties to any member of his or her staff,[69] and this delegation has generally taken place since the *Act* came into force.

## NEWFOUNDLAND AND LABRADOR

The Commissioner for Legislative Standards in Newfoundland was given jurisdiction under the *House of Assembly Act*[70] in 1993 and the *Conflict of Interest Act, 1995*[71] for members of Parliament and other public officials, respectively. From 2006 to the time of writing, the commissioner was Vic Powers, who also holds the completely separate position of Chief Electoral Officer. This situation is not common in Canada, as most ethics commissioners are employed exclusively in the ethics capacity.

Mr. Powers's duties and powers are similar in nature to the other regimes described above. Perhaps the most notable difference is that he is not required to make members' public disclosure statements available on the Internet.[72] A member of the public must make an appointment and find his or her way to the commissioner's office to look at physical copies of disclosure statements.[73] This may seem like a small matter, but in the era of digital communication, this provision is already grossly outdated.

## SASKATCHEWAN

In 1975 the Law Reform Commission of Saskatchewan was asked by the province's attorney general to prepare a report on conflicts of interest with respect to members of the assembly and appointed provincial officials. The request was inspired by a draft conflict of interest bill put forth by the government. The commission's report was released in early 1977,[74] and by 1979 members of the Legislative Assembly of Saskatchewan had their first conflict of interest legislation in place.[75]

Despite this new legislation, however, a huge scandal befell the Conservative caucus in the late 1980s and early 1990s, when it was revealed that all thirty-eight members approved the diversion of 25 per cent of their individual communications allowances to numbered companies. Several of those members were also convicted of fraud when it was proven that they had received illegal payments from the numbered companies that had been set up.[76]

Very clearly in response to this scandal, an independent commissioner was appointed under new conflict of interest legislation passed in 1993.[77] This legislation has since been expanded to include: specific prohibitions against the use of insider information; provisions restricting members from having a private interest in government contracts; and a requirement that disclosure statements be filed by all members. These rules are in line with the best practices that have been adopted elsewhere in Canada. The office has been lauded for its success at moving past the damage done by the Conservative Party through the communications allowances scandal. In fact, in 2014 the legislature even signaled its confidence in the office when it established the *Lobbyist Act*[78] and appointed the Conflict of Interest Commissioner as Saskatchewan's first Registrar of Lobbyists.

## NORTHWEST TERRITORIES

The *Legislative Assembly and Executive Council Act*[79] was passed in the Northwest Territories in 1999, establishing the territory's first conflict of interest commissioner. The commissioner has jurisdiction over complaints from members of the legislative assembly and members of the public, but interestingly, there is no dedicated website to help people understand how these complaints should be filed. At the time of writing, the only way to contact the commissioner was through a local phone number[80] or an online search for the commissioner's personal contact information. There is certainly an opportunity to modernize this process, as is the case in Yukon. In 2016, the commissioner was David P. Jones, an Edmonton lawyer and former law professor, and co-author of a leading text on administrative law. Jones was also the commissioner for Yukon.

Legislation in the Northwest Territories also stands apart from that of other Canadian jurisdictions in that it allows the commissioner to conduct an investigation and then, if necessary, direct that a further inquiry be held before a "sole adjudicator."[81] In advance of the need for any inquiry, the legislative assembly, in consultation with the commissioner, approves a list of sole adjudicators who are either judges, retired judges or people who have served (or who serve) in another province or territory in a position similar to the conflict of interest commissioner. If an investigation by the commissioner leads to a preliminary determination that in inquiry is appropriate, a sole adjudicator from that list is then appointed by the commissioner. This is a rather unique process that effectively provides for a separation between the primarily advisory function of the commissioner, and the inquiry function of the sole adjudicator (Quebec also separates these two functions). The adjudicator can choose to hold the inquiry in public or in private and the person or people who are the subject of the complaint are compelled to to give evidence. A few inquiries by sole adjudicators have taken place, including one involving Premier Floyd Roland in 2009.[82]

## PRINCE EDWARD ISLAND

Prince Edward Island's *Conflict of Interest Act*[83] was amended in 1999 to more closely resemble Ontario's 1994 legislation. But despite its narrow title, the *Act* actually gives the commissioner broad jurisdiction over "Prince Edward Island parliamentary convention."[84] Up to the time of writing, however, parliamentary convention was never used in PEI as a standard against which to judge a member's conduct, whereas it now has a long and interesting use in Ontario.

The PEI commissioner's office has received relatively few complaints since its establishment, and there has fortunately been very little controversy about the ethical conduct of the province's parliamentarians. Two controversies are worth mentioning, however, the first being the 2009 firestorm over the province's Provincial Nominee Program (PNP). The PNP dealt with immigrant investment in PEI and was accused of operating in a manner that effectively auctioned off preferential treatment to certain individuals wishing to immigrate to the province. The auditor general investigated the PNP and filed a report that drew attention to the fact that three members had financial interests in small businesses with some involvement in the PNP controversy. Those members had actually sought and received clearance letters from the commissioner before the businesses in which they had interest made applications to the PNP program,[85] but the auditor general had concerns about the commissioner's decision. He took the liberty of recommending that the legislative assembly review the *Act* in order to clarify what qualifies as a conflict of interest.[86]

The three members who were the subject of the auditor general's report responded by asking the commissioner to provide another opinion about whether they had in fact put themselves into conflicts of interest. The commissioner issued a public report concluding that the

MLAs were not in conflicts and that the auditor general did not have a full enough understanding of the legislation. The report also clarified the applicable rules so that there would be no confusion in the future.[87]

A second major controversy took place in 2015 when allegations surfaced that Commissioner Neil Robinson was himself in a conflict of interest as a result of an investment he had made in an e-gaming (i.e., internet gambling) company. Provincial legislators had been considering regulating the e-gaming industry, and it had become a rather hot topic. Controversy arose when it came to light that the commissioner had advised the leader of the Opposition, Steven Myers, not to file a complaint against another member for accepting a trip from a private firm that was deeply involved in the e-gaming file. Critics said that the commissioner should have been fully aware of the public debate about e-gaming, and that he should have recused himself from any conversations on the matter due to the fact that he had a financial stake in the debate.[88] Commissioner Robinson resigned his position in early 2015 before the legislature could vote on whether it had retained its confidence in his ability.[89] Notably, this is the only case of an independent ethics commissioner resigning in Canada in the midst of a controversy about his or her own conduct.

## NEW BRUNSWICK

New Brunswick's *Conflict of Interest Act* was assented to in 2000.[90] It replaced legislation from 1978 that designated a superior court judge to act as the conflict of interest commissioner. The legislation was modeled after that of Ontario, but it also included a few additional items. For example, the commissioner can recommend that a financial penalty be imposed on a member who violates the *Act*. The commissioner can also recommend that any member who violates the legislation be required to reimburse the Crown for the legal fees and disbursements associated with the cost of any investigation.

Provincial legislation allows for complaints to be made by anyone willing to file an affidavit setting out the grounds for their belief that the *Act* has been breached. The commissioner publishes all annual reports, investigation reports and information bulletins on the office's website. Much like in Newfoundland, however, members' public disclosure statements were not available online as of 2017, and must be requested by an individual who is capable of visiting the Office of the Clerk of the Legislative Assembly. Again, this section of the *Act* is clearly outdated and needs to be corrected to enable the public to engage with the information that has been collected and disclosed.

## NUNAVUT

Nunavut enacted its *Integrity Act* in 2001.[91] The resulting integrity commissioner also has duties under the *Nunavut Elections Act,*[92] including the power to issue "compliance agreements."[93] The commissioner can allow a person who has committed an offence under the *Elections Act* to enter into a compliance agreement where that person, in exchange for a stay of proceedings, must agree to pay restitution for their breach; make an apology; seek atonement in accordance with Inuit *Qaujimajatuqangit*;[94] perform community service or refrain from doing some other action that has been mutually agreed upon.

Nunavut's *Integrity Act* has incorporated many of the best practices already adopted in Canada, but it also remains outdated with respect to public disclosure statements. Specifically, although the blank statement is available online for anyone to download,[95] members of the public must contact the Office of the Clerk of the Legislative Assembly to arrange to view public disclosure statements that have been completed and filed. Finalized public statements are not available online.

## MANITOBA

The Law Reform Commission of Manitoba released a report in 2000 entitled *The Legislative Assembly and Conflict of Interest.*[96] This report looked at the legislation in place throughout Canada with the aim of correcting some of the deficiencies in Manitoba's legislation. It found that an independent officer of the legislature was needed for the administration of conflict of interest legislation in Manitoba. The *Legislative Assembly and Executive Council Conflict of Interest Act* was then amended in 2002 to include provisions requiring the appointment of a part-time conflict of interest commissioner.[97]

Given that the commissioner is not full time, the Legislative Assembly of Manitoba has also decided that he or she should not receive complaints or conduct investigations into alleged violations of the *Act*. The commissioner's primary responsibilities are to meet with the members, to provide them with advice about avoiding conflicts of interest and to receive their yearly disclosure statements. An individual wishing to make a complaint must file an affidavit and pay a $300 security for costs to the court before filing an application to the Court of Queen's Bench to request that a judge hear the complaint. If the application is accepted then a hearing will be held.[98]

## YUKON

The Yukon *Conflict of Interest (Members and Ministers) Act* was enacted in 1995.[99] It was rather unique because, instead of appointing a single commissioner, it required that the province appoint a three-member commission. The commission had not yet been appointed when the legislature passed *An Act to Amend the Conflict of Interest (Members and Ministers) Act* in 1996, which reconfigured the commission to "up to three members."[100] The Honourable E.N. (Ted) Hughes was then appointed in 1996 as Yukon's first sole conflict of interest commissioner. Hughes was replaced in 2002 by David Phillip Jones, Q.C., who still holds the position at the time of writing.[101] Curiously, the commissioner is not an officer of the legislature, in contrast to Yukon's ombudsman, for example.

The commissioner's duties mirror the best practices that have been adopted across the country, but they also include similar obligations to deputy ministers and cabinet and caucus employees.[102]

## NOVA SCOTIA

The Nova Scotia legislature passed the *Conflict of Interest Act* in 2010.[103] The *Act*, which replaced legislation from 1991[104] designating a superior court judge to act as the conflict of interest commissioner, came into force on March 29, 2011. The new legislation is an improvement over the previous model, but it ignores many of the best practices that have already been embraced in other Canadian jurisdictions. For example, the commissioner is not an officer of the House of Assembly. Furthermore, the commissioner has no dedicated website, no public email address and is not required to file or publish annual reports to inform the members and the public about the office's work. Absolutely no information about the commissioner's activities is publicly available unless a member of the provincial legislature discloses an opinion they have received. Members do file disclosure statements in Nova Scotia, as they do in the other provinces and territories, but they are made available on the House of Assembly website as one large scanned file full of members' handwriting — the public would have to painstakingly sift through if they had any question about a member's private interests.[105] Similar to Ontario, the Nova Scotia commissioner does not have jurisdiction to accept complaints (or requests for opinions) from the public. Overall, the Nova Scotia legislation leaves much to be desired, and it will be important for legislators to update it so that it more fully takes into account the public's interest in having meaningful government transparency and accountability mechanisms in place.

## QUEBEC

In 1982, Quebec passed *An Act respecting the National Assembly*.[106] The purpose of this legislation was to stipulate the operating rules of the National Assembly of Quebec. It set out rules of ethical conduct, including provisions about conflicts of interest, and it also created the role of the jurisconsult.[107] The jurisconsult is an individual responsible for providing confidential advisory opinions to members of the National Assembly about conflicts of interest and what are called "incompatibilities of office." It has been said that the creation of the jurisconsult is the first instance of a legislative assembly in Canada appointing an individual whose job it was to advise parliamentarians on code-of-conduct matters.[108]

It was not until 2010, in reaction to several ethics scandals involving the government of Premier Jean Charest, that legislation was passed to create the office of an ethics commissioner along the lines of the other provinces and territories. The new legislation was called the *Code of Ethics and Conduct of the Members of the National Assembly*[109] and, interestingly, it renewed, rather than removed, the function of the jurisconsult. Under the new *Code*, the jurisconsult would remain available for members who were seeking advisory opinions on "ethics and professional conduct," though such opinions would not be binding on the ethics commissioner.[110] Although the two advisors have an odd parallel jurisdiction in this regard, the commissioner also has responsibility for conducting investigations into alleged violations of the *Code*. Members of the National Assembly were hesitant to eliminate the jurisconsult position because the new ethics commissioner would not only have advisory power, but also have the right to undertake investigations into violations on his or her own initiative (i.e., without having to first receive a complaint). Members wanted to be assured that there was someone to whom they could ask questions without also taking on the risk that the person might open a formal investigation. It is perhaps out of the members' own sense of self-preservation that the jurisconsult position remains in place today.

To deal with the confusions that soon arose, the Office of the National Assembly adopted a *Regulation respecting the rules applicable to the Ethics Commissioner concerning conflicts of interest* and a *Regulation respecting conflicts of interest involving the jurisconsult* on March 1, 2012. These regulations were adopted under sections 71 and 111 of the *Code*. In February of 2015, the ethics commissioner published his first *Report on the implementation of the Code of ethics and conduct of the Members of the National Assembly*,[111] under section 114 of the *Code*. In it, the commissioner expresses no concern about the office of the jurisconsult and makes no recommendations about how the dual jurisdiction might be varied. This unique aspect of Quebec's conflict of interest regime is an interesting variation on the Canadian legislative model.

## THE HOUSE OF COMMONS

After several prime ministers' less-than-perfect attempts to establish useful guidelines,[112] Paul Martin's government spearheaded the creation of meaningful conflict of interest legislation in 2004. The effort to establish an overall ethics regime for Parliament was motivated by the revelations that eventually led to the sponsorship scandal (discussed in Chapter 1). The new system included a process for creating a code of conduct for MPs and a more stringent code of conduct for cabinet ministers; the appointment of an independent ethics commissioner for the House of Commons, cabinet and order-in-council appointments; the appointment of an independent ethics officer for the Senate; and a process to create a code of conduct for the Senate.

The Martin government had to overcome some major hurdles to enact this legislation. It was especially difficult to convince the Senate — even one with a Liberal majority — that having ethics rules and an independent commissioner would be useful for preventing conflicts of interest and enhancing the body's public image. As a reaction to the scandals faced by the Chrétien government during its last years in office, Chrétien had introduced legislation that would have created one code of conduct for both the Senate and the House of Commons. It would also have created one ethics commissioner to advise MPs, senators and public office holders and to investigate alleged ethical breaches. In its consideration of this bill, the Senate concluded that it required its own ethics officer and its own conflict of interest code. The Chrétien proposal consequently died in the upper house. The Martin government reintroduced amended ethics legislation that empowered the Senate to choose its own ethics officer and to develop its own code of conduct. The new legislation passed and Dr. Bernard Shapiro, retired Principal of McGill University, was appointed Parliament's first ethics commissioner in 2004. In 2005, the Senate chose Mr. Jean Fournier, a retired senior federal public servant, to become its first ethics officer.

The legislation required the prime minister to "consult" with the leader of every recognized party before appointing an ethics commissioner. Despite this requirement, Opposition leader Stephen Harper was apparently not pleased with how the consultation process unfolded. The media echoed this discontent when it began to criticize Shapiro's appointment on the grounds that he lacked extensive experience with government ethics regimes.[113] Harper became progressively more critical of Shapiro, and once he became prime minister he was reportedly reluctant to cooperate with the commissioner in his first investigation of an alleged breach of the rules.[114]

Only a few months after the Conservative Party took power in 2006, the government introduced the *Federal Accountability Act*.[115] It was intended to fulfill Harper's election promise to create higher standards of ethics and accountability in government. The legislation, as originally introduced, would have abolished the ethics commissioner and the Senate ethics officer, replacing them both with a new parliamentary conflict of interest and ethics commissioner. Predictably, the Senate objected to the merger of the offices, which caused the minority government to amend the bill to continue the separate Senate ethics officer in an attempt to get it through Parliament. Bernard Shapiro chose to resign as ethics commissioner, and he refused to stand for the new position.

On July 9, 2007, Mary Dawson, a career lawyer in the federal Department of Justice, was appointed conflict of interest and ethics commissioner under the *Parliament of Canada Act*.[116] Commissioner Dawson was appointed for a renewable seven-year term and has since been reappointed for a two-year term and two more six-month terms. The commissioner may only be removed for cause by the Governor in Council on the address of the House of Commons.[117]

The *Federal Accountability Act* passed by the Conservative government included the *Conflict of Interest Act* for public office holders, which replaced the *Conflict of Interest Code for Public Office Holders.* Commissioner Dawson also has jurisdiction over the *Conflict of Interest Code for Members of the House of Commons,*[118] which was initially adopted by the House in April 2004 and has since been amended on several occasions. The *Code* is an appendix to the Standing Orders of the House of Commons. Interestingly, ministers and parliamentary secretaries are subject to both the *Act* and the *Code.*

As of 2017, the *Code* applied to all 338 members of the House of Commons and was very similar to the legislation passed in Canada's provinces and territories. It deals with conflicts between public and private interests and empowers the commissioner to receive disclosures, give advice, investigate complaints and issue reports. The *Code* does not require members to divest assets and it does not restrict members' outside activities. It does require them to recuse themselves from matters that could give rise to a conflict of interest, and it requires that they inform the commissioner about any material changes in their assets, liabilities, other interests, sponsored travel or gifts and benefits received. The *Code* has also been the subject of some criticism because it does not require members to meet with the commissioner on an annual basis.[119] Rather, it permits the commissioner to choose to require a meeting with the member after reviewing the member's private statement. Ian Greene has argued that annual face-to-face meetings with ethics commissioners or their senior staff ought to be mandatory for legislators because there is good reason to believe that these meetings help reduce the number of investigations conducted into violations of the rules.[120]

The *Act,* in addition to applying to cabinet ministers, applies to more than three thousand public office holders, including ministers and parliamentary secretaries. The rules are very similar to the *Code,* but with a few notable exceptions. First, those subject to the *Act* must not engage in outside employment, nor are they permitted to own certain specified assets. If they do own such assets (for example, an asset that a government decision or policy could have an impact on) prior to their appointment, then they must sell them to an arm's-length third party or place them in a blind trust, the specific requirements of which are set out in the *Act*. Second, the commissioner has the power to issue compliance orders and to issue administrative monetary penalties (AMPs) of up to $500. AMPs may be issued when a public official does not meet the reporting deadline set out in the *Act*. Deadlines exist for such things as filing annual private disclosures, reporting material changes to those disclosures, reporting the receipt of gifts or benefits, reporting recusals from matters due to conflicts of interest, reporting outside activities and reporting travel, to name a few. The commissioner's website reports that sixty-eight administrative monetary penalties were issued between 2009 and the end of 2015.

## THE SENATE

The Office of the Senate Ethics Officer was established through amendments to the *Parliament of Canada Act*.[121] The ethics officer is understood to be independent and is appointed in consultation with the leader of every recognized party in the Senate and after approval by a Senate resolution.[122] The officer is appointed for a term of seven years and may be reappointed for one or more terms of up to seven years. The officer can only be removed for cause by the Governor in Council on the address of the Senate. Jean T. Fournier, a career public servant who had served under both Liberal and Conservative governments, was appointed to the position on April 1, 2005. Fournier was appointed by consensus of both the Liberal and Conservative leaders in the Senate (an appointment process that was strikingly different from the one used to appoint Bernard Shapiro, as detailed above), which seems to have helped him to quickly gain the members' trust. Fournier was succeeded by Lyse Ricard on April 5, 2012.

Ms. Ricard administers the *Ethics and Conflict of Interest Code for Senators,* which includes providing opinions and advice, administering a disclosure process, answering inquiries, publishing a public registry, offering outreach and educational activities and filing annual reports. Senators must declare when they reasonably believe that either they or their family members might benefit from a matter before the Senate or a committee in which they are a member. Senators must also refrain from participating in votes from which they may benefit, and they must in some cases withdraw entirely from proceedings before a committee if it is reasonable to believe that a conflict might arise.

The Senate has been the subject of much negative press since 2013, but these scandals have mostly revolved around expenses, not conflicts of interest. Small changes were made to senators' residency rules, but it is very likely that further changes are forthcoming. In fact, the first Senate ethics officer, Jean Fournier, has publicly stated that the rules are insufficient and that they must be expanded.[123] This will be an important challenge for the Senate as it moves forward.

## THE FUTURE OF ETHICS COMMISSIONS

There is no denying that ethics commissions represent an improvement over previous models, but this does not mean that they are perfect. Ethics commissioners are appointed under legislation passed by the very individuals over whom they must exercise jurisdiction (i.e., legislators). This is in itself a conflict of interest, though it is arguably an unavoidable one. It is therefore important to critically examine ethics commissions and the work they are empowered to do. For example, it is important to ask what the role of ethics commissioners ought to be. Should they be seen as protectors of the public interest, of public officials, or both? It matters a great deal how we characterize the role of an ethics commissioner. In Ontario, for example, unlike in some other jurisdictions, the integrity commissioner cannot accept complaints from members of the public. As a result, no report will ever be published unless a complaint comes from a member or from the executive council. This legislative structure hardly allows the commissioner to act in the public's interest.

Regardless of how specific regimes are structured, however, opportunities to improve ethics commissions all across Canada clearly exist. As mentioned earlier, the beauty of Canadian federalism is that new practices can be tested by one jurisdiction and then adopted by others if they prove successful. To ensure that the standards our elected officials are held to continue to reflect evolving public expectations, the following recommendations are offered:

- Information about members' personal assets must be available online and must be searchable, sortable and downloadable. Ethics commissioners must be given the power to investigate on their own initiative, and the public must be allowed to make complaints. Commissioners must be able to draw attention in their annual reports to public disclosures that demonstrate a violation of the legislation. If a minister, for example, had purchased an income property even though the legislation says he or she cannot do so, and then refused to dispose of his or her interest in that asset, the commissioner ought to be able to draw attention to that violation in an investigation or annual report. If we are going to fund these offices and expect them to have an impact, then it should not be left to a member of the legislature or a member of the public to figure out that there has been a violation.

- Sunset clauses and mandatory public consultations must be built in to every jurisdiction's legislation so that the rules will continue to reflect evolving social values. This problem is quite obvious when we remember the fact that Nova Scotia's legislation requires none of the commissioner's work to be made public. Furthermore, the Nova Scotia office does not even have a website or a publicly disclosed email address. If we want these offices to protect the public interest, then public opinion must play a meaningful role in how we decide what rules to put in place.

- Legislators must have mandatory face-to-face meetings with their ethics commissioner or a senior staff member of their commissioner's office, and mandatory ethics training must be provided to members and their staff.

- More consideration must be given to how ethics regimes can expand beyond mere conflicts of interest to the promotion of good ethical conduct more generally. Ontario's experiment with parliamentary convention provides one example of how this could be done, but it is certainly worth exploring other options as well. A jurisdictional expansion of this nature might also allow commissioners to provide opinions about apparent conflicts of interest, depending on how the rules are structured.

- Finally, the method of selecting ethics commissioners must be enhanced so that an all-party committee in each legislature publicly advertises for the position, conducts interviews and then recommends to the House. These appointments must be completely free of even the appearance of partisan manipulation.

## CONCLUSION

Overall, ethics commissions have proven to be an excellent and well-received innovation. Research demonstrates that the number of conflict of interest scandals reported in the media has gone down in most jurisdictions since an ethics office was established, and sometimes the change has been dramatic.[124] Despite this positive development, challenges still lie ahead. Perhaps the biggest is ensuring that legislation continues to reflect Canadians' ever-changing social values. One way to do this is to make the public aware of the rules that are in place so that they can help to pressure legislators to continue to strengthen those rules. We have seen in this chapter that every jurisdiction in Canada has basic rules in place, but that there are still many jurisdictions that have not adopted some important and widely accepted practices. Legislators ought to feel pressure to bring those regimes up to date. Ethics commissions must continue to move forward if they wish to remain relevant in this constantly evolving and highly engaged digital world.

| Table 1 | | |
|---|---|---|
| The Creation of Independent Ethics Commissioners | | |
| Province | Year of Appointment of First Commissioner | Title |
| Ontario | 1988 | conflict of interest commissioner |
| British Columbia | 1990 | conflict of interest commissioner |
| Alberta | 1992 | ethics commissioner |
| Newfoundland & Labrador | 1993 | commissioner for legislative standards |
| Saskatchewan | 1993 | conflict of interest commissioner |
| Yukon | 1996 | conflict of interest commissioner |
| Northwest Territories | 1999 | conflict of interest commissioner |
| Prince Edward Island | 1999 | conflict of interest commissioner |
| New Brunswick | 2000 | conflict of interest commissioner |
| Nunavut | 2001 | integrity commissioner |
| Manitoba | 2002 | conflict of interest commissioner |
| House of Commons | 2004 | conflict of interest and ethics commissioner |
| Senate | 2005 | ethics officer |
| Quebec | 2010 | ethics commissioner; (1982 jurisconsult) |
| Nova Scotia | 2011 | conflict of interest commissioner |

# CHAPTER 6
# MONEY IN POLITICS: THE ETHICS OF ELECTION FINANCE REGULATION AND EXPENSE CLAIMS OVERSIGHT

## Lori Turnbull, Ian Greene and Robert Shepherd

Money has an important and legitimate role to play in elections. It is the primary vehicle for political expression, as it enables individuals to indicate their support for candidates and their parties by making donations to campaigns. In pledging support for these people and groups, we offer support for their ideas and plans, and give them the resources they need to advance their platforms in the arena of political competition. In this way, the public has an opportunity to affect the tone and substance of public debate. And, let's face it: campaigns cost a lot of money. The world of strategic communications is complex and expensive, and politicians who intend to be serious contenders need donations to finance their campaigns.

Though the flow of money in elections is important and legitimate, it must also be regulated so that money does not become *too* important or get misused. We must avoid both the perception and the reality of undue influence in elections. This is the objective that motivates several election finance regulations in Canada today. The Parliament of Canada places legal limits on the amount that donors can contribute to political campaigns so that wealthy donors do not acquire excessive influence over political actors. Any donation over $200 must be disclosed, so that the public knows who is donating to whom and in what amounts. Further, we limit the amount that candidates can spend, so that personal wealth does not confer excessive advantage on some competitors over others.

Although there is a clear ethical justification for regulating the influence of money in political campaigns, the state's obligation to protect freedom of expression and the right to participate meaningfully in elections serves as a countervailing force. A balance must be struck between the two. The Supreme Court of Canada acknowledged and worked through this tension in *Figueroa v. Canada* (2003) and in *Harper v. Canada* (2004). The court ruled that while spending limits do place a restriction on section 2(b) of the *Charter of Rights and Freedoms*, which protects freedom of expression, the violation is justified on the grounds that spending limits create a level playing field for political competition. Ultimately, this serves to protect the individual's right to participate meaningfully in democracy, because it affords a robust exchange of ideas. The political marketplace is to be a fair and democratic forum where a variety of ideas are exchanged and debated on their merits, and where financial wealth does not determine the prominence and force of a particular idea or message.

We must also avoid the misuse — whether in reality or perception — of public money by our representatives. To this end, Parliament uses guidelines to spell out the proper use of public funds by Members of the House of Commons and the Senate, including rules related to travel claims, living allowances and other expenses associated with members' official duties. The perception or reality of greed, largesse or indulgence among the political class is damaging to the credibility of all politicians and the institutions they represent. Therefore, there is a public interest in ensuring accountability and transparency with regard to parliamentarians' use of taxpayers' money in relation to public reimbursements for election expenses.

Though federal and provincial elections finance regimes have evolved and become more comprehensive over the years, written rules can never cover every ethical transgression; there is, inevitably, a gap between the letter of the law and the public's sense of what it means to be ethical. Actions can be legal but offensive, and there can be significant political cost when politicians test the public's patience in this regard.

To explore in more depth the space between legal and regulatory obligations on the one hand and ethical norms on the other, this chapter considers an extraordinary example of ethics issues as they relate to expense claims: the case of Senator Mike Duffy. Duffy went to trial in 2015 on thirty-one charges, including bribery, fraud and breach of trust. Many of these related to Senator Duffy's use of the money allotted to him for living expenses, travel and the purchasing of services to support his Senate work. There was also one bribery charge in connection to money given to him by then chief of staff to the Prime Minister, Nigel Wright. The Duffy case represents just one strand of the broader Senate expense scandal, which left the institution's reputation in tatters. Even though Senator Duffy was acquitted of all charges, the case exposed gaps and loopholes in the Administrative Rules that govern senators' use of funds for travel, per diems and other expenses. The case serves as evidence that legal exoneration does not mean that all is well on the ethical front: Senator Duffy's actions still strike many Canadians as questionable, which is what really matters when it comes to public trust in our political actors and institutions.

Before providing a case study of Senator Duffy's trial, we review the suite of electoral finance regulations that exist in Canada.

## ELECTORAL FINANCE REGIMES

### Federal Electoral Finance Laws

Political candidates and parties in Canada have two major sources of revenue: electoral expense reimbursements and political contributions from eligible donors. Registered political parties can receive reimbursement for up to 50 per cent of their eligible election expenses, as reported in the party's election expense return form. Candidates are eligible for partial reimbursement, provided the candidate wins at least 10 per cent of the popular vote in his or her riding.[1] From 2004 to 2015, registered political parties received a per-vote subsidy on an annual basis, roughly equivalent to $2 for each vote received in the previous election. The most popular parties received the most money, but all parties benefitted from having a guaranteed, pre-determined source of income each year. The per-vote subsidy was introduced by Prime Minister Jean Chrétien, but was gradually phased out by the Conservatives under Prime Minister Stephen Harper, after they won a majority government in 2011. There were two reasons for this change. From a policy perspective, the Conservative government thought that taxpayers should not be subsidizing political parties. But from a more self-serving perspective, the Conservatives were doing far better than the other federal parties in terms of fundraising.

Only Canadian citizens or permanent residents can contribute to political campaigns. It is now illegal for trade unions or corporations to contribute, though this was not always the case. These organizations were the source of substantial financial contributions prior to Prime Minister Chrétien's 2003 amendments (which came into effect in 2004 and were later expanded by Prime Minister Harper in 2006–7). Before 2004, there had been no caps on the contributions that either individuals or trade unions and corporations could make. Today, however, trade unions and corporations cannot contribute at all, and individuals can contribute a maximum of $1,550 per election to each registered party,[2] as well as the same amount in total to all registered candidates, nomination contests and registered riding associations. In the event of a party leadership contest, individuals can contribute $1,550 in total to all leadership candidates.[3] From an ethics perspective, these limitations serve an important purpose. Specifically, they seek to remove both the reality and the perception of undue influence by reducing the potential for an individual or group to donate enough money to sway political decisions. Section 119 of the *Criminal Code of Canada* therefore makes it an indictable offence to "corruptly" give or receive something of value, with intent to either bribe or to be bribed.

In addition to limitations on the size of contributions, amounts of over $200 must be included on a list of donors, which is made public by Elections Canada. Such disclosures are aimed at improving transparency by making the list of donors public, and ensuring voters are informed about the source and amount of contributions to political officials.

Both candidates and political parties are subject to spending limits as well, so that even if a party is highly successful at soliciting donations, or its membership is particularly wealthy, they cannot gain unfair advantage simply by outspending their competitors. The spending limits are calculated by Elections Canada using a formula that includes the number of electors on the preliminary or revised list in each electoral district and the number of days in the campaign. To provide some context, the Conservatives, Liberals and New Democrats adhered to spending limits of $54,936,320 each in the 2015 election. Limits can and do vary for federal parties, depending on the number of candidates they officially endorse. At the candidate level, spending limits for the 2015 election ranged from roughly $170,000 for candidates running in Prince Edward Island to $279,228 in Kootenay-Columbia, British Columbia.

Both spending and contribution limits are enforced by the Commissioner of Canada Elections. If the commissioner believes that there is evidence of a serious violation of the *Act*, he or she can refer the case to the Director of Public Prosecutions, who decides whether to prosecute based on the likelihood of obtaining a conviction.[4]

In 2014, Dean Del Mastro, former MP and Parliamentary Secretary to Prime Minister Stephen Harper, was convicted of election fraud for violating the election spending limits. "Mr. Del Mastro . . . was convicted of three electoral offences: overspending, failing to report a personal contribution of $21,000 he made to his own campaign and filing a false report."[5] He was unsuccessful in appealing his conviction and sentence, at which point the judge reminded Del Mastro that "the offences [he] committed . . . are serious and do strike at the heart of our democratic electoral process."[6] He was sentenced to one month in jail, and eighteen months of probation.

In 2016, the issues of "cash-for-access" fundraising events attracted the attention of the public and the media. Ministers in the Trudeau government had organized a number of fundraising dinners for which attendees were asked to pay up to $1,500. This amount is within the federal limit for annual contributions, and seems small enough to avoid undue influence. And yet, those seeking to influence government policy are more likely to attend such events since they are more likely to pay the price of admission. For example, Finance Minister Bill Morneau was the star attraction of a $500-a-person fundraising event in Toronto in November 2016. Barry Sherman, chairman of the pharmaceutical company Apotex, helped to organize and sell tickets for the event. The negative publicity stemming from the cash-for-access nature of the event led the Liberal Party to issue new guidelines that prohibited those lobbying the government from attending or organizing such events. As a result, Sherman stopped selling tickets and declined to attend. However, in October, before the new Liberal policy was announced, Morneau attended a $1,500-a-person fundraiser in Halifax. The event was attended by "bankers, mortgage brokers and a member of the Halifax Port Authority" who was considering applying for substantial funds from the federal government.[7] Though the conflict of interest and ethics commissioner has described such fundraisers as "not very savoury," neither were they contrary to the conflict of interest rules then in place.[8]

In reaction to media and opposition critiques of these events, in early 2017 the Trudeau government announced that it would introduce legislation to increase the transparency of fundraising events without lowering the contribution limit of $1,550. The proposed legislation would apply to fundraisers organized for cabinet ministers, party leaders and party leadership candidates. Such events would need to be publicly accessible, advertised in advance and open to the media. Reports detailing how many attended and how much was raised would need to be filed soon after the events.[9]

The controversy surrounding these events is another indication that when it comes to ethical standards in politics, public expectations change over time, and increasingly higher expectations are not unusual.[10] The challenge for political parties is to be proactive rather reactive in their formation of ethical standards.

## Provincial Electoral Finance Laws

It has been argued that "provincial political systems . . . serve as laboratories to examine how different regulatory regimes affect political financing."[11] When the state of provincial electoral finance legislation is examined, several laboratory experiments can be observed.

Table 2 presents a summary, as of January 2017, of the state of provincial electoral finance rules. Five provinces have banned corporate and union donations, while one, New Brunswick, has placed limits on such donations. Six provinces have placed annual limits on individual donations to political parties ranging from a low of $100 in Quebec, to a high of $12,000 in New Brunswick (divided between the party and the candidate). However, two of these have allowed additional donations during an election period. Four provinces have no limits at all. Nine provinces have set limits on party and/or constituency spending during campaigns (the outlier is New Brunswick). Two provinces, Manitoba and British Columbia, have some party spending limits outside election periods. Six provinces provide taxpayer-subsidized programs to support parties so that the burden of public fundraising can be reduced, and five provinces have limited the amount that can be spent by third parties during elections, following suit with the federal third-party spending limits described above.

The range of provincial rules reflects the fact that they are often passed in reaction to local political crises. Until 2017, Alberta allowed up to $30,000 in annual individual donations, but in 2016, the NDP government, with the support of the Wildrose Party, spearheaded legislation to reduce the annual limit to $4,000. In part, this change was a reaction to the perception that the previous Progressive Conservative government was beholden to its major donors.[12]

In Ontario, prior to enacting new electoral financing rules in the fall of 2016, Ontario's Liberal government had been under attack in the media for several months concerning their "pay-to-play" fundraising events. Until the end of 2016, the annual limit for individual political contributions in Ontario was $9,975 during non-election periods, and in the Liberal administrations of Dalton McGuinty and Kathleen Wynne, individual cabinet ministers were assigned individual fundraising goals of up to $500,000 annually. Some ministers organized fundraising dinners that cost attendees close to the annual limit. These events were criticized because only the wealthy could afford to buy tickets, and if they were willing to spend nearly $10,000 to attend, it was assumed that favours were likely expected in return.[13] The media's critique of this fundraising activity was so intense that in September 2016 the Wynne government introduced radical changes to Ontario's electoral financing rules, reducing annual contribution limits to $3,600 (split $1,200 each amongst party, constituency and candidate during election periods) and prohibiting all members of the legislature from attending any fundraising events.[14]

Ontario's electoral financing situation is indicative of how changes in the rules may not be subject to immediate public reaction. In the 1997 edition of *Honest Politics*, we reported that the annual limit for personal donations in Ontario was $750, up from $500 a few years earlier. However, shortly after publication, Mike Harris's Progressive Conservative government raised the limit substantially. Following the Harris formula, by early 2016 the total annual individual donation limit had risen to $33,250.[15] It is noteworthy that Dalton McGuinty, elected in 2003, did not restore the limits previously set by the Liberals in 1995. The likely reason was that the Ontario Liberal Party had learned how to rake in more funds using the Conservatives' higher limits. Eventually, though, public pressure resulted in the new and more sensible contribution limits, which took effect in January 2017.

### Table 2
### Provincial Campaign Finance Rules Summary as of January 2017[16]

| Prov | Corporate & Union Donations | Personal Annual Donation Limit, Non-Election Years | Personal Donation Limit during an Election Campaign | Party Spending Limits during campaigns | Subsidy from govt? | 3rd Party Spending Limit? |
|---|---|---|---|---|---|---|
| B.C. | No limit | No limit; Out of Prov donations OK | No limit; Out of Prov donations OK | Yes | No | Yes |
| AB | Banned | $4,000 overall | None | Yes | No | Yes |
| SK | No limit | No limit; Out of Prov donations OK; Charities OK to donate | No limit; Out of Prov donations OK; Charities OK to donate | Yes | No | No |
| MB | Banned | $3,000 | None | Yes | Yes | No |
| ON | Banned | $1,200 to party $1,200 to constituency | Additional $1,200 to candidate | Yes | Yes | Yes |
| QC | Banned | $100 for each party; Anonymous donations banned | Additional $100 for each party | Yes | Yes | Yes |
| NB | $6,000 for party, plus additional $6,000 for candidate | $6,000 for party, plus additional $6,000 for candidate | Nothing extra | Yes | Yes | No |
| PEI | No limit | No limit; Out of Prov donations OK | No limit | Yes | Yes | No |
| NS | Banned | $5,000; Anonymous donations banned | Nothing extra | No | Yes | Yes |
| NL | No limit | No limit; Out of Prov donations OK | No limit; Out of Prov donations OK | Yes | Yes | No |

The four provinces with election financing regimes most open to undue influence are Saskatchewan, British Columbia, Prince Edward Island and Newfoundland and Labrador. None of these provinces, as of 2017, has banned union or corporate donations, set limits on the annual amounts of personal donations to parties or prohibited out-of-province donations; Saskatchewan even allows donations from registered charities. The lack of rules leaves these provinces open to undue influence and political scandal.

## Salary Supplements for Leaders from their Parties

It is not uncommon for political parties to provide their leaders with salary top-ups or to cover some personal expenses. These supplements are meant to encourage potential leaders to assume a position that is arguably not well-paid from public funds, compared with similar positions in the private sector. Leadership positions also involve having to face a good deal of pressure and criticism.

For example, in 2016 the *Globe and Mail* reported that British Columbia Premier Christy Clark, who earns about $200,000 a year as premier, also received between $30,000 and $50,000 a year from the B.C. Liberal Party in recognition of the additional work she does for the party.[17] Payments like this raise a number of questions. First, the Liberal Party is paying Clark from funds that it raises from donors who receive tax credits for their contributions — in essence, a form of taxpayer subsidization. Second, Clark attends cash-for-access fundraising events "at which attendees can pay $20,000 or more to gain privileged access."[18] It would be difficult to avoid undue influence when the premier knows who these donors are, and that some of their donations may be funding her salary top-up. A member of the provincial Opposition referred the issue to the B.C. conflict of interest commissioner, who interpreted the *Act* narrowly and found no real or apparent conflict of interest.[19]

In another example, in April 1996 the *Globe and Mail* reported that Ontario Premier Mike Harris had received substantial payments from his riding association to cover personal expenses over the years. In 1994 alone, these expenses totaled at least $18,000, and included $7,000 for upgrading his Toronto residence, $2,000 for meals and entertaining, $1,000 for golf club dues and fees and nearly $1,000 for dry cleaning. The people who covered these expenses received tax credits ranging from 44 per cent to 75 per cent. In other words, Harris's party expenses were subsidized by Ontario taxpayers.

At the request of the leader of the Opposition, Integrity Commissioner Gregory Evans investigated. He reported that Harris had not been in violation of the *Act* as written. However, the tone of Evans's report implied that political parties must exercise caution when making payments to elected members. He stated that if a gift or benefit were provided to a member, the "apparent purpose [of which] is to 'use' the office of the member as lobbying for the benefit or the donor," that gift would be unacceptable under the *Act*. From this perspective, he noted that although the disclosure of payments from political parties is currently not required under the *Act*, "whether such disclosure would be prudent is another matter."[20]

However, paying salary supplements to party leaders in order to encourage them to take on the job is unlikely to end. Our view is that salary supplements from parties are acceptable under the following conditions:

- The gifts are *not* tax-subsidized.

- Persons receiving such gifts report them as taxable benefits on their income tax returns.

- Donors are made aware that their contributions are going into a fund for the personal benefit of the candidate rather than to fight an election campaign.

- There are limits to the single-source amounts that can be donated to the party's special fund for salary supplements to safeguard against the possibility of undue influence.

An absolute annual limit of $500 per source might be appropriate, because this amount is small enough that it would be unlikely to result in undue influence.

- Payments should be fully and publicly disclosed pursuant to conflict of interest rules.

These kinds of ethics controversies could be headed off by political parties if they were to draft their own internal, enforceable codes of ethics, as recommended by the Royal Commission on Electoral Reform and Party Financing in 1991.[21]

## NON-STATUTORY PARLIAMENTARY REGULATIONS AND EXPENSE CLAIMS

Members of Parliament and senators are regulated by non-statutory rules dictating how they spend the public money allotted to them. The Board of Internal Economy, a House of Commons committee, adopts policies governing MPs' use of their office budgets, entitlements and allowances, including funds for travel, housing, living and hospitality. The Standing Senate Committee on Internal Economy provides senators with guidelines and rules for their use of public funds to staff their offices, travel, obtain lodging close to Parliament Hill and to cover other expenses related to their official responsibilities. Though these rules do not have legal force or effect outside the House of Commons or the Senate, members can be sanctioned internally. That said, these rules can and do overlap with the law. Filing a false travel claim, for example, is not only a breach of internal rules but an act of criminal fraud, as illustrated by the case of Senator Raymond Lavigne (discussed in Chapter 4).

Campaign finance regimes are meant to regulate the use and influence of money in electoral politics. The rules are designed to create openness and transparency around political contributions so that Canadians know where candidates and parties acquire their money.

This standard of openness and transparency extends to MPs' and senators' use of public funds while in office. We put our trust in them to
use our money properly, and we also trust that they will not take unfair
advantage of the benefits to which they are entitled once they assume
public office. The regime also limits the presence of money in politics
by setting caps on the amount that political actors can receive or spend,
which provides a level playing field for the competition of political ideas,
making it possible for the voter to make a fair and informed choice
between candidates. Failure to abide by these rules, either in perception or reality, has serious consequences for the relationship between
Canadian legislators and citizens. With this in mind, we turn to a case
study of the effects of allegations regarding the misuse of public funds
and undue influence.

The case is that of Senator Mike Duffy, which lasted roughly from
December 2012 to April 2016. Senator Duffy's story is part of a larger
narrative concerning the misuse of funds in the Senate. As the case was
building, three other senators, each of whom claimed their primary
residence was outside the Ottawa area, were also accused of filing inappropriate claims relating to housing. In addition, a report released by
the Auditor General of Canada in June 2015, following an investigation
into other senators' expense claims, found that thirty current or former
senators had incurred inappropriate expenses, made claims that were
not related to parliamentary business or filed claims that lacked supporting evidence. The report recommended that nine of these cases be
referred to the RCMP; it also found that there was a "lack of independent oversight in the way Senators' expenses are governed."[22] The Duffy
trial and its findings show that the rules regulating senators' expense
claims, residency claims and use of public funds for contracting work
were vague and incomplete, undermining their ability to help create a
culture of ethics in the Senate. The Duffy case also involved allegations
of undue influence, as the political leadership of the federal Conservative Party was accused of attempting to bury the scandal. It was in this
context that Senator Duffy was charged with bribery for accepting a

cheque from the prime minister's chief of staff to cover the costs of repaying his expenses.

## Case Study: The Expense Scandal of Senator Mike Duffy

### BACKGROUND

Mike Duffy was named to the Senate in December of 2008 by then Prime Minister Stephen Harper to represent the province of Prince Edward Island. In 2012, Senator Duffy's PEI residency became the subject of intense public debate and scrutiny. Though he claimed living expenses for his time in Ottawa, it was well known that he and his wife owned a home in Kanata, which is less than thirty kilometres from downtown Ottawa. Prior to his appointment to the Senate, Mr. Duffy worked as a journalist for CTV in Ottawa. He and his wife lived in their Kanata home at the time, and also owned a property in Cavendish, PEI. Duffy was not the only Senator in public difficulty at the time: Senators Patrick Brazeau (Conservative), Mac Harb (Liberal) and Pamela Wallin (Conservative) were also accused of falsely claiming primary residency outside of the Ottawa area. In February 2013, the Senate Committee on the Internal Economy announced that the four senators' residency claims would be audited.[23]

Though Senator Duffy insisted that his primary home was in PEI and not Ottawa, he publicly volunteered to repay the expenses he had claimed for his work in Ottawa. He made this payment, which totaled $90,172, in March 2013. Two months later, Canadians learned that Senator Duffy had received a cheque for this entire amount from the chief of staff to the prime minister, Nigel Wright. All of this occurred while an external forensic audit of Senate expenses was underway.[24]

Once the public became aware of the cheque, Mr. Wright announced his resignation. Mr. Harper has always maintained that he had no prior knowledge of an exchange of money between Wright and Duffy, and that he did not approve this transaction. In his statement to the media on the day of his resignation, Mr. Wright corroborated Prime Minister

Harper's version of events, insisting that he "did not advise the Prime Minister of the means by which Sen. Duffy's expenses were repaid, either before or after the fact."[25]

In November 2013, the Conservative-dominated Senate voted to suspend Senators Duffy, Brazeau and Wallin without pay for the remainder of the session in light of the allegations against them (Senator Harb had retired in August of that year). There were allegations that the Prime Minister's Office (PMO), anxious to take the oxygen out of the scandal and to appear responsive on the matter of Senate corruption, had inserted itself into Senate business by strongly encouraging Conservative senators to vote in favour of suspending their peers. Since Duffy, Brazeau and Wallin had each been appointed by Prime Minister Harper, there is some logic to the claim that the PMO had a political interest in distancing itself and the Conservative Party from a Senate expense scandal. This is understandable, particularly in light of the fact that the two main opposition parties, the Liberals and the New Democrats, were enjoying strong positions in the lead-up to the fall 2015 election. The Liberals had elected Justin Trudeau as their new leader in the spring of 2013 and were steadily gaining in the polls. Because the Senate expense scandal had focused predominantly on the three Conservative senators, the governing party, by contrast, was the subject of a host of negative publicity.

The case against Duffy came to a head in July 2014, when the RCMP laid thirty-one charges, including bribery, fraud and breach of trust. Apart from treason, there are no more serious charges for a politician. To be accused of bribery, fraudulent expense claims and breaching the public's trust strikes at the heart of one's legitimacy as a public official.

## INVESTIGATION AND ISSUES

The charges against Senator Duffy fell into four themes or categories: bribery, in relation to the roughly $90,000 Senator Duffy received from Nigel Wright; fraudulent expenses, stemming from the claim that his primary residence was in PEI; inappropriate expense claims for political rather than parliamentary activity; and those related to contracts that Senator Duffy paid using Senate funds for ineligible services or projects.

First, the bribery charge against Senator Duffy garnered significant attention because of its seriousness but also because of its one-sided nature: Though Senator Duffy was charged with accepting (or at least intending to accept) a bribe from Nigel Wright, Mr. Wright himself was not charged with offering a bribe. But how could Mr. Duffy accept a bribe that was not offered? One explanation is that, while Duffy might have intended to receive a bribe, Mr. Wright did not intend to offer one. It all comes down to intent and whether either individual stood to gain from the outcome. Mr. Wright insisted that he made the decision to cover Duffy's expenses on his own and that there was no *quid pro quo* of any kind. In other words, Mr. Wright, who is independently wealthy, claims to have offered the money voluntarily, and that Mr. Duffy accepted it with no strings attached. However, though the Senate's code of conduct requires the public disclosure of all gifts over $200 to the Senate ethics officer, there was no recorded disclosure for the Duffy-Wright transaction. Moreover, the $90,000 payment, while not considered criminal by the RCMP, may have violated the *Conflict of Interest Act*, to which Wright was subject. At the time of writing, the Senate ethics officer and Parliament's conflict of interest and ethics commissioner were investigating potential violations of the Senate code and the *Conflict of Interest Act*, respectively. The rules governing investigations by these officers did not allow them to carry on an investigation while court proceedings were underway, hence the delay in their investigations.

During Senator Duffy's trial, Mr. Wright was called as a witness for the Crown. During his testimony he released hundreds of pages of emails and messages between himself, other members of the Harper PMO, Senator Duffy, the senator's lawyer and other high-ranking Conservative senators. The messages related to Senator Duffy's claim that his primary residence was in PEI and that his claims to housing and living expenses while in Ottawa were justified. The emails revealed a clear, coordinated effort by the PMO and the Conservative leadership in the Senate to make the controversy go away by arranging a repayment strategy for Senator Duffy and to have him removed from a Deloitte audit on senators' expenses. For example, an email from Mr. Wright to Senator Duffy indicated Wright's concern that the Deloitte audit would find that his primary residence was Kanata rather than PEI. In turn, Senator Duffy's lawyer wrote that since "his apparent ineligibility for the housing allowance stems from his time on the road on behalf of the party, there will be an arrangement to keep him whole on the repayment. His legal fees will also be reimbursed." But when the Conservative leadership learned how much Senator Duffy really owed in February 2013, it balked at offering the funds for repayment. For his part, Nigel Wright wrote: "I am beyond furious. This will all be repaid."[26]

The second category of charges also stemmed from living and housing expenses that Senator Duffy claimed while working in Ottawa as a senator; he was allowed to do so because he claimed PEI as his "residence." To represent a particular province in the Senate, the *Constitution Act 1867* makes clear, an individual must be "resident" in the province that he or she represents. Although Senator Duffy owns a home in the Ottawa area, he claimed that his primary home was in PEI. The prime minister's legal advisor at the time, Benjamin Perrin, warned him that it was questionable whether Duffy was really a resident of PEI, and that he was "taken aback" when Prime Minister Harper rejected his opinion.[27]

Questions about Senator Duffy's true residence came to light in December 2012. As mentioned earlier, he was not the only one. Senators had been asked to provide documentation to prove their residency by January 31, 2013. This was the first time since 1867 that senators were asked to provide such documentation. Senator Duffy tried to meet the requirement by expediting his acquisition of a PEI health card before the deadline. When asked why he did not have one to begin with, he explained that he has a serious heart condition that requires quick access to quality health care and that he held an Ontario health card for this purpose.

The third category of charges related to the travel and expense claims that Senator Duffy filed, and the allegation that they were related to political rather than parliamentary business. The difference between the two is not easy to parse; indeed, people often conflate the two. However, senators' roles as public representatives must be distinguished from their roles as members of a political party. For example, travelling with a parliamentary committee is, in legal terms, public business in "pith and substance," while attending a party's annual convention is not.

Though this comparison seems straightforward enough, matters become more complex if MPs' and senators' parliamentary and party work blend. Senator Duffy's travel and expense claims were largely related to trips that served both parliamentary and political purposes. For example, if the senator was travelling on parliamentary business but also served as the keynote speaker at a Conservative Party fundraiser, should the taxpayer pay for his flights, or should the party contribute as well? Senator Duffy's trial revealed a number of examples where he headlined fundraising events for other senators and MPs. Prior to his appointment as a senator, Duffy was a high-profile journalist with much personal charisma. Once appointed to the Senate, he was a good fundraiser for the Conservative Party, and other caucus members would often invite him to make guest appearances in their ridings if he was planning to be in the area anyway. The question is: When party business piggybacks on parliamentary travel, who should pay? What if the time spent on party business is longer than the time it took for the senator to attend a business meeting or make a government announcement?

To make matters more confusing, both the House of Commons and the Senate acknowledge, whether implicitly or explicitly, that partisan work is not entirely separable from parliamentary work. For example, the House of Commons allows MPs to claim the expense of travelling to their annual caucus retreats. These are party events, but because they are also seen as integral to MPs' parliamentary work, the taxpayer pays. Likewise, Duffy's lawyer, Donald Bayne, argued in court that the Senate's rules acknowledge that partisan activity is an inherent part of a senator's job.

The fourth and final category of charges relates to contracts that Senator Duffy signed and paid using Senate funds. Senators are permitted to use public money for services and projects relevant to their parliamentary work, but the Crown argued that many of Senator Duffy's payments, including to a make-up artist and a fitness trainer, were inappropriate. There were also allegations that Senator Duffy received kickbacks from these contracts. This was especially relevant in light of the fact that much of the money was paid to companies owned by his friend's family. Another contract that garnered significant attention during the trial was for a speech called "Why I'm a Conservative." The speech was written by columnist L. Ian MacDonald, who was paid $7,000 for his work. He was paid by Maple Ridge Media, a company owned by Senator Duffy's friend, Gerry Donahue, because Senator Duffy used Donahue as a "general contractor" to manage his Senate contracts. To put it simply, Senator Duffy wrote cheques from his Senate account to Maple Ridge Media which, in turn, used that money to write cheques to cover the costs of contracts, such as the one paid out to Mr. MacDonald. But according to Senator Duffy, "as long as it's Senate money for Senate work, it's all 100% appropriate."[28]

## FINDINGS

Senator Duffy was exonerated on all thirty-one charges. Mr. Bayne's successful defense of his high-profile client was premised on the claim that the Senate rules were loose, vague or, in some cases, non-existent. Therefore, even if common sense suggests that Senator Duffy's actions were offensive, the trial was not about common sense. It was about the rules (and laws) that existed at the time in question, and whether they were breached. It is entirely possible that a senator's actions could be ethically questionable but completely legal. In light of this, Senator Duffy's exoneration might leave a negative impression for those who disagree with the way he conducted business.

In dismissing the bribery charge against Senator Duffy, Justice Vaillancourt took the opportunity to express his shock at the willingness of the PMO to direct senators and to interfere in an independent audit, all with the objective of making the politically damaging Duffy story go away. The PMO actually provided senators with *scripts* to use when discussing the issue of Senator Duffy's residence and related expenses, and also approached Deloitte during their independent review of senators' expenses "to either get a peek at the report or part of the report prior to its release to the appropriate Senate authorities or to influence the report" in some way.[29] Legally, it was Senator Duffy who was on trial, but it was the members of the PMO who received the most stinging indictment from the judge's ruling. Nigel Wright's emails revealed that the PMO placed significant pressure on Senator Duffy to play along so that the scandal could be put to rest.

Senator Duffy insisted that he was a resident of PEI, which meant that his expense claims were legitimate. However, the PMO concluded that this claim was not resonating with the public, and that the expenses would have to be repaid in order to restore Duffy's reputation, not to mention that of the prime minister who had appointed him. The Conservative Party was initially willing to provide the repayment, and to cover Senator Duffy's legal fees as well. However, when party officials learned that the payment totaled over $90,000, they had a change of heart, and Nigel Wright stepped forward with his own funds. There was no attempt by Senator Duffy to bribe anyone: the judge described him as a "pawn," not an aggressor attempting to extract a benefit.

When the issue of residency claims was explored in Senator Duffy's trial, it became evident that the Senate's rules on this had been vague or non-existent. Until the expense scandal began, senators had never been asked to prove residency, but instead were asked to swear an oath that "the information provided about their living expenses is true."[30] The Senate Administrative Rules did not define the concept of "primary residence," nor did they indicate any criteria for determining it. Furthermore, evidence presented during the trial demonstrated that Senator Duffy consulted a number of authorities, including the prime minister himself, the PMO and the Conservative leader in the Senate, Marjorie LeBreton, to ensure that he met the residency requirement for serving as a senator for PEI. They all assured him that he did. And, as Justice Vaillancourt points out, the senator did this early on, in advance of any accusations. This means that there was no *mens rea* for fraud or breach of trust.[31]

On the issue of submitting travel expense claims for activities that were primarily partisan rather than public, the court accepted the defence's evidence and arguments to the effect that the Senate Administrative Rules allowed senators to submit expenses for partisan activity, as long as this activity did not occur during a writ period or as part of a nomination process. Therefore, Senator Duffy's expenses were permissible. As stated, the Senate Administrative Rules considered partisan activity to be part of a senator's job, thereby rejecting the dichotomy between public and partisan business. Expenses connected to partisan activities were no less eligible than any other expenses related to a senator's work. Further, there were no limitations on submitting expenses for partisan activity, apart from the fact that these activities could not be conducted during a writ period or part of a nomination process. Even trips that the Crown argued were of a personal nature, including funerals, were absorbed under the umbrella of the Senate's public business.

With respect to the charges connected to contracts administered by Maple Ridge Media, a company owned by Senator Duffy's friend, the Crown argued that the senator and his friend had devised a "slush fund" with taxpayers' money. By writing cheques directly to Maple Ridge Media, the senator made it impossible for the Senate to conduct meaningful scrutiny of his expenditures, as the arrangement had the effect of concealing the nature and recipients of contracts as well as the services obtained. In defense of Senator Duffy, Mr. Bayne reiterated his client's argument that as long as it was "Senate money for Senate work," and there were no kickbacks or other forms of waste or corruption, there is no illegal activity. Further, there is nothing in the Senate Administrative Rules that prevents a senator from hiring a third party to manage his contracts, as Senator Duffy did. In fact, these rules specified that "a Senator is to have full discretion over and control of the work performed on the Senator's behalf by the Senator's staff."[32]

## DISCUSSION

This case study exposes a serious lack of oversight with regard to senators' use of taxpayers' money. As shown, Senator Duffy was the only individual subject to legal censure, but from an ethical perspective both the PMO and the Senate itself were the subjects of intense scrutiny and criticism. Even as Senator Duffy was exonerated, both institutions were tainted. Since Senator Duffy's trial, the PMO has been entirely repopulated, as the Conservative government was defeated in the October 2015 election. Under the Liberals the PMO promised to do things differently; openness and transparency were themes of both the Liberal Party platform, and the mandate letters to cabinet ministers that were released publicly on the prime minister's website.

In addition, one of the Liberal government's key priorities has been Senate reform. Instead of continuing the practice of appointing party loyalists, Prime Minister Trudeau made appointments only after the Independent Advisory Board for Senate Appointments provided him their merit-based recommendations. This approach is a clear break from the past, and it suggested a desire on the part of the PMO under Justin Trudeau to distance itself from the Senate expense scandal. A question remained, however, as to whether such a merit-based process was used as cover for appointing government-friendly senators. The first batch of Senate appointments appeared to show a notable predisposition toward liberal-minded appointees.[33]

The message that resonates throughout Justice Vaillancourt's written decision is that there were no clear guidelines against which to measure Senator Duffy's behaviour. The institution was not able to hold senators to account for their use of public funds, as the rules that existed were too flexible and vague to be able to communicate clear standards of behaviour. Therefore, practices that raised eyebrows — such as Senator Duffy's use of a third party to manage his contracts, which meant that Senate administration was not able to track where the money was going and for what purposes — were not contrary to the rules. So, even though this invited the suspicion that the senator was receiving kickbacks from contracts, it was not possible for the judge to find criminal intent on Senator Duffy's part. Likewise, though Senator Duffy's decision to fly from one partisan event to another using taxpayers' money may not have met the ethical "smell test" for many Canadians, this was, according to Senate rules, acceptable since partisan activities were part and parcel of parliamentary business.

A logical conclusion to draw, after reading Justice Vaillancourt's decision, is that the Senate Administrative Rules should be wholly reconsidered so that a case like Senator Duffy's does not occur again.[34] The system itself was broken, and Senator Duffy was merely using the resources available to him, albeit in several creative ways. Indeed, following the Senate expense scandal, the rules were revamped and tightened. It is now an annual requirement that Senators submit proof of residency, for example. Jean Fournier, former Senate ethics officer, argues that senators need a mandatory annual refresher course on expense claims rules, and that the validity of claims must be determined not by the Internal Economy Committee, which is in a conflict of interest by doing so, but by an impartial official who is accountable and has the ability to reject claims not sanctioned by clear rules.[35]

Senator Duffy continued his work as a senator for PEI, though he never rejoined the Conservative caucus. He continued to submit living expenses for the time he spent in Ottawa. At the time of writing, neither the Senate nor the government has determined whether to take action against senators who may have been appointed unconstitutionally, or simply wait until they retire. Beginning in 2015, the government at least established a clear standard of residency for the appointment of senators going forward.

The judge concluded that Senator Duffy's actions were not illegal, but whether they were ethical is another matter completely. Judge Vaillancourt's sense of ethical propriety was offended more by the actions of the PMO than of Senator Duffy. Describing the PMO's handling of Senator Duffy's predicament, he wrote: "The political, covert, relentless unfolding of events is boggling and shocking."[36] As for Senator Duffy, the judge acknowledged that some might be "uncomfortable"[37] with his way of doing business, but that such a feeling "does not even begin to approach proof of criminal conduct beyond a reasonable doubt."[38] It was not Judge Vaillancourt's job to pronounce on the ethics of Senator Duffy's actions, and public opinion is not a perfect ethical compass either. As Kernaghan and Langford point out in their book *The Responsible Public Servant,* "a negative reaction to the media's portrayal of your decision does not make it the wrong ethical choice."[39] That said, there is a political cost to offending the public's sense of what it means to be ethical. Senator Duffy, an appointed member of the upper chamber whose job is secure until he reaches the age of seventy-five, can be said to be relatively immune from political cost, but the Harper Conservatives can be sure that Senator Duffy's trial, which extended into the election of 2015, contributed to their defeat.

## CONCLUSION

Senator Duffy's case speaks to the implications of a vague regulatory system and, in so doing, raises an oft-cited question in the study of public and political ethics: What is the best way to encourage ethical behaviour among public officials? Should we use a values-based approach that puts ethics in a positive light by enumerating the values by which public officials should abide, such as honesty and integrity? Or, should we take a rules-based approach that prohibits specific behaviours that are deemed unethical, such as bribery and waste? Judge Vaillancourt's conclusions suggest that Senator Duffy's behaviour was within the rules because they were weak and/or non-existent. Clearer, more comprehensive rules might have either discouraged him from acting as he did or, at the very least, provided a mechanism to hold him to account. These are the advantages of the rules-based approach. On the other hand, values-based regimes have the capacity to be more comprehensive if they are applied in good faith, since public officials might take a broad, aspirational interpretation of values and, therefore, hold themselves to a higher standard of ethics. Of course, public officials might also interpret them narrowly, in which case the values-based approach loses its desired effect.

John Langford and Ralph Heintzman gave voice to this debate in an exchange published in *Canadian Public Administration*. Langford argued that the values-based approach is a "dead end," that the definition of values is too subjective an enterprise to support a strong ethics regime and that the approach leaves little guidance for resolving conflicts between values when they arise.[40] Heintzman responded by arguing that, without values, ethics regimes lack the solid foundation required to encourage responsible and ethical individual behaviour.[41] The "rules versus principles" debate is, of course, a false dichotomy; there is no reason that a mature ethics regime cannot incorporate both approaches in a complementary fashion. That would seem to be the ideal. In the case study reviewed here, it would seem that both values and rules were largely absent.

In this book, we have emphasized the importance of a commitment to shared democratic values, an understanding of elected officials' duty to maintain those values and the importance of appropriate review agencies to ensure compliance. Actions that are not illegal are not necessarily ethical, which is why the legal-judicial system is only one part of the rules and procedures used to promote ethics in our political system. The use of money in politics can be problematic in numerous ways — from the ways in which parties raise funds to fight elections, to how they spend these funds so as not to have an unfair advantage, to the appropriate strictness of expense claims rules. These are issues that Canadians have wrestled with since 1867. We suggest that over time, through the dissemination of values and the strengthening of review agencies, some progress is being made. In particular, public attitudes are shifting with respect to the behaviours of public officials, especially on matters related to the benefits afforded by public office. The bar continues to be raised, which may not be such a bad thing.

# CHAPTER 7
# ETHICS OF LOBBYING AND INFLUENCE[1]

## Robert Shepherd

## CANADA'S LOBBYING REGULATION REGIME IN CONTEXT

Lobbying is about exercising influence, and it is a legitimate activity in democratic societies. Citizens have a right to make their views known to policy-makers for the purpose of making interventions that are relevant, effective and transparent. For example, Ontario's definition of lobbying is: "Communication with a public office holder in an attempt to influence: the introduction, development, amendment, passage or termination of legislative proposals, bills, resolutions, regulations, policies or programs; decisions to transfer any interest or asset of, any business, enterprise or institution that provides goods or services; procurement decisions; and, the awarding of grants, contributions or financial benefit."[2] The aim of regulating lobbying activities is to ensure that there is fairness and transparency with respect to who is attempting to access and influence political decision makers between elections. There is an ethical obligation on the part of lobbyists, regulators and persons being lobbied to respect the public's right to know the facts about attempts to influence.[3] Lobby legislation was introduced in Canada federally in 1989 in response to concerns about the influence of consultant lobbyists over unfair access to national policy debates.[4] Several attempts at lobby legislation had occurred before 1989, but two key events raised public awareness of the need for rules on lobbying. First, a Newfoundland fisherman, Ulf Snarby, wanted a fishing licence and approached Frank Graves of Government Consultants International (GCI) to set up a meeting with then Fisheries Minister John Fraser in 1984. According to Stevie Cameron, Fraser was "outraged to find that Snarby [had] paid to have the meeting set up."[5] Second, there was controversy over a 1988 decision of the Mulroney-appointed board of Air Canada to purchase a fleet of aircraft from Airbus Industrie, a European consortium, rather than the US Boeing Corporation. Karl-Heinz Schreiber, a lobbyist for Airbus, arranged for Airbus to acquire the services of his friend Frank Moores, Newfoundland premier from 1972 to 1979 and a close friend of Prime Minister Brian Mulroney. After Mulroney became prime minister in 1984, Moores started a lobby firm in Ottawa, which became "the biggest lobby firm in Ottawa, with billings of close to $5 million a year."[6] In 1985, Brian Mulroney fired the Liberal-appointed board of Air Canada and replaced it with his political friends, including Frank Moores. Shortly afterwards, Air Canada began to consider how it would replace thirty-four of its older Boeing 727 aircraft. By acting for both Air Canada and Airbus, Moores was in a conflict of interest, but there were no rules in place at the time to control such conflicts. Moores was eventually forced to resign his seat on the Air Canada board. Later in 1988, the Mulroney-appointed board awarded Airbus Industrie the contract to replace Air Canada's fleet, and Air Canada was privatized.[7]

Since then, lobbyist legislation has been adopted in eight provinces and a growing number of Canadian municipalities in response to scandals that have highlighted two main concerns: 1) a desire to make influence on government decisions, and attempts to influence transparent, and 2) the need to regulate influence and attempted influence.[8] Making transparency a priority of lobbying laws has understandably created some confusion regarding the object of regulation.[9]

In general, individual lobbyists must register with the appropriate registrar of lobbyists (federal, provincial or municipal) if they are attempting to influence government policy. When they register, they must summarize who they are lobbying, and for what purpose, and this information is posted on a public website to promote transparency. Some kinds of individual contacts with public officials do not require registration. For example, in some jurisdictions, only lobbying that is remunerated requires registration, while in others, all lobbying, whether paid for or not, is a registrable activity. Some jurisdictions consider *any* attempts to influence a public official to be the main criterion for regulation, rather than focusing only on those activities where remuneration was a part of the lobbying activity.

Most lobby legislation in Canada comprises the following basic elements: a statement of legislative purposes and principles; outline of the scope of what kinds of lobbyists are targeted by the legislation; what lobbyists must disclose about their activities; specifying what activities warrant registration; identifying activities that are exempt from registration; a list of individuals, organizations and jurisdictions that are captured or exempted from lobbying regulations; prohibitions under the legislation (e.g., contingency fees under contracts); ethics provisions and codes of conduct for lobbyists; timelines for registration; the creation of registries and how the public can access them; appointment and powers of registrars or commissioners; and offences and penalties for breach of legislation and/or codes.

All legislation identifies various categories of lobbyists. "Consultant lobbyists" are individuals hired on a contract basis to influence public officials. "In-house corporate lobbyists" are employees who work within and on behalf of a private business. Lastly, "in-house organization lobbyists" are employees who lobby on behalf of their non-profit or trade organization. Canadian jurisdictions refer to some or a combination of these types.

## ETHICS AND LOBBYING

The ethics of lobbying concerns the moral obligation to ensure that all activities aimed at influencing government decision makers are made transparent, and follow appropriate standards of practice. To this end, legislation provides essential tools such as registration and regular disclosure requirements. Several jurisdictions in Canada also use codes of conduct to identify accepted standards of practice for lobbyists. Some are enforceable, with powers afforded to registrars and commissioners to investigate breaches and apply penalties, while others are more aspirational in nature with no enforcement provisions.

Ensuring compliance with transparency provisions is a challenge. For example, there are lobbyists who believe that their activities do not constitute lobbying and who attempt to persuade legislators that this is the case. The ethical concern is that individuals or organizations will either ignore, avoid or reject registration as it applies to them.[10] The success of lobbying legislation depends on lobbyists respecting the rules to register and disclose their activities. As soon as individuals and organizations observe an unfair or incomplete application of the rules, the legislation's effectiveness is jeopardized.

Lobbying legislation attempts to reduce the potential for inappropriate practices by establishing codes of conduct that set out standards in a jurisdiction regarding respect for democratic institutions, transparency, use of confidential information, and against the placing of public office holders in conflicts of interest.[11] Inappropriate practices include the purchasing of access to officials through tickets to events where lobbyists are positioned to discuss issues with governmental officials out of public view. These types of activities can create ethical dilemmas for government officials who may wish to speak with organized interests, while not wishing to favour, or appear to favour, particular private interests. Codes of conduct provide an accepted standard that all lobbyists must agree to follow.

Codes of conduct also serve to protect public office holders. The public has a right to know that public officials are discharging their duties in a non-prejudicial manner. By understanding the limits placed on those wanting to access them, public office holders will have the ability to decide between those events that respect the standard and those that do not.

Another area of ethical concern is post-employment of public officials once they terminate their positions. It is sometimes the case that individual lobbyists are former ministers or senior officials who, having exited their positions, use their connections to land contracts or act on behalf of others who want government contracts. Access to decision makers offers the potential for former public office holders to affect a policy or regulation that benefits their private interest. To prevent such unfair advantage, legislation requires a *cooling-off period* during which time former officials are prohibited from lobbying their former employer. Post-employment rules may be contained either in lobby legislation, or conflict of interest legislation, or both. Post-employment rules prevent the possibility that former public office holders will have unfair advantage using their contacts to serve their own or someone else's private interests.

Three cases pertaining to problematic lobbyist activities are examined in this chapter. The first regards a former Conservative MP, Rahim Jaffer, who used his position to influence officials over a procurement decision for green energy. The second recounts the lobbying activities of a lawyer and party official, Alfred Apps, who believed lobbyist rules did not apply in his case. And the third discusses the *indirect* lobbying activities of MyChoice/MonChoix, and provides an example of a benefactor, an advocate, or private interest funding a grassroots campaign to influence government. The first of these cases demonstrates the importance of transparency provisions, the second the need for standards of practice and the third the role of integrity in lobbying activities.

## Case 1: Rahim Jaffer and Patrick Glémaud: GPG Corporation

### BACKGROUND

On April 8, 2010, the *Toronto Star* reported that former Conservative

MP Rahim Jaffer had formed a company with a friend, Patrick Glé-maud, who had previously worked as a lawyer in the federal Department of Justice. The company, Green Power Generation (GPG), was created to seek out income opportunities in promoting green energy. The *Toronto Star* found that Mr. Jaffer, who was an MP from 1997 until 2008 and also the chair of the Conservative caucus in 2006, claimed that he was an expert in obtaining government funding and that he had "access to a green fund." However, since he was no longer an MP, these claims were arguably overstated.[12] Canada's Green Infrastructure Fund (GIF) was established as part of "Canada's Economic Action Plan," and was announced in the federal budget on January 27, 2009. The plan called for $12 billion in new infrastructure spending over two years, and included an additional $1 billion over five years for the GIF, which covered potential sustainable energy projects.

Various *Toronto Star* articles detailed a meeting between Mr. Jaffer and one of his prospective clients, Mr. Nazim Gillani, the CEO of International Strategic Investments, who boasted in an email that "Mr. Jaffer has opened up the Prime Minister's Office to us." When this email came to light, the federal lobbying commissioner received several complaints from MPs and their staff that Mr. Jaffer was not registered as a lobbyist.

Specifically, between April 10 and 27, 2010, three MPs filed complaints with the federal commissioner of lobbying detailing the possible violations of the *Lobbying Act*, and the *Lobbyists' Code of Conduct*. On April 10, 2010, Liberal MP Marlene Jennings alleged that the principals of GPG had failed to register, and that Mr. Glémaud had previously registered as a consultant lobbyist in 2009 but failed to indicate that he was a former public office holder. On April 10, Liberal MP Mark Holland alleged that Mr. Jaffer and Mr. Glémaud had met with Mr. Brian Jean, the Parliamentary Secretary to the Minister of Transport, Infrastructure and Communities, who was responsible for approving projects under the $1 billion GIF. Mr. Holland complained that the meetings between the parties had sought the awarding of a "grant, contribution or other financial benefit" and thus necessitated the filing of a return under the

*Lobbying Act.* Finally, on April 27 Liberal MP Francis Valeriote alleged that Mr. Glémaud had violated the *Lobbying Act* when he failed to register as a lobbyist after conversations he had with staff employed by the Honourable Gary Goodyear, the minister responsible for the Federal Economic Development Agency for Southern Ontario. Mr. Glémaud had met with the minister's director of operations on behalf of Sustainable Ventures Inc. to discuss potential funding opportunities.

## INVESTIGATION AND ISSUES

The federal lobbying Commissioner opened an administrative review on April 12, 2010, and a formal investigation in May, after receiving complaints from the three MPs. Under the *Lobbying Act,* if there are reasonable grounds to believe that a breach of the legislation may have occurred, any ongoing investigation must be suspended, and a peace officer advised about the possible offence. In October 2010, after an in-depth investigation, the Commissioner determined there were adequate grounds to refer the case to the RCMP for criminal investigation. In March 2011, the RCMP informed the commissioner that it would not be pursuing a prosecution against either Mr. Jaffer or Mr. Glémaud.

The RCMP decision, however, did not preclude the commissioner from considering a further investigation of those aspects of the complaints where there may have been a violation of the *Lobbyists' Code of Conduct.* On April 5, 2011, the commissioner determined there were indeed sufficient grounds under the *Lobbyists' Code of Conduct* to continue an investigation. A final report was completed in December 2011.[13] Several questions were investigated regarding Mr. Jaffer's and Mr. Glémaud's activities, including:

1.  Did Mr. Jaffer engage in unregistered lobbying when he attempted to arrange a meeting between a former minister and a not-for-profit, and when he communicated with the Department of Industry regarding a government policy?

2. Did Mr. Jaffer and Mr. Glémaud engage in unregistered lobbying when they communicated with public office holders about leasing the rooftops of federal buildings for solar power generation facilities, funding for a solar electricity generation facility and funding for a proposed electricity generation and waste disposal infrastructure project?

3. Did Mr. Jaffer and Mr. Glémaud engage in any activity requiring registration as in-house lobbyists when they communicated with public office holders about funding for a mercury capture test involving another company they were associated with called RLP Energy Inc.?

4. Did Mr. Glémaud engage in any activity on behalf of RLP Energy Inc. that required registration as a consultant lobbyist?

Questions three and four are differentiated on the basis of type of lobbying activity. Registration and reporting requirements would be different based on whether RLP Energy Inc. was considered an in-house or consultant lobbyist as indicated in the first issue below.

With respect to Mr. Glémaud's activities, the investigation also asked the following:

1. Did he engage in unregistered lobbying when he communicated with staff in the Office of the Minister of State (Science and Technology), to discuss the Southern Ontario Development Fund?

2. Did he breach the *Lobbying Act* by failing in an earlier registration to disclose that he was a former public office holder?

## Issue: Influence and Registration

In their efforts to generate income for GPG, Mr. Jaffer and Mr. Glé-maud met with companies involved with green energy in order to assist these companies with preparing project proposals that could be funded. The companies did not retain GPG, nor did they pay GPG any professional fees. However, the parties understood that compensation would be contingent on a successful proposal. Given the nature of their relationship, questions were raised about who Mr. Jaffer and Mr. Glémaud were acting for when submitting proposals. Depending on the answer, reporting obligations may vary between different types of lobbyists. In-house corporate lobbyists must register if their activities constitute a "significant part of duties" regarding the development of legislative proposals, the introduction or processes of passing bills, the making of amendments to regulations, the development of amendments to policies or programs and the awarding of any financial benefit. In these cases, the senior officer of the corporation must file a return no later than two months after the lobbying activity has occurred. If they undertake such activities, and also if they are paid to arrange meetings or communicate with public officials, consultant lobbyists must register as well. In addition, success fees (contingency payments) were also prohibited under the *Act* as of 2008.[14]

## Issue: Influence and the Lobbyists' Code of Conduct

The *Lobbyists' Code of Conduct* came into force on March 1, 1997, and an amended version has been in effect since December 1, 2015. In essence, the appropriate standards of practice are similar. Whereas the *Act* is concerned with lobbyists' registration requirements, the *Lobbyists' Code of Conduct* provides standards of practice when they are engaging in lobbying activities. If indeed Mr. Jaffer and Mr. Glémaud were seen to be using their past experience to influence the granting of applications, this would be a violation of the *Code of Conduct*. In addition, the rules state that such individuals must identify themselves as lobbyists with clients.

## FINDINGS

It was found that both Mr. Jaffer and Mr. Glémaud had not registered as in-house lobbyists for GPG, nor as consultant lobbyists. As such, the Commissioner ruled that in five instances their communications with public office holders required registration under the *Act*. Their failure to do so also gave rise to breaches of the professionalism, transparency and conflict of interest rules under the *Code of Conduct*.

The report concluded by highlighting the importance of transparency. Because Jaffer and Glémaud did not register or identify themselves as lobbyists, "individuals and organizations with an interest in the status of the activities of Green Power Generation remained uninformed, and were thus misled about the existence of lobbying activity." The report also concluded that, "GPG was a commercial enterprise created . . . with the intention of generating revenue."[15]

During the investigation, Mr. Jaffer and Mr. Glémaud were afforded the opportunity to respond before the report was made public. Mr. Jaffer argued that GPG did not make money, file any financial returns or open a bank account. Neither did GPG pay Mr. Jaffer or Mr. Glémaud for their services, which is a prerequisite for registration. But it was noted that GPG "had embarked upon a commercial enterprise" and that Jaffer and Glémaud "expected to benefit financially from any successful applications for funding that they were able to obtain." This was sufficient under the *Act* to meet the definition of "payment." There was also no evidence to demonstrate that Jaffer or Glémaud were communicating on behalf of GPG on a voluntary basis, rather than as part of a commercial enterprise, which again met the *Act*'s definition of payment. Mr. Jaffer also argued that the proposals submitted on GPG letterhead were simply summary proposals, and not detailed enough to be complete, but it was found that "requests for government funding are considered to be 'communication in respect of the awarding of a grant, contribution or other financial benefit' even if the requests are not lengthy and detailed proposals."[15]

Significantly, GPG was dissolved on July 6, 2010, and the federal government did not fund any of the projects that were the subject of the investigation.

## DISCUSSION

This case raises some important issues regarding the ethics of lobbying. First, the intention of the *Act* and the *Lobbyists' Code of Conduct* is to make lobbying activities transparent. According to the lobbying commissioner, registration is required "whether or not a lobbyist achieves the desired outcome"; "whether or not the lobbyist has been explicitly hired as a 'lobbyist' by the client"; "whether or not a corporation or organization has generated revenue"; and whether or not requests for government funding are considered to be communication in the awarding of contracts or other benefits.[16] Mr. Jaffer and Mr. Glémaud showed little evidence that transparency was their main concern. Although it is difficult to demonstrate *mens rea* in this case, it is likely accurate to say that had registration been foremost in their minds, the post-employment rules alone would likely have prevented any lobbying at all.

Second, a key principle in the *Lobbyists' Code of Conduct* is "integrity and honesty." Both Mr. Jaffer and Mr. Glémaud appear to have knowingly communicated with public officials about potential grants. Despite being unregistered, Mr. Jaffer in particular advertised that he had access to decision makers, implying that he could have an effect on their funding decisions. That this would not be considered lobbying defies reasonable argument. In addition, such claims of access are not only a misrepresentation of facts, but the expectation of preferential treatment as a former MP and chair of the Conservative caucus, would indicate that communications with officials were likely occurring outside of public view.

Third, with respect to dealing with clients with honesty and integrity, Mr. Jaffer came up short. He claimed that what he considered to be access was within the rules. Not only can these dealings be considered a violation of the *Code of Conduct*, but he must also have thought that the lobbying rules did not apply to him, or if they did, that he would not be implicated by them. An argument can be made that self-interest was the main motivation, which only contributes to public perceptions of improper behaviour of politicians, and a culture of entitlement.

Fourth, the case also highlights the professionalism on the part of some public office holders who decided not to meet with Mr. Jaffer and Mr. Glémaud. The troubling thing is that other public office holders *did* meet with them, demonstrating that they either did not know or understand the rules regarding influence, or that they felt an obligation to meet with Jaffer and Glémaud because of their previous relationship. Either way, these individuals could be seen as contributing to non-transparent lobbying activities by failing to speak up with their superiors, or worse, fueling the perception that government processes unfairly advantage insiders.

Finally, the case makes it clear why post-employment rules must be in place. Although the length of a cooling-off period is debatable, that a former minister can have access to former colleagues for reasons of financial gain calls into question the processes designed to ensure due process and fairness in the awarding of grants and other public resources.

## Case 2: Chris Mazza, Alfred Apps and ORNGE Ambulance Service

### BACKGROUND

Ontario's aeromedical program was established with the assistance of Sunnybrook Hospital at Toronto's Buttonville Airport in 1977. It was expanded that year to include on-board paramedics and, in 2002, several base hospitals in Sioux Lookout, Thunder Bay, Sudbury, Timmins and Toronto were amalgamated under the new Ontario Air Ambulance Base Hospital Program. In 2005, a non-profit entity was created, Ontario Air Ambulance Services Company (OAASC), to coordinate all air ambulatory services for the province. A year later, OAASC changed its name to ORNGE to reflect the colour of its aircraft. In 2005, a volunteer board of directors was appointed to focus on "providing air ambulance and critical care land service to patients in Ontario."[17] Ontario's Ministry of Health and Long-Term Care handed the central dispatch for the service over to OAASC in 2005. OSAAC (and later ORNGE) outsourced its operations to private operators who provide aircraft, pilots and paramedics for twelve bases across the province. In 2006, ORNGE received a provincial budget of $730 million over five years, and between June 2009 and January 2011 it borrowed $300 million to finance the purchase of aircraft and a new head office. Services were extended in 2011–12 to include certain land ambulance services under provincial contract. It also subcontracted to independent service providers to transport patients and organs.[18]

In 2006, ORNGE CEO and founder Chris Mazza received an annual salary of $870,000; he reported only $285,000 of that publicly. In December 2011, a *Toronto Star* investigation, with the assistance of a whistle-blower who was a former senior employee of ORNGE,[19] revealed that Dr. Mazza was receiving a $1.4 million annual salary through a newly-created consulting company named ORNGE Peel, formed to avoid the public reporting of ORNGE executives' salaries.[20] When the scandal broke, the Ministry of Health claimed it lacked the ability to collect information from ORNGE to effectively carry out the ministry's oversight responsibilities, even though there was a clause in the original Performance Agreement with ORNGE that allowed the ministry to examine the books of ORNGE at any time with due notice. Allegations were made in the media about questionable procurement decisions and management practices. For example, under Mazza's direction, ORNGE used its government funding to create a charity called JSmarts to teach youth how to safely engage in high-risk sports. In December 2011, Health Minister Deb Matthews asked Ontario's auditor general to investigate the salary issue, and ORNGE operational performance more generally, including the questionable procurement of contracts with AugustaWestland Helicopters, an Italian manufacturer from which ORNGE Global (a for-profit subsidiary) received a

$6.7 million "payment" as part of a purchase of twelve helicopters.[21] Mazza went on indefinite medical leave in late December 2011 due to mental health issues.[22]

On January 24, 2012, as the salary scandal and mismanagement allegations gained traction in the media, eighteen managers were dismissed, and the JSmarts program was closed. A new board of directors was appointed by the Minister of Health on January 25, following the resignation of its chairman, Mr. Rainer Beltzner.

On February 2, 2012, Health Minister Deb Matthews announced the winding up of for-profit entities that ORNGE had created, while the parent organization, the ORNGE air ambulance service, would continue to exist. She announced that,

> Today, the for-profit ORNGE Global GP, and ORNGE Global Holdings LP went into receivership, essentially ending their existence. As a result, Dr. Chris Mazza, President and CEO, and Maria Renzella, chief operating officer, have been terminated and ORNGE advised us that no severance has been offered. These are vitally important and necessary steps needed to restore the confidence of Ontarians in the leadership team responsible for Ontario's air ambulance service.[23]

On February 16, 2012, the Ministry of Health asked the Ontario Provincial Police to investigate various financial irregularities, including the management of ORNGE's for-profit and charitable entities. The OPP was called after forensic auditors from the Ministry of Finance found that $1.2 million in loans had been made to former CEO Chris Mazza, and that a $6.7 million payment made by AgustaWestland was channelled back to ORNGE as part of a purchase of twelve helicopters.[24]

On February 17, 2012, the Ontario government introduced legislation, as well as a new performance agreement with ORNGE, aimed at improving oversight and limiting the company's ability to make procurement decisions or sell assets without government approval.[25]

On February 23, 2012, the *Toronto Star* uncovered reports of unqualified ORNGE staff carrying out operational management responsibilities. The OPP also reported that AugustaWestland had made kickback payments to ORNGE, and that ORNGE had granted interest-free loans and cash advances to Dr. Mazza, who was also identified as one of the creditors of ORNGE Global companies.

On March 21, 2012, the auditor's report was tabled in Ontario's Parliament. It concluded that the Ministry of Health lacked the ability to oversee ORNGE's operations given the corporation's unwillingness to supply information.[26] It found, for example, that while funding was increased by 20 per cent between 2006–07 and 2010–11 based on misleading information provided by ORNGE, patient transfers actually decreased by 6 per cent. In addition, it received $165 million to perform inter-facility patient land transfers, projected at 20,000 annually when in reality that number was 15 per cent of projected estimates. The provincial auditor also raised serious questions about overall provincial oversight of ORNGE, especially with respect to its annual allocation and ORNGE loans. The audit also found that ORNGE's provincial funding increased by $50 million over five years starting in 2012, but that the Ministry of Health had failed to demand an accounting of those funds. In addition, the audit found that ORNGE bought more aircraft than it needed, and a fleet of land ambulances that was unused. Moreover, ORNGE executives had sold the building that housed the company's headquarters, which had been bought using public money, then leased it back for 40 per cent above market price. The result was a profit of $9 million that went to ORNGE executives.

A legislative probe by the Ontario Public Accounts Committee into the mismanagement at ORNGE was struck in March 2012, and the committee completed its work in September. On December 26, 2012, Deb Matthews responded to questions about the lack of oversight by claiming that, "because ORNGE was a federally incorporated charity, legislative options were not available."[27] However, the 2005 performance agreement, which was still in effect at the time, indicated that the province possessed several tools, including the performance of audits, responsibility over board appointments and performance of members and the authority to demand accounting of all procurement contracts. Such measures were not exercised until early 2012 after complaints had arisen. Ministry officials explained that action could not take place earlier because board members had to resign voluntarily, and because only the board could authorize the release of information, excuses that have little credibility when checked against the Performance Agreement.

Several witnesses appeared before the committee, including Mazza's one-time executive aide, who testified that he had been ordered to create illegal documents meant to mislead provincial auditors, and that when he refused to write back-dated justifications for several purchase decisions, he was fired.[28] These allegations came on the heels of Premier Dalton McGuinty's refusal to testify in front of the committee about the meetings he had with ORNGE executives.

Dr. Mazza was called to testify on July 18, 2012. He insisted that he had done nothing wrong, and that he had "always acted with the best interests of the public of Ontario." In his last two years at ORNGE, he was paid $4.6 million, including salary, bonuses, cash advances and two housing loans. In total, Mr. Mazza was paid $9.3 million between 2006 and 2012. He insisted that all compensation was sanctioned by board decisions.

### Enter Alfred Apps

When ORNGE was created in 2006, the company hired the firm of Fasken Martineau, which had represented the Ontario Air Ambulance Base Hospital Program since its inception in 2002, to serve as official legal counsel. Alfred Apps, a partner with Fasken Martineau from 1991 to 1993 and again from 2001 to 2010, was added to ORNGE's legal team in 2007.

Apps's exposure to ORNGE was allegedly "intermittent and focused on specialized work related to corporate structuring and structured finance."[29] According to the *Toronto Star*, Mr. Apps played a major role in brokering several procurement arrangements, including one in 2008–09 that raised $275 million to purchase new helicopters and aircraft. He was also involved in setting up several for-profit companies and two charities on behalf of ORNGE.[30] In total, ORNGE paid out $11 million to create these for-profit companies and charities (ORNGE Foundation and JSmarts).

In 2010, Mr. Apps was named chairman of one of these for-profit companies, and tried to raise at least $15 million from investments on Bay Street to support the business.[31] Approximately $9.55 million was paid to Fasken Martineau between 2003 and 2012.[32]

In the course of his various duties, Mr. Apps sent emails in December 2010 (dated December 7 and 15) to Premier Dalton McGuinty's office as well as Ministry of Health officials (he also copied the Deputy Minister of Health) to request a meeting so that ORNGE could brief the government about its plan to create additional for-profit ventures. These emails were exposed to the media late that fall, raising questions as to whether they constituted lobbying.

Triggered by negative media attention, Fasken Martineau's regional managing partner, Mr. Martin Denyes, submitted a letter to Ontario Integrity Commissioner Lynn Morrison, with the emails attached, on January 13, 2012, arguing that "Mr. Apps takes the view that he was not engaged in consultant lobbying because the meeting discussed in these emails was not for the purpose of lobbying."[33]

On January 30, 2012, Mr. Denyes sent another letter to the integrity commissioner formally requesting that an advisory opinion be provided as to whether the communications were registrable activities under the *Act*.

On February 3, 2012, two letters were submitted by the Integrity Commissioner to Fasken Martineau with an advisory opinion: one to Mr. Denyes as the author of the request, and a second to Mr. Apps as the recipient of that request.

It is interesting to note that Mr. Apps was president of the Liberal Party of Canada from May 2009 to January 2012, which provided him the appearance of access to various political networks in Ontario, including that of the premier. He continued to work on ORNGE files as a lawyer, having resigned his partnership status over that period.

## INVESTIGATIONS AND FINDINGS

In her February 3, 2012, letter to Mr. Denyes, the commissioner was of the opinion that "Mr. Apps was engaged in lobbying [in 2010] as defined by [Ontario's *Lobbyists Registration Act*], and he was required to register his activities," and that "Mr. Apps was acting as a consultant lobbyist . . . The emails evidence Mr. Apps' clear intention to arrange a meeting with public office holders."[34]

On February 10, 2012, Mr. Apps confirmed that he understood the advisory opinion, and that no further communication was made on the subject after December 31, 2010. However, he requested clarification of the opinion, and argued that ORNGE was a client of Fasken Martineau, that the firm was providing legal services, that he did not bill for services related to the emails and that he was not paid for drafting or sending emails on the subject, as he was an employee at the time and therefore did not share in the profits of the firm.[35] In her response to this letter, the Commissioner indicated that she had "considered the information . . . and it does not lead me to a different opinion."[36]

Mr. Apps was called before the Ontario legislature's Standing Committee on Public Accounts on April 18, 2012, where he testified that he "never lobbied this government, for anything in respect of ORNGE."[37] Apps argued that he never arranged meetings with elected officials, despite memos tabled with the committee indicating otherwise.

As for the substance of these memos, and the request for meetings, committee chair Frank Klees suggested that attempts to set up meetings with government officials were being made at the time that ORNGE was being asked to consolidate its debt position, and prepare financial reports. Mr. Klees suggested that the meetings were intended to fend off consolidation attempts, as ORNGE was preparing a bond offering and did not want Ministry of Finance interference. Mr. Apps disagreed, and indicated that the meetings had an informational purpose.[38]

On April 23, 2012, Mr. Apps sent a separate letter to the Commissioner in which he elaborated on the discrepancies between his understanding of his activities and those defined in the *Act*. In particular, he raised questions about solicitor-client privilege, and how there might be a conflict between those obligations and the lobbyist's requirement to register.

On August 2, 2012, Commissioner Morrison was called before the public accounts committee, in part to respond to this case, where she raised the issue of compliance with the *Act*. She said that because the opinion was requested more than one year after the email traffic, there was "no mechanism to file a registration retroactively."[39]

Ultimately, the commissioner had no investigatory powers to pursue the matter further. As a result, she used the correspondence with Fasken Martineau and Mr. Apps as an educational opportunity to issue an interpretation bulletin so that lawyers would be aware that solicitor-client privilege does not excuse them from compliance with the lobbyist rules. In March 2012, Mr. Apps resigned from Fasken Martineau to join the firm Wildeboer Dellelce LLP, where he worked until November 2015. No criminal or other charges were laid.

## DISCUSSION

This case raises ethical questions about ORNGE's management practices, especially its use of public funds. It shows how a culture of unethical management and entitlement ultimately stained the reputation of Premier Dalton McGuinty, and contributed to his resignation on July 12, 2013. This was in addition to other abuse of trust scandals, such as the cancellation of gas-fired electrical generating plants,[40] that dogged Ontario's Liberal government at the time.

The case shows a history of abuse of trust at ORNGE, which fueled speculation by some that, beyond the emails brought to light in the case, non-transparent lobbying may have occurred. Based on Mr. Apps's letters to the commissioner, it is clear that there was not only a lack of understanding about how Ontario's *Lobbyist Registration Act* should be applied, but that consideration of its application was not raised until the emails were made public. This could suggest that the *Act* was not considered in the course of arranging the meetings, or an intention to avoid it. Either way, that the commissioner was not approached until a year later suggests that lobbying rules were considered only when scandals occurred.[41]

The case shows that solicitor-client privilege does not apply to the arranging of meetings with ministers and officials; indeed, this activity qualifies as lobbying under most legislation throughout Canada. Despite exchanging several letters with the commissioner, it is not clear from his testimony before the Public Accounts Committee that Mr. Apps had fully accepted the advisory opinion. To ensure absolute clarity that solicitor-client privilege did not exempt lawyers from the lobbying rules, guidance was issued by Ontario's Office of the Integrity Commissioner in 2011.[42]

The case also underlines the need for individuals and organizations to remain vigilant about new lobbyist requirements, and to act in a transparent manner. As more jurisdictions embrace lobbying legislation, it will become more difficult to claim ignorance of the rules, and even harder to ignore them altogether. It is apparent that Fasken Martineau did not apply sufficient oversight to ensure that lobbying rules were followed. Again, it was not until emails were made public that the firm acted. This does not mean the firm intended to breach the *Act*, but rather that the monitoring of compliance was ineffective.

Finally, as president of the Liberal Party, Mr. Apps ought to have known that he had influence in Liberal circles, and should have been aware of lobbying rules. The fact is that Mr. Apps wanted to make connections between ORNGE and provincial officials apparently without the public knowing, which speaks to the perceived intentions of the meetings. If these meetings were *informational*, as Mr. Apps suggested, and he had in fact been aware of the *Act*, there would have been no rational reason not to register.

## Case 3: MyChoice/MonChoix and the Tobacco Lobby

### BACKGROUND

Another case illustrates what may be considered improper indirect influence: *astroturfing*, the practice whereby a grassroots or citizen-based organization, usually with very few members, pursues a communications strategy that is closely tied to third-party funding such as funding by a private corporation, and that aims to effect change to a public policy, regulatory or other issue.[43] The logic is that it is more effective to have a group of experts or citizens to promote the desired outcomes espoused by a private entity, and to proffer the appearance of working for the public good. It also allows these private entities to operate behind a cover of community concern. Astroturfing is distinct from direct lobbying, examples of which we saw in the first two cases in this chapter. It is also different from what is commonly referred to as grassroots lobbying, which occurs when positions are stated to the general public, funding sources are member-driven and usually modest *and* citizens beyond the group's membership are called to advocate with decision makers for change to a law, regulation or other issue.

Where direct influence and communications are more clearly captured in lobbying regulations, indirect or grassroots lobbying efforts are sometimes more difficult to make transparent. By contrast, astroturfing (the term alludes to "grasstops")[44] is considered by regulators to be a form of unethical indirect lobbying because there is usually an intention to conceal or obfuscate the source of influence or funding, and to engage in lobbying where the real agent(s) behind the effort cannot be discerned.[45] The prevailing wisdom in lobbying legislation is that by making funding sources transparent, the nature and authenticity of lobbying events can be validated.

In the digital age, when messages can be communicated quickly and websites and other social media platforms can be accessed almost instantaneously, mobilizing such indirect efforts has become a big business. This makes it all the more important for decision makers to know the source of communications and funding sources. This enables them to establish whether such communications are.legitimate expressions of grassroots concerns, or whether they are manufactured or directed by private interests. The sheer volume of messages to which legislators are exposed makes the urgency for transparency in grassroots lobbying of fundamental importance.

The MyChoice case exemplifies astroturfing. MyChoice is a so-called citizen-based group that advocates for the right to smoke in public places. It was supported by the Canadian Tobacco Manufacturer's Council, which comprises several large tobacco companies. MyChoice's efforts are predicated on the assumption that if it advocates for the right to smoke through a membership, the message will resonate better with decision makers than if they came directly from the funding agent(s).

## CALLS TO ACTION

MyChoice.ca was a nonprofit smokers' rights group established in September 2004 with the aim of fighting back against the Canadian government's attempts to ban smoking in certain outdoor areas and in private cars and homes. The group's president was Nancy Daigneault, who described the organization in a speech to the Public Affairs Association of Canada in the following terms:

> MyChoice.ca is funded by the Canadian Tobacco
> Manufacturers' Council. MyChoice.ca is not a voice for the
> tobacco industry. We are an independent, registered non-
> profit organization. We are membership driven. Unlike many
> other associations, our members are not companies or other
> associations, but individuals.[46]

In early 2005, the organization expanded to include a French-language website, MonChoix.ca. At that time, an amendment to Quebec's 1998 tobacco law was being drafted that would ban smoking within nine metres of public spaces or workplace entrances. With the support of the Tobacco Manufacturer's Council, a public ad campaign was funded and launched by MonChoix.ca under the premise that to "increase awareness and persuad[e] people is more effective than prohibiting and restricting behaviours."[47] The group stated expressly that "our positions and opinions will be those of our members."

In October 2005, Ms. Daigneault claimed that the organization had grown to more than twenty-three thousand members who wanted to curb government funding for smoking-cessation products, speak out for fair taxation of tobacco products, influence the passing of balanced laws and encourage the respectful treatment of smokers.[48] The goal was to ensure that smokers could speak for themselves in the ongoing policy debate.

Between 2005 and 2008, the organization appeared at many public events and was featured in several media articles. But in December 2008, Imperial Tobacco withdrew its funding, stating that it had elected to refocus its corporate priorities and address the trade of contraband cigarettes. Because Imperial Tobacco was the organization's principal source of funding at that point, MyChoice/MonChoix ceased its operations.

## ISSUES AND DISCUSSION

In its various public interactions, MyChoice/MonChoix repeatedly claimed that it was independent of the tobacco manufacturers who were funding it. Although the organization did not promote smoking, it did advocate for the right of smokers to be included in public policy discussions about anti-tobacco measures. As of October 2007, only six jurisdictions in Canada had lobbying regulations in place. In each of those jurisdictions, indirect lobbying was identified as an increasingly important focus of regulation. The question for legislators was the value that transparency adds in cases such as this. In Ontario, provisions were introduced in 2012 which prohibit direct communications through grassroots campaigns that target public office holders on behalf of clients without first registering those activities. The provisions state that:

> Lobbyists engaged in developing and/or managing grass-
> roots communication campaigns may not have direct

communications with public office holders on behalf of their
client (in the case of consultant lobbyists), or their employer
(on behalf of in-house lobbyists). Because the lobbyist is
not involved in direct communications, this may lead to the
incorrect conclusion that registration is not required. In fact,
registration is required.[49]

The MyChoice case raises two important issues concerning the
transparency of lobbying activities: the sources of influence regarding
the indirect lobbying activity, and the sources of funding supporting
those activities. First, in cases of astroturfing, though there are few
members there is plenty of funding, which suggests that the group's
legitimacy may be in question. The problem with astroturfing is that it
"chok[es] out any semblance of organic ground-borne movements that
decades ago pushed issues like civil rights, and the end of wars."[50] Decision makers listened to the messages of these movements, because they
could discern whether there was support from citizens. Astroturfing as
a strategy defeats the ability of decision makers to distinguish between
legitimate messages and fabricated ones. The *business* of astroturfing
has further had the effect of raising the level of cynicism among political and bureaucratic decision makers to the extent that petitions are
largely ignored.

Returning to the matter of lobbying regulation, all communications
with governmental decision makers must be transparent so as to allow
them, and citizens, to make informed choices that affect the public
good. When private entities call on governmental decision makers to
effect change to a policy, regulation or other issue, the source of these
calls should be clear to establish clear motives and interests. The essential point is that calls to action on the part of any grassroots campaign
aimed at governmental decision makers is a form of lobbying, making
registration necessary for the public good.

Second, with respect to funding, the central question is the activity
the public requires to be transparent. As forms of indirect lobbying,

grassroots campaigns and astroturfing are often difficult to distinguish, thereby placing their legitimacy in question. For Stephanie Yates, identifying a threshold amount of external funding beyond those generated through fees or donations would shed light on the major influencers of grassroots campaigns, thereby making transparent possibly the true nature of the messages. Several jurisdictions in Canada now have such requirements. However, the issue now is ensuring compliance with those rules, and curbing non-transparent lobbying activities orchestrated by such groups.

## CONCLUSIONS

As was concluded in *Honest Politics* (1997), non-transparent lobbying "has often been tolerated as an inevitable part of the political process."[51] Though the authors indicated that the registration of lobbyists was a step in the right direction, they called for a greater commitment to ethics commissions at the provincial level. Up to 2016, only eight provincial jurisdictions have lobby regulations in place, with legislation still pending in Saskatchewan and New Brunswick. The passage of such legislation has failed in the Northwest Territories, and its need was denied outright in Yukon. Former Yukon premier Daniel Pasloski has argued that the territory is "too small" for a lobbyist registry and that "this government is not going to make it harder for people to talk to the government."[52] Such misunderstanding of the value of lobbyist registries to make communications in those offices transparent indicates that much work is still needed.

*Honest Politics* (1997) also emphasized the need for "a solid consensus among elected officials at all levels that undue influence is unacceptable."[53] Although in 2017 there is greater acceptance of this idea in principle, the fact remains that nurturing a political culture in which undue influence is unacceptable is still a challenge. Post-employment rules are particularly important, and despite Canadian jurisdictions having some of the most rigorous in the world, abuses still occur. Again, although the need for such rules is acknowledged publicly, officials still demand that these be limited both in terms of their scope and the powers granted to independent and non-partisan ethics commissioners to enforce them. A culture of entitlement persists as a result.

That said, several jurisdictions have independent and non-partisan commissioners or registrars responsible for enforcing lobbying rules and managing registries. Especially encouraging is the fact that many large municipalities, including the Ontario cities of Toronto, Ottawa, London and Brampton, have adopted lobbying regulations and registries, and that provincial legislation extends to municipalities in Quebec and Newfoundland. Outside of Quebec, the challenge is to provide offices with effective instruments to enforce the legislation. Currently, enforcement powers generally remain with police agencies, as legislative offences are considered a criminal issue. Although using the criminal law for enforcement may be appropriate for habitual non-compliance, it makes little sense in areas for enforcing routine registration and disclosure provisions. Attempts have been made in some jurisdictions to allow registrars and commissioners to apply administrative monetary penalties for such offences, but these are not widely supported by their legislatures. The net effect is that enforcing compliance is very difficult. At the federal level, only three convictions have been made under the *Lobbying Act* since 1989; the last one, with a major fine of $50,000 on three counts under the *Act*, being the most significant to date.[54] The message appears to be resonating that convictions are becoming more severe, although the effort needed to obtain such convictions under the *Act* remains significant.

With respect to regulators' emerging priorities, one that came to the fore in 2016 was the issue of cash-for-access fundraisers. Such fundraising events are organized with the promise, stated or unstated, that donors will have exclusive access to ministers who will listen to their concerns. For example, under Premier Kathleen Wynne, the Ontario Liberals have since 2013 held over two hundred such fundraisers, raising almost $20 million for the party. Most striking about these figures is that 159 of these events were private affairs with fifty or fewer guests.[55] Although political parties may claim that these events are open to anyone, there is the potential for a perception of undue influence given high-profile donors' access to ministers. In addition, in some jurisdictions, including Ontario, such events are non-registrable, and despite claims that there is no undue influence, the fact remains that few people would consider making such *donations* without the promise of exclusive access to senior cabinet ministers. In addition, corporate and union donors know that as long as these events are non-registrable, short of an outright ban on ministers attending such events, the practice will continue in some form. Even then, influence may simply shift to other individuals who have the ear of ministers. Figuring out how to address this kind of influence, especially regulating private events, will be a major challenge for all Canadian jurisdictions. And yet even if there was a registration provision for such events, it is unclear how that would be enforced, especially since many of these fundraisers, particularly private ones, are not publicized. Prime Minister Trudeau announced in January 2017 that legislation would be introduced that would increase the transparency of such events without lowering the contribution limit of $1,550. This means that such events will likely continue with high entry costs. For purposes of lobbying regulation, such events would have to be made public in advance, and considered a registrable activity. These two conditions would likely make such events unappealing to both the traditional donors and public office holders invited to attend. Ultimately, paying for access denies a fundamental democratic right for all citizens to have equal access to political representatives.

Another emerging issue is the need to make digital communications and indirect lobbying efforts transparent. Recent federal guidance on grassroots communications provisions (sections 5 and 7 of the federal *Lobbying Act*) recognizes the increasing effects of platforms like Facebook and Twitter. Equally important are sophisticated calls to action in digital advertisements, letter writing campaigns, internet petitions or other calls to action by paid lobbyists and employees.[56]

As shown in the MyChoice case, lobbyists representing large corporate interests are becoming more sophisticated at influencing decision makers through third parties. Such activities have the potential to distort public discourse and misrepresent popular sentiments on public issues. A great deal more analysis of lobbying rules will be needed to curb such practices, and to find creative ways to bring transparency to indirect lobbying. Although more people are becoming engaged in such lobbying, "it remains increasingly difficult to identify those people when they're standing in a crowd of others who may have far less measured, and certainly less earnest, interest in the issue at hand."[57] In this respect, it will be a challenge for legislators and regulators to recognize abuse, and build the tools necessary to address it.

Lobbying continues to hold the public's attention in Canada, and more jurisdictions, especially at the municipal level, are recognizing the value of regulating communications between lobbyists and public officials. The ethical value of lobbying regulations is in the assurance they provide that access will be fair and transparent. From a democratic perspective, citizens want to know what messages are being delivered to public officials so that they can make informed judgments on matters of public policy. But the fact lobbying techniques continue to change and evolve in reaction to government regulation presents a challenge. It is important that regulators continue to enjoy the commitment and understanding of public officials to support the democratic principles that underlie lobbying legislation. The alternative is to face a decline in confidence in our political actors and institutions, because they can be swayed unduly by power and influence.

# CHAPTER 8
# WHISTLE-BLOWING
# AND ETHICAL PRACTICE[1]

## Robert Shepherd

## WHISTLE-BLOWING IN CONTEXT

A recent addition to public ethics regimes in Canada is the enabling of public servants and others to *blow the whistle* on things like corruption, fraud, misconduct, abuse of authority, mismanagement and other forms of wrongdoing without jeopardizing their careers or personal safety. From an ethical perspective, whistle-blower legislation is often expressed as a dichotomy between two competing dilemmas: the extent to which loyalty to the employer or institution prevails at the expense of acknowledging and addressing wrongdoing, and ensuring integrity and accountability in government.[2] Despite advances in ethical oversight, whistle-blowing is a misunderstood form of ensuring ethics in practice, as loyalty only holds when it is earned. Whistle-blowing is most often defined as "the disclosure [by] organization members (former or current) of the illegal, immoral or illegitimate practices under the control of their employers to persons or organizations that may be able to effect action."[3] This is a reasonable description of the disclosure of organizational *insiders* to some entity, either within or outside that institution, with the intention of effecting change. However, in the public sector, the term "whistle-blower" is often applied more broadly to *anyone* who discloses wrongdoing, and who either may require protection from reprisal or support to ensure that the disclosure is taken seriously.

When the definition is broadened in this way, public institutions have wide discretion when it comes to setting the scope of what qualifies under legislation as areas for potential disclosure. The US Government Accountability Office, for example, defines whistle-blowers narrowly as "individuals who use free speech rights to challenge abuses of power that betray the public trust."[4] By contrast, the Committee on Legal Affairs and Human Rights of the Parliamentary Assembly of the Council of Europe defines whistle-blowers as "concerned individuals sounding the alarm in order to stop wrongdoings that place fellow human beings at risk."[5] Transparency International occupies the middle ground by describing a whistle-blower as "any public or private sector employee or worker who discloses information [related to corrupt, illegal, fraudulent or hazardous activities] . . . and who is at risk of retribution."[6] Such definitions raise important implications for how whistle-blowing is reflected institutionally, and they relate to local legal, ethics and social arrangements.

In the United Kingdom, the *Public Interest Disclosure Act 1998* (*PIDA*) was borne out of several highly publicized events that many believe could have been prevented had whistle-blowers been given the means to come forward.[7] One of the most notable cases was the sinking of the ferry *MS Herald of Free Enterprise* after it left the port of Zeebrugge on March 6, 1987. The sinking, which resulted in the deaths of 193 passengers and crew, was attributed to negligence on the part of the assistant boatswain, who was asleep in his cabin when he was supposed to close the bow door. However, the official inquiry placed even greater responsibility on the supervisors, and a culture of poor management and communication at the operating company, Townsend Thorsen. The inquiry heard from employees who raised concerns on five separate occasions about company practices. It concluded that company loyalty and employees' contractual obligations were valued more than safety and communication.[8] Since the introduction of *PIDA* in 1998, the United Kingdom has been regarded as a model because it balances provisions for internal disclosure, which can be made within and outside the hierarchical lines of authority, with external disclosure through a regulator where appropriate.[9] This offers the advantage of protecting the interests of the employer on matters of confidentiality, and the interests of employees and the public for disclosing information related to workplace wrongdoing or corruption.[10] This model has since been instituted in several countries, including Canada.

Canada's whistle-blower legislation was also preceded by common law provisions that provided protections within an employer-employee relationship. Such measures attempted to balance an employee's duty of loyalty to their employer with the right to individual freedom of expression. Over time, greater emphasis would be placed on good-faith disclosures of alleged wrongdoing rather than loyalty considerations.[11] In 1985, the Supreme Court ruled in a case involving an appellant who lost his position at Revenue Canada after criticizing government policy on metric conversion.[12] It was found that it would be possible for a public servant to make a disclosure contrary to their duty of loyalty, although the court concluded that "a public servant must not engage . . . in sustained and highly visible attacks on major government policies."[13]

The federal government and several provinces and territories have since developed legislation to protect public employees. These fall into one of three types: the two-branch model (i.e., two authorities share the responsibility to protect whistle-blowers based on the nature of their disclosures); the integrated model (i.e., authority falls to a single external parliamentary body covering all types of disclosures); and the two-step model (i.e., disclosures by individuals can be made internal to a department/ministry, or an external body usually attached to a parliament). Canada uses variations of all three types as follows:

1. Two-branch model: labour board and ombudsman
   (Manitoba, New Brunswick and Nova Scotia), or integrity
   commissioner and labour board (Ontario and Quebec).

2. Integrated model (Saskatchewan, Alberta and Yukon).

3. Two-step model (federal government).[14]

At the federal level, the *Public Servants Disclosure Protection Act* was enacted by the Paul Martin government in 2005 in response to the sponsorship scandal, as a way to protect federal employees from retaliation, but did not come into force. In 2006, the Gomery Commission report on the sponsorship scandal recommended that the act be "significantly improved" by broadening the class of persons authorized to make disclosures and the list of wrongdoings open to disclosure.[15] After the 2006 election, the *Act* was amended by the new Conservative government as part of the *Federal Accountability Act 2006*, and came into force in 2007. This approach most closely corresponds to the Transparency International model, which opens up the whistle-blowing process not only to federal employees but to members of the public as well. The *Act* allows for the following types of disclosures to be investigated:

- Contravention of any Act of Parliament or provincial legislature, or of any regulations made under any such Act, with certain explicit exclusions;

- Misuse of public funds or public assets;

- Gross mismanagement;

- Any act or omission that creates a substantial and specific danger to the life, health or safety of persons or to the environment;

- A serious breach of a code of conduct established by the treasury board and applicable to the public sector or a code of conduct established within a specific organization of the public sector;

- Knowingly directing or counselling a person to commit one of these wrongs.[16]

It is possible that some complaints may not fall within the scope of the *Act*. For example, abuses of authority or abuses arising from improper staffing practices may be covered by collective agreements or other legislative tools. The *Act*'s limitations have been the subject of much attention by advocacy groups and the media, leading some to conclude that it may not be as effective as it could be, as evidenced by the fact that the number of disclosures to the office has been dropping steadily since 2007.[17] Confidence in the federal system can be attributed to past results, and according to some commentators these have not been significant. Some whistle-blowers, including one discussed in this chapter, believed it was preferable to use the media rather than internal processes as there were few assurances the latter would work to their advantage.

## ETHICS AND WHISTLE-BLOWING

In the public sector, whistle-blowing is regarded as a means to support and even encourage integrity in government. It also provides a means for holding public officials to account for the work they do and to ensure that employees are treated fairly.[18] Employees should expect to work in safe environments where they will not be forced to condone others' unethical or illegal behaviour. A whistle-blowing system, if instituted properly, can encourage a *speak-up* culture in which individuals feel welcome, comfortable and safe to raise concerns.[19] Such systems provide several benefits, including reducing the costs of misconduct through early detection; improving employee enfranchisement; safeguarding the integrity of the management system; deterring future wrongdoing; maintaining public confidence by demonstrating that an organization is being openly monitored and so that it complies with laws and expectations of integrity; and creating positive public perceptions.[20]

Despite these advantages, whistle-blowers face several challenges in Canada. First, public servants do not have a legal obligation to disclose information about wrongdoing. Second, most whistle-blower legislation is clear about the types of disclosures that can be made, which may restrict other disclosures from being examined and investigated. Third, the processes to make and investigate disclosures tend to be complex. Such rules mean that investigations are sometimes lengthy, thereby adding to whistle-blowers' personal costs. These processes, though they are meant to ensure that disclosures are made for the right reasons and fall within the scope of legislation, sometimes make investigation difficult as evidentiary rules may be restrictive. Fourth, organizational leaders may not be committed to whistle-blowing protection, thereby further complicating the resolution of disclosures. Such lack of commitment may be reflected in reprisals against whistle-blowers. Finally, it is advisable for whistle-blowers to have legal representation, the cost of which may far exceed what employers are willing, able or required to reimburse.

The following cases provide some examples not only of the challenges associated with whistle-blowing, but of the important ethical questions about integrity in public institutions, the accountability of public officials to honour their responsibilities and organizations' obligation to do the right thing for the communities they serve. They also show that public servants have a duty to serve ethically, and to raise questions when institutions do not honour their obligations to citizens.[21] The case of Edgar Schmidt exemplifies circumstances when loyal public servants carry out their legal responsibilities that may be contrary to the preferences of the government. The case of Richard Colvin demonstrates a need for whistleblowing provisions in circumstances when government action may be removed from public view. Finally, the case of Sylive Therrien shows how abuses of authority can affect the conduct of departmental responsibilities, which may be contrary to individual values.

## Case 1: Honouring Legal Obligations — The Case of Edgar Schmidt

### BACKGROUND

Prior to joining the federal government, Edgar Schmidt worked in a private law practice in Manitoba for ten years before completing a graduate degree in legislative drafting in 1993. He joined the federal Department of Justice in 1998 as legal counsel to the parliamentary Standing Joint Committee for the Scrutiny of Regulations, and moved to the Legislative Services Branch in 1999, where he remained until his retirement in 2013. As director of the branch, he gave legal advice on legislation-related questions, and trained other lawyers in his craft. He was well regarded and received several awards and satisfactory performance ratings.[22]

A key part of the branch's role was to ensure that any proposed legislation was consistent with section 4.1 of the *Department of Justice Act*, which reads:

> . . . the Minister shall, in accordance with such regulations
> as may be prescribed by the Governor in Council, examine
> every regulation transmitted to the Clerk of the Privy Council
> for registration pursuant to the *Statutory Instruments Act*
> and every Bill introduced in or presented to the House of
> Commons by a minister of the Crown, in order to ascertain
> whether any of the provisions thereof are inconsistent
> with the purposes and provisions of the *Canadian Charter
> of Rights and Freedoms* and the Minister shall report any
> such inconsistency to the House of Commons at the first
> convenient opportunity.[23]

Section 3 of the *Bill of Rights* and section 3 of the *Statutory Instruments Act* also contain provisions for similar reviews that are required by law.

Schmidt observed that since 2008, these provisions were increasingly being ignored by ministers. Over the course of a decade, he made several attempts to address his concerns internally, with a final, unsuccessful attempt in July 2012.[24] In this final attempt, he contacted the public sector integrity commissioner, who declined to investigate because it was decided that the necessary information was protected by solicitor-client privilege. In addition, it was also decided that no wrongdoing as defined in the *Public Servants Disclosure Protection Act* had occurred.[25]

In December 2012, Schmidt filed a claim in Federal Court, alleging that:

> Since about 1993, with the knowledge and approval of the
> Deputy Minister, an interpretation of the statutory examination
> provisions has been adopted in the Department to the effect
> that what they require is the formation of an opinion as to
> whether any provision of the legislative text being examined is
> manifestly or certainly inconsistent with the *Bill of Rights* or the
> *Charter* and, in the case of proposed regulations, whether any
> provision is manifestly or certainly not authorized by the *Act*
> under which the regulation is to be made.[26]

Schmidt argued that section 4.1 of the *Act* was being interpreted so as to require that the minister be informed *only* if it was found that proposed legislation was more than 95 per cent likely to be defeated by a *Charter* or *Bill of Rights* challenge, and whether *any* reasonable argument can be made in favour of its consistency. In his view, such interpretations were inconsistent with the intent of the *Department of Justice Act*. As such, Schmidt sought the guidance of the court regarding the current interpretation by ministers, and to clarify the department's obligations under the *Act*.[27]

For its part, the Department of Justice denied any wrongdoing, arguing that its legal obligations were being met.[28] It also attempted to quash the claim on several grounds, including solicitor-client privilege, though this was rejected by the court.[29] At this point, the Canadian Civil

Liberties Association intervened in the case, arguing that "(1) the government has a responsibility to ensure that its proposed laws comply with the *Charter of Rights and Freedoms*; and (2), the Minister of Justice has an obligation to report serious concerns about compliance to Parliament, and, in turn, Canadians."[30]

Schmidt was suspended without pay the day after filing his claim. Schmidt then began negotiating a graceful exit from the department. He reached a settlement in May 2013, thereby ending his suspension on the condition that he take early retirement with a decreased pension.[31] On March 2, 2016, Federal Court Justice Simon Noël released his decision. He rejected Schmidt's arguments and ruled that the Crown had met its obligations under the *Act*, including that the stipulation that "credible argument" criteria (e.g., claim, warrant, evidence) be maintained.[32] Schmidt appealed the decision to the Federal Court of Appeal in April 2016, arguing that Justice Noël made errors in fact and law.[33]

## INVESTIGATION AND FINDINGS

As this appeal is still in process as of April 2017, this case study must rely on the Federal Court ruling. Justice Noël ultimately rejected Schmidt's requests for relief.[34] He came to this conclusion after examining several factors. First, it was found that there were slight inconsistencies between the French and English versions of the *Act*. For example, different language, such as "ascertain" versus "verifier," were used in the different versions. In English, the use of "ascertain" is less direct, whereas in French "verifier" indicates a more active intent. The judge also examined the history of the *Act*, and drew important conclusions about the original intent of the drafters. In this respect, the duties of different parties (i.e., courts, parliamentarians, minister) were considered in light of practices in other Westminster jurisdictions, including Australia and New Zealand. The court considered whether Schmidt's interpretation would create a conflict with cabinet confidence conventions, and came to the conclusion that cases that had come before the Supreme Court of Canada were treated seriously, suggesting that the Crown took its responsibilities with respect to the *Charter* equally seriously.

The judge also concluded that each party to the *Act*'s *Charter* provisions has separate responsibilities in upholding the *Act*'s intent, including that "Parliament must not place its duties on the shoulders of the other branches, notably on those of the Minister of Justice."[35] Further, he found that "the only possible interpretation to be given to the examination provisions is that the 'credible argument' standard is correct."[36] Finally, he argued that it was unreasonable to expect a government to undermine itself and its legislative agenda by providing "ammunition" to opposition parties.[37] To guard against any disadvantage to citizens, it was suggested the Court Challenges Program be re-established to provide additional oversight.

That said, there is little indication that the Department of Justice conducted a formal internal review of its benchmarks for informing the minister of an inconsistency, as it was not introduced into evidence. Some thought that had it been introduced, solicitor-client privilege may have been violated, which also explains in part why the public sector integrity commissioner was unwilling to investigate. The court did, however, interpret Schmidt's suspension as a reprisal, which led it to find that Schmidt's legal costs should be remunerated.

## DISCUSSION

The Schmidt case is interesting for a number of reasons, not least of which is that it involves a senior public servant's attempt to hold the government to account for the manner in which it respects the law under an Act of Parliament. Specifically, the Department of Justice has an obligation to ensure that any bill coming before Parliament is consistent with the *Charter of Rights and Freedoms*. Schmidt, having served in the department for some time, observed that section 4.1(1) of the *Act*, which requires a check for consistency, was only being respected on an intermittent basis. The department's negative reaction to this was noteworthy, hence our reason for highlighting this case.

Perhaps the most obvious observation in this case is that, had the department understood that it was not respecting the law, the appropriate steps could have been taken to avoid prolonging what was perceived by a senior public servant to be wrongdoing. That this case went so far as a court challenge should have indicated to departmental officials that there was a serious problem. Instead, the department created the perception that it valued its own reputation, and by extension the government's, more than the opportunity to correct officials' and ministers' faulty practices. That public funds were used to defend such wrongdoing further highlights the problem. As Schmidt put it: "If the court finds that what the minister and deputy minister have been doing wasn't consistent with the law — then you'll have a situation where all the resources of the state were devoted to defending wrongdoing, and none toward rectifying it."[38]

Second, from an ethical policy perspective, few institutions play a more important role in maintaining the balance of power between governments and citizens than the courts. When the state's resources are brought to bear on citizens (and public employees) who try to hold power to account, this raises ethical questions about fairness and due process under the law. The Court Challenges Program was created in 1994 to "provide financial assistance for important court cases that advance language and equality rights guaranteed under Canada's Constitution."[39] The program was eliminated in 2006, and with it another lever of government accountability[40] until 2017, when the Liberal government announced that the program would be reinstated.[41] Between 2006 and 2017, public servants had to make their case before the court without support on matters such as this, and take the chance of bearing the cost. Although it could be argued that this case should not have required court intervention, it nonetheless creates obstacles for individuals coming forward on public accountability. In addition, a key role of the state is to encourage democratic participation, not stifle dissent, especially from within its own ranks. Schmidt felt an obligation under the law and his responsibilities within the workplace to provide parliamentarians with access to all of the information they needed to make informed choices. That pressure was needed to compel appropriate behaviour from decision makers to respect the public good is a common theme in public administration. Third, this case highlights the importance placed on departmental and government reputation versus the public good. Schmidt believed that the public good was being compromised, and that his duty of care was also being compromised. In principal-agent theory, if organizational goals are consistent with individual aims, there is often little challenge. However, when these fall out of step there are often challenges that can lead to the outcomes shown in this case: reprisals for Schmidt, and ultimately a court challenge.

Fourth, this case raises important questions about the government's obligation to release information. Adam Dodek, a law professor, expressed concern that the Crown invoked and then withdrew the claim that Schmidt had violated solicitor-client privilege by "revealing the contents of four department policy documents in his court filings." This, he argued, suggests that the department may have been abusing this privilege in the past and withholding information about internal policies that do not constitute legal advice, including access to information requests.[42] Although not a central concern in this case, it does again raise some ethical concerns about the obligations to respect the spirit of the law, and to make information available so that citizens can make informed opinions.

Finally, and perhaps most importantly, the case highlights the department's suppression of a "speak-up culture." Indeed, Justice Noël was very clear about the effect of the department's reprisals in this regard: "The day after the filing of [Schmidt's] statement, bang: 'You're suspended . . . It's unbelievable . . . Your client [Department of Justice] has done everything it could to kill this thing. The court doesn't like that . . . Canada is still a democracy."[43]

## Case 2: Addressing Misconduct: The Case of Richard Colvin

### BACKGROUND

Canada began contributing to the military effort in Afghanistan in December 2001, three months after the attacks of September 11, 2001. By 2005, Canadian Forces had assumed a role in the Kandahar district as part of the Provincial Reconstruction Team (PRT), and Canadian troops were engaged in combat with the Taliban as well. As part of these combat operations, Canadian forces regularly captured Taliban combatants. Despite an "abundance of evidence"[44] regarding Afghanistan's poor record in human rights, especially relating to torture, detainees were frequently turned over to the Afghan National Security Forces and, more often, the National Directorate of Security (NDS). These transfers took place under a December 2005 agreement which did not include any right of access to Afghan detainees for Canadian personnel. The majority of information regarding detainees was communicated to Ottawa via Canadian personnel on the ground, and was not made public. It was long alleged that, though Ottawa knew about the torture of detainees, it continued to honour the 2005 agreement anyway. Allegations of torture became public in 2007 due to a complaint by University of Ottawa law professor Amir Attaran, and a number of stories of detainee abuse that were prepared by the Canadian Press. When asked to verify these stories, the federal government denied there had been any evidence of torture; indeed, it prepared a media strategy to this effect rather than admit publicly that it knew about the mistreatment of Afghan prisoners.[45] The story was made even more compelling by the fact that Canadian troops captured six times more prisoners than the British, and twenty times as many as the Dutch.[46] Many of these individuals were picked up on suspicion of violence or because of unproven denunciations.

In May 2007, the Chief of the Defence Staff, General Rick Hillier, announced that the transfer agreement had been modified. Detainee monitoring would now be the responsibility of the Department of Foreign Affairs and International Trade (DFAIT), whose job it would be to monitor prisoners and prevent potential abuses.[47] Despite these modifications, Canadian officials lost track of many transferred detainees, and torture continued unabated. To many experts, this constituted violation of the United Nations Convention Against Torture, which prohibits prisoner transfers when there is evidence of torture. Specifically, article 12 of the Geneva Convention makes prisoners the responsibility of the detaining party.[48]

One of the officials responsible for monitoring Afghan detainees transferred under the agreement was Richard Colvin, a Canadian diplomat. Colvin replaced Glyn Berry as political director for the PRT in January 2006, after Berry was killed by a car bomb. In April 2007, Colvin was appointed second-in-command of the Canadian embassy in Kabul, where he served for seventeen months. Colvin took meticulous note of the conditions in which Afghan detainees were held, and he observed many instances in which torture had taken place. As required, beginning in May 2006, he reported his observations in seventeen emails and reports to his superiors in Afghanistan and in Ottawa, which were copied to seventy-seven officials.[49] He later explained in his affidavit to the Military Police Complaints Commission (MPCC) that he copied so many people because he wanted to be sure his concerns were heard, and because the chain of command was complex and confusing.[50] In June of 2006, the Afghan Human Rights Commission reported that one-third of prisoners handed over by Canadian forces were tortured.

In February 2007, Amnesty International Canada, the British Columbia Civil Liberties Association and University of Ottawa law professors Amir Attaran and Errol Mendes drew public attention to the issue and called for a formal investigation.[51] Despite protests of ignorance by government officials, it was later uncovered that a meeting had been held between Colvin and senior Canadian officials on March 9, 2007, and that Colvin had explicitly indicated that "the NDS tortures people: that is what they do, and if we don't want detainees tortured, we shouldn't give them to the NDS."[52] Colvin had reported on several occasions that many detainees were not combatants or "high-value" targets, but rather "just local people: farmers; truck drivers; tailors, peasants — random human beings in the wrong place at the wrong time." He also reported that, "according to our information, the likelihood is that all the Afghans we handed over were tortured. For interrogators in Kandahar, it was standard operating procedure." Colvin indicated that when he raised these concerns, he was told to stop emailing his observations and to communicate verbally only.[53]

Before leaving Afghanistan in 2007, Colvin summarized his concerns in a five-page memorandum to David Mulroney, then deputy minister responsible for the Afghanistan Task Force.[54] In that memo, Colvin made a number of scathing criticisms of internal processes related to this mission, including:

- The absence of a formal "dissent channel" in the Canadian Foreign Service;

- The abuse of detainees was first apparent in April 2006;

- Interdepartmental meetings in Ottawa revealed a "collective lack of understanding" of the issues and ethical implications, and reluctance of the Department of National Defence (DND) to acknowledge the abuses;

- Despite recommendations for improvement of the transfer process, the military resisted, arguing that it would place additional demands on personnel;

- Instead of investing in resources to address transfers, Ottawa decided instead to invest in public affairs staff in Ottawa;

- DND Headquarters wanted nothing in writing regarding detainee transfers;

- Colvin stated bluntly in his memo that, "I have never before in my 15-year career been told that, internally, we must lie to each other."[55]

In 2008, the MPCC under Peter Tinsley launched an inquiry into whether the federal government had in fact violated the *Geneva Conventions*. Attempts were made by the federal government to shut down the investigation by, among other things, refusing to extend Tinsley's mandate. In addition, of the twenty-two public servants summoned to testify, several indicated that they had received threatening letters from the Department of Justice discouraging their participation. In the end, only Colvin agreed to testify, despite several attempts to prevent him using national security provisions under the *Canada Evidence Act*. Such attempts failed.[56] In October 2009, Colvin's affidavit was made public. It contradicted the government's claim that there was no evidence of torture.[57]

In November 2009, Colvin was subpoenaed by the MPCC, and was called to testify before a newly created Special Committee on the Canadian Mission in Afghanistan. Between November and December 2009, the government heavily censored the documents Colvin provided to the MPCC. In addition, the Conservative government did not renew Tinsley's mandate, despite his direct responsibilities for leading the investigation. Finally, Parliament was prorogued on December 30, 2009, at the request of Prime Minister Stephen Harper, further delaying the House and MPCC investigations.

In April 2010, the Canadian forces announced through the Department of National Defence that it was aware of the torture of Afghan detainees. As the House investigation into the scandal continued, the courts rejected applications by the Conservative government in September 2011 to strike Colvin's testimony. The government also requested that the amount of evidence that could be used by the MPCC in its final report be restricted, and this request too was rejected. In October 2011, the United Nations published a report that confirmed the torture of

Afghan detainees. The Canadian forces mission in Afghanistan ended in July 2011, and Richard Colvin was appointed first secretary in the intelligence office at the Canadian embassy in Washington.

## INVESTIGATION AND FINDINGS

Although the MPCC launched two investigations into the treatment of Afghan detainees, there is no evidence that the government initiated its own internal investigation, despite pressure to do so by the special parliamentary committee. The first MPCC investigation, launched in 2007, looked into a complaint that three detainees had possibly been mistreated by Canadian soldiers. It concluded in 2008, and reported that Canadian forces had treated the detainees humanely and that the complaint had been based on speculation due to redactions on a document obtained under the *Access to Information Act*.[58] The second MPCC investigation was launched in 2008, and focused on the question of whether military police had failed in their duty to investigate the transfer orders given by Canadian commanders in Afghanistan between May 3, 2007, and June 12, 2008. In 2012, the MPCC's final report stated that the military police carried out their duties responsibly, and that there was no indication that an investigation into illegal treatment of detainees was warranted. The report also showed evidence of extensive efforts on the part of the government to withhold evidence pertaining to the inquiry.[59]

The House of Commons Special Committee on the Canadian Mission launched its investigation in 2009 under a minority government, and before the completion of the MPCC inquiry. An election was also scheduled for May 2011, which gave the Conservative government cause to be concerned about the committee's findings. Having subsequently won a majority, the Conservative government closed the parliamentary investigation before a report could be tabled. Prior to that, however, 362 heavily redacted documents were released under a 2011 agreement with opposition parties, which cut out critical records presented by Colvin.[60]

Colvin's testimony before the House of Commons appeared on the national news. The coverage showed government lawyers attempting to undermine Colvin's credibility, calling his reports second-hand and implying that what he had seen had been fabricated by the Taliban.[61] However, he was defended by former diplomats and opposition parties who supported his testimony.[62] Defence Minister Peter MacKay also attacked Colvin in Parliament, arguing that Colvin lacked credibility, and accused him of being a "dupe" of the Taliban. He also hinted that had Colvin made the revelations earlier, there would have been consequences. "Mr. Colvin is a member of the public service who has a job in Washington. As far as I'm concerned his job is there for him," said MacKay, before adding: "I suspect that promotion (to Washington) took place, or it did take place, long before he gave his evidence yesterday."[63]

Several MPs, including Cheryl Gallant, worried about the government's, and the Afghan mission's, reputation, while Conservative MP Jim Abbott questioned Colvin's credibility, and even hinted that his accounts were fabricated. Former military commanders also came forward to testify that there was no evidence of torture, taking the public attack on Colvin's credibility even further.[64] What's more, the Crown refused to pay Colvin's legal fees in full until 2010, despite an internal requirement to do so.[65]

## DISCUSSION

Colvin's case is similar to Edgar Schmidt's in that it relates to holding the government to account for its legal responsibilities. What differentiates the case, however, is that Colvin believed the federal government had an ethical obligation to protect Afghan detainees from harm and to respect the *Geneva Conventions.* Despite the meticulous evidence provided to senior officials, the Crown's response was to deny that it had the relevant information, and later, to argue that all due diligence was taken in the handing over of detainees. To this was added the public denunciation of Colvin in Parliament, and the outright rejection of the evidence by former military officials. Although not all of the evidence was made public, it was compelling enough to warrant two MPCC investigations, and the creation of a special committee to examine them. Such events raise a number of ethical considerations, including those related to the transfer process itself, Canadian processes of due process and accountability and of the treatment of Colvin in particular.

First, in his testimony Colvin raised the question of how the determinations to turn over detainees were made. Colvin alleged that many detainees were innocent of any crimes, and were simply in the wrong place at the wrong time. Should not Canadian forces, he wondered, first carry out an initial vetting of these individuals prior to any transfer? If such vetting had been completed, by what criteria? And why did Canadian transfers far exceed those of other nations? Even if officials on the ground were unaware of the Afghans' record of torture, was there no obligation to ensure due process? The only other explanation is that the information gleaned from detainees by CSIS and other agencies was valued much higher than that of due process. This of course raises bigger questions of Canadian moral authority on issues of human rights.

Second, it is clear from this case that Colvin believed he had a legal and moral obligation to report his findings to senior officials in Afghanistan and Ottawa. Though Colvin did not consider himself a whistle-blower, preferring to call himself a "loyal public servant of the Crown,"[66] he was ultimately labeled as one.[67] It is also clear that the formal reporting processes used at the time were regarded by senior officials as inappropriate, and for that reason reporting was considered to have caused the government some embarrassment. Outside of these formal lines of communication, the Department of Foreign Affairs had no internal mechanism to voice dissent. That is, there was a denial of due process for Canadian officials working abroad. More importantly, this was a case where Colvin was forced to choose between honouring the transfer agreement and ensuring that detainees were not knowingly treated badly, and governmental priorities for securing information on terrorist activities in the region. Colvin could not reconcile these purposes, and we can infer that he ultimately weighed ethical and legal obligations over governmental policy.

Third, Colvin was essentially ordered not to report his observations up the chain of command, but instead remain quiet in an effort to protect the reputation of the Afghan mission and that of the government of the day. Typical of almost all whistle-blowing cases is the use of reprisals to silence or remove the complainant. This case is clearly no different: Colvin was passionate about his responsibilities in Afghanistan, and that of the Canadian mission generally. He felt an obligation to remain true to the Canadian values of fairness and due process. That the government elected to deny Colvin's accusations, and then block efforts to acknowledge the evidence being provided in good faith, shows questionable decision making, which likely inadvertently fueled Colvin's efforts to make this issue public. The lack of internal processes through which Colvin could work left few options for reporting his observations. Senior officials' failure to question government policy on detainee transfers also serves to weaken organizational culture, which in turn breeds intimidation, duplicity and misguided individual and organizational duties. Such a culture, established from the top, also gives unspoken permission to rank-and-file employees, including military personnel, to look the other way when abuses are apparent. It establishes a norm that it is better to remain quiet than come forward with information. It also provides support for those individuals who willingly encourage the government's attempt to carry out wrongdoing with impunity, either out of a lack of understanding of the constitutional principle of the rule of law, or a willful disregard for it.

Finally, the case raises questions about parliamentarians' and oversight agencies' access to untainted information when looking into the detainee issue. The information provided was typically highly redacted, thereby limiting Parliament's ability to hold the government to account. Equally important, ethical questions can be raised about interventions into investigations to limit the availability of evidence, and to use that evidence to question government policy. Again, questions of due process were raised at home with respect to Colvin's treatment. In addition, the government used the prospect of a plum transfer to Washington to encourage his silence. Colvin was placed in the position of having to choose between doing the right thing and the prospect of personal gain.

## Case 3: Abuse of Authority: The Case of Sylvie Therrien

### BACKGROUND

Sylvie Therrien is a former Employment Insurance (EI) fraud investigator at what was then the department of Human Resources and Skills Development Canada (HRSDC). She was first hired in the EI program in 2010, and later moved into her new position as a fraud investigator in October 2012, after her original position was cut. Soon after assuming this new role, Therrien and other investigators became uncomfortable with departmental instructions to make the EI program more efficient. Specifically, investigators were instructed to meet quotas of $35,000 to $40,000 in direct cuts each month, and by restricting benefits and targeting what the department believed were groups abusing the system, such as Indigenous peoples.

According to Therrien, "the goal was not to detect fraud, but to create it."[68] For Therrien, the program's purpose had shifted from one of supporting EI claimants while understanding that there was occasional abuse of the benefits system, to one that considered every claimant a potential abuser who had to be investigated.[69] Rather than assessing each case on the basis of its merits, fraud inspectors were instructed to comb through case files to find any reason to deny benefits. Changes were later made to the EI program that empowered investigators to conduct surveillance of claimants.[70] Therrien often complained to senior management that she was ordered to deny benefits for minor reasons and that she felt pressured to save the department money. She also claimed that she was verbally abused for not meeting departmental quotas.[71]

When Therrien raised these concerns with senior management, she was ordered to maintain her silence or face consequences.[72] Increasingly vocal, Therrien was shunned by her co-workers, who feared reprisals from management if they were seen to be sympathetic to Therrien's position. Having received little internal support, Therrien decided to go public in January 2013. She provided records of the quotas to *Le Devoir*, which ran a story on February 1 highlighting the quota system, and how officials' remuneration was tied to the cuts.[73] When questioned about the matter the minister responsible, Diane Finley, denied any quota existed. This was repeated in a departmental statement published online, which stated that Therrien was not a whistle-blower because the practice of investigating claims without quotas had been in place for some time:

> Ms. Therrien claims to be "blowing the whistle," but this is not
> a matter of whistleblowing. Let's be perfectly clear: there are
> no so-called "quotas" for Employment Insurance fraud, and
> Service Canada employees are not subject to consequences for
> failing to meet any such "quota."[74]

Despite these government denials, *Le Devoir* received other documents on February 25, 2013, that appeared to substantiate Therrien's claims. In fact, one document specifically pointed to the fact that fraud investigators' performance was calculated in part on the basis of savings to the EI program.[75] The incentives were to deny claims, which amounted to quotas. According to Therrien, "you highlight some things, you ignore some things, you manipulate the facts. It's easy."[76] A second document showed weekly reports on the amounts of benefits denied, and the intrusive investigations practices of investigators. Stories in *Le Devoir* appeared soon after that documented how investigators frequently "spy on EI claimants" when fraud is suspected.[77] According to Therrien, only about 3 per cent of claimants actually cheat on their benefits applications.

Not long after these stories appeared the minister was forced to admit publicly that such performance objectives existed.[78] However, Finley also maintained that EI fraud was rampant. She claimed that investigators blocked $500 million in ineligible payments. When verified in the

*Public Accounts,* it was found that fraudulent claims amounted to $158.8 million in 2012–13 involving 112,693 cases, a 25 per cent increase over the previous year. However, it was explained that much of this increase was a result of the fact that many were unaware of EI policy changes from the year before.[79] Also in February 2013, *Le Devoir* uncovered a performance appraisal that provided evidence of an annual target of $485,000 worth of cuts to the EI program.[80] When confronted with this evidence, the department maintained that it was not a quota, but rather a target.[81] Human Resources Minister, Jason Kenney, also maintained that the allegations were false.

As of 2016, Therrien works as an educational assistant for the francophone school board in British Columbia. When employed with HRSDC she earned approximately $60,000 a year, while in 2016 she earned approximately $25,000 a year. This case attracted much attention at the federal level, and Therrien was even courted, unsuccessfully, by the federal Liberal Party to run as an MP in 2014.[82]

## INVESTIGATION AND FINDINGS

By the spring of 2013, HRSDC managers suspected Therrien of leaking documents to the media in contravention of the federal *Communications Policy of the Government of Canada 2006*, and they began an investigation in March 2013. On May 13, 2013, Therrien was suspended without pay. In her departure letter, she was instructed not to speak negatively against the government, as per the department's *Code of Conduct for Employees*.[83] The investigation was concluded on October 15, 2013, and her employment terminated. By analyzing her web usage and email content, the department was able to trace the leaked documents to Therrien.[84] Her security clearance was revoked in October 2013 for violating both the communications policy, and the departmental code of conduct.[85] In practical terms this meant that she was fired. Publicly, the department justified this action by claiming Therrien had ignored internal avenues of dissent and had released documents not intended for public disclosure.[86] Nine days after her termination, HRSDC indicated that its employees, "do not face consequences for missing so-called quotas," and that the process for finding savings had been in place for decades.[87] But this practice was flagged in a 2003 auditor general report that concluded that "generating savings has become an end in itself as savings objectives are based on previous savings achieved and not on program compliance objectives ... Furthermore, the problem with how savings are calculated could also lead to inappropriate behaviour by investigation and control officers."[88]

In addition, the HRSDC investigation concluded that Therrien should have approached the Office of the Public Sector Integrity Commissioner if she had serious concerns. Under the *Public Servants Disclosure Protection Act*, all complaints would be investigated, and the whistle-blower protected from reprisals. Therrien claimed to be unaware of this process, and that she felt that her only option was to approach the media.

In July 2013, Statistics Canada reported that the number of EI beneficiaries was decreasing at a faster rate than the number of unemployed Canadians. For example, in May 2013 Statistics Canada indicated that "only 37.7 per cent of unemployed Canadians received regular EI benefits — a proportion lower than at any time since World War II."[89] Slowly, reports appeared that substantiated the Conservative government's singular obsession with balancing the budget at the expense of merit-based programming such as EI.

After the conclusion of the departmental investigation, Therrien attempted to have the public sector integrity commissioner investigate. Therrien subsequently filed a grievance claim before the Public Service Labour Relations and Employment Board (PSLREB), seeking financial compensation for her termination, and to have the termination decision overturned. According to her claim, insufficient notice was given to defend against the allegations, and that the department had no right to terminate her.

The public sector integrity commissioner declined to investigate, arguing that Therrien was not protected under the *Public Servants*

*Disclosure Protection Act* and because there was no wrongdoing within the definition of the *Act*. Her request was also rejected because she had approached the media, and because she had already filed a complaint to the PSLREB.[90] She subsequently appealed the commissioner's decision to the Federal Court, but this too was rejected in 2015.[91] Therrien subsequently filed an appeal with the Federal Court of Appeal, whereby the court delivered a rebuke of the public sector integrity commissioner in its decision on January 17, 2017. The court found that the commissioner violated Ms. Therrien's rights to procedural fairness by misleading her counsel about the type of evidence needed to make her case. The court also found that it was unreasonable for the commissioner to dismiss Therrien's case when it was unclear whether the PSLREB would hear her complaint. Finally, the court ruled that the commissioner's refusal to act was "incompatible with the intent and purpose of the *PSDPA*, which is designed to provide protection from reprisals to public servants in addition to the rights they possess under the *PSLRA* [*Public Servants Labour Relations Act*]."[92]

Despite the ruling of the Federal Court of Appeal, the commissioner refused to reopen Therrien's complaint. Instead, the commissioner has opted to await a decision of the PSLRB adjudicator. Therrien's counsel protested this decision in January 2017, arguing that the decision introduces another unreasonable delay. More importantly, the PSLREB complaint does not address the issue of reprisals, a matter that can be dealt with independently by the public sector integrity commissioner.[93] Therrien always maintained that, "I didn't do anything wrong. I was following my conscience."[94]

## DISCUSSION

Therrien's case highlights the fate of those who make disclosures in the absence of whistle-blowing provisions or adequate oversight mechanisms. Therrien approached the Office of the Integrity Commissioner after leaking documents to the media, by which point it was no longer possible to protect her from reprisals. Despite this aspect of the *Act*, Therrien questioned whether "mismanagement" as defined under the *Act* should still be investigated by the office. In addition, Therrien believed that confidence in the *Act* and the office was low, as many whistle-blowers had lost their jobs. The case points to the complexity, both in terms of process as well as the personal toll on the individual, of making disclosures, even with disclosure protection. Equally important, this case raises several questions.

First, with respect to the issue of loyalty as an argument against whistle-blowing, Vandekerckhove and Commers[95] maintain that "loyalty is a virtue only to the extent that the object of loyalty is good." In this case, Therrien observed that she must exercise loyalty to the government at all times. However, she also felt an obligation to prevent harm to EI claimants. The objects of those duties were incompatible. From the perspective of Vandekerchhove and Commers, when such conflicts occur, the duty of care to the claimants would usually take precedence. Therrien had a choice to make regarding the way in which she disclosed information. She decided to use internal management channels first, which is arguably the appropriate course of action. This allows the department to respond to her concerns, as was the case with both Schmidt and Colvin. And, like the other cases, officials preferred to protect their public reputation rather than examine the merits of the concerns. Receiving no satisfaction from these officials, Therrien decided to take her concerns to the media. One can certainly argue that she should have sought advice before proceeding. Whether the outcome would have been different is a matter of speculation, as it is likely that Therrien calculated the costs of approaching the media, knowing that she might lose her job, or at least be subject to reprisals.

Second, the case raises questions of merit regarding the adjudication of benefits applications. One could argue that fraud investigators were placed in a position to decide between the government's attempt to cut costs and the needs of EI applicants. It also raises questions as to whether performance in cases like this ought to be measured on the basis of budget quotas. There appeared to be a cost-recovery model in place that justified the positions of investigators to the extent that *savings* were applied to salaries, even if indirectly. At a minimum, the values that support such a model could be seen as questionable given that the rationale for EI is to support citizens through rough times. That an economic lens is used to justify public positions alters that rationale by treating applicants as potential abusers of the system rather than as needy recipients.

Third, the case raises ethical questions about Therrien's decision to leak documents to the media. Therrien had a duty to serve her minister, and ultimately Parliament. However, given that Parliament was unaware of HRSDC's changes to EI policy, one could ask if public servants have a responsibility to inform the chair of an appropriate House or Senate committee when mismanagement and other issues are raised. Should this responsibility be exercised in advance of public disclosures? As servants of the executive branch, such disclosures would also be seen as whistle-blowing, since Parliament's role is to scrutinize.

Fourth, the case raises issues related to the rule of law. The law — in this case EI legislation and regulations — should be applied as impartially as possible. If the government's objective is to cut costs, then the proper course of action is to amend either the legislation or the regulations to account for changes in coverage. The government's objective should not be achieved surreptitiously through internal directives that may violate the rule of law.

Fifth, the case makes a sound argument for whistle-blowing protection legislation. Ministers, the government of the day and senior bureaucrats operate to some extent without routine oversight. Many oversight regimes tend to be complaints-driven. This means that governments can act with considerable discretion in their routine management responsibilities. At what point do senior officials, or any public officials for that matter, have a responsibility to call government policymakers to account for their decisions? The challenge is a very old one: public servants must serve the government of the day, even if there is widespread disagreement with its decisions. Public servants often face ethical dilemmas regarding matters of conscience versus institutional priorities and decisions. In this case, the government's priority was to balance the budget despite the apparent costs for those affected by government programs. Was authorizing surveillance of EI applicants, especially as these relate to privacy rights, and the right not to be intimidated by the state, a reasonable use of authority? The answers to such questions vary according to the judgments of those asked.

Finally, the case raises the breadth of discretion afforded to agents of Parliament, and the manner they choose to enforce legislation for which they are responsible. The Therrien case shows that the commissioner could have proceeded with an investigation of the complaint, but elected instead to take a less risky decision to await the PSLREB decision. It brings into question the role of the office to safeguard process versus serve the needs of whistle-blowers. This is a fine balance to maintain, but an argument can be made that the low number of investigations that have been carried out by PSIC can be attributed to concerns for systems and process, over the needs of the complainants to be heard.

## CONCLUSIONS

Including a whistle-blowing mechanism in an ethics regime in any organization can be controversial for a number of reasons. The most notable of these is that its contribution to that regime is often misunderstood as an outlet for staff and employees to be disloyal. The fact is that a whistle-blowing system, if viewed positively, is vital to an organization's health. It encourages people to come forward whenever wrongdoing is observed. Organizational leaders should pause to consider that uncovering abuses actually protects their public face as well as their economic position.

The major challenge, even for those organizations with an established whistle-blowing process, is shifting the organizational culture to accept that speaking out about mismanagement, abuse or other ethical breaches is not disloyal because those who disclose usually do not regard *themselves* as disloyal. As indicated in the case studies presented in this chapter, the individuals involved saw themselves as loyal public servants beholden to the public good and the interest of the Crown. The majority of whistle-blowers first attempt to use internal processes to lodge their complaint.[96] That said, despite the promises made by the federal government to support whistle-blowing protection under the *Federal Accountability Act 2006*, few resources are made available to cover individuals' legal or other costs.[97] This invariably sends the message that government is not completely supportive of whistle-blowing and that the burden of speaking out will be left to the individual. Equally important, whistle-blowers will only use external mechanisms when the organization has taken no action, or when facing reprisals. This suggests that there is much that organizations can do to create the conditions whereby whistle-blowing becomes an accepted way to forge a speak-up culture. In the absence of a whistle-blowing system, public servants are actually denied an acceptable way to show their loyalty, and contribute to organizational improvement. Ultimately, whistle-blowers just want to be heard and valued.

Ignoring complaints or engaging in overt or even veiled reprisals may sometimes discourage individuals from speaking out, which may ultimately cause more problems for organizations. Each of these cases shows the negative effects of attacking the complainants. More importantly, they show that such overt attacks embolden those individuals inclined to wrongdoing and suppress the voices of those who would improve the organization's work. In the absence of effective whistle-blowing mechanisms, individuals may get the idea that going public is the safest way to protect themselves. The organizations in this chapter were not committed to open internal communication. In fact, no complainant in these cases saw themselves as whistle-blowers until they were forced to behave in that manner.

These cases also demonstrate that even having a whistle-blowing process does not guarantee that wrongdoing will be addressed, or that whistle-blowers will be protected. When reputation, loyalty and self-protection are valued more than service-oriented values such as protecting the public good, whistle-blowers will be subject to reprisals and exposure. The psychological and physical costs of such repercussions can be debilitating, but the benefits for coming forward are often extensive as well. In the Colvin case, for example, a new policy was crafted to deal with detainees. For Therrien, the rationale for investigating EI claimants was subject to intense review, and changes in policy were made. Were it not for dedicated individuals, ethical lapses in these policies would likely not have been exposed.

Lastly, it should be noted that public servants in Canada are, for the most part, highly ethical people who want to do what is right. Sometimes, however, institutions and some people within them do not conduct themselves with the same degree of integrity. In the Colvin case, it was observed that there was no established process for reporting wrongdoing, and that in fact, there was also no way to align bureaucratic and political priorities. This provides a glimpse into what happens when political priorities (in this case) take precedence over ethical practice in the field. There may have been practical reasons for this, but in the end, Canadian values of fairness and due process were compromised. Balancing operational expediency with the public good is the essence of ethical reasoning.

# CHAPTER 9
# MUNICIPAL ETHICS ISSUES

## Gregory Levine and Naomi Couto

An Ontario mayor admits under oath that he has not read the *Municipal Conflict of Interest Act* and seems to delight in his ignorance and bellicosity, much to the horror of the court and observers. Another cries out that she has complied with that very *Act* but her actions nonetheless betrayed conflicts of interest not covered by legislation. Still another municipal leader in another province has colleagues who defend his ostensible compliance with conflict of interest rules and yet his involvement in a development project so offends a provincial government that he is driven from office. Motivated sometimes by self-interest and other times by misguided notions of the public interest and who speaks for it, municipal politicians too often end up in questionable, troubling situations and, in turn, this leads to calls for ethics reform.[1]

Municipal government performs tasks that are essential to modern public life. As much as any other order of government, municipal government ought to function in a climate of mutual respect and equality buttressed by not only an understanding of fair play, but the actual display of fairness in both government and administration. Too often, municipalities, especially but by no means exclusively at the political level, fall far short of our best aspirations for democratic governance. The response to lapses in ethical conduct has been the articulation of concepts of appropriate conduct coupled with various enforcement mechanisms. In short, an assortment of ethics regimes, which vary in procedure and effectiveness by province and even within provinces, has been created.

Municipal ethics regimes have undergone considerable change in the last decade. New rules, new mechanisms and new officers have been adopted to promote ethical conduct in the municipal sector. This chapter outlines rules, policies and practices related to the ethical conduct of elected municipal officials as well as lobbying laws which govern those who contact elected officials.[2] It also highlights cases and reports to illustrate some of the ethical problems encountered at the local level and some of the difficulty in dealing with those problems.

This chapter begins with an overview of ethics issues typically faced by municipal governments and a summary of how they are typically dealt with. It will then proceed to several case studies that illustrate how some municipal councillors have abused voters' trust. We devote this chapter to municipal ethics regimes because, unlike the federal and provincial governments, they are not parliamentary systems. They sometimes imitate federal and provincial ethics reforms, but they need to adapt these to their structure of government and the specific kinds of issues that local governments deal with.

## THE RULES FOR ELECTED OFFICIALS: OVERVIEW AND KEY TERMS

The ethical conduct of municipal councillors across Canada is governed by legislated rules concerning conflict of interest and corruption. Increasingly, they are subject as well to codes of behaviour, which, among other things, deal with inappropriate use of civic property, improper influence of office and inappropriate treatment of staff and the public.

## Corruption

Corruption is the purposeful misuse of power, or the inducement to misuse power, for ends other than those prescribed by law, and is the most serious form of abuse of trust enshrined in criminal law. In Canada, corruption is a criminal offence, and includes such things as bribery and fraud on the government. Municipal corruption is a separate offence within Canada's *Criminal Code* which for all intents and purposes revolves around either an official using his or her position to gain a benefit, or someone else conferring a "benefit" to get something from an official.[3]

Municipal corruption has been a concern since the country was founded. Indeed, it has been the topic of commissions of inquiry for over a century. Consider for example the Cannon Commission, which outed corruption in the administration of early twentieth-century Montreal; or in the modern era, consider the recently concluded Charbonneau Commission, which found corruption coursing through the veins of city halls in Quebec, as well as those of the province's construction industry.[4]

Corruption strikes at the heart of democratic government. When a councillor takes money to vote a certain way on a rezoning,[5] for example, it demeans government and governance, works unfairness on others involved in the process and fouls the decision rendered or action taken by the municipal council.

Corruption is among the most severe forms of misbehaviour in public office, and in a sense is the most retrograde of ethics violations. For this reason it has been criminalized. But it is not the only ethics problem. Inappropriately acting on a conflict of interest and engaging in misbehaviour short of corruption are problematic as well.

## Conflict of Interest

Conflict of interest in the public sector, in its most general formulation, is the clash of a private interest with a public duty.[6] The media and the public often conflate conflict of interest with corruption, but they are not the same. People have various interests, some of which may come to clash with their public duties. Having the interest is not the problem, but what one does about it is.[7] If one plows ahead without concerning oneself with the issue, one does run the risk of either acting unfairly or acting corruptly, or both. If one declares a conflict and does not take part in decision making and so on, ethical transgressions will not occur.

Across Canada, municipal conflicts of interest have traditionally been formulated in terms of financial or pecuniary interests.[8] This is unlike legislation for members of provincial legislatures, which typically refers to private interest generally,[9] as shown in Chapter 5. Increasingly, however, municipal codes of conduct refer to conflict of interest generally, and not simply to financial or pecuniary interests.[10]

The core of conflict of interest rules is that no one should put his or her self-interest ahead of his or her public duty: the public interest must take precedence. Municipal politics offers many opportunities to further one's own interest over and against the public interest. Land deals and contracts for services are two areas that seem to present difficulties. Consider the Wascana land matter in Saskatchewan or the World Class Developments concern in Mississauga, or numerous other smaller "deals" that have arisen from time to time across Canada, which have raised conflicts issues.[11]

## Unethical Behaviour

There are behaviours short of corruption, which can impair the fair and decent operation of government and administration. Increasingly, such misbehaviours are being codified at or for the municipal level. These codes may take a variety of forms. There may be blanket legislation covering all municipalities, as in British Columbia, or a legislated template that allows municipalities to adopt their own individual codes, as in Quebec, or codes could be left entirely to municipalities to create, as in Ontario.[12] Among the misbehaviours these codes try to address are improper or inappropriate influence of office, misuse of insider information, misuse of civic property and abuse of the public and municipal staff. Each of these can destroy the credibility of government, and work great harm on institutions and the individuals they serve.

## Improper or Inappropriate Influence of Office

Typically, current codes of conduct prohibit the use of office for anything other than official duties.[13] Hence, the influence of decision making at the political or administrative levels for private reasons is a focus of concern as well.[14]

Influence may be seen as the power to act on persons or things and the power to produce an effect without using force.[15] It is not about physical force but is surely about coercion in some sense. Holding office opens doors but also carries with it power, sometimes real, sometimes perceived. It is one thing to call an administrator on behalf of a constituent, but quite another to have the administrator respond to one's personal interests and requests. And yet even the former may be problematic. Using office to promote one's own interests rather than the public interest is wrong, as illustrated by the Rob Ford case below.

## Improper or Inappropriate Use of Civic Property

Clearly, using public property for private interest or gain is wrong. For instance, the use of municipal business cards to promote private business, or glad-handing on behalf of one's business at a council meeting, are both clearly inappropriate. Civic policies often allow for a certain amount of personal use of civic property by officials and employees (e.g., use of email or phones, use of computers for professional training). Such policies are important in creating fair and creative workplace environments, but their usage should not be abused.

# RULES FOR LOBBYISTS

Municipal lobbyist registration and regulation is relatively novel in Canada, although corrupt behaviour by lobbyists at any level has been the subject of criminal law for some time. What is more recent is the registration of municipal lobbyists and the regulation of offensive and inappropriate behaviour short of criminality by those lobbyists. As shown in Chapter 7, registration and lobbyist disclosure systems aim at allowing those who are governed to see who is trying to influence those who govern, while lobbying conduct is centred on ensuring that an otherwise lawful activity is carried out appropriately.[16]

Lobbyist registration and regulation systems were still relatively uncommon in Canadian municipalities as of 2017. In Ontario, Toronto, Ottawa and Hamilton have or are establishing such systems.[17] In British Columbia, Surrey has a single-purpose system focussed on land development applications.[18] In Ontario the *Municipal Act* provides a framework for establishing a registry, but it does not require municipalities to establish registries (except in Toronto). If they do, the registry must include those who contact public office holders, including both councillors and civic employees, and they must create a code of conduct for registrants.[19] These codes are specific to their municipalities. Toronto's code, as well as its articulation of lobbying types and registration processes, is elaborate, in some ways mimicking the federal and provincial schemes described in Chapter 7.[20] It includes such requirements for lobbyists as not offering gifts when they lobby, clearly identifying their clients, providing accurate information and so on. Ontario's *Municipal Act* prohibits the acceptance of contingency fees.

Quebec has taken a different approach in that the province registers municipal lobbyists and provides a set of rules for lobbyists.[21] The province's *Lobbying and Transparency Ethics Act* prohibits various activities, including the charging of contingency fees and lobbying by former municipal politicians during what are typically called "cooling-off periods."[22]

Lobbyists have the potential to bring public office holders into conflicts of interests and inappropriate conduct situations. This means that lobbyists have much potential influence and their conduct bears regulation and scrutiny.

## ENFORCEMENT MECHANISMS

Just as ethics rules have grown, so have methods of enforcement. At the municipal level, pecuniary conflict of interest has typically been regulated through court processes; this remains so in Ontario and B.C., and indeed in most provinces. Of course, corrupt behaviour has been and remains a crime, and it too has been dealt with in the courts.

In the context of council and committee meetings, bad behaviour has been dealt with through council procedures. With the rise of codes of conduct in Ontario has come the establishment of local or municipal integrity commissioners. In Quebec, though, the formalization of codes of conduct has occurred in tandem with the centralization in Quebec City of non-criminal municipal ethics law procedures and decisions through its Municipal Commission, described below.

### Courts

Courts are the enforcement mechanism prescribed in Ontario's *Municipal Conflict of Interest Act*, in the conflict of interest and inappropriate behaviour sections of B.C.'s *Community Charter*, in Quebec's *Lobbying and Transparency Ethics Act* and in the lobbying sections of Toronto's *Municipal Code*.[23] Courts are effective to the extent that they make binding decisions subject to legitimate appeal. They bring a seriousness, solemnity and finality to ethics problems. On the other hand, they are slow and costly. Cost is especially problematic because it often falls to electors, or residents of municipalities, to assume the cost of pursuing through litigation councillors who may be seen to be in conflict of interest[24] or guilty of other misbehaviours.[25] This is a cost which most people cannot bear, and so the result is minimal enforcement of the law and an inappropriate level of security for those in office.

### Tribunals

Tribunals have a smaller role in municipal ethics law in Canada than in the United States. To be sure, in the area of access to information, a key area of government ethics law, information and privacy commissioners in many provinces provide a tribunal mechanism for dealing with appeals of or reviews of access request refusals in municipalities, and related record decision requests. In the area of conduct, though, there is nothing approaching the panoply of municipal ethics commissions in Canada like there is in the United States. The American commissions operate as tribunals and often have extensive powers to punish those who engage in misconduct.

In Canada, by contrast, while some ethics commissioners have administrative penalty powers, and in Ontario some municipal ethics commissioners have the power to issue orders,[26] Quebec is the first and only province to have municipal conduct matters involving councillors handled by a tribunal — the Commission municipale du Québec.[27] This is a relatively new development, although by 2017 there have already been about a hundred decisions.[28] The advantage of this system is that it is less costly than courts. A disadvantage is that it hinges on a mechanism for screening complaints that involves a provincial ministry. This step seems unnecessary, and could open the system to bias and inappropriate interference.

## Ministerial Control

In some instances, provincial ministers may be able to influence or control ethics processes or enforcement, although this is not as common as court methods. In Quebec, complaints about members of council are first sent to a provincial minister whose office vets the complaints, and then sends those that may be justified for inquiry to the Commission municipale du Québec.[29] This has the advantage of weeding out ostensibly frivolous and vexatious complaints, but it may also result in a diminution of the right to complain.

In Saskatchewan, members of council may be removed by order-in-council when it is deemed in the public interest to do so.[30] This was done in the Wascana case discussed below. This procedure has the advantage of avoiding gridlock at the municipal level when a member's conduct is so egregious it hurts the council. But as in the Wascana case, even where a council is operating despite a member's questionable behaviour, it may be necessary to remove an elected official for self-serving and egregious conduct.

## Integrity Commissioners and Ethics Ombudsmen

Commissioners who act as specialty ombudsmen at the local level are new in Canada, although a number of provincial ombudsmen have had jurisdiction over municipalities for some time and have been able to deal with aspects of misconduct at the municipal council level.

Ontario has allowed municipalities to establish integrity commissioners who are empowered to investigate complaints when councillors are alleged to have breached their councils' codes of conduct. These commissioners' most basic function is to investigate and report an opinion on whether a code rule has been breached and to recommend what to do about it.[31] In turn, council is to impose a sanction where appropriate.[32] Councils may assign other functions to a commissioner — educational and advisory functions, for example, are increasingly common.[33] The ability to settle or resolve complaints is often included in codes, but the method of achieving settlement is often unstated.[34]

The advantage of having integrity commissioners is that the municipalities fund them, and residents do not have to go to great expense to get some level of accountability from local councillors. But the downside is that commissioners typically have no power to give orders, and their reports may be dealt with politically or expediently by councils, thus failing to fulfill the intent of the codes.

The commissioners themselves are also vulnerable, as there are no mechanisms to ensure their security. Tenure of office is not legislatively established, nor are indemnity or insurance requirements.[35] If integrity commissioners are left unprotected in this way they will be vulnerable to lawsuits which, in turn, might inhibit them from making controversial decisions.

However, we should keep in mind that municipal integrity commissioners represent a relatively new innovation in Canadian public sector ethics regimes. They will therefore face challenges as they mature.

## CASES

### 1. The Curious Case(s) of Rob Ford

The late Rob Ford saw himself as the champion for those anti-intellectual, anti-government Ontarians who were sure they were being cheated by the elites. Despite being the son of a wealthy family, he played the "everyman" card to the hilt. City staff and councillors often described him as obnoxious and erratic as he berated and bullied his way through the mayoralty. His behaviour, described by many as lacking in honour and dignity, perplexed those who saw it as an affront to good government and governing with integrity and, in a sense, delighted those who considered him an everyman.[36] Ford's populist appeal was successful in spite of his drug use and alcoholism. Ford was a sight to behold as he made headlines around the world, but his life story is beyond the focus of this chapter.

By using his office to further his own agenda, Ford ran afoul of the City of Toronto's *Code of Conduct*. Ford's entanglement with conflicts of interest began in 2009, when he was a city councillor. Ford was a well-known football enthusiast and high school football coach. He established the Rob Ford Football Foundation, which was administered by the Toronto Community Foundation and which purchased football equipment for secondary schools. The foundation obviously needed funds and Ford solicited such funding. How he did so led to a complaint in 2009 and a subsequent investigation and report.

Ford had sent letters soliciting funds for his foundation using city letterhead, the City of Toronto logo and his city hall return address, and he included in his letters his City of Toronto business card and a promotional sticker from his family's company. A private citizen who had received the solicitation lodged a complaint with the integrity commissioner. The commissioner wrote to Ford to advise him that further to the City of Toronto's *Code of Conduct for Members of Council*, he must separate his council work from his charitable activities because some of those receiving his solicitations, especially developers and lobbyists, might feel pressured to donate to his charity in order to gain his support. No formal inquiry was established, and Ford agreed that the promotional stickers for his family's company should not have been included in the letters. The integrity commissioner received a second complaint about Ford's solicitations in early 2010, this time from another city councillor. The commissioner again handled the complaint informally, and wrote to Ford to explain why his solicitations were prohibited by the *Code of Conduct.* At no time up to then did Ford repudiate the advice from the commissioner.

In May 2010, the integrity commissioner received a third complaint that Ford was continuing to carry on the solicitations for his charity using city letterhead and city staff; the complainant was uncomfortable because Ford had announced that he would run for mayor, making the breach of the *Code of Conduct* even more serious. Ford had apparently disregarded the two letters that he had received from the commissioner. As a result, the commissioner opened a formal investigation.

The commissioner found that from 2008 to the time of the investigation in 2010, about $40,000 had been donated to the Rob Ford Football Foundation, including $3,150 donated by registered lobbyists.[37] During the investigation, Ford conceded that he used city staff to do the mailings. He stated to the commissioner that he "did not understand"[38] why he could not use city letterhead and city staff to help solicit funds for a "charitable cause," and he never attempted to establish an arm's-length relationship with the Rob Ford Football Foundation. As well, he rejected the notion that the source of donations might influence his decision making; he maintained that he could not be "bought."[39]

The integrity commissioner summed up Ford's misconduct in the following way:

> Where a Councillor asks someone to give money to a personal
> cause in his or her role as Councillor and underlines that
> role by putting the request in an official format, that is, on
> Councillor letterhead, this is a use of the influence of office

for a cause that is not part of the Councillor's public duties. Councillor Ford described this as an "inconsequential complaint about the use of letterhead" but the complaint is not just about the letterhead, the envelope or the embossed gold seal imprinted with the councillor's name. It is about the role of the councillor, which is symbolized by all of these formal items. Councillors make significant decisions by voting in council and committees, by having access to fellow councillors, to the Toronto public service and to the public at large through the media. Councillors make decisions, set policy and determine how taxpayers' money will be spent. A councillor's correspondence with the public is a reminder of that role and it is in that context that the use of the letterhead must be measured.

The problem with using one's influence, even for a good cause, is that such behaviour can be received in many different ways. The recipient may wish to do business with the city, lobby the city or be appointed by the city. Alternatively, the individual may work for the city or appear as an advocate for other citizens. The recipient may have made a deputation before committees or community councils. The recipient could take such a request as a way to gain an advantage by making a donation. Alternatively, as in this case, recipients could feel uncomfortable for declining to donate . . .[40]

Ford seemed to have no understanding that using civic letterhead, business cards and the like, as a means to influence and pressure his constituents was wrong, Devoid of anything approaching a solid understanding of conflict of interest, he at least seemed to understand that using staff for his private purposes was problematic.

Ford was found by the commissioner to have breached the *Code* in 2010 when he was a city councillor. As a result, he was required to reimburse the lobbyists who had donated to the Rob Ford Football Foundation.[41] This never happened.[42] On February 7, 2012, after Ford became mayor, council voted twenty-two to twelve to rescind its prior sanction. Ford participated in this discussion and in the subsequent vote. This set the stage for one of the most bizarre conflict of interest cases in modern times as well as for a confusing decision by the Divisional Court of Ontario.

Prior to the February 7 motion, and over the course of a year, the integrity commissioner sent Ford six requests to comply with the order. Ford disregarded these requests. In 2011, Ford had become mayor, at which point he finally replied that he had been in touch with a number of donors, and three of them indicated that they did not want reimbursement. The commissioner noted that seeking forgiveness in this way was also a breach of the *Code*. This was reported to council and the commissioner sought council support by asking that it require Ford to present proof of reimbursement.[43] Instead, in February 2012 council rejected the recommendation and rescinded the original order: the mayor had the votes.[44] By any objective measure this was a sad day for ethics in government.

The mayor and possibly a majority of councillors seemed not to understand why it is wrong to use influence, civic property, or civic symbols for their own ends. Some no doubt would say that the monetary penalty imposed on Ford by council was inappropriate, and as shown below, this became a critical point for the courts. It is noteworthy that amongst those who felt the penalty was inappropriate, no one appears to have suggested another sanction. And not one councillor challenged the decision of the integrity commissioner that Ford's use of civic resources to raise funds for his charity was inappropriate. Instead, the focal point of debate became the ethics of the mayor's involvement in the council's decision in 2012, to rescind its prior decision of 2010 which required him to reimburse those from whom he had inappropriately solicited funds.

An elector in Toronto, Paul Magder, challenged Mayor Ford in court, claiming he had no right under the *Municipal Conflict of Interest Act* to participate in a discussion and vote which involved his private financial interests. Mr. Magder claimed the mayor should be disqualified from office, since that was the only penalty available in the *Act* for Ford's actions. Mr. Magder succeeded at the trial level but the Divisional Court overturned the decision.[45]

Some observers have concluded that the mayor got off on a technicality, and left it at that. However, there are important lessons that can be gleaned from the court decisions. They convey how difficult it is to deal with ethics issues in the court arena, and they illustrate how tough it is for judges to disqualify members of council given their fundamental respect for the fact that they are dealing with elected representatives. As well, the legislation at the time provided no option other than dismissal from office for punishing violations of provincially-mandated conflict of interest rules.

At the trial level, Justice Hackland did not accept that error in judgment would allow Ford relief from disqualification. Indeed, Ford intended to speak to the reimbursement issue in council, and to participate in and to influence the debate. Ford was also clearly, and in some sense wilfully, unfamiliar with relevant legislation (i.e., the requirements of the *Municipal Conflict of Interest Act*). Ford had been warned not to participate by another councillor, but he did anyway. Aware that there were no lighter penalties to administer, Justice Hackland did not take the step of disqualification lightly, but he did apply it, correctly from our perspective.

The Divisional Court, through a series of mental gymnastics worthy of the Olympics, reversed the decision. Ultimately, the court held that the city had no authority to compel Mayor Ford to reimburse those from whom he solicited funds. Absent this power, the question of conflict of interest became moot and so the disqualification was overturned and the populist mayor stayed in office.

A detailed analysis of this decision is beyond the scope of this chapter. From a legal perspective, however, the distinction between penalties and sanctions, and remedial measures in relation to *Code* breaches, was an issue. Only two sanctions or penalties were authorized by the *Municipal Act* at that time — a reprimand, or the suspension of pay for up to three months.[46] The Divisional Court found the reimbursement requirement of the *Code* and the council to be punitive in nature, and found the city had no basis to authorize it. Both courts recognized that municipalities could impose remedial measures — for example, requiring an apology — but the Divisional Court was clear that remedial measures could not be punitive.

The consequence of this decision in law is that it becomes more difficult to have any Ontario mayor or councillor punished for participating in debates which involve pecuniary interests that engage them in a conflict of interest. Indeed, a new defence seems to be "I thought what council was doing was wrong or illegal and so my interests would not matter."[47] The consequences for code drafting are that remedial measures and penalties must be clearly delineated. Remedial measures must not be punitive in any way.

The consequences for politicians, particularly those who really do not give much thought to ethical matters, is that ethics laws are either toothless or very forgiving — either of which is, presumably, quite acceptable for them. For the public that cares about such issues, the laws become a little less comprehensible, and the powerful just seem to be able to do what they want. What recourse is there in the case of someone like Ford, who says he had not even read conflict of interest legislation, willfully disregarded warnings about participating in a vote where he has a clear financial interest, and where a court essentially created a new defence for what most people would intuitively understand to be an arrogant action tinged with more than a modicum of inanity? Beyond this, no one disagrees that the *Code* had been breached, and yet the mayor ultimately went unpunished for that as well. This is not a good story for those seeking good governance and clear ethics rules. However, in November of 2016, the Ontario government introduced legislation to amend the *Municipal Act* and the *Municipal Conflict of Interest Act* that would allow judges to choose from a range of sanctions if a mayor or councillor is found to have been in a conflict of interest. The new options would include a reprimand, suspension of remuneration for up to three months, removing the member from office, disqualifying the member from running for municipal office again for up to seven years, and requiring financial restitution for financial gain.[48]

## 2. Meetings and Mayor McCallion

In September of 2009, media reports claimed that longstanding and popular Mayor Hazel McCallion of Mississauga had taken part in meetings involving the City of Mississauga and business interests promoting a hotel development deal that could have benefitted her son. A month later, Mississauga's council requested a judicial inquiry, which was established and headed by Justice Douglas Cunningham. In October 2011, Justice Cunningham reported that the mayor had been in a conflict of interest position vis-à-vis her son's business dealings — albeit not necessarily in respect to council meetings.[49] The judicial inquiry was conducted in two phases, one concerned with a transaction involving the restructuring of a utility, and the other involving a land transaction and the potential development of a hotel complex. This discussion focuses on the latter phase.

Mayor McCallion believed that Mississauga's city centre would be enhanced by the development of a five star hotel, and to that end she facilitated meetings between people who might promote such a development. This seems fairly typical — until one realizes that the mayor's son, Peter McCallion, was an associate of one of the principal players in this possible deal, World Class Development (WCD). Though the mayor's son claimed he was merely a real estate agent, the inquiry found that he was a principal figure and investor in the development company.[50] Other potential investors were aware of Peter McCallion's involvement.[51] From a general ethics perspective, it is not difficult to see that any involvement on the part of the mayor in promoting something that could benefit her son could be problematic.

Mayor McCallion understood that her son had a financial interest in the WCD project. At first she characterized this interest as a commission, but ultimately she understood that her son was more than a real estate agent, and had a significant interest in the success of WCD and its proposed development.[52] The way she understood the *Municipal Conflict of Interest Act* was that her son's involvement in the WCD project should not stop her from advocating for the project, and that she only had to declare a conflict if the matter went before council or committee meetings.[53] She did not see that her actions outside of official committee and council meetings were problematic or alternately, if she did, she was at least satisfied that she was complying with the law as she understood it. She believed she could intervene on WCD's behalf in various negotiations because to her mind such a development was in the city's interests.

Some of the land in downtown Mississauga that WCD wanted to develop was owned jointly by two pension funds: the Ontario Municipal Employees Retirement System (OMERS), and the Alberta Investment Management Corporation (AIM). The mayor was heavily involved in negotiations respecting OMERS, AIM and WCD, which would have transferred land for the kind of development she wanted for Mississauga. The Cunningham report details the mayor's efforts. This extensive involvement need not be detailed here; suffice it to say that the mayor met with people in OMERS and AIM and did a great deal to facilitate a land sale which would be used in WCD's project. The mayor was also heavily involved in discussions of the agreement of purchase and sale, and in subsequent discussions of conditions and extensions in respect to that agreement. The mayor had no involvement with city staff in these negotiations or subsequent development application issues.

Though, as we saw, the mayor believed she had met the ethical obligations laid out in the *Municipal Conflict of Interest Act*, Justice Cunningham found otherwise. His report states:

There is considerable evidence that the mayor frequently intervened with the vendors in relation to WCD . . .

I accept that the mayor's interest in the WCD Project was driven principally by her desire for a four or five star hotel in Mississauga and not simply by a desire to assist her son. However, the fact that the mayor may not have acted primarily to further her son's pecuniary interests does not end the conflict of interest analysis, nor does it take into account questions surrounding apparent conflicts of interest. The mayor should have been more wary of using her influence where her son stood to gain financially from the transaction . . .

In this case the mayor actively promoted WCD's interest at many different stages of the transaction when she knew that her son had a pecuniary interest in WCD. In pushing the interests of WCD, and by extension Peter McCallion, the mayor acted in the face of a clear conflict of interest and used the influence of her office, albeit outside her legislative role. It is no answer for the mayor to say this was done for the benefit of the City of Mississauga when her son stood to make millions of dollars if the deal were concluded.

I find that, once Mayor McCallion learned her son had a pecuniary interest in WCD (which she knew from the outset), she should have refused any involvement in the project.[54]

This finding is significant because it reminds us that dealing with conflicts of interest and influence of office may take us beyond legislated rules and may engage the common law. Justice Cunningham followed Professor David Mullan's argument that common law rules still applied, that the municipal conflict of interest legislation was not a complete code. This is important not only from a legal perspective, but also because it reflects a common-sense view that should prevent council members from thinking that ethics rules, and in particular conflict of interest rules, only apply in a very restricted sense to the limited spaces of meetings of council and committees.

The mayor learned little from Justice Cunningham's report. She said "I did nothing wrong" and that the charge that she had been in both a real and an apparent conflict of interest was merely Cunningham's opinion.[55] His opinion indeed — one the city asked for when it set up a judicial inquiry. Cunningham's report contained numerous recommendations for change both to the *Municipal Conflict of Interest Act* and to Mississauga's *Code of Conduct*. As well, it contained substantive changes to the law and to the role of and protections for integrity commissioners. In November of 2016, the provincial government introduced legislation that would implement a few of the commission's recommendations, although Mississauga has incorporated parts of his recommendations into its code of conduct for councillors.

What should we learn from this case? For starters, one might readily conclude that the arrogance of some politicians knows no bounds. What else would drive someone in a position of such importance to act in a land deal in which one's son figured so prominently? Will we learn that intention is not always enough to buttress propriety — that sometimes one has to absent oneself even if we consider a potential conflict of interest to be minor? It is hard to know what to conclude about the defiance of the mayor in the face of Justice Cunningham's findings. Moreover, there are similarities between Ford and McCallion. They are both "right" presumably by virtue of their elected position, but not based on any substantive understanding of law, morality or ethics as these relate to conflicts of interest. Perhaps their transgressions were not considered serious enough, either by the courts or the public, to be a "firing" offence.

Next, we consider a case where a civil leader became involved in a conflict of interest, and was not allowed to continue in office.

## 3. The Reeve and a Land Deal Too Far

In February 2015, Kevin Eberle, the reeve (president of the municipal council) of the Rural Municipality of Sherwood in Saskatchewan
— which encircles Regina — was removed from office because of his
involvement in a land deal.[56] The national media duly reported the
event,[57] which followed an inspection and inquiry into the RM of
Sherwood.[58] The Minister of Government Relations was "shocked and
disgusted" and the inquiry officer said that the chance to make lots of
money interfered with the reeve's "moral compass."[59]

In 2013, the Great Prairie Development Corporation announced a
plan to develop Wascana Village in the RM of Sherwood. Amendments
in the Official Community Plan (OCP) were made to accommodate the
development. Prior to the announcement, the RM also withdrew from
a joint planning agreement with Regina, although in late 2013 the RM
and the city subsequently signed a memorandum of understanding to
promote collaborative planning, and three committees were established
to do this.

Wascana Village was to be a high-density residential development
in the RM southeast of Regina. OCP amendments and a plan of subdivision were presented to the council of the rural municipality. OCP
amendments were conditionally approved at the end of 2013. A concept
plan was to be submitted by the developer, and at the time of writing of
the inquiry report it had not been submitted.

The major landowners in the development area were Kevin Eberle
and his wife. They owned 467.2 acres, while Eberle's cousin and his
cousin's wife owned 107 acres; Marathon Properties owned a further
167 acres. The developer attempted to buy the land from these owners.
Because of concerns about possible conflicts of interest, in June 2014
the Saskatchewan Minister of Public Relations appointed Justice Ron
Barclay to inquire into the situation.

Justice Barclay's report on the Wascana Village development outlines
the steps taken to bring this project to fruition. Many of these steps —
for example, zoning and OCP amendments — involved the RM. There

were also interactions between the municipality and the provincial government as approvals were necessary.

The Wascana Village development was huge and was agreed to by the RM very hastily in 2012.[60] The reeve did declare a conflict before the matter was discussed. Two years later, a concept plan that met none of the conditions required was also hastily agreed to.[61]

Questions were raised with Justice Barclay about the development. For example, a petition was presented to him that raised questions about the costs and benefits of such a development, and noted the reeve's interest in the matter.[62] In addition, a consulting firm had been hired to gage residents' and stakeholders' views; it found that there was no interest in a suburban development.[63] Furthermore, it was found that the rural municipality did no "due diligence" with respect to the developer.[64]

In his report, Barclay states the following:

> I am left to wonder what would cause good, honest,
> hardworking Councillors to pursue the Wascana Village
> Development through the torturous years I have outlined . . .
> I am left to wonder what part Reeve Eberle played with the
> other councillors during this period of time. I am also left to
> wonder what part the Developer and the RM retaining the
> same lawyer throughout much of this period played . . . I am
> left to conclude that the Council blindly (no cost benefits
> analysis, no mandate, no due diligence) pursued the Wascana
> Village Development for the simple sake of development.[65]

It was not Barclay's mission to investigate council per se but his comments nonetheless help us understand what brought the reeve into disrepute.

At issue for the inquiry was whether the reeve had a pecuniary interest, what the nature of the interest was, and how that interest played out in the governance of the rural municipality. In terms of the pecuniary interest, four attempts were made to conclude purchase and sale agreements respecting the lands held by the Eberles. The agreements were worth considerable sums of money, but none of them closed. Another profit-sharing agreement was attempted which would have netted the Eberles something in the range of $57 million were the development to come to fruition. Moreover, there were lands being retained by the Eberles and their cousins which would be used for a further development, the Estates at Wascana Village, a development idea never disclosed to the rural municipality.[66]

It is significant that the agreements were themselves conditional on the OCP and related zoning changes. Clearly, the reeve would have had pecuniary interests in such matters as they came to council.[67] Indeed, there was no time after the Wascana project was announced in May 2012 when the reeve would *not* have had a pecuniary interest.

The inquiry assessed the reeve's and the council's conduct as it related to conflict of interest in the *Municipalities Act*, the official oath sworn by members, the RM of Sherwood's *Code of Ethics* and the common law of conflict of interest. In assessing the provisions of the *Municipalities Act*, Justice Barclay found that the barest of declarations was required when a matter came before council; that influencing a vote relates to actions before a vote; the oath of office requires faithful, impartial behaviour and not profiting from office; and that the common law duties respecting conflict of interest are not as narrow as those in the *Municipalities Act*. In this regard, he followed the lead of Justice Cunningham's analysis of conflict of interest and the common law, and cited several court decisions.[68]

Reeve Eberle declared a conflict each time the matter came to council, but no detail was provided. At one point the rural municipality's solicitor indicated to the reeve that he would have to disclose that he had a disqualifying personal interest, and not simply an interest.[69] Moreover, the reeve's continuing involvement in related aspects of the matter (i.e., questions related to the OCP and the zoning) were problematic.[70]

Justice Barclay noted that the OCP changes were brought about as a result of the development project in which the mayor clearly had an interest.[71] Had this been a "community of interest" situation, the reeve would have been exonerated, since it would have involved a situation in which the reeve was one of amongst many potential beneficiaries. However, he acted on legal advice, and the majority of council supported the OCP changes. The forwarding of OCP plans directly to the developer was found by Barclay to be inappropriate, and a breaking of trust with the municipality. Beyond this, Justice Barclay detailed related aspects of the development in which the reeve figured and attempted to influence (from water matters to zoning issues as well as meetings on other matters).[72] The reeve also attempted to conceal his involvement with the Wascana development. Justice Barclay found that he did not disclose his interest to all councillors in zoning matters, that he did not disclose the profit-sharing agreement he ultimately agreed to and that, indeed, he was concerned about revealing any records that might have showed his involvement with Wascana.[73]

In sum, Justice Barclay stated:

> I find that Reeve Eberle had a serious conflict of interest and failed to act in accordance with his Oath, and in the best interests of the RM. Instead he sought to advance Wascana Village in numerous respects, most notably, directing the RM's CAO Ms. Kunz to withhold unfavourable documents, procure a water source and destroy documents . . .

> Reeve Eberle's actions were highly inappropriate for an elected representative of a municipality. His actions do not withstand public scrutiny and violate trust reposed in him.

> Reeve Eberle's actions fall far below any standard by which I was asked to assess his conduct. Unfortunately, the opportunity to earn significant profits has interfered with his moral compass . . .

In sum, the conduct of Reeve Eberle, as outlined above,
coupled with his lack of recognition of the effect of this
conduct, and lack of remorse, has left me to conclude that
serious damage has been done to the office of Reeve as well as
to the integrity and credibility of the RM as a whole.[74]

Like Mayors Ford and McCallion, the reeve displayed an unwillingness to confront the ethical wrongs he had participated in. This was
partly the result of the reeve's ignorance, and partly a result of his arrogance, or what we might describe as a type of entitlement in which
elected officials think they are entitled to do what they want

But whether ignorance or arrogance, the Wascana development story
is staggering. How could an elected official not withdraw or resign
when he or she was so significantly involved in such a massive deal?
It is interesting that the common law looms large in this case in a way
it did not in judicial review initiated by Sinclair Stevens discussed in
Chapter 3, and that the municipality's code of ethics figured so little. It
is significant that the oath of office played an important evaluative role
as, of course, did the conflict of interest sections of the *Municipalities
Act,* which are similar to others across Canada.

## 4. Toronto Computer Leasing and External Contracts Inquiries

In each of the previous cases we have considered ethical dilemmas
faced by prominent municipal councillors. Each case illustrated ethical problems, and presented the findings either of a court, or a judicial
inquiry. In this last case what is highlighted is the persistence of those
who sought to ensure that ethical standards prevailed — to find out
what really happened and to set it right. We refer to the results of the
*Report of the Toronto Computer Leasing and External Contracts Inqui-
ries,* better known as the Bellamy Report.[75]

In late April 2001, Bas Balkissoon, a member of the Toronto City
Council, started asking questions. He had seen a memo making reference to the city's "current technology lease provider," but no one

around him seemed to know who that was. On the council's agenda was approval of the "photocopier report," which recommended leasing city photocopiers from the technology lease provider, but when Councillor Balkissoon asked city staff to provide a copy of the city's contract with that provider so he could ascertain whether that contract included photocopiers, he encountered a stone wall. As a result, "Inside the Chamber, the photocopier report was no longer just routine business. It started a battle for higher principles of public accountability."[76] The photocopier report didn't name the company from which millions of dollars' worth of technology would be leased. On April 23, Auditor Jeff Griffiths let Balkissoon know that he had spoken to the city's Information and Technology Division and that someone there would have an answer to his question. That someone was Lana Viinamae, the city's Director, Computer Operations and Telecommunications, who informed Balkissoon that the "current technology lease provider" and the city's "vendor of record" for leasing was MFP Financial Services Ltd. This raised many questions, so Councillor Balkissoon held the photocopier report so that it could not be approved without further inquiry, discussion or information from staff.[77]

Holding the report had caused a stir in the Council Chamber:

> Councillors were asking questions. As Lana Viinamae made her way out of the Chamber, she bumped into lobbyist Jeffery Lyons. He wanted to know what was going on down on the Council floor. She told him Councillor Bas Balkissoon was asking lots of questions about leasing.

> As the Council meeting continued, another councillor approached Councillor Balkissoon: Did he know MFP's Dash Domi was Tie Domi's brother? Tie Domi, the famous hockey player? Mr. Balkissoon said that was irrelevant. Why would it matter if an MFP salesman's brother played for the Toronto Maple Leafs?

On the second day of the Council meeting, Councillor
Balkissoon had a surprise visit. A security guard came into
the Chamber to tell him that "Jeff" wanted to see him in the
Council lounge. Off he went to the lounge, looking for City
Auditor Jeff Griffiths. But it wasn't Mr. Griffiths who was
waiting for him—it was Jeff Lyons.[78]

For the next few months, allegations of wrongdoing and undue influence kept surfacing, until in February of 2002, city council authorized
a judicial inquiry into computer equipment and software leases by the
city. Justice Denise Bellamy was appointed to conduct the inquiry. In
October 2002, city council wanted another inquiry into other contracts
entered into by the city, and Justice Bellamy was appointed to conduct
the second inquiry. As she did not begin the inquiry until December,
she was able to combine both inquiries, and a four-volume report covering both mandates.[79]

The events and cover-ups that the inquiry unravelled went back in
time to before the amalgamation in 1998 of several municipalities to
form the City of Toronto. Justice Bellamy's report into the shocking
events leading up to the photocopier report reads like a detective novel,
with a long list of actors and events that even Hollywood fiction and
scandal would have a hard time scripting. This is all well documented
in Volume I of Bellamy's report: *Facts and Findings*.[80] Although Volume
I is a fascinating read, what is most pressing for us here is the content of
*Volume 2: Good Government*. Here, Justice Bellamy writes:

The issue at the heart of these vulnerabilities is trust.
Specifically, it is trust in public officials who spend public
money. Those with control of public funds have a special
duty of trust to the public. They must discharge their duty of
trust fairly and objectively and they must be seen to be doing
so. That should be obvious. So why is it that trust is broken
so often?

Democracies must handle the taxpayers' money, but the structures of democratic government have become sufficiently complicated that people are unable to track their tax dollars day to day. But government consists of human beings. Both politics and the civil service attract bright, ambitious, dedicated people. And some people in both politics and the civil service are susceptible to human failings like incompetence, greed, and dishonesty. All of them regularly work with the ingredients for scandal. With each new scandal, public trust is eroded.[81]

This is the heart of the matter when thinking about the lack of awareness, responsibility and ethics that key actors listed in the Bellamy Report did or didn't exhibit. Both the Toronto Computer Leasing Inquiry and the Toronto External Contracts Inquiry — so intertwined they became a single inquiry — revealed that many of the same people played a role in both. As Justice Bellamy examined the six large IT transactions between the City of Toronto and outside suppliers before and after amalgamation, she and her staff became aware, over their three and a half year inquiry, that a lack of ethics, a sense of entitlement and self-serving interests had come to pass as the norm for many with power in those chambers — councillors, lobbyists and senior staff. We know, however, as Bellamy noted, "Judicial inquiries have no power to put people in jail, find them guilty of crimes, fine them, or find them liable to pay damages. An inquiry is simply an investigation, and the commissioner's report is simply findings of fact and statements of opinion, which should not be perceived as findings of criminal or civil liability."[82]

As with the examples above and so many others like them in Canadian cities, we are left to think about what "honest politics" means and who the bearers for attaining honest politics must be. Clearly, the theme of entitlement runs through that surge of power that many of the political actors in our examples felt they could use as personal leverage. We chose in this last example not to name the bad actors (we recommend reading the Bellamy Report) but rather to generally consider that it takes others in those offices to call bad governance into question. Councillor Balkissoon and others like him took it upon themselves to challenge the ethics and political decisions they saw as suspect. These are the types of men and women who also work for the public in city halls across Canada. To complement and surpass much of the valid cynicism and anger towards government, we need to also tell the stories of those that stand up in the name of justice and ethical behaviour. We need to consider that educating for good governance must also take place in our schools, in employee training sessions throughout municipalities and in the hiring of integrity commissioners, but most importantly, in supporting those that work to make sure ethical policy and procedure are in place and followed.

## LESSONS LEARNED

One can legitimately wonder how much has been learned as a result of municipal ethics regimes, how much has been window dressing for the cynical and not meaningful or effective enough for the sincere and how much more (or less) will have to be done to create a truly democratic local polity that embodies and reveres mutual respect, equality and fair play. Chapter 18 of Machiavelli's *The Prince* begins thus:

> Everyone admits how praiseworthy it is in a prince to
> keep faith, and to live with integrity and not with craft.
> Nevertheless our experience has been that those princes who
> have done great things have held good faith of little account,
> and have known how to circumvent the intellect of men by
> craft, and in the end have overcome those who have relied on
> their word.[83]

Machiavelli goes on to discuss ways of contesting, which include the use of law and the use of force. He concludes that because the first is often insufficient, the prince must have recourse to the second. Does it not seem this way far too often? In our day and age, coercion through physical force is rare, but force created by conflicts of interest, bullying and deception can have even more powerful results than physical force. One can envisage a pack of local princes who are quite prepared to cast off integrity and to use their offices to get their way and beyond that ultimately to serve themselves.

For every Ghandi and for every Mandela, there seem to be cadres of politicians willing to demean the body politic to maintain self-serving power. And yet, hope springs from the work of people devoted to making governance better by making it ethical. From those who teach ethics in government and administration, to those who work and act ethically, to those who organize and maintain ethics regimes, there is a spectrum of hope.

A former Ontario Ombudsman, writing in the *Toronto Star*, described Ontario's municipal ethics system as an "epic fail."[84] He was wrong, but it would be just as inaccurate to say it has been an unqualified success. No province has found *the* answer to municipal ethics problems.

Enforcement is a major part of any solution, and there is much to be done. Moving from the court system to the use of integrity commissioners, as in Ontario, is part of the answer. Quebec's centralized, yet accessible, ethics tribunal system presents another template which, over time, may ultimately have more traction. Both are relatively informal systems that provide a more useful and accessible framework than court-based systems. Whatever method ultimately evolves, it must be nurtured, and its commissioners protected, through such classic means as ensuring security of tenure, providing liability insurance coverage for the commissioners, and indemnification for any damages not covered by the insurance.

There are indeed problems to be sorted out — problems in behaviours, in rules and in enforcement of rules, and in the approaches to creating and enforcing rules. To be sure, conflict of interest remains an issue, and its definition must be expanded at the local level. The panoply of misbehaviours identified in various codes also needs elaboration.

Codes themselves need greater clarity and need, more importantly, to become part of the cultures of municipal government. Over-reliance on codes and extreme codification, that is, attempting to detail every potential misbehaviour and all the conditions leading to it, would not be sensible. But we are a long way away from that. The best codes have some detail and some explanation, and these are the codes that should be held up as examples.[85] Codes, though, are not enough. The long struggle ahead is about embracing fair play and genuinely embracing the principles of democracy, as outlined in the first three chapters of this book. Of course, this is a timeless struggle, but there are immediate concerns as well, because our municipal institutions are threatened by ignorance and malice made worse by new technologies and social media. The formalization of rules is not enough. We need to encourage their cultural adoption and to inculcate a genuine belief in the values underlying democracy.

Whether provincial and municipal governments will muster the courage and determination to create and enhance effective municipal ethics systems remains to be seen. There have been meaningful initiatives and plenty of setbacks. Age old questions of right and wrong will always face those in whom we place our trust. Well-constructed and supported ethics systems have the potential to help those we trust meet the ethical challenges before them.

# CHAPTER 10
# DIRTY HANDS, DECEPTION AND DUPLICITY

## David P. Shugarman and Shaun Young

On September 26, 2002, thirty-two-year-old Maher Arar, a Montreal resident with dual Canadian-Syrian citizenship and degrees in computer engineering and telecommunications, was on a flight back to Canada after vacationing with his family in Tunisia. The trip required two connecting flights, one in Zurich, one in New York. When he landed at New York's JFK airport he was detained by American immigration authorities. A little over a week later, Mr. Arar found himself a shackled captive in Amman, Jordan. Shortly thereafter he was transferred to a Syrian jail, where, in an attempt to prove he was an Al Qaeda operative, he was subjected to constant interrogation, threats and torture for almost a year. The Syrian government ultimately acknowledged that its "investigators" were of the view that Mr. Arar was neither a member of Al Qaeda nor a terrorist threat.

Before he was kidnapped, transferred illegally to another country, unjustly imprisoned and subjected to torture, Mr. Arar had not been charged with any crime by US authorities. He was, rather, the victim of what in US intelligence parlance is known as an "extraordinary rendition," a term that refers to the practice of transferring suspected terrorists to locations outside the purview or jurisdiction of the US legal system where local authorities specialize in torture with the co-operation of US intelligence agencies.

As a result of a rigorous public inquiry into what happened to Mr. Arar and why, Justice Dennis O'Connor, the inquiry's commissioner, concluded, "I am able to say categorically that there is no evidence to indicate that Mr. Arar has committed any offence or that his activities constitute a threat to the security of Canada."[1] After he was finally released by Syrian authorities and returned to Canada, it was discovered that the RCMP had provided the FBI and the CIA with misleading information indicating that Mr. Arar might be an Al Qaeda agent. In the words of Justice O'Connor, "it is very likely that the American authorities relied upon information provided by the RCMP in making the decision to remove Mr. Arar."[2] To repeat, there was never any substance to this allegation.

Complicating matters even further, after Mr. Arar's return to Canada "his torment did not end, as some government officials took it upon themselves to leak information to the media, much of which was unfair to Mr. Arar and damaging to his reputation."[3] As a result of these leaks, media organizations reported that inside sources in government and security circles were saying that Arar was fabricating his claim of being tortured and that there was evidence that he had links to Al Qaeda. As Commissioner O'Connor's investigation showed, these leaks of ostensibly classified information were meant to smear Mr. Arar's reputation. The leaks also were meant to rationalize the actions and interests of those officers who alleged that Mr. Arar was an agent of a terrorist organization. The leaked information was so persuasive that at least one Canadian journalist opined that providing classified information — which was, unknown to the journalist, actually *disinformation* — was justifiable if it was in defence of intelligence agents' good intentions and investigative work. So it is acceptable, from this perspective, to violate strictures on leaking classified information when it is in the interests of intelligence agents or agencies. This defence for breaking rules and laws is quite different from a case in which a whistle-blower leaks confidential information to expose wrongdoing by those in authority. By contrast, justification of spreading misinformation based on good intentions is an open door to the manipulation of opinion and judgment by those occupying privileged positions of power shielded from accountability and transparency. In Commissioner O'Connor's words, "based on this reasoning, since the public does not have access to classified information, leakors can pick and choose what is released to suit their purposes."[4]

There are many disturbing aspects to the Arar story, best set out and best appreciated in Commissioner O'Connor's reports. Here we want to emphasize the particularly dangerous and not uncommon tactics and strategy associated with officials protecting their turf. Innuendo and smear tactics were employed to create further suspicions about Mr. Arar, to mobilize opinion amongst the public and within senior government ranks to discredit him. Both personal needs to cover up mistakes, and institutional priorities were defensively conjoined by these "inside sources," and that involved firing away at the person whose innocence threatened to expose earlier bungling. These efforts were an attempt to eclipse the slipshod way that certain RCMP officers changed their meagre suspicions into what they claimed were probable facts, which were then passed on to American agents leading up to the apprehension of Mr. Arar. What was additionally reinforced and repeated with these leaks were attempts by government officials throughout Mr. Arar's ordeal to provide rationales for the deception involved in his unlawful imprisonment and the cruelty he subsequently suffered. Fortunately, neither the prime minister, nor his Defense Minister during the time of Mr. Arar's imprisonment and release were prepared to accept further attacks on him. Prime Minister Chrétien agreed to set up the public inquiry. Fortunately too, the next PM, Stephen Harper, after considerable negotiations with Mr. Arar's legal team, agreed to an official apology "for any role Canadian officials may have played in what happened to Mr. Arar, Monia Mazigh [Arar's spouse] and their family in 2002 and 2003."[5] The apology was accompanied by a compensatory payment of $10.5 million for his suffering and an additional $1 million for his legal expenses.

Cruelty and deception played a prominent role in the treatment of Maher Arar. When government officials claim these methods are instrumental to the national interest, we find the workings of "dirty hands." In the saga of Maher Arar, our leaders did not succumb to the temptation of dirty hands, but as we will see, that has not always been the case.

## DOING WRONG IN ORDER TO DO RIGHT

Perhaps the most serious challenge to integrity in politics comes when our leaders and their associates believe they are justified in using duplicitous measures and other immoral tactics to accomplish goals that they believe will advance the public good. Such leaders flout laws and moral conventions for the sake of goals they consider to be so important (for example, safeguarding national unity, protecting the security of the state from foreign invasion or subversion, countering terrorist or racist organizations, bolstering confidence in the dollar) that failing to achieve them will result in disaster. The use of deceit, trickery and force has a long tradition in politics and has been justified by a number of thinkers — most notably, the Italian political theorist Niccolo Machiavelli — as necessary for the greater good. In other words, they have argued that it is sometimes necessary to do wrong in order to do right because the ends justify the means.

When lying, breaking promises and concealing the facts are carried out in the name of the public good, the political leaders who commit or authorize and justify such acts are known as politicians with "dirty hands." The image of dirt, which can also be understood to mean blood (that is, someone with blood on his or her hands), conveys the notion that the actor is tainted or guilty of doing something terribly wrong in his or her dealings with others. In this chapter, we will review and criticize the justifications for dirty-handed behaviour. We will consider several famous examples of dirty-handed politics, including Watergate and the Iran-Contra scandal in the US, and the RCMP "dirty tricks" campaign in Canada, and we will argue that there is no justification for such behaviour in a peacetime democracy. We will also draw attention to examples of unethical conduct that have much in common with dirty-handed activities but should nevertheless be seen as markedly different.

As noted in Chapter 9, Machiavelli observed that in the exercise of power,

> Everybody recognizes how praiseworthy it is for a ruler to
> keep his word and to live a life of integrity, without relying
> on craftiness. Nevertheless . . . in practice . . . those rulers who
> have not thought it important to keep their word have achieved
> great things, and have known how to employ cunning to
> confuse and disorientate other men. In the end they have been
> able to overcome those who have placed store in integrity.[6]

Machiavelli was describing Italian politics as he saw it in the sixteenth century. And he made it clear that this context was one of widespread corruption marked by intense factionalism, violence, intrigue and duplicity. But as the preceding quotation makes clear, it is not only when dealing with dishonest opponents that dishonesty is usefully employed. What Machiavelli tells us is that in the real, tough world of politics, honest politicians, like nice guys, often finish last.

In *The Prince*, Machiavelli wasn't satisfied with presenting only a shockingly realistic picture of the struggle for power in his times. He also offered counsel — recommendations and advice — to would-be rulers. And rather than criticize duplicity and ruthless behaviour, or direct leaders to reorient their conduct, Machiavelli counselled more of the same: if people want power they have "to learn how not to be good"[7] because "a wise ruler cannot and should not keep his word when doing so is to his disadvantage." Such a ruler "is often obliged in order to hold on to power, to break his word, to be uncharitable, inhumane, and irreligious . . . [Though] he should do right if he can . . . he must be prepared to do wrong if necessary."[8]

There are various ways of summarizing this extreme version of what is known in political philosophy as consequentialist ethics but which also has much to do with an actor's purposes, intentions and commitments to a cause. Proponents of this philosophy believe it is not what you do to reach a goal, but reaching it that matters. "So if a ruler wins wars and holds on to power," says Machiavelli, "the means he employs will always be judged honorable and everyone will praise him." It is very important to remember that the context in which Machiavelli wrote was unconstrained by constitutional rules or democratic values and procedures. In sixteenth-century Italy, people didn't gain office through democratic elections; they were either handed power or they seized it. Would-be rulers got away with doing nasty things because there was no rule of law. Furthermore, Machiavelli assumes that it is up to these individuals to determine the preferred outcome as well as the means used to achieve it. And when the public is involved, their overwhelming concern is with a politician's success. In the end, the only thing that counts is a successful outcome. As Machiavelli wrote, "in the behaviour of all men, and particularly of rulers, against whom there is no recourse at law, people judge by the outcome."[9]

This is not to say that Machiavelli was uninterested in the nature or the value of these outcomes. There is ample evidence in his writings to indicate that he hoped strong leaders would reduce rampant corruption, establish a system of law and order and rid Italian states of foreign armies and influence. However, he argued that one needs to be in power first to be able to accomplish these worthy goals. The primary goal of any ruler is thus attaining and/or maintaining power. This seems at first glance to be a general truth about all politics and all politicians everywhere and at any time. But, as we shall argue below, the logic involved in both the prescriptive and descriptive elements of Machiavelli's analysis — a logic of the morality of dirty hands — is incompatible with the principles of democracy that inform our own politics. When dirty hands come into play, it is because democratic norms have either been ignored or flouted.

Two characteristics of the "dirty hands" approach to political action need to be emphasized if we are to appreciate its appeal to practitioners and commentators. Both characteristics underlie many peoples' belief that committing dirty deeds is justified in various conditions. First, dirty hands is different from an amoral or cynical "anything goes" approach to politics.[10] The willingness of decision makers to act immorally or illegally stems from the notion that at a certain point, in extreme situations, a different and higher morality takes precedence, one that is especially applicable to the struggle for power and one that trumps all other moral considerations.

Second, the assumption of a higher morality or overriding set of principles is believed to distinguish public life, with its special calling and professional responsibilities, from normal, everyday activity. This distinction is sometimes referred to as the difference between public duties (and public morality) on the one hand, and private duties (and private morality) on the other. Both of these concepts — the notion that some moral principles trump others, and the idea that there are two moralities, public and private — are closely related. The alleged higher morality — which ironically legitimizes committing base acts — is associated with the special duties and more complex ethics that come into play once one enters the realm of politics.

## MODERN MACHIAVELLIANS: POLITICS AS WAR

Over the past five hundred years a long list of political thinkers and actors have subscribed to Machiavelli's views. Modern Machiavellians view the obligation to "do wrong in order to do what is right" as an ethical paradox or dilemma, one that lies at the heart of politics and which has to be confronted by any conscientious, responsible leader. The dirty-hands position seems to have no single ideological home. It has been advocated by left-wingers, right-wingers and those in the centre of the political spectrum. "All means are good when they're effective," says Hoederer, a central character in Jean-Paul Sartre's aptly named play, *Dirty Hands*.[11] Hoederer is the leader of a Communist party in an East

European state emerging from the carnage of the Second World War. He is a modern-day Machiavelli who boldly articulates a justification for dirty hands. He contends that in the struggle to achieve worthy, desired ends, any leaders worth their salt will have to get their hands not only dirty but bloody. Only infantile idealists and the indecisive think they can govern innocently.

In the early twentieth century, the German political sociologist Max Weber (generally considered a liberal for his time) argued that, because "the decisive means for politics is violence," a special kind of morality must be applied to politicians: They must, in Weber's words, "be willing to pay the price of using morally dubious means, [even] dangerous ones" that could have "evil ramifications."[12]

Communist revolutionary and theorist Leon Trotsky took the position that all measures that united the revolutionary working class and contributed to advancing the goal of liberation were not only "permissible" but "obligatory."[13] An almost identical rationale was set out by Barry Goldwater, the Republican Party's 1964 American presidential candidate. In his acceptance speech at the Republican convention, Goldwater proclaimed that "extremism in the defense of liberty is no vice." Here in other words is the view that there is a world of difference between "their" morality and "ours." And because "theirs" is criminally deficient and dangerous (really a bogus morality), "we" can do anything to make ours triumphant.[14]

Though he was ridiculed by his Democratic opponents, Goldwater accurately summed up the mentality that informed American foreign policy throughout the Cold War. This dirty-hands mentality also figured significantly in the Vietnam War. As David Halberstram pointed out in his book on the Kennedy and Johnson presidencies, a central component of their thinking during the Cold War was

> the idea that force justified force. The other side did it and
> so we would do it; reality called for meeting dirty tricks
> with dirty tricks. Since covert operations were part of the

> game, over a period of time there was in the high levels of the
> bureaucracy, particularly as the CIA became more powerful,
> a gradual acceptance of covert operations and dirty tricks as
> part of normal diplomatic-political maneuvering.[15]

Since the September 11, 2001, terrorist hijacking of passenger jets and attacks on the World Trade Center in New York and the Pentagon in Washington, many liberal democracies have bolstered their security apparatuses in ways that reflect the mentality and tactics of the Cold War, but with a new emphasis on electronic surveillance. The reach of such covert surveillance is formidable, intrusive and growing. Making sure that Canada's various security agencies conduct such surveillance in accordance with statutory provisions and the *Charter of Rights* is of great importance. There are highly trained, bright, sincere and well-intentioned people working in these agencies who are convinced that the things they are doing to discover and counter terrorist networks are in the country's best interests; they are protecting us against the enemy. So if too much information is inappropriately gathered, if domestic communications and activities are improperly collected and shared with other governments, if sometimes incomplete or badly misinterpreted information is transmitted to allies, these can all be treated as "inadvertent" or as unfortunate complications stemming from allegedly "necessary" crossings of legal lines for the right reasons. We will return to discuss further the ethical issues that bear on developments in the security field later in the chapter.

At this point it is important to draw attention to the tendency to slide from monitoring foreign threats to intrusively spying on one's own citizenry. In fact, Machiavelli drew no distinction between the politics of one realm and the politics of the other. As we have seen, thinkers and politicians as different as Trotsky, Weber, Hoederer, Kennedy, Johnson and Goldwater all share Machiavelli's perspective on the essential demands of statecraft. So too do ostensibly democratic theorists like American political scientist Michael Walzer, who declares that "the men who act for us and in our name are often killers," and who claims that the defining characteristic of a moral politician is that he has dirty hands and knows it.[16]

Now, if we accept this perspective we must concede that politics is more often than not another name for war and the politician a warrior. This view has clear implications, for, as Thomas Hobbes stated almost four hundred years ago, "force and fraud, are in war the two cardinal virtues."[17] So, according to the tough-minded adherents of dirty-hands strategy, only those willing and able to use these "virtues" as tools have what it takes to attain their goals. A skillful politician will know how and when to fight dirty against an unscrupulous opponent. If politics is often a dirty game, then even good politicians will have to get their hands dirty if they want to bring about desired ends. And getting dirty involves a wide ambit of action: misleading all or some of the public, lying, concealing information, breaking promises, flouting the law, using and abusing individuals or entire groups of people and killing. Some or all of these acts are not only acceptable to those who advocate the use of dirty hands, they need to be done, given particular situations, and therefore, ought to be done. They are morally right because they bring about a great good or prevent disasters. And the great good outweighs and compensates for the deviousness and the harm some people are subjected to along the way.

The trouble with this perspective is that force and deception are not tools of democratic politics; they are tactics and strategies in warfare. When politicians start dirtying their hands, they have abandoned their democratic sensibilities and succumbed to the protective/aggressive instincts and ruthless determination of embattled warriors. Their behaviour is a consequence of the breakdown of politics or the absence of conditions and processes of democratic practice.[18]

Let's look at some of the forms that a dirty-hands approach takes. Several of these examples were in the 1997 edition of *Honest Politics*, but because they are necessary for an appreciation of the dangers of using dirty-handed tactics, they bear repeating. While this is a book about Canadian politics, some of the examples that follow are from the United States.

There are several reasons for this. First, Watergate and Iran-Contra are classic cases of dirty-handed thinking and practice. Second, it is no secret that Canada's intelligence-gathering networks and security services have long had a close working relationship with their American counterparts and have been greatly influenced by US policies and priorities. Third, like so many things American, trends in campaign styles and tactics are often imitated by Canadian strategists. Finally, the American examples provide us with a useful reminder of what we should avoid in our political culture.

## EXIGENCIES OF WAR

As the following examples show, dirty-handed tactics are often used in war:

- An advance squad is ordered into an area to draw enemy fire and faces almost certain death — though they aren't told this is highly probable — but this allows a large battalion to take up an advantageous position elsewhere and also permits headquarters to pinpoint the whereabouts of enemy positions for air strikes. Consequently, some soldiers are sacrificed for a "good cause." The tragedy of the Canadian army's Dieppe raid comes to mind in this context: on August 19, 1942, five thousand men of the 2nd Canadian Infantry were sent across the English Channel to land on the shores near Dieppe, a small city on the northwest coast of France. The point of the raid was to test the German defence installations. Within nine hours, over nine hundred Canadian soldiers were killed and almost two thousand were forced to surrender. From the perspective of Allied planners, this sacrifice was necessary because of what could be learned. Generals dirtied their hands with their soldiers' blood. War historians have argued about the reasons for the debacle, but many have held the view that the lessons learned from the failed assault did prove helpful in later amphibious attacks, especially the D-Day landings of June 6, 1944.

- Despite the fact that America's military had virtually defeated the Japanese by the late summer of 1945, in August of that year US planes dropped atomic bombs on two militarily insignificant cities, Hiroshima and Nagasaki, in order, purportedly, to force the unconditional surrender of Japan to end the Second World War and avoid losing thousands of American soldiers in a ground invasion; so, incinerating hundreds of thousands of Japanese civilians was regrettable but "worth it" (though clearly not to the Japanese populations of those cities).

These examples apply cost-benefit calculations to dirty-hands situations and deliberations. It is a cost-benefit analysis that rationalizes ruthlessness and deception; it sacrifices principles and people to higher causes. The classic examples come from war.

In these cases, of course, the people who pay the costs — with their lives — are not involved in the decisions affecting them. This is war, after all, not democracy. The enemy is not invited to participate in decision making, nor are one's own soldiers. Nevertheless, so long as they are mindful of the criteria for a just war on one hand and what constitutes just conduct *in* war on the other (though there is room for disagreement, and of course pacifists would reject both categories), there will be times in extreme situations like Dieppe and Hiroshima when leaders may be justified in authorizing covert operations, deception, concealment and the use of force that may unavoidably harm innocents, non-combatants, and even their own civilian and military population.

## DIRTY CAMPAIGNING

Election campaigns that resort to false promises, tricks and negative advertising provide further examples of dirty-hands: The metaphor of war is unfortunately easy to apply to election campaigns "the battle for the ballot" involves "mobilizing" workers and supporters, pits one side's "troops" against the other's, and provides "ammunition" (that is, excuses and arguments) for denigrating and duping the enemy, while concealing a party's real intentions.

## Making False Promises

An all-too-common dirty-handed manoeuvre is to promise to do one thing during an election campaign and then do the opposite once elected:

- Lyndon Johnson campaigned for the US presidency in 1964 by claiming that he was committed to peace, in contrast to his opponent, who would immerse America in war. All the while his administration was planning to escalate the war in Vietnam, which it did shortly after Johnson's victory.

- Pierre Trudeau campaigned against wage and price controls in the 1974 federal election, only to introduce them within months of being re-elected.

- Brian Mulroney treated free trade with the United States as a non-issue in his 1984 campaign. He explicitly dismissed it, only to embrace it once in office.

- The Liberal Party, when in opposition during the early 1990s, continually berated the Conservatives for introducing the GST and indicated that the tax would go if they were elected. After becoming the governing party they contended that there was no viable alternative to the GST, though it might be improved through harmonization with provincial sales taxes.

- The first NDP government in Ontario history decided a public automobile insurance system was off their agenda within a year of making it a central plank in their election campaign.

Having convinced themselves of the importance of their goals, politicians may often sincerely believe that their election is in the public interest; and so they lie, "justifiably" and with good intentions, assuming that the truth is too complex for the voter or that a different position (the one they really hold) is not yet acceptable but will be eventually.

In opposition to this line of reasoning, American philosopher and ethicist Sissela Bok's critical comment on Lyndon Johnson's deception about Vietnam applies as well to Trudeau's phony campaign against wage and price controls, Mulroney's misleading comments on free trade prospects, Chrétien's attack on the Tory GST policy and Bob Rae's skittish commitment to a government-run auto insurance system. As Bok wrote,

> Deception of this kind strikes at the very essence of democratic government. It allows those in power to override or nullify the right vested in the people to cast an informed vote in critical elections. Deceiving the people for the sake of the people is a self-contradictory notion in a democracy, unless it can be shown that there has been genuine consent to deceit.[19]

In times of war, it is arguable that citizens in a democracy will expect their government and military command to conceal many things, engage in covert activities and deceive their own citizens when such actions are necessary to deceive an enemy. And in peacetime, citizens accept (that is, consent to) police use of unmarked cars and radar traps to catch speeders and stakeouts to monitor and prevent criminal activities. But the false promises made by politicians referred to above are all examples of a party's posture during a democratic election when people expect to make decisions on the basis of what a party is committing itself to do if elected. The idea that in each of these cases the electorate was somehow complicit in an elaborate con game orchestrated by the political parties is difficult to fathom. The proposition that it is democratic for citizens to disenfranchise themselves by suspending their critical decision-making rights and capacities is logically and practically incoherent. It is tantamount to saying that as an expression of their freedom, free persons will voluntarily submit themselves to slavery. "Democratic dirty hands," like "free slaves," *is* an oxymoron, but ethical politics is not.

The law of contracts does not apply to political promises, so a failure to honour political commitments is not illegal, just immoral. Under our political rules the only recourse "betrayed" voters have is to wait until the next election to punish a government that breaks its promises. In the meantime, however, issues may change, the party has an opportunity to fudge its policies again and it may offer retroactive excuses for why it changed its position. The comment of a Liberal cabinet minister on Sheila Copps's victory in a Hamilton by-election provides an example. The by-election was held because Copps was embarrassed into resigning by an earlier pledge to keep the Goods and Services Tax (GST). Without offering any evidence to back her up, Revenue Minister Jane Stewart said Copps's victory was another indication that "Canadians are beginning to realize the G.S.T. is a necessary evil."[20]

The examples of politicians reneging on their promises or simply making false ones show how elected officials can thumb their noses at the electorate. Parties tend to espouse issues that have considerable resonance with voters who want clear alternatives, but party leaders may not really be committed to implementing the alternatives in the first place. Even if we assume they are motivated by public-spiritedness — that they break their promises because they genuinely believe that keeping them won't benefit the public or that they believe *their* governing, rather than that of another party, is best for the country — it still amounts to double dealing and scorn for the democratic process. Indulging in bogus promises purportedly in the interests of the people is almost always a deception that serves only the interests of the party or party leaders. For example, in mid-February 2017, PM Justin Trudeau announced that his government was taking electroral reform off its agenda. During his successful election campaign in 2015 he maintained that the country needed a more just, more proportionately representative alternative to Canada's long-standing, single-member, simple plurality (also known as first-past-the-post) system. Mr. Trudeau promised that the 2105 federal election would be the last ever held using the simple plurality system. Cynical commentators contend this promise was simply a ruse to attract progressive voters. Others suggest that the implications of the promise were never carefully thought through. Either way, there was an ethical lapse.

## Deceptive and Negative Advertising

Political advertising in the mass media and especially on television has become a central feature of election campaigns. While alerting voters to the disastrous consequences they will face if they elect the wrong party has long been a staple of electoral tactics, a new emphasis has recently developed on deceptive and negative advertising that exaggerates the other party's or party leader's failings. It is in keeping with a dirty-hands approach to electoral competition.

In the 1988 American presidential election, George Bush's campaign team created posters and TV ads stating that his opponent, Michael Dukakis, "opposed virtually every weapons system developed." The Bush organization also ran a series of television ads that carefully juxtaposed words and pictures to imply that Dukakis as governor of Massachusetts granted furloughs to 268 first-degree murderers who went out to rape and kidnap. As Kathleen Jamieson points out in her study of deceptive campaigning in America, these were patently false claims, and Bush's team knew it. Dukakis's campaign ran ads indicating that Bush had voted to "cut" Social Security, which was also untrue.[21] During the 2016 presidential election campaign, Donald Trump, having several years earlier contributed significantly to the lie that President Obama hadn't been born in America and thus held the office illegitimately, maintained that his Democratic opponent, Hillary Clinton, would also be an illegitimate occupier of the office. In speech after speech Trump kept saying that Mrs. Clinton belonged in jail because she used her email in criminal ways when she was Secretary of State. He also said that he saw on TV Arabs in New Jersey celebrating when the twin towers in Manhattan were destroyed by terrorists in 2001; that the Democrats were rigging the election; and that an unidentified "they" in Mexico were sending "their" rapists, killers and drug dealers to the US. All of these allegations were put out by Mr. Trump in support of his claim that he alone could save America from "dangerous" Mexicans and Muslims and he alone understood the dangers of foreign threats. Not a shred of evidence supporting these allegations was ever produced. Mrs. Clinton was never charged with anything. Adding to his litany of lies, Mr. Trump, who was elected through the US's electoral college system despite Mrs. Clinton receiving almost three million more votes across the nation, claimed that he "knew" that his opponent garnered more votes only because millions of people voted illegally through rigged voter fraud. Again, no evidence for this allegation was produced by Mr. Trump, his campaign team, a single reputable media source or any law enforcement agency.

However, Canadians need to be wary of becoming comfortably self-righteous about how our campaign strategies play out in contrast to those of our southern neighbour. In the Canadian general election of 1993, the Tories ran a television ad that focused attention on former Liberal leader Jean Chrétien's face. As a result of a childhood disease, one side of his mouth drooped. The Tory ad implied that electors couldn't trust a man who looked like that. And early in 2017, as a result of investigative media exposure, it was revealed that Nick Kouvalis, the campaign manager for the Conservative Party leadership hopeful Kellie Leitch, had tweeted falsehoods about the Justin Trudeau Liberals pouring "billions" of dollars into international aid organizations and giving three hundred and fifty million dollars to a designated international terrorist organization. Mr. Kouvalis subsequently admitted he was spreading the lies to provoke and divide left-wing supporters of the

Liberals.[22] In this example, it is important to emphasize, the media's revelations were not about the disreputable antics of a minor backroom political organizer. In addition to managing Kellie Leitch's campaign for the Conservative leadership, the activities of Mr. Kouvalis as a political operative included engineering successful campaigns for two Toronto mayors (Rob Ford and John Tory), and advising the premier of B.C. on her re-election planning.

Normal regulations and laws against false advertising and defamatory statements don't apply to political campaigning, so these ads are not illegal, but they are certainly sleazy. They show that at least some key members of election campaign teams are so bent on winning that they will authorize any misleading and negative publicity — however inaccurate or unfair — that they think will garner votes. One positive result of the Conservatives' negative advertising attack on Chrétien was that it proved counterproductive. Hundreds of thousands of Canadian voters, including many Tory politicians, were so disgusted by the cruel and shameful attempt at character assassination that the ad was pulled within days of its appearance. And the positive results of investigative journalist's reporting on Mr. Kouvalis's deceptive practices were his admission of the wrongs he engaged in and his exit from the campaigns he was helping direct. In addition, he apologized for calling an academic a traitor to Canada because the latter criticized Ms. Leitch's campaign for focusing on the alleged dangers associated with welcoming Muslim refugees and immigrants.

## Dirty Tricks and Watergate

The Watergate scandal is a dramatic example of how a dirty-hands mentality, the sense that one is in a war that must be won at all costs, infected US domestic politics, and especially the Republican Party's campaign strategy. Watergate led to a demand for President Richard Nixon's impeachment, and it ultimately resulted in his resignation.

Soon after he took office in 1968, Nixon and his top advisors became concerned that government documents and strategies relating to the war in Vietnam had been leaked to the press. To counter these leaks, they set up their own intelligence-gathering unit called "the plumbers." A former National Security Council advisor named Daniel Ellsberg had released hundreds of pages of documents, later known as the Pentagon Papers, that added up to a history of government obfuscation regarding the war. In an effort to smear Ellsberg's reputation, the plumbers broke into the office of his psychiatrist. They were after medical records that might tarnish Ellsberg's credibility. The enemy was no longer the Soviet Union and their "proxies" but other Americans.

In fact, the Nixon White House had drawn up an "enemies list" comprised of prominent Americans who were actively involved in mobilizing opposition to the war and to the Nixon administration. It wasn't long before the targeted enemy became the opposition Democratic Party. The plumbers were therefore authorized to break in to the party's national headquarters (located in the Watergate office building) and plant listening devices so they could find out what the enemy was up to. But the break-in was botched, and the plumbers were caught in the Democratic offices and arrested by Washington police on June 17, 1972.

Just four days after the plumbers were caught, President Nixon told his chief of staff that he didn't think there would be an uproar across the country. "Breaking and entering" said Nixon (on the audio tapes confiscated from his office), "is not a helluva lot of crime." Furthermore, he said that "most of the people" would not be outraged by "the Republican committee trying to bug the Democratic Headquarters" because they would "think that . . . this is routine — that everybody's trying to bug everyone else: it's politics."[23] In other words, Nixon felt that Americans believed it was normal and acceptable for all parties to use dirty tricks to get elected. He was wrong. He was forced to resign and almost all his lieutenants involved in the plumbers' activities were disgraced and sent to jail.

Despite the Nixon administration's notoriety and the heightened concern about ethical conduct on the part of senior decision makers in the US government, the dirty-hands defence resurfaced with President Reagan's administration involvement in the Iran-Contra affair in the 1980s, which is a case study we will come to shortly.

## FOR REASONS OF STATE AND NATIONAL SECURITY

The term "reason of state" (in French, *raison d'etat*) refers to the idea that the interests of the state, especially its national security, are the first priority for political leaders and therefore come before all other moral considerations. This argument is often adopted by prime ministers, presidents and defence ministers to maintain state secrecy and covert operations; it also serves those associated with spy agencies as a ready justification for their activities, no matter how morally questionable they may be. It can be too easily aligned with Machiavellian dirty-hands practices.

### RCMP Dirty Tricks and their Aftermath

Around the same time as Watergate, and two decades before the Iran-Contra affair, the RCMP's Security Service was operating very much along the lines first followed by Nixon's plumbers and later by Oliver North and his associates in the Iran-Contra affair (which we discuss below). Over a period of approximately five years beginning in the early 1970s — but in a few instances stretching back to the 1950s — our national police force committed a long list of dirty-handed illegal acts.

This was a time of considerable anxiety on the part of government security agencies and conservative forces in society in general. The 1960s in North America had been marked by the Black civil rights movement, mounting protests against the war in Vietnam, an anti-nuclear weapons consciousness, campus radicalism and the development of articulate and militant student groups, including anarchists and socialists, demanding major social change. Many of these movements had offshoots in Canada, and in addition, many Canadians became critical of what they saw as American imperialism and the Americanization of Canada's culture, economy and foreign policy. A left-wing segment of the NDP, known as the Waffle, called for an independent and socialist Canada and received considerable coverage in the media and on campuses across the country; some left-wing magazines and radical activists spoke about the need for an extra-parliamentary opposition, given what they regarded as the conservative nature of parliamentary parties and the truncated nature of participation offered by traditional electoral politics. On top of all this, Quebec nationalism was becoming a powerful force, and a small but articulate — and in a few instances violent — portion of the nationalist movement was agitating for a socialist revolution. In October 1970, two small cells of the Front de Liberation du Quebec (FLQ) whose membership didn't number much more than those of the two cells, kidnapped first James Cross, the British trade commissioner in Montreal, and then Pierre Laporte, a cabinet minister in the Quebec government. Laporte was subsequently murdered by his kidnappers.

In response to these events and movements, Canadian security forces decided to "protect" Canada in much the same way the conspirators involved in Watergate and Iran-Contra sought to defend America. Here are some examples of their protection:

- In a joint operation, officers from the Quebec Provincial Police, the Montreal Police force and the RCMP broke into the offices of a left-wing news agency in Montreal and stole various documents and files.

- The RCMP broke into offices containing Parti Québécois membership lists and financial information where they copied and removed some material.

- The RCMP's criminal investigations branch conducted about four hundred break-ins without warrants, mainly in B.C.

- The RCMP spied on the NDP, the Waffle and other left-wing movements and placed operatives on campuses.

- The force electronically bugged MPs. The most famous incident was the bugging of the solicitor-general, who was responsible for the RCMP.

- In contravention of the *Post Office Act*, hundreds of pieces of mail were opened by security investigators.

- Several agents burned down a barn that they believed was a meeting place for radicals.

- Some officers stole dynamite.

- Security personnel engaged in a campaign of disinformation by sending out phony communiques with false signatures of Quebec radicals that were calculated to incite other radicals to violence.

- When trying to recruit informers, officers used threats and force to get co-operation.

- They obtained confidential medical files on various left-wing leaders to spread rumours about their mental stability.

- They organized surveillance of almost all candidates running for election.

- The force was found to be in possession of papers that had been stolen from a left-wing Toronto research organization called Praxis, which had its offices broken into and torched in December 1970. Seven years later, a Tory backbencher revealed that the Canadian government in the early 1970s — much like the Nixon government

— had compiled an enemies list of twenty-four people
who were associated with a so-called extra-parliamentary
opposition. The list had apparently been based on names
found in the Praxis files. To this day the break-in and
arson remain unsolved.

• The force had a paid informant in a neo-Nazi Toronto
organization called the Western Guard. The informant
did more than inform; he took an active role in a swastika
painting and window smashing series of raids on offices
and homes of Jews and communists.[24]

In response to considerable pressure from the media and opposition parties after some of these operations became public, the Pierre
Trudeau Liberals established The Royal Commission of Inquiry into
Certain Activities of the RCMP, which soon became known as the
McDonald Commission. The inquiry found that our security force
shared the same kind of siege mentality that was exhibited by American administrations and intelligence agencies during the Cold War.
The inquiry also drew attention to RCMP officers' dismissive attitude
towards complying with the law: they did so without compunction
whenever they were convinced that the justness of their cause — getting the bad guys — required ignoring legalities. When the former chief
of security services in Quebec testified before the commission he said
his officers were accustomed to breaking the law in order to protect the
country. "We were used to living with certain illegalities. They were so
commonplace they were no longer thought of as illegal." When he was
asked by one of the commissioners how he felt about breaking the law,
the officer replied that one either "betrays one's duty to protect the public
or break[s] the law."[25]

What was clearly lacking in the training and standards of the force
and what also seemed neglected by the force's political masters was
a serious appreciation of the rule of law. In 1969, Mr. Justice Bora

Laskin, in a unanimous judgment of the Ontario Court of Appeal, declared that

> the recognition of 'public duty' to excuse breach of the criminal law by policemen would involve a drastic departure from constitutional precepts . . . Legal immunity from prosecution for breaches of the law by the very persons charged with the public duty of enforcement would subvert that public duty.[26]

One very practical and central problem that surfaced in the investigation of RCMP dirty tricks was the dilemma a police officer faces when asked to carry out orders that require laws to be broken: The officer is subject to internal discipline if an order is disobeyed and liable to prosecution for a criminal offence if it is obeyed. This appears to be a classic case of a professional being caught between a rock and a hard place in trying to discharge public duties.

In 1980, the Canadian Bar Association tried to address the issue of an officer's duty when confronted with orders to commit dirty deeds: "The solution to the dilemma is not to give an immunity to prosecution for obedience to orders. The solution is to give immunity from disciplinary action for obedience to the law."[27] The association's recommendation is as pertinent for whistle-blowers, moral politicians and honest cops today as it was then.

Yet an examination of the incidents of RCMP wrongdoing indicates that practically none of the Mounties found it difficult to extricate themselves from the dilemma addressed by the Bar Association. And this was apparently the case because they didn't think there really was much of a dilemma. There was no evidence that any Mounties either questioned or refused orders that involved law breaking. A Mountie who was involved in the 1972 barn burning proudly told the McDonald Commission of Inquiry that he and his fellow undercover officers did what they did because "the ends justified the means at that time."

The conviction that their actions were right (even though illegal) was reinforced by the general understanding that involvement in such activities would not hurt one's career. To the contrary, there were numerous examples of officers being promoted for carrying out their orders.

So one of the prime inducements as well as one of the seductive traps of dirty-handed activity by intelligence officers and security personnel is the opportunity to combine career security with national security, personal interest with the national interest. The same Mountie who offered the Machiavellian dirty-hands rationale told the McDonald Commission that most of his comrades who were involved in surreptitious activities continued to have very good careers.

It is in the interest of both the officer giving the orders and subordinates carrying them out to conceal their activities not only from the targets of their skullduggery but from the purview of any impartial third party. They believed that what they were doing was in the public interest, so the deception and concealment were also justified.

The parallel with politicians and especially those with cabinet-level powers, is close. A politician who refuses to go along with her party when it lies or makes false promises has to choose between fidelity to principles of integrity and democratic accountability or loyalty to her party. If she chooses the former she risks party discipline, exclusion from the caucus and losing the opportunity to run for the party again. If she is a cabinet minister she risks betraying cabinet solidarity and being stripped of her portfolio. Again, if she can be convinced by colleagues that the motives for lying or other breaches of integrity are "good" ones because the public good will be advanced, then she may still feel troubled but also righteous about the regrettably necessary, unpleasant thing(s) done.

It is true that politicians have public duties that the rest of us don't have. They make laws, we don't; they can instruct police to carry machine guns rather than pistols, we can't; they can authorize a government intelligence agency to eavesdrop on our email, telephone conversations, even our talk around the dinner table and in the bedroom;

they can pass or revoke laws that reward companies that specialize in strike-breaking; they can exclude or permit the hiring of replacement workers when unions are on strike; they decide whether highway patrols will use photo radar to catch speeders or not; whether there will or won't be inspections of the safety of the vehicles we drive and the food and water we consume; if bridges and roads are constructed and maintained; whether the taxation rules are progressive or regressive; and if our health-care system is functioning properly. What this should tell us is that public officials have a greater — not lesser — responsibility to be scrupulously honest with citizens than most of us have in our day-to-day dealings because their actions affect far more people and are authoritative, and because they have a trust to uphold.

Despite all the revelations brought to light by two commissions of inquiry into RCMP dirty tricks (one set up by the Province of Quebec known as the Keable inquiry, the other being the federal government's royal commission that we've referred to as the McDonald inquiry), neither the solicitor general, at that time the minister responsible for the RCMP, nor a single member of the federal cabinet felt obliged to resign; nor was one asked to do so by the prime minister. Instead, the politicians in charge either claimed ignorance of RCMP wrongdoing or implied that in trying to deal with potential threats to national security members of the security forces might have erred slightly on the side of overzealous — which was excusable given the circumstances — but otherwise were doing the job they were meant to do.

A number of senior RCMP officers testified that they believed they were doing what the government of the day wanted and expected them to do, although there may have been no explicit instructions to that effect. When faced with the Trudeau government's stubborn refusal to take responsibility for the huge number and succession of dirty tricks, the McDonald Royal Commission blamed the security force for getting out of control.

Nevertheless, in a clear admission that something was terribly wrong with the direction of Canada's security service, on July 14, 1984, the

Trudeau government replaced the RCMP Security Service with a civilian agency, the Canadian Security Intelligence Service (CSIS). In an attempt to avoid a repetition of RCMP errors and to keep the security service under control, the *CSIS Act* mandated a review agency, the Security Intelligence Review Committee (SIRC), and another monitoring office, the Office of the Inspector-General, to conduct investigations and review CSIS activities.

Since its establishment, CSIS has had its mandate considerably expanded, especially as a result of the *Anti-terrorism Act* of 2015. That act now empowers CSIS to *disrupt* threats from abroad and, when necessary, even on foreign soil. What that means is that a civilian intelligence-gathering agency created to separate its function from police and quasi-military activities has now been given police and quasi-military powers. One of its review institutions, the inspector general, has been abolished, and it now reports to the Minister of Public Safety and Emergency Preparedness. Our intelligence service has now become an intelligence *force,* and it remains to be seen if dirty-tricks campaigns will return. The responsibilities and pressures on the SIRC and the Minister of Public Safety and Emergency Preparedness to see that that does not happen are considerable.

Recently, Canadians have learned through investigative journalism and reports by our SIRC and the Office of the Communications Security Establishment Commissioner (OCSEC) that two of our major security agencies have been engaged in serious abuses of their power. CSIS collected taxpayers' confidential filings from the Canada Revenue Agency without obtaining warrants, and subsequently misled the Minister of Public Safety and Emergency Preparedness that it had destroyed all improperly obtained material, though it still had the data on file.[28] And in its annual report of 2015 the OCSEC revealed that our major cryptology agency, the Communications Security Establishment (CSE), unlawfully transferred metadata that could provide personal identification of Canadians' phone calls and online activities to a number of intelligence services among our allies. CSE authorities claimed that the problem had to do with a failure of the software that was supposed to eliminate the possibility of exposing Canadians' identities.[29]

It is no surprise that organizations like the RCMP, CSIS and CSE have expertise in deception; that, after all, is a key facet of their calling. They are there to crack codes and communications of potential threats, and they are continually working on encryptions to prevent the hacking, penetration, disruption and possible destruction of Canadian communications and institutions. We may be moving into a political and security environment where there are inconspicuous closed-circuit television cameras on every block and in every building, listening devices able to access any phone, and electronic surveillance techniques capable of monitoring every email and all uses of the internet. In such an environment, a return to a Cold War mentality could well mean that those who hold unorthodox views and dissenting opinions on issues of public policy, especially those at odds with security agencies, will be treated as subversive, and subjected to harassment and worse. What is additionally worrisome is that these agencies, or agents within them, may be so zealous at pursuing their goals and so good at deception that they will believe it is in Canada's interests to ignore their political masters, be duplicitous with their watchdog committees and judicial authorities and find ways to get around the law. In the autumn of 2002 a Toronto lawyer named Rocco Galati managed to get CSIS to admit that it had been spying on his communications with two of his clients for at least a decade, a clear violation of solicitor-client privilege. It is not clear that either the SIRC or the Minister of Public Safety and Emergency Preparedness knew or did anything about these violations.

Also vexing is the fact that watchdog agencies may be headed by people with highly dubious qualifications. In 2004 a former Tory cabinet minister, Chuck Strahl, was appointed by the prime minister as the chair of the SIRC. Mr. Strahl, who had little background in intelligence work or the committee's responsibilities prior to his appointment, resigned after two years when it was revealed that he was a lobbyist for Enbridge's Northern Gateway Pipeline project while CSIS was involved in the surveillance of environmental groups and First Nations who opposed the pipeline. Strahl's immediate predecessor, Dr. Arthur Porter, also had to resign when it became public knowledge that he had close ties to a notorious foreign arms dealer; shortly after his resignation and move to the Bahamas, Porter was charged with numerous counts of fraud and other crimes by Quebec's anti-corruption unit. At the time of writing, Justin Trudeau's Liberal government was preparing legislation for the creation of a parliamentary security committee that will have powers to review a number of major intelligence services and report to either the prime minister, the Minister for Public Safety and Emergency Preparedness, or both. Clearly the onus is on elected leaders to see to it that our security agencies are attentive and efficient and not permitted to engage in dirty tricks — as CSIS did in the Heritage Front affair in 1994, which was discussed in the 1997 edition of *Honest Politics* — or thumb their noses at civil liberties and assume that citizens are the enemy. With respect to the Iran-Contra affair, to which we now turn, elected leaders either authorized, condoned or appeared to look away as illegalities were egregiously committed and dirty hands were active.

## The Iran-Contra Scandal

Between 1984 and 1986 key figures in the Reagan administration were secretly involved in activities that contravened congressional stipulations and Reagan's own stated policies. The president's national security advisor, Admiral John Poindexter, and Poindexter's assistant, Lieutenant Colonel Oliver North, with the co-operation of the director of the CIA and various agents, organized a scheme to sell arms to Iran in exchange for the release of Americans who had been kidnapped in Lebanon by Iranian-backed terrorists. They also organized the channelling of funds from the arms sales and other sources to support rebels in Nicaragua (called "Contras" because they were against the left-wing Sandinista government, which the US opposed).

The first part of the scheme was clearly at odds with President Reagan's public condemnation of Iran as a terrorist nation and his efforts to get Congress to pass a law forbidding the sale of arms to Iran. And the second part, the financial and military support of the Contras, violated an explicit congressional ban on such activities.

Once the conspiracy was exposed and the principal actors in the covert operations were subjected to congressional investigations and criminal indictments, many commentators were surprised at how brazen North and Poindexter were in maintaining the justness of their deceit. On a number of occasions, North indicated that lying was second nature to anyone involved in covert actions. In testimony before one of the congressional hearings into Iran-Contra, North declared that

> it is very important . . . to understand that this is a dangerous world; that we live at risk and that this nation is at risk in a dangerous world . . . By their very nature covert operations are a lie. There is great deception practiced . . . [and] the effort to conduct these covert operations was made in such a way that our adversaries would not have knowledge of them or that we could deny American association with it, or the association of this government with those activities. And that is not wrong.[30]

Asked if the operations weren't also designed to be kept from Americans, North replied that this was the only way they could be kept from the enemy. And when he was asked how he could defend his actions in terms of democratic principles, his response echoed the rationale of the Nixon White House during the Watergate scandal: he did it, he said, "because we have had incredible leaks, from discussions with closed committees of the Congress." In other words, anyone outside a tight circle of committed loyalists and specialists in deception was suspect. Summing up the rationale for the operation, North stated that "we had to weigh in the balance the difference between lies and lives." And in response to congressional committees, and later when he defended himself against twelve criminal charges in a jury trial, North offered the defence of a dutiful soldier: He was properly following orders from his superiors and everything he did was authorized from above.[31]

When professional liars like North are put on the defensive, they claim that if people only understood their motives better and the situations with which they have to deal, they would be viewed as great patriots having to spread noble lies. They ask that we defer to their judgment and trust them. The trouble with their claims, unfortunately, is that the very nature of their arguments and practices prevent the public from evaluating the seriousness of the situation or worthiness of the motives, means or goals. And we are being asked to trust those who are masters of deception. An appeal for trust is difficult to uphold when it comes from such a source.

There is an additional factor that came to light in the Iran-Contra machinations: Though the individuals and companies that fronted the trading made profits of $16 million, curiously, only about $4 million was funnelled to the Contras. It is not unfair to infer that in this case dirty hands found their way into pockets filled with money, thus casting additional doubt on the supposed nobility of the cause.

On sound democratic grounds, citizens should be wary of deferring to bureaucratic, political or policy elites, because such people find it easy to treat their own particular interests as equivalent to the general interest. Their cause — getting re-elected, securing immunity from public scrutiny and immunity from criminal investigations — is seen to be at one with the nation's cause. "The freer they are from public scrutiny and public judgment," notes Robert Dahl, "the more likely they are to be corrupted" by the exercise of power.[32] Dahl adds that the corruption is not necessarily venal. But as was the case in the Iran-Contra scandal, using the necessity of protecting state secrets as a cover certainly facilitates concealing private aggrandizement.

## The Shelley Martel Affair

In December1991 Shelley Martel was a twenty-eight-year-old Minister of Northern Development in Ontario's NDP government. Around that time the government had reached an agreement with the Ontario Medical Association that included a cap on medical billings of over $400,000 a year, with a portion of billings beyond that sum having to be rebated back to government coffers. This greatly upset some doctors in the province, particularly a number of high-billing specialists in Martel's home riding of Sudbury. These doctors continually criticized the NDP government. In turn, members of the government saw these doctors as a threat to the viability of the health-care system.

At a party in Thunder Bay, Martel got into an argument with a Tory organizer who felt the government was treating the physicians unfairly. Martel apparently responded that she knew of a Sudbury doctor who was probably guilty of over-billing and that the government was thinking of charging him. This seemed to indicate that Martel had confidential information from the health ministry, as well as confidential information from the attorney general's office. Within days, Martel's comments were in the news and the legislature. As Thomas Walkom reported, it became a "full-fledged political scandal" within a week.[33] Martel's reputation and career subsequently took a nosedive; the situation was exacerbated when she voluntarily asked to take a lie detector test to show that she was telling the truth when she said she lied about having information about the doctor. A legislative committee eventually concluded that she had told the truth about having lied, and so she stayed in the cabinet. But, in 1994 Ontario's privacy commissioner reported that Martel had violated that *Privacy Act* in another incident, and she resigned.

According to Walkom, the Martel affair, combined with the government's flip-flop on auto insurance and its surprising support for casinos, shattered the NDP's reputation for integrity, and the party never recovered the public's trust. Comparing Richard Nixon, Oliver North and the RCMP's dirty tricks to the foolishness of a rookie Ontario cabinet minister seems like equating the outrageous with the ludicrous, and not a little unfair. Indeed, Martel's conduct pales beside that of the individuals we've discussed previously. The point, though, is to emphasize what can happen to a talented, generally conscientious young politician when the perceived rightness of the cause and the treatment of dissenters as enemies overshadow all other considerations.

## Jean Chrétien and the Sponsorship Scandal

A more recent example of the lengths that even an astute and enormously successful leader will sometimes go to when he believes he's fighting a battle for a great cause is former Prime Minister Jean Chrétien's reaction to criticism of his office's role in the administrative failings and corruption that attended his government's largely secretive Sponsorship Program (discussed in Chapters 1 and 2). During a speech he gave to a mainly Liberal audience in Winnipeg in late May 2002, Mr. Chrétien had this to say:

> Perhaps there was a few million dollars that might have been stolen in the process [of carrying out the Sponsorship Program]. It is possible. But how many millions of dollars have we saved the country because we have re-established the stability of Canada as a united country? If somebody has stolen the money, they will face the courts. But I will not apologize to Canadians . . . With the circumstances in November of 1995, I had to make sure that the presence of Canada was to be felt in Quebec.[34]

This is an almost classic defence of dirty hands: If there were wrongs committed they were nonetheless minor and worth it once one looks at the big picture and considers the good reasons for, and the overall success of, the actions undertaken; and besides, some of those implicated will pay the price. But it's not something leaders should apologize for — rather, they should be thanked. From this perspective, the Sponsorship Program was part of the struggle to defeat an enemy trying to tear Canada apart. As one of Mr. Chrétien's biographers has noted, for our former prime minister, politics was war.[35] Most Canadians, however, were not as grateful as Mr. Chrétien thought they should be. His popularity sank, he resigned to avoid a rebellion within his own party and in the next election the Liberals were defeated.

## DIRTY HANDS VERSUS DEMOCRATIC TRUST

When we say that public office is a public trust with obligations we mean that elected representatives assume the role of trustees, with the duty of acting to protect and advance the best interests of their fellow citizens. And that, in turn, means they must not allow their decisions to be influenced by anything other than the welfare of the citizenry they have undertaken to serve.

Furthermore, the trust relationship associated with democracy should not be confused with either the blind faith expected of religious fundamentalists or the blind trust established for corporate investments on behalf of public servants who want to avoid conflicts of interest. With respect to information and considerations that bear on decisions made in citizens' interests, the duty of a government is to provide full and frank disclosure at all times. In the examples of fraud or real conflicts of interest covered in earlier chapters, there was a clear breach of trust. But the betrayal of trust by public officials for private purposes does not seem to fit the case, generally, of dirty-handed politicians who genuinely believe that they are acting for the common good and do not seek or receive a special favour in return.

The two types of corrupt practices overlap, however, because the nature of the trust relationship has been undermined in similar ways, though for different reasons. In both cases the truth is concealed from us or we are deliberately misled while rules, regulations and laws are violated. A couple of examples of the abuse of democratic trust will help to illustrate how it differs from dirty hands.

### The Muzzling of Government Scientists

In 2007, approximately one year after Stephen Harper first became prime minister, a "Media Relations Policy" was implemented by Environment Canada. That policy included a requirement that any inquiry from any reporter concerning "politically sensitive" topics, such as climate change, fracking or, indeed, almost any subject related to the environment, could not be addressed until it had been considered by the Privy Council Office (PCO) — this in addition to the existing ability of the Environment Minister to deny reporters' requests to speak with any scientist employed by Environment Canada.

By most accounts, the policy resulted in the effective "muzzling" of scientists employed not only by Environment Canada, but, indeed, by all other government departments, ministries and agencies (e.g., the Department of Fisheries and Oceans; Natural Resources Canada; Health Canada).

As the consequences of the policy became clear, numerous organizations and individuals began to protest the government's actions. For example, Democracy Watch documented a number of clear examples of the government preventing scientists from speaking about their research or certain topics, and initiated an e-letter campaign asking Canadians to write to Prime Minister Harper to indicate that they would not "accept the muzzling of federal government scientists."[36]

Demonstrations were also held on Parliament Hill to protest the situation. The *Huffington Post Canada* ran a series entitled "Stifling Science," and an editorial in a March 2012 issue of the widely read and internationally respected journal *Nature* called upon the Canadian government to provide much greater freedom to its scientists to share their research and expertise, noting that "[p]olicy directives and e-mails obtained from the government through freedom of information reveal a confused and Byzantine approach to the press, prioritizing message control and showing little understanding of the importance of the free flow of scientific knowledge."[37] And in February 2013 Democracy Watch and the Environmental Law Clinic at the University of Victoria jointly filed a formal complaint with the federal information commissioner, in essence asserting that scientists employed by the federal government were being unlawfully prevented from sharing their research and expertise with either the press or the public in general. That month also witnessed Rick Mercer devote the "Rick's Rant" segment of his show the *Rick Mercer Report* to the muzzling of federal government scientists.

These examples represent merely some of the reactions to the restrictions the federal government placed upon its scientists. In April 2013, the information commissioner agreed to investigate whether the government's restrictions violated the *Access to Information Act*, focusing on the following seven government bodies: the Canadian Food Inspection Agency; Environment Canada; the Department of Fisheries and Oceans; the Department of National Defence; Natural Resources Canada; the National Research Council of Canada; and the Treasury Board. As of September 2016, the report had yet to be released. But it should be noted that at no time during the controversy did the government justify its restrictions on the basis that they were necessary to protect the public interest.

## The Gas Plants Scandal

In 2005 and 2009, the Government of Ontario awarded contracts to build new gas-fired power generating facilities in Mississauga and Oakville, respectively. Local, vocal opposition to the proposed plants arose, and on October 7, 2010, the Minister of Energy announced that construction of the Oakville facility had been cancelled.

On September 7, 2011, Premier McGuinty announced that a provincial election would be held on October 6, 2011. The so-called 905 region, which includes Oakville and Mississauga, is a key battleground in Ontario elections. Trailing in many polls, the Liberal Party promised on September 28, 2011, that, if returned to power, it would cancel construction of the Mississauga facility as well. The Liberals secured a minority government, and on October 7, 2011, the Minister of Energy announced that construction of the Mississauga facility was being cancelled.

Soon thereafter the estimates committee of the Ontario legislature, dominated by the two opposition parties, initiated an investigation of the government's cancellation of the two gas plants. In May 2012, the committee adopted a motion that gave the Minister of Energy, the Ministry of Energy and the Ontario Power Authority two weeks to provide "all correspondence, in any form," related to the cancellations.[38]

In July 2012, the committee was presented with five hundred pages of emails, letters and PowerPoint presentations; unsurprisingly, opposition members of the committee were dissatisfied with the response to its request, and in August 2012 a member requested that the Speaker of the Legislature determine whether the former Minister of Energy was in contempt for failing to provide all of the information requested by the committee. On September 13, 2012, the Speaker — a Liberal MPP — declared that there was a *prima facie* case for holding the former Minister of Energy in contempt of the legislature, and ordered the former minister to comply with the committee's motion. Between late September and mid-October 2012, the committee was provided with approximately 56,500 pages of records, but none originated from political staff in the minister's office.[39]

In March 2013, the Standing Committee on Justice Policy began its review of the contempt charge against the former Minister of Energy. During the review the minister's former chief of staff testified that he could not provide any documents to the estimates committee because, as a matter of habit, he kept a "clean inbox" — by which he meant that he deleted his emails daily. A few days after that testimony a member of the committee filed a complaint with the Information and Privacy Commissioner of Ontario (IPC), requesting that she investigate "what appears to be a breach of protocol and a violation of the *Archives and Recordkeeping Act* and the *Freedom of Information and Protection of Privacy Act*."[40]

The IPC tabled her report in June 2013.[41] In it, she stated that "the practice of indiscriminate deletion of all emails sent and received by the former Chief of Staff was in violation of the *Archives and Recordkeeping Act, 2006 (ARA)* and the records retention schedule developed by

Archives of Ontario for ministers' offices." She also suggested that "[i]t truly strains credulity to think that absolutely no records responsive to the Estimates Committee's motion and the Speaker's ruling were retained."[42] The commissioner's report also noted that in the course of her investigation she had been told that Premier McGuinty's chief of staff, David Livingston, had asked the secretary of the cabinet (i.e., the senior civil servant) how to erase the hard drives of government computers. Two days after the report was tabled the OPP launched an investigation into potential wrongdoing by Livingston and the premier's other staff.

After seizing a number of government computers and retrieving some emails, the OPP concluded that it was likely that Mr. Livingston and the premier's deputy chief of staff, Laura Miller, had employed a computer consultant — Peter Faist, who was also Ms. Miller's life partner — to "wipe clean" the hard drives of the computers of staff who had been involved with the gas plants file, especially from September 2011 onwards. According to the OPP, such an action would constitute a "criminal breach of trust" because it is illegal in Ontario to provide administrative access to government computers to anyone who does not possess the necessary security clearance, as was the case with Mr. Faist. In December 2015, charges of breach of trust, mischief in relation to data and misuse of a computer system to commit mischief were laid against both Mr. Livingston and Ms. Miller. Their trial is scheduled to begin in September 2017.

Is it possible to identify a reasonable, non-partisan justification for either destroying or severely restricting public access to government-generated information (and, in the case of government scientists, their expertise)? While there is nothing unusual or inherently wrong with governments managing the flow of, and access to, information they possess and restricting the ability of their employees to engage in certain types of public commentary, the above-noted actions certainly seem to exceed any reasonable understanding of the legitimate or typical parameters associated with such management.

Did those responsible for either the muzzling of scientists or the destruction of information genuinely believe that such actions were necessary to protect the public interest? To be generous, it is immensely challenging merely to identify a plausible, persuasive, neutral hypothetical justification for such actions, never mind one that supports the claim that they were done to protect the public interest. Indeed, such muzzling and destruction runs contrary to a foundational principle of responsible democratic government — namely, that government be open and transparent so that citizens can be aware of how their government behaves and hold it accountable for its actions (or lack thereof). The fact that the research and/or opinions of federal government scientists might conflict with government policy, for example, does not prevent the government from pursuing any policy, especially when the government controls a majority of the seats in the House of Commons. The only inescapable constraint against the government pursuing a chosen policy in such a situation is whatever legal impediments already exist.

It is difficult, then, not to conclude that the muzzling of scientists and the erasing of emails was done because of a fear that public knowledge of that information would jeopardize the political "capital" and future "attractiveness" of the government in question (and, in the case of email messages and documents, perhaps render certain individuals vulnerable to legal prosecution). In other words, it is difficult not to believe that the governments involved in the aforementioned activities purposely impeded the public's access to certain information[43] merely to avoid the negative political consequences associated with being fully forthcoming and transparent.

Sometimes there is a blurred line between duplicitous moves to hold on to power for power's sake and those orchestrated by dirty-hands practitioners for (what they believe are) worthy causes; and sometimes it is tempting for leaders to blur those lines. In doing so they can claim that their deceptive conduct wasn't done to maintain or gain power, but only to accomplish an esteemed result. But what needs be remembered, we maintain, is that *both* those kinds of motivations and their related actions involve serious infringements of democratic values such as integrity, fairness, and transparency.

Our representatives are not elected to treat us like children or compliant lambs ready to be shepherded this way or that way. We elect them assuming that we deserve to be treated with mutual respect, that they will look after our best interests, and that they must be accountable to us.[44]

Democracy provides a public space for differences of opinion over policy options, debate over strategic goals and argument about the range of alternatives and their practical and moral appropriateness. Democratic sensibilities acknowledge and encourage a public discourse replete with appeals and arguments meant to persuade, to mobilize opinion and support, to direct collective preferences this way rather than that. What energizes representative democracy is persuasion, not manipulation, force of argument, not force of arms, honest politics, and not lies and deception.

Except for the most extreme exigencies of war or insurrection, democracy rules out the right of any elite, whether self-appointed or elected, to decide what and how much information the public can be trusted to have — when it can handle the truth and when it needs to be lied to. This means that governments cannot arrogate to themselves the role of moral guardian or parent. Paternalism and democracy are like fire and water: they don't mix. A defence of dirty hands turns on paternalism and turns off democracy. Dirty-hands advocates claim that morally dubious acts are committed because not doing them would be disastrous. But what could be more disastrous than the breakdown of democracy and the absence of trustworthiness?

## COMPROMISE

It is sometimes thought that a compromise is tantamount to dirty hands in that it entails selling out or abandoning one's principles, and therefore betraying the trust of supporters/electors who expected such principles to be promoted. As one advocate of compromise has stated,

"Arrangement of compromise belongs today to specialists . . . the politicians. Let these moral middleman do this dirty work for you."[45] According to this double-edged meaning of compromise, democratic politics and dirty-handed negotiations go together. But there is another understanding of compromise, which holds that dirty work, in the sense of sacrificing one's moral integrity, is not required by the give-and-take of democratic politics.

The idea of compromise as a reasonable middle way or balance between extreme demands has some affinities with the notions of moderation and the "golden mean" that Plato and Aristotle recommended as great practical virtues. Neither were democrats, however, so close parallels should be avoided. But the kernel of an important idea is there: moderate political policies usually result in better political outcomes than extremist politics.

In her 1993 Massey Lecture, Jean Bethke Elshtain notes a discussion she had with a former Czechoslovakian dissident who was elected to the Prague Parliament after the 1989 Velvet Revolution. The new legislator said that compromise is something of fundamental importance to a democracy — something that many Czechs weren't used to but would have to learn. "In a democracy, compromise is not a terrible thing. It is necessary. It lies at the heart of things because you have to accept that people are going to have different views, especially on the most volatile matters and the most important issues."[46]

Ambivalence about the meaning and value of compromise is nicely underlined by Arthur Kuflik, who notes that the word has both "a pejorative and honorific sense." He outlines four criteria that indicate when it is morally right to try to accommodate views and positions different from your own. He says we should be prepared to scale down our own demands and be prepared to accept those of others whenever our priorities are reflections of "non-moral interest rather than considered moral conviction"; are "based on moral convictions that we now perceive to be mistaken"; are clearly ones that need balancing "against other legitimate claims" to achieve a "more comprehensive view of the matter that is in dispute"; or are clearly biased because of our emotional closeness to a situation. We need to ask what our views would be if we could look at the situation objectively, imagining that there is no dispute, realizing "that reasonable differences of opinion are possible, and that a peaceful settlement achieved through a fair process that fosters mutual understanding and respect is of great moral significance in its own right."[47]

Kuflik emphasizes that what need *not* be compromised according to these criteria is moral integrity. Extrapolating from Kuflik, we would say that willingness to compromise, within limits, is a fundamental democratic disposition that complements the democratic sensibilities of accepting majoritarian decisions, respecting minority rights and treating others as equals. Compromise facilitates decision making and is an estimable procedure for resolving conflicts respectfully and peaceably. The process of compromise actualizes the proposition that ethical decision making in politics often requires not only tolerance of differing interests and claims, but mutual accommodation. Sometimes parties may choose to work out their differences through direct negotiated settlement, and sometimes they may elect to bring in an impartial third party to mediate or arbitrate. Regardless of the approach, everyone will not necessarily see eye to eye on tough questions; rather, the disputants will probably have to accept some things they don't like or want.

Kuflik adds that in some instances compromise is not only inappropriate, "it is reprehensible."[48] His example is the Munich accord that Neville Chamberlain arranged with Adolph Hitler just prior to the start of World War Two. Insofar as compromise implies searching for a middle way and splitting differences, there are clearly some midpoint solutions that are unacceptable, such as accommodating an abusing parent or husband intent on continuing the abuse. Authorizing police or crown attorneys to reach an agreement with a wife batterer not to press charges as long as the abuser reduces the incidence of abuse by, for example, 50 per cent, is not an acceptable compromise. A compromise that countenances prejudicial or ill-treatment of someone is not a moral one. These distinctions illustrate the notion that compromising one's morality is the opposite of a moral compromise.

There is both a procedural and substantive aspect to any compromise, and both have to meet certain conditions if a particular compromise is to count as morally acceptable. An honourable democratic compromise, as we intimated earlier, is one that recognizes limits. And the limits that apply are our commitment to moral integrity and the principles of democracy. Clearly, what must be avoided are compromises that countenance deception or bribery. As well, a compromise is unacceptable if it sanctions the threat or use of force to frustrate the will of the majority, to violate fundamental human rights or to distribute primary social goods unequally without advancing the life chances of the least advantaged. Such compromises do not meet the criteria of honourable, democratic principles. In this regard, forging a successful moral compromise consistent with democratic principles is one thing and achieving success with dirty hands quite another.

## CONCLUSION

The examples we have considered demonstrate the dangers involved in accepting dirty-hands justifications for deceiving citizens. This defence is extremely elastic. It includes cases in which individuals knowingly do something wrong and plan it in advance, and cases in which something goes wrong as a result of incompetence or human error and the officials involved decide a cover-up is in order; it applies to election campaign trickery and false promises which, ironically, have parallels with the dirty tricks and disinformation campaigns waged by covert security and intelligence agencies.

If we accept the argument that those in charge, or — in the case of political parties in an election — those who believe they should be in charge, can lie to us because they have our best interests at heart, *even* when they cover up actions that have jeopardized our interests, then we can never require them to account honestly for what they do or to correct their mistakes. Nor can we be informed participants in the decisions that affect us.

Dirty-hands practices destroy integrity. When lying, deception and breaking promises become regular practices, the bonds of trust among citizens, as well as between citizens and their representatives, are unravelled. John Stuart Mill was right when he spoke of "the trustworthiness of human assertion" as the foundation of "social well-being" and its "insufficiency" as the greatest factor threatening "civilization, virtue and everything on which human happiness on the largest scale depends."[49]

Breaking promises and deceiving the electorate undermines the trust relationship between citizens and their representatives. These actions betray the responsibility that governments are obligated to fulfill. The result may be success for a party or faction but it signals a failure of the democratic process. The repercussions of such a failure are considerable: the deterioration of the trust relationship contributes to cynicism, and the provision of opportunities increases for charismatic charlatans to preach salvation through simplistic solutions about the cleansing of politics. This failure leads to a loss of faith in the role of governments, an erosion that seems to be happening in Canada and the United States. If no politicians do the positive things they promise, the electorate will understandably be receptive to calls for the downsizing of government initiatives and institutions and the temptation to leave everything up to the market, because at least businesses have a clear agenda to produce useful, saleable goods and services and to make a profit for their shareholders.

However, there is also an upside to citizen reaction to government perfidy. While many politicians have debased the democratic currency, they haven't managed to alter the electorate's demand for honest politics. Voters handing overwhelming defeats to British Columbia's Social Credit government in 1991, Saskatchewan's Conservative government in 1991 and the federal Conservative government in 1993, and then rejecting the federal Liberal government in 2006, demonstrate the electorate's indignation and irritation with governments that provide cover for unscrupulous activities.

Religious fundamentalists answer to their God, military officers to their commanders, revolutionaries to history and egoists to themselves, but politicians in a democracy are accountable to the people. Dirty-handed conduct subverts both the process that ensures accountability and the maintenance of trust. Dirty-handed politicians undermine the principles and values that are integral to democracy and that is why their conduct is unacceptable and incompatible with honest politics.[50]

# CHAPTER 11
# WHY ETHICAL POLITICS IS ESSENTIAL

## David P. Shugarman and Ian Greene

On May 9, 1992, twenty-six coal miners were killed in an underground explosion in Nova Scotia's Westray Mine, which had opened just nine months earlier. Before the opening, federal and provincial bureaucrats with expertise in the coal mining field, as well as other industry figures, strongly advised against the mine's development. Serious doubts were expressed about the mine's safety, and the company's viability given the abundance of coal on the market. Nevertheless, Westray received political and financial support from both the provincial and federal Conservative governments. Together they provided in excess of $20 million in subsidies to the mine's owner as well as a loan guarantee that covered 85 per cent of the company's $100 million bank loan. The federal Public Works Minister, one of the mine's chief supporters, was also the MP for the riding where the mine was constructed.

Soon after the disaster, the Nova Scotia government established an inquiry, which reported its findings in 1997. The inquiry revealed, in the words of its commissioner, "a story of incompetence, of misman-agement, of bureaucratic bungling, of deceit, of ruthlessness, of cover-up, of apathy, of expediency, and of cynical indifference."[1] Among the factors contributing to the tragedy were the management's insufficient attention to mine safety, and lax supervision of occupational health and safety standards by provincial inspectors. On top of this, three provincial government departments failed to apply regulations and laws bearing on mine safety. Furthermore, a Nova Scotia government official removed records relating to the mine so they could not be accessed through the province's freedom of information law because they were thought to be "politically embarrassing."[2] Eventually, and largely as a result of Commissioner Richard's report, the Nova Scotia government apologized to the families of the victims for the way the Westray matter was handled.

Let us here re-emphasize one of our central concerns: reneging on promises, hoodwinking electors, neglecting ministerial responsibilities, using public office for personal purposes and private gain or to advance the interests of the already privileged — these are all wrongdoings which seriously mar the trust relationship between citizens and their representatives. Such actions signal a failure of democratic processes and they turn people off politics. A disconnect between citizens and their representatives seems to be happening in many liberal democracies and the possibility of such a rupture developing here could have worrisome consequences for Canada's democratic body politic. Recent public opinion sampling in this regard offers distressing evidence: our citizens' trust in politics and politicians is weak.

In a survey of Canadians recently conducted by researchers at Ryerson University, a majority expressed the view that politics is a dirty game, and over 60 per cent of respondents felt that engaging in politics would tend to corrupt normally honest people. Almost a fifth of those surveyed indicated that they had stopped voting because of political dishonesty.[3] However, while *some* politicians — and note that we do not say *most* — have debased the democratic currency, they haven't managed to lessen the electorate's disapproval of dishonest politicians. Indeed, of those surveyed who were under thirty-five, over half said they would switch party affiliation if they believed their preferred party was acting unethically. Clearly many Canadians are *not* passive once they become aware of political misconduct. As we noted in Chapter 10, again and again they have tossed out offending governments seeking re-election.

A further upside to the recognition and intolerance of governmental wrongdoing and ethical impropriety is the general acceptance by all political parties of the usefulness of independent agencies and officers tasked with the review and oversight of a wide array of decision-making procedures to both check ethical misconduct and support the enhancement of an ethical political culture.

Our view is that honest politics is not only attainable in a democratic country — it is essential to ensure that the fundamental democratic value of mutual respect is taken seriously. It is often said that ethical politics is an oxymoron. Yet this is usually expressed in frustration. Serious ethical deficiencies have existed in Canadian politics because the infrastructure and education needed to support honest politics were lacking. Since the 1997 edition of *Honest Politics* was published, ethics offices with independent commissioners have been created for federal and provincial governments, and in several dozen municipalities, indicating that this approach is having an educative influence on more and more jurisdictions. As the examples in this book have illustrated, serious breaches have continued even where these new offices have been instituted. However, more recent ethical breaches have tended to occur in areas not previously covered by comprehensive ethics regimes; conversely, well-established ethics regimes have led to fewer breaches. For example, there were far fewer allegations of conflicts of interest involving members of legislatures in the 2010s than there were in the 1980s and 1990s, and this change is concurrent with the establishment of the offices of independent ethics and conflict of interest commissioners.[4] In the 2010s, scandals have been concentrated in areas such as municipal politics, where ethics regimes are only beginning to develop. And abuse of expense claims, often related to inflated notions of entitlement, have taken place in jurisdictions lacking proper oversight procedures and clear regulations.

There are some who will conclude that any attempt to improve ethical standards in Canadian politics is as futile as teaching good manners to swine. However, it should be remembered that at one time in the common law tradition, judges did not enjoy a high reputation. Before the advent of judicial independence in the Anglo-Canadian legal tradition, judges had a reputation for being corrupt and amenable to undue influence. Today, thanks to a general acceptance of the principles of fairness and impartiality in the courts, and the attention that judges themselves pay to ethical issues, judging is one of the most respected professions in our society. Many good lawyers aspire to become judges, in spite of a possible drop in pay, because a judicial appointment is symbolic of a successful career. The same transformation needs to occur — and we believe can occur — with respect to elected officials.

We close here with a summary of the essential arguments made in this book and we offer a road map for the path we can take to bolster ethical politics in Canada.

## WHY ETHICAL POLITICS IS ESSENTIAL TO A STABLE DEMOCRACY

The essential ingredient for ethical politics is mutual respect, which is the foundation of the basic democratic principles of social equality, free and fair elections with deference to the majority, protection of minority rights, freedom of expression, and integrity. Mutual respect means that we have a duty to treat others with civility and as intrinsically important as ourselves, just as others have a corresponding duty to treat us with respect. The observance of this fundamental principle in the political world takes courage and integrity, and it takes constant attention, vigilance, work and education. As history shows, we have not reached the standards of democracy practiced today in Canada and other advanced liberal democracies without a great deal of struggle and, unfortunately, bloodshed.[5] We argue that in order for a democracy to survive and thrive there must be a critical mass of citizens who understand, practise and promote mutual respect.

The democratic principles that go along with the exercise of mutual respect lead to crucial ethical duties on the part of politicians and public servants. First, they must always act as trustees of the public interest rather than serve private or special interests. Although the concept of "the public interest" is complex, the examples of abuse of trust we presented in Chapters 1 through 4 clearly indicate what is *not* in the public interest. We have also emphasized the duty of impartiality that is connected to implementing the law and administering governmental programs. The third duty that our representatives must fulfill is to be prepared at all times to account for their behaviour and decisions with transparency and integrity, and to take responsibility for mistakes that are bound to occur.

Two important legal principles buttress the ethical duties we have outlined. First, the rule of law in the broadest sense, which we argued in Chapter 2 means that "a legal framework is provided for social co-operation, and everyone's conduct is subject to non-arbitrary regulation." Second, the duty of fairness, which implies that people interacting with the public service, courts or tribunals deserve procedural proprieties: to be heard and treated respectfully and impartially.

Public officials who take these principles seriously and who try to apply them in their day-to-day work are an essential bulwark for democratic government.

## CANADIAN ACCOMPLISHMENTS

We have argued that democracy, always a work in progress, proceeds through stages. Earlier struggles focused on the recognition of equality for women as well as men, and for all races and social classes, along with equality in suffrage. Next came the quest for better recognition of human rights, which in Canada included the advent of the *Charter of Rights and Freedoms* in 1982, and significant judicial decisions and legislative enactments since that time.[6] Beginning with reactions to the conflict of interest scandals that arose across Canada in the 1980s, there has been a new emphasis on the promotion of ethical politics using codes of conduct, new legislation and new independent officers as resources for setting coherent standards and expectations of acceptable exercises of authority.

As of 2017, we have independent conflict of interest commissioners and rules for every province and territory, the House of Commons and Senate and a number of municipalities. The federal government, most provinces and some municipalities have registrars, rules and, in some cases, accompanying codes of conduct that apply to lobbyists. Many jurisdictions have strict rules on post-employment activities that prevent revolving doors and privileged access for retired politicians. Federal electoral financing and spending rules have become stricter, as have those of some provinces and municipalities, in an effort to curtail the undue influence of money in the electoral process. Some jurisdictions have tightened expense claims rules for public officials to prevent entitlement abuses. Several jurisdictions have enacted legislation that supports legitimate whistle-blowers, and this legislation is becoming more effective through trial and error. All of these changes have helped to tackle corruption in politics and the public sector. And the reduction of corruption in the public sector is an essential ingredient for an increase in trust in our institutions and elected politicians,[7] which in turn encourages more people of integrity to put their names forward for public office.

## WHAT CANADIANS NEED TO WORK ON

We have identified several areas where improvements and reforms are needed to prevent the erosion of the improvements to our public sector ethics regimes:

- Patronage needs to be abolished as a means of recruitment for all public sector positions. Ideological preference is not acceptable as a criterion for judicial, administrative, tribunal or governor-in-council appointments that require impartiality and high competence, though it may play a role in the small number of appointments that are connected with implementing a party's platform, such as ministerial staff.

- Some provincial conflict of interest regimes should provide searchable online information about members' disclosable assets and liabilities. All conflict of interest commissioners could be afforded the authority to investigate on their own initiative instead of waiting for complaints to be filed. Annual face-to-face meetings between commissioners and members of legislatures should be mandatory, not optional. The method of selecting some of the independent commissioners should be reformed to prevent the appearance of partisan manipulation. Sunset clauses on ethics legislation would be a useful tool to require periodic review and updating, and consideration should be given to broadening the rules beyond conflicts of interest to promote ethical behaviour in general. Although there are clear challenges in setting the criteria for such rules of behaviour, we nonetheless believe that in a non- or multi-partisan fashion, legislators should make the attempt to explore with each other standards that they can agree on to promote mutual respect and democracy.

- Provinces without annual limits on financial contributions to parties and candidates should set limits at $1,500 or less, and legislators need to engage in debates about what contribution limits are necessary not only to prevent undue influence, but also to ensure that one's financial ability to attend fundraisers is not a factor in obtaining the ability to meet politicians. Union and corporate donations should be prohibited, as well as donations from out-of-province donors, and from charities. Individual contribution limits at fundraising events should be low enough to avoid "cash-for-access" dealings. In addition, there is some merit in (re) introducing per-vote subsidies that provide reliable and sustainable income for political parties. Such subsidies provide voters with some confidence that their votes matter, but more importantly they remove some incentives for political parties to engage in "unsavoury" fundraising activities. The widespread criticism in 2016 of cash-for-access fundraisers with $1,500 limits that form part of an annual individual contribution limit of $1,500 suggests two conclusions. First, Canadians are interested in promoting ethical politics. Second, Canadians' ethical expectations may increase over time, and political parties that are tone deaf to these changes imperil themselves.

- All jurisdictions should continually monitor their procedures for approving expense claims for elected officials, and as much as possible, adjudication of expense claims disputes should be carried out by a neutral third party. Some possible candidates for this role are offices of auditors general, all-party committees of former elected officials, or an independent firm that specializes in public audit. The goal is to prevent a repeat in any jurisdiction of a situation like the Senate expenses claims scandal of 2013–16.

- Provinces, territories and large municipalities without rules for lobbyists and lobbyist registration procedures ought to create the conditions necessary to advance rules, registries and codes of conduct. Lobbying is a legitimate activity in Canada so long as the opportunities to lobby are fair, transparent and accessible to everyone. From this perspective, careful attention needs to be given to the relation between lobbying and partisan fundraising events so that lobbyists do not create conflicts of interest.

- It is important to update Canada's access to information laws, as well as to provide the authority to lobbying and conflict of interest commissioners for alternative monetary penalties that can penalize offenders directly rather than having to work through criminal justice systems that take much time and effort without any guarantee of effect.

- The federal, provincial and municipal governments should take steps to promote a "speak-up" culture in the public service. There must be strong internal mechanisms in ministries and departments to investigate wrongdoing so that public servants have the means to speak up without fear of reprisal. The goal should be that honest whistle-blowers will not feel compelled to go to extraordinary lengths to expose what they believe to be inappropriate conduct or unethical activity. This requires a change in public service culture that encourages speaking truth to power, rather than unbridled loyalty to power.

- Municipal government may well be the one area where corruption is most likely to occur, and it has definitely been the last to develop effective ethics regimes. Large municipalities have increasingly large sums of money to spend on infrastructure and other projects, and municipal politicians and public servants may not be as aware as their provincial and federal counterparts of the dangers posed by conflicts of interest, unregulated lobbyists and loose election financing rules. However, there are some meaningful initiatives that provide hope for the future, including the creation of local integrity offices and officers that provide oversight over procurement.

- All political parties must accept the fact that dirty-hands practices erode integrity in government, and they should take meaningful steps to promote an internal culture of political integrity.

## Promoting Ethics within Political Parties

Among the recommendations of the 1991 Royal Commission on Electoral Reform and Party Financing was the proposal that Canadian political parties develop their own internal codes of ethics. And yet, to date, no party has adopted what we could properly call a code of ethics.[8] This is regrettable, because the less the parties are able to ensure high ethical standards themselves, the more likely it is that ethical standards will have to be imposed on them from the outside. As well, many aspects of our politics, such as campaign tactics, constituency events and voter mobilization might benefit from parties themselves having to deal effectively with actual or potentially dubious practices before they have to be addressed by an external body.

Codes of ethics for parties are important for three reasons. First, even with the most carefully drafted legislation, unscrupulous people will find loopholes. It is far better to have brief, easy-to-understand legislation that politicians can be trusted to comply with most of the time, than complex legislation designed to plug every loophole. Like the *Income Tax Act*, complex laws do not make for inspiring reading, and they open the door to those who specialize in getting around the legislation rather than complying with it. If political parties were to create their own high quality ethics regimes, there would be less pressure for complex and lengthy legislation.

Second, lying, negative advertising and dirty-handed politics are difficult if not impossible to control through legislation. The best way to promote integrity in public life is for elected officials to take primary responsibility for setting standards.

Third, the process of developing a code of ethics is an education in itself. Those involved in developing such codes ought to think carefully about the basic principles of democracy and how they relate to their party's objectives and activities. If carefully planned, this process can lead to the internalization of ethical values, and this is a powerful weapon on behalf of integrity.

With meaningful codes of ethics our parties might be able to significantly reduce overzealous partisans' ability to unwittingly tarnish the party's reputation. For example, during the 2011 election Michael Sona, an overly keen and unscrupulous Conservative Party staffer in Guelph, Ontario, arranged for nearly seven thousand "robocalls" to be sent to a list of possible non-Conservative voters with false information about where they were supposed to vote. Sona was convicted of violating the *Canada Elections Act*, and sentenced to nine months in jail and a year of probation.[9] If the Conservative Party had had a code of ethics and had ensured that its volunteers had read and signed off on it, this might have helped to prevent such an embarrassing incident.

It is worthwhile considering why the parties have resisted developing these codes. Janet Hiebert has suggested that activists tend to see their parties as private organizations with little public accountability.[10] This may seem odd to those who consider that parties play a pivotal role in setting the public policy. But it can be explained in part by politicians' rather dismal reputation, which draws a disproportionate number of self-interested persons into politics. Being self-interested, they would tend to emphasize the private rather than the public nature of their party. For example, Allan Kornberg's study of the twenty-fifth Parliament found that between half and one-third of the members of the Conservative and Liberal Parties were motivated to enter politics primarily by personal reasons, such as a desire to advance their own careers. Only the New Democrats were motivated primarily by a desire to serve the public and to advance the party's ideology.[11] And Maureen Mancuso's study of British MPs in the late 1980s shows that one-third of them — she calls them "entrepreneurs" — had fairly low ethical standards. These MPs viewed their office almost as a business, rather than a calling. In the grey areas of conflict of interest, and in determining the scope of activities that can be conducted in the name of constituency service, these particular MPs were guided by the principle of "anything goes."[12] It would not be surprising to find that in Canada a significant number of elected officials are similarly motivated. It would be hard to persuade these "entrepreneurs" that codes of ethics are desirable.

This may change if one political party develops a credible code and attracts significant new public support because of it. Eventually, the other parties might feel pressured to develop their own codes to maintain public support, and they could end up competing to establish the most effective code. In our view, a political party that intelligently pursues honest politics is more likely to lead by example — and thereby encourage the other parties and the less ethical elements in the media to raise their standards — than to be defeated by ethical lapses.

What form should a party code of ethics take? It should be brief and clear. There should be a statement outlining the basic principles of democratic government together with the values of the party from which the more specific elements of the code are derived. A definition of conflict of interest would be useful, along with a statement affirming the duty of party members to remove themselves from such situations. Similarly, there should be a definition of undue influence and a condemnation of activities that promote undue influence, especially in relation to the financing of election and leadership campaigns. The importance of providing equal opportunities for all party members to participate in party activities, regardless of their gender, race, ethnicity, age, physical disability or sexual orientation should be stressed. There should be a commitment to respect the activities of other parties and their members, especially during election campaigns, along with constraints on negative advertising. A statement affirming the value of integrity and condemning dirty-handed politics would be useful. And there needs to be an internal enforcement mechanism utilizing an independent integrity officer, and this mechanism needs to be explained. This list does not exhaust the topics that a party's code of ethics might cover, but we think that the issues discussed above should all be considered.

## Ethics Audits

One way to promote accountability in politics is the use of periodic ethics audits. In 1995, the Office of the Auditor General of Canada published its first ethics audit of the federal public service, and additional ethics audits have taken place since.[13] The first audit included a survey of public servants to assess their awareness of ethics-related rules and issues in the public sector. It also reviewed the extent and effectiveness of ethics training programs in the federal public service. The report indicated that ethical standards among federal public servants were relatively high, but areas of weakness were detected. For example, a tenth of those surveyed saw nothing wrong with accepting a free weekend of skiing from an agency receiving benefits from their department, and nearly a third saw nothing wrong with hiring a relative on a $20,000 untendered contract. Recommendations were made for dealing with these ethical deficiencies through better ethics training. The auditor general would not be the appropriate agency for conducting an ethics audit of elected members or a political party, but the auditor general's report demonstrates both the practicality and the utility of the ethics audits.[14] Some provinces also regularly carry out ethics audits, a good example of which came from Manitoba in 2014.[15]

Elected officials at every level, as well as political parties, could benefit from periodic ethics audits. An objective set of procedures could be developed to evaluate the extent to which a particular government or a party was adhering to generally accepted ethical standards. Such audits could be conducted by an independent research organization, such as a public policy research institute or a centre for practical ethics affiliated with a university.[16] Our view is that such measures would go a long way towards ensuring public accountability for ethical standards in politics.

## Ethics Education

As the American philosopher and democratic theorist John Dewey emphasized, education should be about "the formation of character, intellectual, moral and esthetic, and not just training in skills and the importation of information."[17] For Dewey, the purpose of a democratic education is building a democratic character. Our aim in this book has been to make a contribution to that kind of education by focusing on the democratic value of mutual respect and the principles and obligations that flow from it, along with the necessary ethical supports that will help sustain and strengthen the workings of our democracy.

It is desirable that as many public officials as possible have a solid grounding in the principles of ethical democratic politics and the process of ethical reasoning prior to becoming politically involved. It is naïve to assume that elected officials can learn what they need to about ethical politics in a crash course after they are elected; elected officials are often too busy for such activities, and bad habits may already have set in. From this perspective, the basics of ethical politics should be covered in courses that deal with Canadian government and politics in high schools, colleges and universities.

Unfortunately, in reality the word *ethics* is rarely mentioned in such courses today. This needs to change, and we think that change is inevitable. In the 1970s, human rights issues were rarely mentioned in Canadian government courses; today, they are considered central. We expect a similar growth of interest in ethical politics as the agencies for promoting honest politics, such as ethics commissioners, become better known, and as more teaching materials become available.

## Political Accountability and Responsibility

The Westray tragedy, as with other scandals that have been revealed by the press, whistle-blowers, public inquiries or independent officers of legislatures, was treated initially by both principals of the company and the provincial government as essentially blameless, an accident. Initially, no one was willing to take responsibility for the disaster. It is too often claimed in such instances that no wrongdoing was ever intended, that what happened couldn't have been helped or that so many factors were involved that it is too complicated to assess responsibility. However, at the inquiry several company and government officials who testified claimed that there was nothing they could have done, and instead, they blamed others for the explosion. Former Nova Scotia Premier Donald Cameron echoed the mine's management and blamed the workers and the union. The denial of responsibility by those who *should* take responsibility and the tendency to shift blame onto others has been called the problem of "many hands."[18] So many people are involved at various stages of decision making and policy implementation that those in authority claim not to have known about particular transgressions. In Canadian parliamentary democracy, however, the involvement of many people should not count as an excuse. This point was emphasized by former Health Minister Monique Begin who, when she wrote to the Krever inquiry into Canada's tainted blood scandal,[19] stated that if there were problems with supervision, monitoring and control in governmental departments, responsibility for questionable policy and mistakes must lie with ministers, not just their subordinates.

Responsibility and accountability are closely intertwined. To have responsibility means that there is also an accountability relationship. Responsibility refers to "the giving and accepting of power or discretion," while accountability involves "compliance with the direction of those who provide that discretion."[20] In a democracy, the elected ministers of a government are held to account by the prime minister or premier who appointed them. Additionally, they and their leaders must answer to the legislature, and by extension to the public. The question of *how* ministers and politicians are accountable is almost as important as to *whom*. They are accountable to their fellow citizens through elections and by being required to publicly disclose their records and their reasons for seeking support to run for office.

While we are not supporters of the traditional view that a minister must always resign as punishment for departmental error, we are disturbed by the current tendency of federal and provincial ministers to shirk responsibility and to refuse to admit that ethical breaches or administrative foul-ups have occurred. To err is human; to admit error and devise a plan to ameliorate the situation is the ethical route because it is honest and respectful of those who have suffered from the error. On the other hand, for the Opposition to insist on the resignation of ministers who take the ethical high road in such situations is itself morally reprehensible.

Although laws and courts are useful for protecting constitutional rights, nullifying jurisdictional trespass, checking criminality and enforcing contractual obligations, there is no law to penalize — nor would any court punish — politicians who break their promises. The electorate is responsible for holding politicians to account. For that to happen we need a vigorously attentive citizenry. In our 1997 edition of *Honest Politics*, we argued that to compensate for the fact that the majority of citizens aren't involved in well-organized, well-financed interest groups and lobbying activities between elections, it made sense to give voters opportunities to voice their concerns over special issues via the recall and referendum processes. We are still of the view that in extraordinary circumstances, such as a government reversing its stance on a key election issue or seeking to introduce a major policy it never mentioned previously, referendums and recalls may still be worth considering as supplements to elections.[21] For example, had there been federal recall legislation in effect in the 2000s, David Emerson may well have been recalled after his audacious switch from Liberal to Conservative shortly after the 2006 election, or he may have decided not to switch because of the near certainty that a recall election would occur. However, were parties to embrace codes of conduct that forbid the arbitrary crossing of the floor within, say, six months of an election, and were more vigorous access to information laws abided by and transparency demanded and practised with the encouragement and attentiveness of conscientious ethics officers, the case for institutionalizing recall systems in extraordinary circumstances and the need for mechanisms to instigate referendums would be less compelling.

With respect to our summary of a number of the measures that can contribute significantly to checking unethical conduct by our leaders, the role of commissions of inquiry with their investigative, reporting and recommendatory functions should not be underemphasized.

This chapter began by drawing attention to the revelatory findings of an important commission of inquiry. We have throughout the book referred to a number of other inquiries that have thrown much needed light on irresponsible actions or inactions by those in authority. It is our view that the appointment of commissions of inquiry in cases of serious allegations of ethical breaches is a positive, at times, crucial, last resort method of promoting ethical accountability.

Some critics, however, are of the opinion that commissions of inquiry lead to protracted, expensive and highly legalistic ventures in fact-finding concerning political responsibility and that, furthermore, they contribute to the erosion of an older, traditional sense of *civitas,* or civic duty.[22] In a somewhat related sense, John Langford and Allan Tupper have indicated their concern that increased reliance on codes of conduct, ethics commissioners, ethical education and principles like the ones we've been emphasizing throughout this book might result in future Canadian governments being "ethically bombarded to death" by utopian "democratic sanitizers."[23]

Our position is that the more obstacles in the way of unethical and corrupt practices, and the more motivations for ethical politics the better. Our examination of the way politics is conducted across the country does not indicate that our elected officials are overburdened with rules and regulations, but rather that they require better and more useful checks and guidelines to help them carry out the jobs they were elected to do.

## CONCLUSION

Although this book has highlighted ethical deficiencies in Canadian politics and their remedies, we should not forget that despite these defects, the ethical standards of many Canadian politicians and public servants are actually quite high compared with other countries. Monique Begin is an excellent example of a highly responsible and honest politician. Begin was Minister of Health and Welfare in successive Liberal governments under Pierre Trudeau. In August 1996, she sent a letter to Justice Krever, head of the inquiry into the tainted blood fiasco. Begin waived any immunity that Justice Krever might grant and noted that she should be asked to testify if her former civil servants were called on to do so.

> If you have to lay the blame, I consider it my duty to take my share of the responsibility. The notion of "ministerial responsibility" is the cornerstone of our executive government. Justice is offended if people at the top are not held responsible for their actions, but employees at less serious levels of the hierarchy are. Public ethics requires that those at the top be accountable.[24]

This is a clear illustration of how responsibility and accountability need to be brought together.

Another outstanding example is Warren Allmand, who was a moral gadfly within government circles for more than three decades. Allmand, who served as solicitor general, Minister for Indian Affairs and Minister for Consumer Affairs in Liberal governments, was dismissed as chair of the House of Commons justice committee on September 1995 by the Liberal Party whip because he voted against the government's budget. According to Allmand, the budget was a disavowal of the party's public platform,[25] and he felt an obligation to hold firm to his principles. "You have to, and I'll continue to do so, if I think we are violating the principles of our party or we are going against what we promised in the election. I'll continue to support the platform I ran on."[26]

Ethical politics is important to most Canadians, and voters are rarely willing to provide ongoing support to governments with a record of corruption. Failing to provide an adequate infrastructure for ethical politics is an invitation to those with baser motives to take advantage of the system.

In 2013, Prime Minister Harper's legal advisor, Benjamin Perrin, quit his job after he learned about the $90,000 cheque that Nigel Wright wrote so that Senator Mike Duffy could claim to have paid back questionable expenses on his own, and after Harper rejected Perrin's legal advice that Duffy's ownership of at least $4,000 worth of property in

Prince Edward Island was not enough for him to qualify as a "resident" for the purposes of representing that province in the Senate. Just before the 2015 election, Perrin, who had been a lifelong Conservative, announced that the Harper government "no longer had the moral authority to govern."[27] In 2010, Munir Sheikh, the head of Statistics Canada, resigned his position in protest over the claim by Industry Minister Tony Clement that the abolition of the long-form census would make no difference to the accuracy of data collected by the agency.[28] Both Perrin and Sheikh provide examples of public servants who give ethical behavior priority.

By making more extensive use of ethics commissioners, improving ethics legislation, encouraging political parties to develop codes of ethics, promoting ethics audits and greater ethical accountability, and enhancing the quality and quantity of ethics education, we can set the stage for an era in the not-too-distant future when ethical politics is considered as much a hallmark of our political system as free elections and judicially monitored human rights.

But all the ethics safeguards in the world will not help a country where too few of its citizens possess a democratic character that is supportive of mutual respect and the democratic principles that derive from it. Someone with democratic character traits is community-minded, tolerant moderate and values social equality. Such a person defends minority rights, finds exploitation of the disadvantaged unacceptable and values freedom and integrity. Fighting political battles fairly and being a good loser are essential to the democratic character. To the extent that citizens feel that they are treated fairly, they have trust in democratic institutions, even when they are on the losing side of a decision. Yet all of us are susceptible to letting our own personal agendas interfere with our public responsibilities. To the extent that we are able to control the "me first" urge in our public duties, we exemplify a sense of democratic character. According to Robert Putnam, party activists need to place loyalty to fellow citizens ahead of loyalty to the party. George Kateb describes this democratic character trait as one of "engaged detachment," and this outlook militates against the temptation to get involved in dirty-handed politics.[29]

Some may consider the quest for democratic character hopeless. The debate about whether human beings are, ought to be or even can be mutually interested rather than singly self-interested is older than recorded history. But until recently, it has been a debate mainly among males. Most mothers we know, as well as fathers who take parenting seriously, have no doubts about the value of concern for others.[30]

There are many factors that, combined, promote a democratic character: a loving and nurturing family environment that engenders a sense of moral consciousness;[31] an education that helps us to understand groups we might otherwise be suspicious about out of ignorance;[32] and enough involvement in community activities to help us appreciate the problems and outlooks of our fellow citizens.[33] But even if these character traits are present in society in significant quantities, their potential energy cannot be harnessed to promote and protect democracy without ethical leadership. A governing regime's ethical tone is enormously influenced by those at the top — the premier or prime minister, the cabinet and the top public servants. Leaders who are considered self-interested and untrustworthy create a malaise in governing circles that tempts public servants to behave unethically to protect themselves.[34] And these factors combine to erode the public's trust in government as a whole. Conversely, if those at the top are perceived as fair and honest, then these values tend to permeate the entire society.

But it is worth remembering that in a democracy, leadership comes from and is representative of the citizenry. As our leaders have a duty to function as moral actors, so all citizens also have a duty to see to it that they live up to their obligations and practice the ethics and principles of democracy.

# CONTRIBUTORS

NAOMI COUTO teaches in the School of Public Policy and Administration, as well as in the Master's of Public Policy, Administration and Law program at York University. Her areas of interest include Canadian criminal justice policy, education policy, ethical theory and processes, practices and power. Her publications include *Violated and Silenced: The Gendering of Justice, An Argument for Critical and Liberal Education: A Synthesis of Ancient and Modern Thought*, and *Rob Ford and the End of Honour*.

IAN GREENE is a Professor Emeritus and Senior Scholar in the School of Public Policy and Administration at York University in Toronto. He was the founding Director of York's Master's program in Public Policy, Administration and Law. Greene's most recent book is *The Charter of Rights and Freedoms*.

GREG LEVINE has had a long career in ethics and law, including his work with the Office of the Ombudsman in British Columbia. He has been the integrity commissioner for several Ontario municipalities, and has written several books on the law of government ethics.

ROBERT SHEPHERD is a professor at Carleton University and president of the Canadian Association of Programs in Public Administration. Prior to 2007, when Shepherd began his academic career, he gained extensive experience working in the federal public service.

DAVID P. SHUGARMAN is a Professor Emeritus and Senior Scholar at York University. He received his M.A. in Political Economy and Ph.D. in Political Philosophy at the University of Toronto. His recent publications include chapters, essays and articles on the commission of the inquiry into the sponsorship scandal, public inquiries and democratic accountability.

IAN STEDMAN is an Ontario lawyer who is currently completing his Ph.D. at Osgoode Hall Law School with a focus on Canada's government ethics regime. His legal career in both the public and private sectors includes the Office of the Integrity Commissioner and Lobbyist Registrar of Ontario and he has worked as an instructor at Osgoode Hall Law School and within the School of Public Policy and Administration.

LORI TURNBULL wrote a PhD dissertation at Dalhousie University on the Canadian approach to tackling conflict of interest issues, and is a professor at Carleton University seconded to the Government of Canada's Privy Council Office.

SHAUN YOUNG is currently a Special Projects Officer in the Office of the Vice-President, Research & Innovation, and a sessional lecturer in political science at the University of Toronto. Prior to this, he spent six years working in public policy development in a number of different Ministries in the Ontario Public Service and has taught at the University of Toronto, Carleton University, York University, Brock University and the University of Ontario Institute of Technology. He is the author or editor of seven books and sixteen essays in peer-reviewed scholarly journals.

# ACKNOWLEDGEMENTS

We acknowledge full responsibility for any errors or omissions in this book.

In the acknowledgements for the 1997 edition of this book, we mentioned several dozen friends or colleagues, without whose assistance or support the book would never have appeared. This book consists mostly of new material, but builds on the framework used in the 1997 volume. We will begin by thanking friends or colleagues whose help was seminal to completing the 2017 manuscript, and then will reiterate our thanks to those key to supporting us in 1997.

Key to the publication of this book was Jim Lorimer, who asked Ian Greene and David Shugarman in 2014 to consider a new edition. This book would not exist without his encouragement, and his gentle but persistent nudging to persuade us that wonderful things can happen in retirement. Jim's long-suffering production editors, Laura Cook and Robin Studniberg, were instrumental in steering the project in the right direction, and we appreciate Lorimer's copy-editing staff, especially Ryan Perks, for their committed work

Ian acknowledges and expresses the greatest appreciation to his wife, Eilonwy Morgan, and his three children — Christina, Philip and Girum — for their patience and understanding on days when the book was all-consuming. David acknowledges the patience and support of his spouse, Linda Scott, for encouraging him to engage in yet another book project during his retirement, and for putting up with him "going back to work."

The two of us only agreed to write this book with the support of six contributors who would do most of the heavy lifting to add new materials to the book. All of them proved to be excellent, compatible colleagues, and each made invaluable contributions. Rob Shepherd made an extraordinary contribution by preparing Chapters 7 and 8, and making significant contributions to several other chapters, all this while serving as President of the Canadian Association of Programs in Public

Administration. It was a privilege to have Gregory Levine, Canada's foremost authority on municipal ethics, as part of our team, and Greg's experience and insight was a guiding light. Ian Stedman is one of the most insightful PhD students whom Ian Greene has ever worked with. He not only took the lead on Chapter 5, but reviewed and improved other chapters. Lori Turnbull is a welcome new voice among the few political scientists who study ethics and politics, and her lead on Chapter 6 was inspiring, particularly considering her secondment to the Privy Council Office from Carleton University, and her duties as a new mother, while the book was being drafted. Naomi Couto, recently hired by the School of Public Administration at York University, helped with Chapters 1 to 3 and made insightful improvements to Chapter 9, and she kept us upbeat and positive when our workload seemed insurmountable. Shaun Young brought his expertise in political philosophy and public administration to bear in Chapter 10, and added the sections on egregious partisanship. Finally, Ian Greene was fortunate to have Jacob Blum as his research assistant in the final stages of the manuscript preparation. Jacob is a multi-talented individual who has already done great public service as a senior administrator in the health field, and as the courageous and honest whistle-blower in the ORNGE episode.

Contributor Shaun Young would like to acknowledge the life-long love and support from his recently deceased aunt, Agnes Dotzko, and the patience during manuscript preparation of his daughters Amy and Faith. Rob Shepherd would like to acknowledge Diane Simsovic and Ian Bron (PhD candidates in the School of Public Policy & Administration, Carleton University) who provided invaluable support for preparing Chapters 7 and 8. Their expertise in areas of lobbying and whistle-blowing was a valuable addition to the substance of those chapters. He would also like to acknowledge the constant support and guidance of his wife, Karen Shepherd.

Naomi Couto, sandwiched between her career and care for her mother, thanks her mother and her siblings for their understanding. Lori Turnbull thanks her infant daughter for sleeping in her snuggly so that mom could work on her chapter. Greg Levine thanks his wife, Joy Parr, for offering encouragement and advice as Chapter 9 came into being. Ian Stedman thanks his wife and beautiful young daughters for his late-night sessions writing and editing for the book.

The manuscript for *Honest Politics* (1997) benefitted greatly from the help of dozens of friends or colleagues of Ian Greene and David Shugarman, a few of whom we mention here. We are indebted to all who participated in the ethical politics workshops at York University in the early 1990s. We would like to thank, in particular, participants Hon. Gregory Evans, Donald C. MacDonald, Charles Campbell and Patrick Boyer for taking time to read our manuscript and to provide us with comments. The late Donald MacNiven was a pioneer in establishing the field of practical ethics, and without his groundwork, this book would not exist. Others who were kind enough to read the 1997 manuscript and advise us were David Baugh and Andrew Heard. Howard Wilson, the federal ethics counsellor, his chief advisor Gordon Parks, and Cornelius von Baeyer, who was with the ethics counsellor's office prior to his retirement, all provided us with valuable insights. Peter McCormick helped us to think more clearly about the recall and other aspects of democratic ethics.

We are particularly indebted to the late Kenneth Kernaghan, who has done so much to promote ethics in the public sector, and who gave us a very detailed commentary for the 1997 manuscript. We learned much from *The Responsible Public Servant*, by Kenneth Kernaghan and John Langford. Ken is greatly missed, and when we encountered the really difficult passages in this book, we envisioned his spirit looking over our shoulders, and asking, "have you really got this right?"

More generally, we wish to record our appreciation and thanks to Tom Pocklington, who set us on our way, whose teaching and writing continue to inspire and who will no doubt find much to disagree with and criticize in what we have written. Others who have significantly influenced our thinking about ethical politics include the late Donald Smiley, who combined a deep sense of ethics and social justice with good humour, and Peter Russell, whose research, student support and public-service contributions have been driven by his commitment to mutual respect and democracy. We are also grateful for help received from Maureen Mancuso, Michael Atkinson, Neil Nevitte and Andre Blais, whose work on the Canadian Political Ethics Project has informed and refined our thinking.

We are grateful to McLaughlin College's administrative assistant, Lilian Polsinelli, and secretarial staff member Vicki Carnavale, and former staff Vicky Perot and Frances Tee for helping us with the preparation of the first manuscript and, in Shugarman's case, easing the burdens of a university administrator at crucial times. In Greene's case, the continued support of Lilian and Vicki was invaluable during the preparation of the 2017 manuscript.

For parts of the 1997 book, we relied heavily on Ian Greene's article, "Conflict of Interest and the Constitution," published in the *Canadian Journal of Political Science* in 1990; we thank the journal for permission to use the article. The Social Sciences and Humanities Research Council not only provided the funding for the three workshops on ethical politics, but also support for related research that was invaluable in the preparation of the 1997 edition.

No project like this can succeed without the support and patience of family members, and those closest to us even provided editorial advice and research assistance for the 1997 manuscript: Eilonwy Morgan, Margaret Bertram, Doris Annear, the late Monty Annear and Linda Scott. Most of all, we are grateful to Jim Lorimer for deciding to publish the 1997 edition, to then editor Diane Young for her tireless and thorough editorial assistance, to Laura Ellis, our copy editor, and to Paul Rynard, our Graduate Research Assistant. Rynard's assistance was invaluable: in many respects there are words, phrases, and sections of the book that are as much his as ours, and he also is responsible for assembling the notes and bibliography. This book is very much a shared project.

— Ian Greene and David P. Shugarman, for Robert Shepherd, Greg Levine, Ian Stedman, Lori Turnbull, Naomi Couto and Shaun Young

# NOTES

## CHAPTER 1

1.  Mr. Justice Isadore Grotsky as quoted in the Honourable E.N. (Ted) Hughes, Q.C., *Report of the Commissioner of Conflict of Interest* (1995–96). http://www.coibc.ca/down/reports/1995-96_annual_report.pdf.

2.  Kirk Makin, "Top court turns down Berntson," *The Globe and Mail*, February 24, 2001. http://www.theglobeandmail.com/news/national/top-court-turns-down-berntson/article25432895/; and The Canadian Press, "Lorne McLaren, 80", *The Globe and Mail*, January 6, 2009. http://www.theglobeandmail.com/news/national/lorne-mclaren-80/article20439603/.

3.  Since there were never receipts or notes made by either or any associate the actual amounts remain a mystery.

4.  *Canada, Report of the Commission of Inquiry into Certain Allegations Respecting Business and Financial Dealings Between Karlheinz Schreiber and the Right Honourable Brian Mulroney*, (Ottawa: Government Publications, 2010), Vol. 1 pp.2&3 and Vol. 2 ch.9, p.363 and passim. Hereafter *Oliphant Inquiry*. Commissioner was Jeffrey J. Oliphant.

5.  Ian Greene testified before the Oliphant inquiry during its second phase, the purpose of which was to devise recommendations to prevent the breaches of integrity documented in the phase one report from occurring in the future. During one of the breaks, Schreiber remarked to Greene, "I don't know what all the fuss is about. What I do is good for everyone. Companies make money, there are more jobs for union members, and I also benefit. Everybody wins."

6.  Office of the Auditor General, "The Sponsorship Program," in *Report of the Auditor General of Canada,* November, 2003 (Ottawa: Office of the Auditor General, 2003), http://www.oag-bvg.gc.ca/internet/English/parl_oag_200311_03_e_12925.html; and Gomery, *Phase I Report,* and *Phase II Report.* http://epe.lac-bac.gc.ca/100/206/301/pco-bcp/commissions/sponsorship-ef/06-03-06/www.gomery.ca/en/phase1report/index.asp.

7.  Gomery, 2005 and 2006, Phase I Report, Executive Summary, 76.

8.  Pierre St-Arnaud, "Ad Exec Jailed in Sponsorship Scandal," *Toronto Star*, June 27, 2007, https://www.thestar.com/news/2007/06/27/ad_exec_jailed_in_sponsorship_scandal.html.

9.  Canadian Press, "Jacques Corriveau Found Guilty on Three Fraud-Related Charges," *Globe and Mail*, November 1, 2016, http://www.theglobeandmail.com/news/national/jacques-corriveau-found-guilty-on-three-fraud-related-charges/article32612692/.

10. Sidhartha Banerjee, "Jacques Corriveau Freed After Getting 4-Year Prison Term for Sponsorship Fraud," *CBC News*, January 25, 2017, http://www.cbc.ca/news/canada/montreal/jacques-corriveau-sentencing-sponsorship-scandal-1.3951190.

11. "Danielle Smith, David Emerson, Belinda Stronach Among High-Profile Defectors," *CBC News*, February 9, 2015, http://www.cbc.ca/news/politics/danielle-smith-david-emerson-belinda-stronach-among-high-profile-defectors-1.2950159; and Bernard J. Shapiro, *The Harper-Emerson Inquiry* (Ottawa, Office of the Ethics Commissioner, March 2006), http://ciec-ccie.parl.gc.ca/Documents/English/Previous%20Offices/

Archives%20from%20the%20former%20Ethics%20Commissioner/Inquiry%20 Reports/Members%20of%20the%20House%20of%20Commons/2006/The%20 Harper-Emerson%20Inquiry%20(March%202006).pdf. Bernard Shapiro, the ethics commissioner for the House of Commons and the cabinet, investigated Emerson's defection. He found that no rules were violated, but recommended that the House of Commons consider how this kind of behaviour might be prevented in the future.

12.  *Toronto Star*, January 12, 1978; and McDonald, *Report of the Commission of Inquiry*.

13.  Immanuel Kant, *Grounding for the Metaphysics of Morals* [1785], 3rd ed., translated by James Ellington, (Indianapolis: Hackett, 1993), 35–36.

14.  Democracy evolves through several stages. At first, there is the struggle for universal franchise, accompanied by fair and free elections. Then there is the human rights advancement period. The next stage is the focus on ethical principles in politics. Of course, these stages overlap each other, depending on historical factors, but the reality is that the Canadian period of focus on ethics and politics did not begin until the human rights period culminated in the *Charter of Rights and Freedoms*.

15.  Macpherson, *Real World of Democracy*.

16.  Supreme Court of Canada, *A.G. Canada v. Lavell* [1973] 38 *Dominion Law Reports* (3d) p. 481.

17.  Polyviou, *Equal Protection of the Laws*.

18.  Greene, *Charter of Rights and Freedoms*, 263 ff.

19.  Sniderman et al., *Clash of Rights*. See also Dominique Clément, Will Silver, and Daniel Trottier, *The Evolution of Human Rights in Canada* (Ottawa: Canadian Human Rights Commission and Minister of Public Works and Government Services, 2012), http://www.chrc-ccdp.ca/sites/default/files/ehrc_edpc-eng.pdf, and Ignatieff 2000.

20.  Marchak, *Ideological Perspectives on Canada*.

21.  Bayefsky, "Defining Equality Rights."

22.  In 1988, the legislature of Newfoundland and Labrador enacted pay equity legislation, but in 1991, during a severe economic downturn, the legislature enacted legislation to defer or cancel pay equity payments, thus disadvantaging many women in particular. In 2004, the Supreme Court of Canada, in the unanimous decision of a seven-judge panel, upheld the 1991 legislation. Although the 1991 legislation was a violation of equality in the *Charter*, it was deemed a reasonable limit, given the severe economic crisis. *Newfoundland (Treasury Board) v. N.A.P.E.*, [2004] 3 S.C.R. 381, 2004 SCC 66.

23.  Malszechi, "He Shoots He Scores"; and see Bashevkin, *Toeing the Lines*.

24.  For example, the Alberta Court of Appeal has had approximate gender equality amongst its sixteen judges since the 1990s.

25.  Susan Delacourt, "Two Liberal MPs Ejected from Caucus Over 'Personal Misconduct' Allegation," *Toronto Star*, November 5, 2014, https://www.thestar.com/news/canada/2014/11/05/2_liberal_mps_booted_from_caucus_over_personal_misconduct_allegations.html.

26.  Laura Stone, "Hunter Tootoo Quit Caucus, Cabinet Over 'Inappropriate Relationship,'" *Globe and Mail*, August 3, 2016, http://www.theglobeandmail.com/news/politics/mp-hunter-tootoo-quit-caucus-cabinet-over-consensual-relationship/article31264673/.

27.  Long and Boldt, eds., with Little Bear, *Quest for Justice*.

28. Greene, *Charter of Rights and Freedoms*, 76 ff.

29. Ibid., 385–403.

30. Dworkin, *Taking Rights Seriously*.

31. Pateman, *Participation and Democratic Theory*.

32. *Globe and Mail*, April 4, 1996, A1.

33. Murray Brewster, "No Need for Inquiry into Afghan Detainee Torture, Liberals Say," *CBC News*, June 17, 2016, http://www.cbc.ca/news/politics/afghan-canada-prisoners-1.3640411.

34. Robert Benzie, "Gas Plant Cancellations Biggest 'Cover-Up' in Ontario History, Tories Say," *Toronto Star*, March 11, 2013, https://www.thestar.com/news/queenspark/2013/03/11/gas_plant_cancellations_biggest_coverup_in_ontario_history_tories_say.html; and Rob Ferguson, "Energy Minister Chris Bentley to Resign His Seat," *Toronto Star*, February 8, 2013, https://www.thestar.com/news/queenspark/2013/02/08/energy_minister_chris_bentley_to_resign_his_seat.html.

35. Robert Fife and Laura Stone, "Duffy Cleared of All Charges as Judge Excoriates PMO under Harper," *Globe and Mail*, April 21, 2016, http://www.theglobeandmail.com/news/politics/duffy-aquitted-of-all-31-charges-in-senate-expenses-trial/article29706093/.

36. See a list of all of the federal, provincial and territorial information and privacy commissioners at: http://www.lop.parl.gc.ca/ParlInfo/compilations/provinceterritory/PrivacyCommissioners.aspx.

37. Evans, *Annual Report, 1994–95*, 15.

38. Canada, Senate of Canada, *Proceedings of the Special Joint Committee on a Code of Conduct*, Issue 9 (Ottawa: Queen's Printer for Canada, November 1, 1995), 9.

39. Chief Justice Lyman Duff in the Alberta Press Bill case, *Re Alberta Statutes* [1938] S.C.R. 100.

40. Fallows, "Why Americans Hate the Media."

41. Canadian political parties are not immune to allowing the use of extreme rhetoric on their social media sites, at least until there are complaints. See Chantal Hébert, "Conservative Party Attracting Unpleasant Odours," *Toronto Star*, August 27, 2016, https://www.thestar.com/news/canada/2016/08/27/conservative-party-attracting-unpleasant-odours-hbert.html.

42. *Globe and Mail*, July 20, 1996, A1.

43. Carter, "Insufficiency of Honesty," 74.

44. For an analysis of the difficulty that this flip-flop caused Liberal MP Sheila Copps, who vowed to resign if the Liberals reneged on their promise, see Greene and Shugarman, *Honest Politics* (1997), chap. 3.

# CHAPTER 2

1. Oliphant 2010, 2 & 3.

2. See Kernaghan and Langford, *Responsible Public Servant*, chap. 3.

3. Canadian Judicial Council, Press release (Halifax, September 20, 1996), 2.

4.    Canadian Judicial Council, *Report of the Canadian Judicial Council to the Minister of Justice* (Ottawa: Canadian Judicial Council, 2009), https://www.cjc-ccm.gc.ca/cmslib/general/Report_to_Minister_Justice_Cosgrove.pdf.

5.    Robson Fletcher, "Justice Robin Camp Tells Inquiry He's Learned from 'Hurtful' Comments He Made at Sex Assault Trial," *CBC News*, September 9, 2016, http://www.cbc.ca/news/canada/calgary/judge-robin-camp-inquiry-testifies-friday-1.3754972.

6.    Information about the Camp inquiry can be accessed on the Canadian Judicial Council website, https://www.cjc-ccm.gc.ca/english/lawyers_en.asp?selMenu=lawyers_bylaw_en.asp.

7.    See Greene and Shugarman, *Honest Politics* (1997), 112 ff.

8.    Canadian Bar Association, Committee on the Appointment of Judges in Canada, *The Appointment of Judges in Canada* (Ottawa: Canadian Bar Foundation, August 1985); and Russell and Zeigel, "Federal Judicial Appointments."

9.    Greene, *The Courts*.

10.    Informal interview by Ian Greene with a former Harper government advisor, May 30, 2016. Greene was told that "ideology in judicial appointments is ingrained in our political system; all parties do it."

11.    Kernaghan and Langford, *Responsible Public Servant*, chap. 7.

12.    Dean Bennett, Canadian Press "Alison Redford Resigns as Alberta Premier amid Spending Scandal," *Huffington Post*, March 19, 2014, http://www.huffingtonpost.ca/2014/03/19/alison-redford-resigns_n_4996450.html.

13.    Re Manitoba Language Rights (Order), [1985] 2 *Supreme Court Reports*, 347.

14.    Rawls, *Theory of Justice*, 235–42.

15.    Dicey, *Introduction to the Study of the Law of the Constitution*.

16.    Greene, *Charter of Rights and Freedoms*, chap. 6.

17.    Locke, *Second Treatise of Government*, 71, 75 (sect. 136, 142).

18.    Smith, "Patronage in Britain and Canada."

19.    See Sara Blake, *Administrative Law in Canada*, 5th ed. (LexisNexis Canada, 2011), 11–17, and 156 ff.

20.    *Canadian Charter of Rights and Freedoms*, sect. 7, http://laws-lois.justice.gc.ca/eng/const/page-15.html.

21.    Jones and de Villars, *Principles of Administrative Law*, 409 ff.

22.    Supreme Court of Canada, *Martineau v. Matsqui Institution Disciplinary Bd.* (No. 2) [1980] 106, *Dominion Law Reports* (3d) 385 at 412. Also see Ibid., 312, 353. More recently, the Supreme Court has expanded the scope of natural justice rather than continuing to develop a separate doctrine of fairness.

23.    Jones and de Villars, *Principles of Administrative Law*, 247 ff.

24.    Wilson, *Book for Judges*.

25.    This worrisome attitude about the corrupting influence of power is taken up again in our concluding chapter.

26.    Presentation by Ted Hughes at Workshop on Ethical Politics, York University, November

21, 1991, with financial support from the Social Sciences and Humanities Research Council of Canada.

27.    See the Annual Reports of the British Columbia Conflict of Interest Commissioner, accessed on August 21 2016, http://www.coibc.ca/annual_reports.htm.

28.    Rawls, *Theory of Justice.*

29.    United Nations Human Development Reports, accessed on August 20, 2016, http://hdr.undp.org/en/data#.

30.    *Toronto Star,* June 15, 1996.

31.    Kernaghan and Langford, *Responsible Public Servant,* especially chap. 2, 3 and 8.

32.    *Canadian Doctors for Refugee Care et al. v. Canada,* 2014, FC 651, para. 2-4.

33.    Ibid., para. 587, 891 and 910.

34.    Stephanie Levitz, Canadian Press, "Liberals Drop Lawsuit over Refugee Health-Care Cuts, Speed Up Resettlement," *Globe and Mail,* December 16, 2015.

35.    Public servants in some jurisdictions, however, already had the benefit of appropriate statutes and regulations. See Kernaghan and Langford, *Responsible Public Servant.*

36.    Mill, *Utilitarianism,* 6.

# CHAPTER 3

1.    Juillet and Rasmussen, *Defending a Contested Deal.*

2.    Whitaker, "Between Patronage and Bureaucracy."

3.    Kernaghan and Langford, *Responsible Public Servant,* 235; and Osborne and Gaebler, *Reinventing Government.*

4.    Weber, *Essays in Sociology.*

5.    Locke, *Second Treatise of Government,* 71, 75 (sect. 136, 142). Locke published these words in 1689.

6.    Whitaker, "Between Patronage and Bureaucracy," 66.

7.    Duffy was eventually acquitted. See Kathleen Harris, "Judge Clears Mike Duffy of All Charges and Slams Prime Minister's Office under Harper," *CBC News,* April 21, 2016, http://www.cbc.ca/news/politics/mike-duffy-trial-rulings-fraud-bribery-senate-1.3545846; Canadian Press, "Patrick Brazeau Gets No Jail Time or Criminal Record Following Guilty Plea," *CBC News,* October 28, 2015, http://www.cbc.ca/news/politics/brazeau-no-criminal-record-jail-senate-1.3292343; and John Paul Tasker and Janyce McGregor, "Patrick Brazeau Clear to Return to Senate as Fraud Charges Dropped," *CBC News,* July 13, 2016, http://www.cbc.ca/news/politics/senator-patrick-brazeau-court-charges-1.3676831.

8.    Greg Weston, "Former Liberal Senator Convicted of Fraud Begins Jail Term," *CBC News,* June 14, 2013, http://www.cbc.ca/news/politics/former-liberal-senator-convicted-of-fraud-begins-jail-term-1.1360706; and Andrew Seymour, "Criminal Charges Withdrawn Against Ex-Senator Mac Harb," *Ottawa Citizen,* May 20, 2016, http://ottawacitizen.com/news/local-news/criminal-charges-withdrawn-against-ex-senator-mac-harb.

9.    Ross Howard, "Liberals, Expect No Favoritism," *Globe and Mail,* February 17, 1994.

10.    Ibid.

11.  Cameron, *On the Take*, 183.

12.  Auron Wherry, "Stephen Harper's Most Unfortunate Appointments," *Maclean's*, July 2, 2015, http://www.macleans.ca/politics/ottawa/stephen-harpers-most-unfortunate-appointments/; and Glen McGregor, "Conservative Government Made More Than 70 Patronage Appointments over Two Days in June," *Postmedia News*, July 7, 2015, http://news.nationalpost.com/news/canada/canadian-politics/conservative-government-made-more-than-70-patronage-appointments-over-last-two-days-of-june.

13.  Cameron, *On the Take*; and Simpson, *Spoils of Power*.

14.  Edward Greenspon, "Job Advertised, but Saved for Party's Friend," *Globe and Mail*, February 6, 1995, Al.

15.  Ibid. and Ross Howard, "Liberals, Expect No Favoritism," *Globe and Mail*, February 17, 1994.

16.  Law Reform Commission of Canada, *Consultative Document*, 39.

17.  Ibid. 39n9.

18.  Brian Bergman, "NS Premier John Savage Resigns," *Maclean's*, March 31, 1997, republished in *Canadian Encyclopedia*, March 17, 2003, http://www.thecanadianencyclopedia.ca/en/article/ns-premier-john-savage-resigns/.

19.  Glen McGregor, "Conservative Government Made More Than 70 Patronage Appointments over Two Days in June," *Postmedia News*, July 7, 2015, http://news.nationalpost.com/news/canada/canadian-politics/conservative-government-made-more-than-70-patronage-appointments-over-last-two-days-of-june. Note the appointments made to the Immigration and Refugee Board.

20.  Shawn McCarthy, "Liberals Won't Force Tories' Late-Term NEB Appointees to Step Down," *Globe and Mail*, January 1, 2016, http://www.theglobeandmail.com/news/politics/liberals-wont-force-tory-appointed-neb-members-to-step-down/article27986653/.

21.  Tu Thanh Ha, "Liberals on Trial over System of Legal Agents," *Globe and Mail*, February, 7, 1996, A6.

22.  Greene and Shugarman, *Honest Politics* (1997), 44.

23.  Tu Thanh Ha, "Liberals on Trial."

24.  Wade Riordan Raaflaub, "The Possible Establishment of a Federal Director of Public Prosecutions in Canada," Parliamentary Information and Research Service, Library of Parliament, March 2, 2006, http://www.lop.parl.gc.ca/content/lop/ResearchPublications/prb0567-e.html.

25.  The method of recruiting deputy ministers used in Alberta, and recommended by Justice John Gomery in his report on the sponsorship scandal, is to stage an open competition, after which the top candidates are interviewed by a selection committee, which makes recommendations and presents a short list to the minister and premier. Such a procedure emphasizes competence, but also allows the premier leeway to choose a candidate who appears best able to implement the government's priorities. See Greene and Shugarman, "Commission of Inquiry."

26.  Sean Fine, "The Secret Short List That Provoked the Rift between Chief Justice and PMO," *Globe and Mail*, May 23, 2014, http://www.theglobeandmail.com/news/politics/the-secret-short-list-that-caused-a-rift-between-chief-justice-and-pmo/article18823392/?page=all.

27.    *Reference re Supreme Court Act*, ss. 5 and 6, 2014 SCC 21; and Sean Fine, "Supreme Court Rejects Harper Appointee Marc Nadon," *Globe and Mail*, March 21, 2014, http://www.theglobeandmail.com/news/politics/marc-nadon-supreme-court-ruling-stephen-harper/article17607585/.

28.    Sean Fine, "Supreme Court Hearings Provide Transparency, Respect to Process," *Globe and Mail*, October 23, 2016, http://www.theglobeandmail.com/news/national/supreme-court-hearings-provide-transparency-respect-to-process/article32486760/.

29.    See Greene 2006, chap. 1. In Ontario and some other provinces, patronage in judicial appointments has been eliminated, but it continues at the federal level. We applaud the Justin Trudeau government for promising to eliminate patronage in federal judicial appointments. See Kirk Makin, "Ontario System Eliminates Patronage in Choosing Judges, Proponent Says," *Globe and Mail*, April 27, 2012, http://www.theglobeandmail.com/news/politics/ontario-system-eliminates-patronage-in-choosing-judges-proponent-says/article4103317/.

30.    See Alison Crawford and Peter Zimonjic, "Justice Minister Announces 24 New Judges in Effort to End National Shortage," *CBC News*, October 20, 2016, http://www.cbc.ca/beta/news/politics/judge-shortage-24-appointments-1.3814275; and Office of the Commissioner for Federal Judicial Affairs Canada, "Appointments to Superior Courts Public Representative on the JACs: How to Apply — Application Form," accessed October 31, 2016, http://www.fja-cmf.gc.ca/appointments-nominations/forms-formulaires/pr-rp/index-eng.html.

31.    *Hewat v. Ontario* (1998), 37 O.R. (3d) 161 (Ont. Court of Appeal).

32.    Ellis, *Unjust by Design*, 87 ff; and Todd Jeffrey Weiler, "Independence, Impartiality, and the Ontario Social Assistance Review Board in 1997," *Journal of Law and Social Policy* 12 no. 7 (1997): 178–201, http://tinyurl.com/kuapfzp.

33.    Ellis, *Unjust by Design*.

34.    See Aucoin, *New Public Management*, chap. 2.

35.    Greene, *The Courts*, 160 ff.

36.    Dimock et. al, *Ethics and the Public Service*, 307.

37.    Canada, Office of the Conflict of Interest and Ethics Commissioner, *Conflict of Interest Code for Members of the House of Commons, S. 2(c)* (Ottawa, Office of the Commissioner, 2016), http://ciec-ccie.parl.gc.ca/EN/Pages/default.aspx.

38.    Parker, *Commission of Inquiry*, 28.

39.    Starr and Sharp, *Ethical Conduct in the Public Sector*.

40.    Kernaghan, "Codes of Ethics," 531. See also Kernaghan and Langford, *Responsible Public Servant*, 124 ff.

41.    Kernaghan, "Ethical Conduct of Canadian Public Servants," 6.

42.    Starr and Sharp, *Ethical Conduct in the Public Sector*.

43.    Greene, "Conlfict of Interest and the Constitution."

44.    A judicial review in 2004 determined that Justice Parker's findings regarding Mr. Stevens's alleged conflicts of interest should be set aside for reasons of an excess of jurisdiction and a breach of procedural fairness by the commissioner. *Stevens v. Canada (Attorney General)* (F.C.), 2004 FC 1746, [2005] 2 F.C.R. 629; and see "Judge Throws Out 1987 Sinclair Stevens Conflict Decision," *CBC News*, December 17, 2004, http://www.cbc.ca/news/canada/judge-throws-out-1987-sinclair-stevens-conflict-decision-1.473755.

45.    Cameron, *On the Take.*

46.    Liberal Party of Canada, "Red Book," 1993, accessed October 16, 2016, https://web.archive.org/web/19961109135653/http://www.liberal.ca/english/policy/red_book/red_index.html.

47.    Margaret Young, "Legislative Summary, Bill C-4: An Act to Amend the Parliament of Canada Act (Ethics Commissioner and Senate Ethics Officer) and Other Acts in Consequence," Law and Government Division, Parliamentary Research Branch, Library of Parliament, February 12, 2004, http://www.lop.parl.gc.ca/Content/LOP/LegislativeSummaries/37/3/c4-e.pdf.

48.    See Canadian Centre for Management Development, *A Strong Foundation: Report of the Task Force on Public Service Values and Ethics* (Ottawa: CCMD, 1996).

49.    John C. Tait, *A Strong Foundation: Report of the Public Service Task Force on Values and Ethics* (Canadian Centre for Management Development, 1996), http://publications.gc.ca/collections/Collection/SC94-72-1996E.pdf.

50.    See Savoie, *What is Government Good At?,* 130–32.

51.    Hughes, *Annual Report, 1993–94*; and Stanbury, *Money in Politics.*

52.    Stanbury, *Money in Politics.*

53.    Greene, "Allegations of Undue Influence," 110.

54.    *Toronto Star,* June 22, 1989, A14.

55.    *Winnipeg Free Press,* August 28, 1988, 9; and *Vancouver Sun,* August 26, 1988, Al.

56.    *Globe and Mail,* August 8, 1987, A8.

57.    *Vancouver Sun,* August 8, 1984, B3.

58.    Kathy Tomlinson, "British Columbia: The 'Wild West' of Fundraising," *Globe and Mail,* March 4, 2017, A8–A9, http://www.theglobeandmail.com/news/investigations/wild-west-bc-lobbyists-breaking-one-of-provinces-few-political-donationrules/article34207677/.

59.    Ibid.

60.    Ibid.

61.    Gary Mason, "Global Ridicule Won't Stop B.C. Liberals' Deceitful Financing Extravaganza," *Globe and Mail,* March 5, 2017, http://www.theglobeandmail.com/news/british-columbia/global-ridicule-wont-stop-bc-liberalsdecietful-financing-extravaganza/article34211267/.

62.    Greene, "Allegations of Undue Influence," 124.

63.    Gary Mason, "Welcome to British Columbia, the Land of 'Pay-to-Play' Events," *Globe and Mail,* January 27, 2017, http://www.theglobeandmail.com/news/british-columbia/welcome-to-british-columbia-the-land-of-pay-to-play-events/article33813233/.

64.    Rob Ferguson, "Ontario Tightens Fundraising Loopholes," *Toronto Star,* November 9, 2016, https://www.thestar.com/news/queenspark/2016/11/09/ontario-tightens-fundraising-loopholes.html.

65.    Sawatsky, *The Insiders.*

66.    Cheney and Brazao, "Moores King of Movers, Shakers."

67. Stark, "'Political-Disclosure' Analysis," 517–18.

68. "EHealth Scandal a $1B Waste: Auditor," *CBC News*, October 7, 2009, http://www.cbc.ca/news/canada/toronto/ehealth-scandal-a-1b-waste-auditor-1.808640. See also "Ontario Government Scrambles to Control OLG Scandal Damage," *CTV News*, August 31, 2009, http://toronto.ctvnews.ca/ont-gov-t-scrambles-to-control-olg-scandal-damage-1.430261. The legislation was amended in 2014 to allow the commissioner to select from any of the province's agencies, boards and commissions. See *Public Sector Expenses Review Act, 2009*, S.O. 2009, c. 20, and regulations, https://www.ontario.ca/laws/statute/09p20.

69. See *Public Sector Expenses Act, 2009*, S.O. 2009, c. 20, section 7: "7. (1) The Integrity Commissioner may require the expenses officer of a public entity selected by the Commissioner to give copies to the Commissioner of all expense claims made by the relevant designated persons during the period described in subsection (2) for expenses that are reviewable under section 3. 2014, c. 13, Sched. 11, s. 1 (1)."

70. Jean Fournier, "Talk is Cheap, Time to Fix Senate's Rules," Hill Times, June 13, 2016, 12–13.

71. Mary Dawson, *The Philpott Report Made under the* Conflict of Interest Act, (Ottawa: Office of the Conflict of Interest and Ethics Commissioner, December 21, 2016), http://s3.documentcloud.org/documents/3245366/The-Philpott-Report.pdf.

72. Kristy Kirkup, Canadian Press, "Jane Philpott Repays $3,700 for Limo Service Owned by Liberal Supporter," *Toronto Star*, August 18, 2016, https://www.thestar.com/news/canada/2016/08/18/jane-philpott-repays-3700-for-limo-service-owned-by-liberal-supporter.html.

73. Terry Pedwell, Canadian Press, "Billing for Orange Juice Was a Mistake, Bev Oda Concedes," *Globe and Mail*, July 31, 2012, http://www.theglobeandmail.com/news/politics/billing-for-orange-juice-was-a-mistake-bev-oda-concedes/article4453440/.

74. Laura Stone, "PMO Denies Aides Were Briefed on Moving Expense Reimbursements," *Globe and Mail*, September 27, 2016, http://www.theglobeandmail.com/news/politics/company-that-moved-trudeau-aides-says-all-clients-briefed-on-costs-of-relocation/article32077868/.

75. Facebook posting by Gerald Butts on September 22, 2016, accessed October 16, 2016, https://www.facebook.com/gerald.butts.54/posts/10154477741530011.

## CHAPTER 4

1. William D. Parker, *Commission of Inquiry into the Facts of Allegations of Conflict of Interest Concerning the Honourable Sinclair M. Stevens* (Ottawa: Ministry of Supply and Services, 1987).

2. *Stevens v. Canada (Attorney General)*, 2004 FC 1746, http://decisions.fct-cf.gc.ca/fc-cf/decisions/en/item/38260/index.do.

3. A detailed analysis of Stevens's business activities, and Parker's conclusion about them in relation to conflicts of interest, can be found in Greene and Shugarman, *Honest Politics* (1997).

4. The ADRG was not truly independent at that time.

5. Parker, *Commission of Inquiry*, 349.

6. Ibid., 29.

7. Ibid., 360.

8. Ibid., 348.

9. Ibid., 353.

10. *Criminal Code*, (R.S.C., 1985, c. C-46), http://laws-lois.justice.gc.ca/eng/acts/C-46/section-380.html.

11. L'Unité permanente anticorruption.

12. "New Que. Anti-Corruption Boss Gets to Work," *CBC News*, March 17, 2011, http://www.cbc.ca/news/canada/montreal/new-que-anti-corruption-boss-gets-to-work-1.998672.

13. "Former Boisbriand Mayor Sentenced to 18 Months in Prison in Municipal Collusion Scheme," *Montreal Gazette*, May 20, 2016, http://montrealgazette.com/news/local-news/former-boisbriand-mayor-sentenced-to-18-months-in-prison-in-municipal-collusion-scheme.

14. The Commission's website, accessed September 2, 2016, https://www.ceic.gouv.qc.ca/la-commission.html.

15. Melinda Dalton, "Charbonneau Commission Report: A Deeper Look at the Recommendations," *CBC News*, November 24, http://www.cbc.ca/news/canada/montreal/charbonneau-commission-report-recommendations-1.3335460.

16. Benjamin Shingler and Elias Abboud, "Michael Applebaum sentenced to 12 months behind bars," March 30, 2017, accessed April 13, 2017, http://www.cbc.ca/news/canada/montreal/michael-applebaum-mayor-sentenced-corruption-charges-1.4046781.

17. "Gilles Vaillancourt Elects Trial by Judge and Jury," *CBC News*, September 4, 2015, http://www.cbc.ca/news/canada/montreal/gilles-vaillancourt-elects-trial-by-judge-and-jury-1.3216402; and Linda Ulai, "Former Mayor Michael Applebaum to Stand Trial on 14 Charges as Preliminary Inquiry Wraps Up," *Montreal Gazette*, June 3, 2015, http://montrealgazette.com/news/local-news/two-new-witnesses-testify-at-preliminary-hearing-for-former-mayor-michael-applebaum.

18. "Lino Zambito Avoids Jail Time for Construction Corruption," *CBC News*, November 9, 2015, http://www.cbc.ca/news/canada/montreal/lino-zambito-corruption-fraud-sentencing-1.3311600.

19. Gomery, *Phase I Report*, 283.

20. Ibid., 14.

21. Ibid., 13.

22. Ibid., 14.

23. See Greene and Shugarman, *Honest Politics* (1997).

24. Gomery, *Phase I Report*, 284.

25. Andy Blatchford, Canadian Press, "Sponsorship Fraudster Chuck Guité Granted Parole," *Toronto Star*, January 2, 2009, https://www.thestar.com/news/canada/2009/01/02/sponsorship_fraudster_chuck_guiteacute_granted_parole.html.

26. Gomery, *Phase I Report*, 284.

27. Ibid., 286.

28. Ibid., 300.

29.   Ibid., 292.

30.   Ibid., 300.

31.   Paul Cherry, "Federal Sponsorship Scandal: Jacques Corriveau 'Floored' by Guilty Verdict," *Montreal Gazette*, November 1, 2016, http://montrealgazette.com/news/local-news/federal-sponsorship-scandal-jacques-corriveau-guilty-on-three-charges.

32.   Ibid.

33.   Sidhartha Banerjee, "Jacques Corriveau Freed After Getting 4-Year Prison Term for Sponsorship Fraud," *CBC News*, January 25, 2017, http://www.cbc.ca/news/canada/montreal/jacques-corriveau-sentencing-sponsorship-scandal-1.3951190. Corriveau appealed his conviction and sentence and was freed on bail. The appeal may not be heard until 2019.

34.   The Liberal Party paid back to the government the funds that Justice Gomery determined that Corriveau and others had illegally donated to it.

35.   Kirk Makin, "Top Court Turns Down Berntson," *Globe and Mail*, February 24, 2001, http://www.theglobeandmail.com/news/national/top-court-turns-down-berntson/article25432895/. Berntson appealed his conviction to the Supreme Court of Canada, where he lost in 2001.

36.   Luke Fisher and John DeMont, "Cogger Convicted of Influence Peddling," *Maclean's*, June 15, 1998, http://www.thecanadianencyclopedia.ca/en/article/cogger-convicted-of-influence-peddling/#h3_jump_0.

37.   Cameron, *On the Take*, 93–98; and Greene and Shugarman, *Honest Politics*, (1997), 64–65.

38.   *Montreal Gazette*, February 10, 1987, A2.

39.   *Globe and Mail*, May 12, 1993, A9; and May 13, 1993, Al.

40.   Ryan Hicks, Canadian Press, "Preliminary Hearing Set for Ex-Deputy Premier Nathalie Normandeau: 7 Face Multiple Charges Related to Normandeau's Time in Jean Charest's Liberal Cabinet," *CBC News*, August 29, 2016, http://www.cbc.ca/news/canada/montreal/normandeau-court-appearance-1.3736998.

41.   Office of the Conflict of interest and Ethics Commissioner, *The Finley Report, Made under the* Conflict of interest Act, March 10, 2015, http://ciec-ccie.parl.gc.ca/Documents/English/Public%20Reports/Examination%20Reports/The%20Finley%20Report.pdf, 1.

42.   Ibid., 2.

43.   Ibid., 5.

44.   Ibid., 14–17.

45.   Testimony of Shawn Graham before Conflict of Interest Commissioner Patrick Ryan, as reported in Hon. Patrick A.A. Ryan, Q.C., Conflict of Interest Commissioner, *Report to the Speaker of the Legislative Assembly of New Brunswick of the Investigation/Inquiry by the Hon. Patrick A.A. Ryan, Q.C. Conflict of Interest Commissioner, Into Allegations by Mr. Claude Williams, MLA for Kent South, of Violations of the* Members' Conflict of Interest Act *by Premier Shawn Michael Graham, MLA for Kent*, February 14, 2013, http://leg-horizon.gnb.ca/e-repository/monographs/31000000047402/31000000047402.pdf.

46.   *Members' Conflict of Interest Act*, M-7.01, SNB 1999, s.4.

47.   Hon. Patrick A.A. Ryan, *Report to the Speaker of the Legislative Assembly of New Brunswick.*

48.    Ibid., para. 108.

49.    Ibid., para. 119.

50.    Ibid., para. 189.

51.    Ibid., para. 190.

52.    Ibid., para. 193.

53.    See Greene and Shugarman, *Honest Politics* (1997), 77-82.

54.    Parker, *Commission of Inquiry*, 35.

55.    Ibid., 37, emphasis in original.

56.    Statutes of British Columbia, 1992, Chapter 54, *Members' Conflict of Interest Act*, Section 2(1) (see Appendix II).

57.    The Hon. E.N. (Ted) Hughes, QC, *Opinion of the Commissioner of Conflict of Interest on a Citizen's Complaint of Alleged Contravention of the Member's Conflict of Interest Act By the Honourable Robin Blencoe, Minister of Municipal Affairs, Recreation and Housing.* British Columbia, Office of the Commission of Conflict of Interest, August 1993. Mimeo, 29-30.

58.    Ibid., 37–38.

59.    Ibid., 39.

60.    Canada, Treasury Board Secretariat, Policies and Guidance, Conflicts of Interest and Post-Employment, "Apparent Conflict of Interest," revised July 23, 2015, https://www.tbs-sct.gc.ca/psm-fpfm/ve/conflict-conflit/aci02-eng.asp.

61.    Neil Wilkinson, *Report to the Speaker of the Legislative Assembly of Alberta of the Investigation by Neil Wilkinson, Ethics Commissioner into Allegations Involving the Honourable Alison Redford, Q.C., Premier* (Office of the Ethics Commissioner, Province of Alberta, December 4, 2013), http://www.ethicscommissioner.ab.ca/media/1063/final-ver-01-dec-03-13.pdf, 48.

62.    Ibid, para. 52(1).

63.    For example, see Jen Gerson, "The Zombie of Alberta Politics: Alison Redford's Misdeeds are Still Haunting the Province," *National Post*, December 4, 2015, http://news.nationalpost.com/full-comment/jen-gerson-the-zombie-of-alberta-politics-alison-redfords-misdeeds-are-still-haunting-the-province.

64.    Charles Rusnell and Jennie Russell, "Alison Redford Chose Last-Ranked Legal Consortium for Alberta's $10B Tobacco Litigation," *CBC News*, November 23, 2015, http://www.cbc.ca/news/canada/edmonton/alison-redford-chose-last-ranked-legal-consortium-for-alberta-s-10b-tobacco-litigation-1.3331001.

65.    Charles Rusnell and Jennie Russell, "Redford Tobacco-Litigation Probe Not Provided All Relevant Documents, Report Says," *CBC News*, April 4, 2016, http://www.cbc.ca/news/canada/edmonton/redford-tobacco-litigation-probe-not-provided-all-relevant-documents-report-says-1.3520271.

66.    Hon. Frank Iacobucci, *Report on the Independent Review Conducted by the Honourable Frank Iacobucci, C.C., Q.C. of Information Relating to an Investigation by the Former Ethics Commissioner of Alberta into Allegations Involving the Honourable Alison Redford, Q.C.*, March 30, 2016, https://justice.alberta.ca/publications/Documents/Iacobucci-Report.pdf, para. 81.

67. Charles Rusnell and Jennie Russell, "Redford Ethics Probe Decision Handed Off to B.C. Due to Potential Conflict," *CBC News,* April 5, 2016, http://www.cbc.ca/news/canada/edmonton/redford-ethics-probe-decision-handed-off-to-b-c-due-to-potential-conflict-1.3522325.

68. Office of the Ethics Commissioner, Province of Alberta, Report of the Re-Investigation by Paul D.K. Fraser, Q.C., Acting Ethics Commissioner, Into Allegations Involving, The Honourable Alison Redford, Q.C., March 29, 2017, accessed April 13, 2017, http://www.ethicscommissioner.ab.ca/media/1787/redford-reinvestigation-decision.pdf.

69. See Greene and Shugarman, *Honest Politics* (1997), 89ff.

70. Steven Chas, "Helena Guergis Fined for Failure to Report Mortgage," *Globe and Mail,* May 20, 2010, http://www.theglobeandmail.com/news/politics/helena-guergis-fined-for-failure-to-report-mortgage/article1576402/.

71. Canadian Press, "Helena Guergis Broke Conflict of Interest Rules: Ethics Watchdog," *Guardian* (Charlottetown), July 14, 2011, http://www.theguardian.pe.ca/News/Canada--World/2011-07-14/article-2653987/Helena-Guergis-broke-conflict-of-interest-rules%3A-ethics-watchdog/1.

72. "Industry Minister Christian Paradis Caught in Conflict of Interest for Rahim Jaffer Dealings," *Toronto Star,* March 22, 2012, https://www.thestar.com/news/canada/2012/03/22/industry_minister_christian_paradis_caught_in_conflict_of_interest_for_rahim_jaffer_dealings.html.

73. Mary Dawson, *The Paradis Report,* Made under the Conflict of Interest Act (Ottawa: Office of the Conflict of Interest and Ethics Commissioner, March 22, 2012), 3.

74. Ibid., 26.

75. Mary Dawson, *Referral from the Public Sector Integrity Commissioner: The Bonner Report Made under the* Conflict of Interest Act (Ottawa: Office of the Conflict of Interest and Ethics Commissioner, February 26, 2015), http://ciec-ccie.parl.gc.ca/Documents/English/Public%20Reports/Examination%20Reports/The%20Bonner%20Report.pdf, 1.

76. Ibid., 11 ff.

77. Ibid., 25 ff.

78. Ibid., 1.

79. Kady O'Malley, "Ethics Watchdog Raps Former Jason Kenney Aide over Gala Tickets," *CBC News,* February 27, 2015, http://www.cbc.ca/news/politics/ethics-watchdog-raps-former-jason-kenney-aide-over-gala-tickets-1.2975243.

80. Mary Dawson, *Bonner Report,* 21.

81. Kady O'Malley, "Ethics Watchdog Raps Former Jason Kenney Aide."

82. Greg Weston, "Former Liberal Senator Convicted of Fraud Begins Jail Term," *CBC News,* June 14, 2013, http://www.cbc.ca/news/politics/former-liberal-senator-convicted-of-fraud-begins-jail-term-1.1360706.

83. Ibid.

84. Canadian Press, "Ex-Senator Raymond Lavigne Denied Early Parole," *CBC News,* August 23, 2013, http://www.cbc.ca/news/politics/ex-senator-raymond-lavigne-denied-early-parole-1.1401452.

85. Ibid.

86.  Dean Bennett, Canadian Press, "Alison Redford Resigns as Alberta Premier amid Spending Scandal," *Huffington Post*, March 19, 2014, http://www.huffingtonpost. ca/2014/03/19/alison-redford-resigns_n_4996450.html.

87.  Ibid.

88.  Charles Rusnell and Jennie Russell, "Alison Redford Ordered Penthouse Suite in Federal Building," *CBC News*, March 28, 2014, http://www.cbc.ca/news/canada/edmonton/ alison-redford-ordered-penthouse-suite-in-federal-building-1.2589713.

89.  Allison Jones, "London, Ont. Mayor Joe Fontana Pleads Not Guilty to Three Fraud Charges," *Maclean's*, May 26, 2014, http://www.macleans.ca/politics/london-ont-mayor- joe-fontana-pleads-not-guilty-to-three-fraud-charges/.

90.  Allison Jones, "London Mayor Joe Fontana Guilty of Fraud, Forgery Charges," *Maclean's*, June   10,   2014,   http://www.macleans.ca/news/canada/london-mayor-joe-fontana- guilty-of-fraud-forgery-charges/.

91.  Mike Donachie, "Exclusive: Former London Mayor Joe Fontana Breaks Silence After Four Months of House Arrest," *Toronto Metro News*, November 14, 2014, http:// www.metronews.ca/news/hamilton/2014/11/16/exclusive-former-london-mayor-joe- fontana-breaks-silence-after-four-months-of-house-arrest.html.

92.  Allison Jones, "Convicted Former London, Ont. Mayor Joe Fontana Spared Jail Time," *Maclean's*, July 15, 2014, http://www.macleans.ca/news/canada/ex-london-mayor-joe- fontana-faces-sentencing/.

93.  Slayton, *Lawyers Gone Bad*, chap. 1.

94.  Fournier, "Talk is Cheap."

# CHAPTER 5

1.   *Conflict of Interest Act*, S.N. 1973, no 113.

2.   *Conflict of Interest Act, 1988*, S.O. 1988, c 17.

3.   Donald C. MacDonald, *The Happy Warrior: Political Memoirs* (Toronto: Dundurn Press, 1998), 75.

4.   *Municipal Act*, RSO 1960, c 249.

5.   *Re Election of Collins*, [1967] 2 OR 41.

6.   Ontario, Ministry of Municipal Affairs, *Report of the Committee on Conflicts of Interest* (Toronto: Queen's Printer, 1968).

7.   See Dick Illingworth, "Province's Policy is Too Loose on Conflict of Interest," *Toronto Star*, September 2, 1986, E4.

8.   *Municipal Conflict of Interest Act, 1972*, S.O. 1972, c 142. (Royal Assent was given to Bill 214 on December 15, 1972).

9.   Illingworth, "Province's Policy." See also Sylvia Stead, "Stricter Guideline on Conflicts is Urged for Cabinet Ministers," *Globe and Mail*, January 12, 1981.

10.  Illingworth, "Province's Policy."

11.  See e.g. Ibid.; and Robert Sheppard, "Conflict of Interest Ontario Proposal is Ethical Buck-Passing, Critics Claim," *Globe and Mail*, July 18, 1987.

12. Ontario, *Statement by the Hon. William Davis, Premier of Ontario, on Guidelines with Respect to Conflict of Interest* (Toronto: Government of Ontario, 1972).

13. Ibid., 1.

14. Ibid., 2.

15. Ibid.

16. Ibid.

17. Ibid.

18. Ontario, *Statement by the Hon. David Peterson, Premier of Ontario, on Guidelines with Respect to Conflict of Interest* (Toronto: Government of Ontario, 1985).

19. Legislative Assembly of Ontario, Standing Committee on Public Accounts, *Report on the Allegation of Conflict of Interest Concerning Elinor Caplan, MPP* (September 1986), 47.

20. Legislative Assembly of Ontario, Standing Committee on the Legislative Assembly, *Report on Allegation of Conflict of Interest Concerning René Fontaine, MPP* (September 1986), Appendix A, 28–30.

21. John B. Aird, *Report on Ministerial Compliance with the Conflict of Interest Guidelines and Recommendations with Respect to those Guidelines* (Toronto: Blake, Cassels & Graydon, 1986).

22. Ibid., 51.

23. *Bill 1, An Act respecting Conflicts of Interest of Members of the Assembly and the Executive Council* (*Members' Conflict of Interest Act*), 1st sess., 34th Parliament, Ontario, 1987 (assented to February 11, 1988), S.O. 1988, c 17.

24. Ibid.

25. Ibid., s 12(2)(a). (This list is simply a summary of the most significant components of the legislation and is not a comprehensive summary.)

26. Ibid., supra note 25, s 10(4).

27. The High Court is now known as the Superior Court of Ontario.

28. *Members' Integrity Act, 1994*, S.O. 1994, c 38.

29. Denise Harrington "Peterson Tells Cabinet to Comply or Be Fired as Conflict Law Passes," *Toronto Star*, February 10, 1988, A11.

30. Legislative Assembly of Ontario, Standing Committee on Administration of Justice, *Report on Conflict of Interest Guidelines* (September 1991), Appendix B, s 15(a).

31. Thomas Walkom, *Rae Days* (Toronto: Key Porter Books Limited, 1994).

32. Ontario, Legislative Assembly, *Official Report of Debates* (Hansard), 1st sess., 35th Parliament, No 73 (December 19, 1990), 2945 (Steven W Mahoney).

33. Ontario, Legislative Assembly, *Official Report of Debates* (Hansard), 1st sess., 35th Parliament, No 74 (December 20, 1990), 3010 (Hon Shelley Martel); see also Legislative Assembly of Ontario, Standing Committee on Administration of Justice, *Report on Conflict of Interest Guidelines* (September 1991), i (Preface).

34. Legislative Assembly of Ontario, Standing Committee on Administration of Justice, *Report on Conflict of Interest Guidelines* (September 1991), Letter to the Speaker.

35. Ibid., 21.

36. *Provincial Offences Act,* RSO 1990, c p. 33.

37. Legislative Assembly of Ontario, Standing Committee on the Legislative Assembly, *Report Regarding Allegations of Breach of the Premier's Conflict of Interest Guidelines Made Against Evelyn Gigantes, M.P.P. and Minister of Housing* (August, 1994), 1.

38. Ibid., 109.

39. Ibid., 110.

40. Ibid., 110–11.

41. Ibid., 136–39.

42. Greene and Shugarman, *Honest Politics* (1997), 140.

43. *Members' Conflict of Interest Act.*

44. *Bill 209, An Act to Revise the Members' Conflict of Interest Act and to Make Related Amendments to the Legislative Assembly Act,* 3rd sess., 35th Legislature, 1994 (as passed by the Legislative Assembly of Ontario December 8, 1994).

45. See Ontario, Legislative Assembly, *Official Report of Debates* (Hansard), 3rd sess., 35th Parliament, no 169B (December 8, 1994).

46. See Ontario, Office of the Integrity Commissioner, *Annual Report, 1994–95* (Toronto: Publications Ontario, 1995), Commissioner's Remarks.

47. Ontario, Office of the Integrity Commissioner, *Annual Report, 1995–96* (Toronto: Publications Ontario, 1996), 1.

48. This preamble was based on the four guiding principles set out by Premier Rae in his guidelines. See *Report on Guidelines,* supra note 33 at Appendix B.

49. See *Members' Integrity Act;* see generally Ontario, Office of the Integrity Commissioner, *Annual Report 1995–96,* 6; Ian Urquhart, "Al Leach Ran Afoul of Rules That Just Aren't Realistic," *Toronto Star,* June 26, 1997, A27; Daniel Girard, "Rules Too Strict, Leach Says Ministers Should Be Able to Act for Constituents, Committee Told," *Toronto Star,* July 16, 1997, A11; and "Blundering on Behalf of Voters," [Editorial], *Hamilton Spectator,* June 27, 1997, A12.

50. Ontario, Office of the Integrity Commissioner, *Report of The Honourable Gregory T. Evans, Commissioner, Re: Ms. Dianne Cunningham, M.P.P., London North,* December 13, 1995, 2.

51. *Lobbyists Registration Act, 1998,* S.O. 1998, c 27.

52. *Cabinet Ministers' and Opposition Leaders' Expenses Review and Accountability Act,* 2002, S.O. 2002, c 34, Sched A.

53. *Public Sector Expenses Review Act, 2009,* S.O. 2009, c 20.

54. *Public Service of Ontario Act, 2006,* S.O. 2006, c 35, Sched A, Part VI.

55. See Ontario Regulation 382/07, *Conflict of Interest Rules for Public Servants (Ministers' Offices) and Former Public Servants (Ministers' Offices);* and Ibid., supra note 55 at ss 66–69.

56. Greene, "Conflict of Interest and the Constitution," 14.

57. Ibid., 4.

58.    *Members' Conflict of Interest Act,* SBC 1990, c 54 [BC MCIA].

59.    *Members' Conflict of Interest Act,* RSBC 1996, c 287, ss 2–3.

60.    Apparent conflicts were added by the B.C. legislature by way of an amendment in 1992 and were modeled after a definition developed by Chief Justice Parker in the Stevens Inquiry that had been conducted in the 1980s.

61.    This opinion has been expressed to Ian Greene by Commissioner Ted Hughes, and two subsequent commissioners in B.C.

62.    Members' Conflict of Interest Act, RSBC 1996, c. 287, s 19(2).

63.    The Province of British Columbia, Office of the Conflict of Interest Commissioner, "The *Members' Conflict of Interest Act –* Proposed Amendments to the *COI Act,*" last modified November 7, 2014, http://www.coibc.ca/act_proposed_changes.htm.

64.    British Columbia, Legislative Assembly, Select Committee on Parliamentary, Ethical Conduct, Standing Orders and Private Bills, *Review of the* Members' Conflict of Interest Act, 5th sess., 39th Parliament (May 14, 2013), https://www.leg.bc.ca/content/legacy/web/cmt/39thparl/session-5/parref/reports/PDF/Rpt-PARREF-39-5-ReviewOfTheMembersConflictOfInterestAct-2013-MAR-14.pdf.

65.    *Conflicts of Interest Act,* S.A. 1991, c C-22.1.

66.    Greene, "Conflict of Interest and the Constitution."

67.    Alberta, *Code of Conduct and Ethics for the Public Service of Alberta* (June 26, 2013), http://www.pao.gov.ab.ca/legreg/code/Code-of-ConductandEthics-printable.pdf.   The Code of Conduct was issued by the President of Treasury Board, Minister of Finance of Alberta.

68.    *Lobbyists Act,* S.A. 2007, c L-20.5.

69.    Ibid., s 11(2).

70.    *House of Assembly Act,* RSNL 1990, c H-10, s 34.

71.    *Conflict of Interest Act, 1995,* SNL 1995, c C-30.1

72.    See *House of Assembly Act,* supra note 70, s 37(4).

73.    Ibid.

74.    Saskatchewan, *Report to the Attorney General from the Law Reform Commission of Saskatchewan, Conflicts of Interest* (March 1977), http://lawreformcommission.sk.ca/Conflict_of_Interest_Report.pdf.

75.    *Members' Conflict of Interest Act,* SS 1979, c M-11.2.

76.    Brian Bergman, "Saskatchewan Tories in Fraud Scandal," *Maclean's,* November 18, 1996.

77.    *Members' Conflict of Interest Act,* SS 1993, c M-11.11.

78.    *Lobbyists' Act,* SS 2014, c L-27.01.

79.    *Legislative Assembly and Executive Council Act,* SNWT 1999, c 22.

80.    Legislative Assembly of Northwest Territories, "Statutory Officers NWT," accessed November 10, 2016, http://www.assembly.gov.nt.ca/about/statutory-officers.

81.    Ibid., s 103.

82.    "N.W.T. Premier's Secret Affair Put Him in Conflict: Report," *CBC News,* October 30,

2009, http://www.cbc.ca/news/canada/north/n-w-t-premier-s-secret-affair-put-him-in-conflict-report-1.795694.

83. *Conflict of Interest Act*, RSPEI 1988, c C-17.1.

84. See Ibid., ss 5(c), 7(1)(c), 12, 28(1)(b), 28(4), 28(5)(c), 29(6)(a), 29(7)(a), 32(1)(d).

85. Prince Edward Island, Legislative Assembly, *Report of the Auditor General to the Legislative Assembly* (2009), 48, http://www.gov.pe.ca/photos/original/ag_report2009.pdf.

86. Ibid., 49.

87. Prince Edward Island, Office of the Conflict of Interest Commissioner, *Report to the Speaker of the Legislative Assembly Reviewing the Findings and Recommendations of the Auditor General Arising from His Audit of the Provincial Nominee Program and Members of the Legislative Assembly* (November 6, 2009), http://www.gov.pe.ca/photos/original/CICPNPrpt.pdf.

88. "PEI Conflict of Interest Commissioner Resigns," *Guardian* (Charlottetown), March 8, 2015, http://www.theguardian.pe.ca/News/Local/2015-03-08/article-4069699/P.E.I.-conflict-of-interest-commissioner-resigns/1.

89. "Neil Robinson Offers Differing View of Conversation with Steve Myers," *Guardian* (Charlottetown), March 10, 2015, http://www.theguardian.pe.ca/Opinion/Letter-to-editor/2015-03-10/article-4071870/Neil-Robinson-offers-differing-version-of-conversation-with-Steven-Myers/1.

90. *Members' Conflict of Interest Act*, SNB 1999, C M-7.01

91. *Integrity Act*, SNu 2001, c 7

92. *Nunavut Elections Act*, SNu 2002, c 17.

93. Ibid., s 231.

94. Although no definition is offered in the statute, this expression is often translated to "Inuit traditional knowledge" or "Inuit traditional institutions."

95. Nunavut, Legislative Assembly, "Integrity Act, Form 1, Annual Public Disclosure Statement," accessed November 10, 2016, http://integritycom.nu.ca/sites/integritycom.nu.ca/files/Annual_Public_Disclosure_Statement_Form_En.pdf.

96. Manitoba, Law Reform Commission, *The Legislative Assembly and Conflict of Interest (Report #106)* (Manitoba: Law Reform Commission, 2000), http://www.manitobalawreform.ca/pubs/pdf/archives/106-full_report.pdf.

97. *Legislative Assembly and Executive Council Conflict of Interest Amendment (Conflict of Interest Commissioner) Act*, SM 2002, c 49.

98. *Legislative Assembly and Executive Council Conflict of Interest Act*, CCSM 2015, c L112, s 20.

99. *Conflict of Interest (Members and Ministers) Act*, SY 1995, c 5.

100. *An Act to Amend the Conflict of Interest (Members and Ministers) Act*, SY 1996, c 2.

101. David Philip Jones and Anne S. de Villars have also co-authored several editions of a renowned text on Canadian administrative law entitled *Principles of Administrative Law* and Mr. Jones has taught at the University of Alberta Law School.

102. *Conflict of Interest (Members and Ministers) Act*, RSY 2002, c 37, s 17(g).

103. *Conflict of Interest Act*, NSA 2010, c 35.

104. *Members and Public Employees Disclosure Act*, SNS 1991, c 4, s 26.

105. Nova Scotia, Nova Scotia Legislature, "Form A: Disclosure Statement on Behalf of Members," accessed November 10, 2016, http://nslegislature.ca/pdfs/committees/hamc/MLADisclosureStatements.pdf.

106. *An Act respecting the National Assembly,* SQ 1982, c 62.

107. The jurisconsult concept is derived from the civil law tradition.

108. Hon. Jacques Chagnon, "An Ethical Framework for Members of the National Assembly of Quebec," *Parliamentarian* 1 (2014): 38–39, http://www.cpahq.org/cpahq/Main/Our_services/Publications/CPA_Publications/The_Parliamentarian/Archived_Issues/Main/Publications/The_Parliamentarian/Archived_Issues.aspx?hkey=fbe8f5c1-8b09-49ac-9061-bc0c25e18ca7.

109. *Code of Ethics and Conduct of the Members of the National Assembly,* SQ 2010, c. 30.

110. Ibid., s 110.

111. Quebec, National Assembly, Ethics Commissioner, *Report on the Implementation of the Code of Ethics and Conduct of the Members of the National Assembly, 2011–2014* (February 2015), http://www.ced-qc.ca/en/rappor"ts/CED-RMEO-2011-2014_2015-04-30_en.pdf.

112. See Chapter 3 for an in-depth discussion of these earlier attempts.

113. Greene, "Evolution of the Office of the Ethics Commissioner in Canada,", 10.

114. Ibid.

115. *Federal Accountability Act,* SC 2006, c 9.

116. *Parliament of Canada Act,* RSC 1985, c P-1, s 81.

117. Ibid., s 82(1).

118. Parliament of Canada, House of Commons, *Standing Orders of the House of Commons,* Appendix 1, *Conflict of Interest Code for Members of the House of Commons* (April 2016), http://www.parl.gc.ca/About/House/StandingOrders/appa1-e.htm.

119. Greene, "Case for Personal Meetings with the Federal Ethics Commissioner."

120. Ibid. This article argues that one of the major weaknesses of the ethics regime for the House of Commons and the federal cabinet is that MPs and cabinet ministers are not required to have annual face-to-face meetings with the ethics commissioner in the way that they are required to in the eight provinces and territories, including Ontario, Alberta and British Columbia, and as is the practice in the Senate. (Greene has argued elsewhere that two other weaknesses in the ethics regime in the House of Commons and cabinet are the methods used for selecting the commissioner and the fact that cabinet ministers must comply with two sets of overlapping rules (Greene 2010).)

121. *Parliament of Canada Act,* supra note 115, s 20.1.

122. Ibid.

123. Josh Wingrove, "Strengthen Senate Ethics Rules, Former Watchdog Says," *Globe and Mail,* November 10, 2013, A9, http://www.theglobeandmail.com/news/politics/strengthen-senate-ethics-rules-former-watchdog-says/article15371275/.

124. Greene, "Evolution of the Office of the Ethics Commissioner in Canada," 13.

# CHAPTER 6

1.    Elections Canada, *Political Financing Handbook for Registered Parties and Chief Agents* (Gatineau, Que.: Elections Canada, 2016), http://www.elections.ca/content.aspx?section=pol&dir=pol/man/ec20231&document=index&lang=e.

2.    Elections Canada, "Limits on Contributions," last modified December 12, 2016, http://www.elections.ca/content.aspx?section=pol&document=index&dir=lim&lang=e.

3.    Prior to limits to leadership campaign contributions being put into place, there were allegations that large donations both in Progressive Conservative and Liberal leadership contests resulted in undue influence, as noted in Greene and Shugarman, *Honest Politics* (1997), 105–107. Furthermore, at the Oliphant Commission inquiry, Karlheinz Schreiber testified that he had donated $50,000 to Brian Mulroney's leadership campaign in 1983. (Oliphant Inquiry, Executive Summary, 7). A donation of that size certainly raises red flags about the possibility of undue influence.

4.    Website for Commissioner of Canada Elections, accessed November 10, 2016, https://www.cef-cce.gc.ca/content.asp?section=abo&dir=bck&document=index&lang=e.

5.    Diana Mehta, Canadian Press, "Ex-Tory MP Dean Del Mastro Loses Appeal over Election Overspending," *Globe and Mail,* April 5, 2016, www.theglobeandmail.com/news/national/dean-del-mastro-ordered-to-serve-sentence-after-losing-appeal-in-election-overspending-case/article29533754/. Also see Colin Perkel, Canadian Press, "Former MP Dean Del Mastro Gets Month in Jail for Election Fraud," *Toronto Star,* June 25, 2015, https://www.thestar.com/news/canada/2015/06/25/convicted-former-mp-del-mastro-finds-out-if-he-goes-to-jail.html.

6.    Mehta, "Del Mastro Loses Appeal."

7.    Robert Fife and Steven Chase, "Drug Company Billionaire Pulls Out of Liberal Cash-for-Access Fundraiser," *Globe and Mail,* November 7, 2016, http://www.theglobeandmail.com/news/politics/chairman-of-canadian-drug-maker-apotex-pulls-out-of-cash-for-access-fundraiser/article32694874/.

8.    Ibid.

9.    Robert Fife and Steven Chase, "Trudeau to End Controversial Cash-for-Access Fundraisers," *Globe and Mail,* January 27, 2017, http://www.theglobeandmail.com/news/politics/trudeau-cash-for-access-fundraisers-changes/article33788333/.

10.    See Mancuso et. al., *Question of Ethics.*

11.    David M. Brock and Harold J. Jansen, "Raising, Spending and Regulating Party Finances in the Provinces," *Canadian Political Science Review* 9 no. 1 (2015): 55.

12.    Carrie Tait, "Alberta Cuts Political Donation Cap, Limits Party Spending," *Globe and Mail,* November 28, 2016, http://www.theglobeandmail.com/news/alberta/alberta-cuts-political-donation-cap-limits-party-spending/article33085219/.

13.    Keith Leslie, Canadian Press, "Kathleen Wynne Comes Clean on Fundraising Quotas for Cabinet Ministers," *National Post,* April 1, 2016, http://news.nationalpost.com/news/canada/kathleen-wynne-admits-ontarios-liberal-cabinet-ministers-have-fundraising-quotas.

14.    Rob Ferguson, "Ontario Tightens Fundraising Loopholes: Staff in Premier's Office and Chiefs of Staff Will Be Banned from Fundraiser," *Toronto Star,* November 9, 2016, https://www.thestar.com/news/queenspark/2016/11/09/ontario-tightens-fundraising-loopholes.html.

15. Government of Ontario, "Ontario Reintroduces Election Finance Reform Bill," [News release], September 13, 2016, https://news.ontario.ca/ghl/en/2016/09/ontario-reintroduces-election-finance-reform-bill.html.

16. Ibid.; and Progress Alberta, "Saskatchewan Has the Worst Campaign Finance Rules in Canada. Here's the Proof," November 1, 2016, http://www.progressalberta.ca/worst_campaign_finance_rules_in_canada.

17. Gary Mason, "Christy Clark's Salary Being Topped Up By Donations to BC Liberal Party," *Globe and Mail*, April 27, 2017, http://www.theglobeandmail.com/news/british-columbia/christy-clarks-salary-being-topped-up-by-donations-to-bc-liberal-party/article29767196/.

18. Ibid.

19. British Columbia, Office of the Conflict of Interest Commissioner, "Opinions," accessed February 3, 2016, http://www.coibc.ca/opinion_default.htm.

20. Hon. Gregory T. Evans, Integrity Commissioner, *Report Re: Mr. Michael Harris, M.P.P. Nipissing* (Toronto: Office of the Integrity Commisioner, May 1996). Mimeo, 5.

21. See Hiebert, "Code of Ethics for Political Parties," regarding how parties could go about drafting internal codes of ethics.

22. Office of the Auditor General of Canada, "Senators' Expenses," 2015, http://www.oag-bvg.gc.ca/internet/English/parl_otp_201506_e_40494.html.

23. Laura Payton, "Senator Mike Duffy Declared Eligible for PEI Seat: 4 Senators Subject to Further Spending Audit as Probe Wraps Up," *CBC News*, February 28, 2013, www.cbc.ca/news/politics/senator-mike-duffy-declared-eligible-for-p-e-i-seat-1.1313497.

24. "Mike Duffy Made Secret Deal with Harper's Chief of Staff During Audit," *CTV News*, May 14, 2013, http://www.ctvnews.ca/politics/mike-duffy-made-secret-deal-with-harper-s-chief-of-staff-during-audit-1.1282015.

25. Bruce Campion-Smith, "Nigel Wright, Stephen Harper's Chief of Staff, Resigns," *Toronto Star*, May 19, 2013, www.thestar.com/news/canada/2013/05/19/nigel_wright_stephen_harpers_chief_of_staff_resigns.html.

26. Record of emails of Nigel Wright from evidence submitted in Michael Duffy trial, 2015. Accessed November 20, 2016 through *Globe and Mail*, http://beta.images.theglobeandmail.com/static/folio/Wright/NigelWrightEmails.pdf.

27. Chris Cobb, "Harper's Former Legal Adviser 'Taken Aback' When PM Rejected Advice on Duffy's Residency Qualifications," *National Post*, August 20, 2015, http://news.nationalpost.com/news/canada/canadian-politics/harpers-former-legal-adviser-taken-aback-when-pm-rejected-advice-on-duffys-residency-qualifications. Soon after this incident, Perrin resigned his position.

28. Mark Gollom, "Mike Duffy Defends Arrangement to Pay Controversial Expenses," December 11, 2015, http://www.cbc.ca/news/politics/mike-duffy-trial-expenses-1.3360532.

29. *R. v. Duffy, 2016*, ONCJ 220 (CanLII), http://canlii.ca/t/gplvk.

30. "Sen. Mike Duffy's Office Asked PEI to Fast-Track Health Card," *CTV News*, February 4, 2013, http://www.ctvnews.ca/politics/sen-mike-duffy-s-office-asked-p-e-i-to-fast-track-health-card-1.1143198.

31. *R. v. Duffy.*

32. Ibid.

33. Kelly McParland, "Trudeau's First Senate Appointees are Exactly the Sort of People You'd Expect Liberals to Appoint," *National Post*, March 22, 2016, http://news.nationalpost.com/full-comment/kelly-mcparland-trudeaus-first-senate-appointees-are-exactly-the-sort-of-people-youd-expect-liberals-to-appoint.

34. See Jean T. Fournier, "Talk is Cheap."

35. Ibid.

36. *R. v. Duffy*, para. 1036.

37. Stephanie Levitz, Canadian Press, "Duffy Cleared of All Charges," *LF Press*, April 21, 2016, http://www.lfpress.com/2016/04/21/duffy-trial-judge-dismisses-some-trust-fraud-charges.

38. *R. v. Duffy*.

39. Kernaghan and Langford, *Responsible Public Servant*, 47.

40. Langford, "Acting on Values."

41. Heintzman, "Public Service Values and Ethics." This debate is reminiscent of the Friedrich and Finer debate. See: Herman Finer, "Administrative Responsibility in Democratic Government," *Public Administration Review* 1 (1941): 335–50; and Carl J. Friedrich, "Public Policy and the Nature of Administrative Responsibility," in *Public Policy*, edited by Carl J. Friedrich (Cambridge: Harvard University Press, 1940).

# CHAPTER 7

1. We acknowledge the contribution of Ian Stedman, PhD Candidate in the Faculty of Law, York University, for providing background research on the case studies.

2. Ontario, *Lobbyists Registration Act, 1998*, S.O. 1998, c. 27. Proclaimed January 15, 1999.

3. Organization for Economic Cooperation and Development, *Implementing the OECD Principles for Transparency and Integrity in Lobbying*.

4. Pross, "Law and Innovation," and Sawatsky, *The Insiders*.

5. Stevie Cameron, "Like Magic," *Report on Business Magazine*, February 1988, 56.

6. Cheney and Brazao, "Moores King of Movers, Shakers."

7. For a description of the Airbus scandal, see Greene and Shugarman, *Honest Politics* (1997), chap. 5, 125 ff.

8. Pross and Shepherd, "Something Borrowed, Something New."

9. Ibid.

10. A. Paul Pross, "The Rise of the Lobbying Issue in Canada: 'The Business Card Bill,'" in Grant Jordan, *Commercial Lobbyists: Politics for Profit in Britain* (Aberdeen: Aberdeen University Press, 1991), 86–91.

11. For example, see the federal code of conduct: Office of the Commissioner of Lobbying, *Lobbyists' Code of Conduct* (Ottawa: Office of the Commissioner of Lobbying, 2015), www.ocl-cal.gc.ca.

12. "Former MP Rahim Jaffer Connected to Alleged Conman," *Toronto Star*, April 8, 2010, https://www.thestar.com/news/gta/2010/04/08/former_mp_rahim_jaffer_connected_to_alleged_conman.html.

13. See Office of the Commissioner of Lobbying, *The Lobbying Activities of GPG-Green Power Generation Corp. and Patrick Glémaud and Rahim Jaffer* (Ottawa: Office of the Commissioner of Lobbying, 2011), https://lobbycanada.gc.ca/eic/site/012.nsf/eng/h_00331.html.

14. *Lobbying Act, 2008*, s. 10.1(1). An individual who is required to file a return under subsection 5(1) shall not receive any payment that is in whole or in part contingent on the outcome of any matter described in subparagraphs 5(1)(a)(i) to (vi) or on the individual's success in arranging a meeting referred to in paragraph 5(1)(b).

15. Office of the Commissioner of Lobbying. "Lobbying Activities."

16. Ibid.

17. ORNGE, "History," accessed February 14, 2017, http://www.ORNGE.ca/AboutORNGE/Pages/History.aspx. The Health Minister appointed a new board in 2012 in reaction to the scandal.

18. ORNGE was responsible for organ transport delivery in Ontario as part of the North American Donor Base.

19. Donovan, *ORNGE*, 11 ff.

20. "ORNGE President was Paid $1.4 Million Per Year," *Toronto Star*, December 22, 2011, https://www.thestar.com/news/canada/2011/12/22/ORNGE_president_was_paid_14_million_per_year.html. Ornge Peel was deliberately created to hide exectuive salaries from the sunshine list. It housed fewer than ten executives. ORNGE contracted the management services of Ornge Peel to run ORNGE.

21. "Ontario Auditor to Dig Deeper into Air Ambulance Executive Salaries," *Toronto Star*, December 15, 2011, https://www.thestar.com/news/canada/2011/12/15/ontario_auditor_to_dig_deeper_into_air_ambulance_executive_salaries.html; See also "Hearing into ORNGE Scandal Ends with Big Questions Still Unanswered," *National Post*, August 2, 2012, http://news.nationalpost.com/news/canada/hearing-into-ornge-scandal-ends-with-big-questions-still-unanswered.

22. Donovan, *ORNGE*, 37.

23. "Founder of ORNGE, Chris Mazza, Fired," *Toronto Star*, February 2, 2012, https://www.thestar.com/news/canada/2012/02/02/ornge_founder_chris_mazza_terminated.html.

24. "Hearing into ORNGE Scandal Ends with Big Questions Still Unanswered," *National Post*, August 2, 2012, http://news.nationalpost.com/news/canada/hearing-into-ornge-scandal-ends-with-big-questions-still-unanswered. Subsequently, AgustaWestland also became embroiled in a bribery scandal in Italy.

25. "ORNGE Scandal: Ontario's Air Ambulance Service on Tighter Leash," *Huffington Post*, February 17, 2012, http://www.huffingtonpost.ca/2012/02/17/ORNGE-scandal-air-ambulance-ontario_n_1285148.html.

26. Office of the Auditor General of Ontario, *Special Report: ORNGE Air Ambulance and Related Services* (Toronto: Queen's Printer for Ontario, March 2012), 7, http://www.auditor.on.ca/en/content/specialreports/specialreports/ORNGE_web_en.pdf.

27. "Deb Matthews: Powerless over ORNGE Because It Was a Federal Charity," *Toronto Star*, December 26, 2012, https://www.thestar.com/news/canada/2012/03/28/deb_matthews_powerless_over_ORNGE_because_it_was_a_federal_charity.html.

28. "ORNGE: Chris Mazza Gave Order to Create 'Illegal' False Documents, Says Ex-Aide," *Toronto Star*, December 25, 2012, https://www.thestar.com/news/canada/2012/08/29/

ornge_chris_mazza_gave_order_to_create_illegal_false_documents_says_exaide.html.

29.  Legislative Assembly of Ontario, Standing Committee on Public Accounts, *Official Report of Debates: Special Report, Auditor General: Ornge Air Ambulance and Related Services,* April 18, 2012, 86(940).

30.  "Hearing into ORNGE Scandal Ends with Big Questions Unanswered," *National Post,* August 2, 2012.

31.  Donovan, *ORNGE,* 40.

32.  "ORNGE Paid Lawyers $11 Million," *Toronto Star,* March 2, 2012, https://www.thestar.com/news/canada/2012/02/03/ORNGE_paid_lawyers_11_million.html.

33.  Fasken Martineau, "Letter to Integrity Commissioner from Martin Denyes," January 13, 2012. Note: all letters cited are on the public record with the Ontario Public Accounts Committee.

34.  Office of the Integrity Commissioner of Ontario, "Letter containing Advisory Opinion to Mr. Martin K. Denyes," February 3, 2012. Letter cites contravention of the *LRA* section 4(10).

35.  Fasken Martineau, "Letter to Integrity Commissioner by Alfred Apps," February 10, 2012.

36.  Office of the Integrity Commissioner of Ontario, "Letter to Alfred Apps," 29 February, 2012.

37.  Ontario, *Official Report of Debates,* April 18, 2012, 91(1009).

38.  Ibid., 92.

39.  Ibid., 673(1310).

40.  See Adrian Morrow, "Ontario Liberals' Gas-Plants Scandal: Everything You Need to Know," *Globe and Mail,* April 1, 2015, http://www.theglobeandmail.com/news/politics/ontario-liberals-gas-plants-scandal-everything-you-need-to-know/article23668386/.

41.  See, for example: "Liberal Alfred Apps Was Warned About Illegality of ORNGE Loan," *BC Blue,* February 17, 2012, https://bcblue.wordpress.com/2012/02/17/liberal-alfred-apps-was-warned-about-illegality-of-ORNGE-loan/.

42.  Ontario, Office of the Integrity Commissioner of Ontario, "Interpretation Bulletin #7: Are Lawyers Who Engage in Lobbying Activity on Behalf of a Client Required to Register as Lobbyists?" (Toronto: Office of the Integrity Commissioner, 2011), http://www.oico.on.ca/home/lobbyists-registration/interpretation-bulletins/lawyers-who-engage-in-lobbying-activity-on-behalf-of-a-client.

43.  See Canada, Parliament, House of Commons, Standing Committee on Access, Information, Privacy and Ethics (ETHI), *Statutory Review of the* Lobbying Act, 1st sess. 41st Parliament, February 9, 2012. Prof. Stephanie Yates (Université du Québec à Montréal), provides evidence regarding the statutory review of the *Lobbying Act,* indicating that "gaps remain" in the regulations.

44.  Mario Cooper, "Winning in Washington: From Grasstops to Grassroots," *Public Relations Quarterly* 38 no. 4 (1993–94): 13–15. The term was first used in print to suggest that messages are often communicated at the grasstops, but have few roots to support them.

45.  See "US: How Grassroots Organizing Has Been Co-Opted," *Newsweek Magazine Online,* August 19, 2009, http://www.newsweek.com/how-grassroots-organizing-has-been-co-opted-78589. The roots of the term emanate from the US. In 1994, the

Clinton administration introduced a health reform bill. Washington based lobby groups mobilized citizens to appear outraged over the bill.

46. Nancy Daigneault, "The Nanny State: Speaking Notes to the Public Affairs Association of Canada," October 27, 2005, http://www.mychoice.ca/en/documents/paac_speech_draft_3.pdf.

47. Monchoix.ca, "Monchoix.ca: A Powerful Voice for Quebec's Adult Smokers.," [Press release], April 5, 2005, http://www.marketwired.com/press-release/monchoixca-a-powerful-voice-for-quebecs-adult-smokers-559222.htm.

48. Nancy Daignealt, "Nanny State"; see also "Tobacco-Fuelled Discussion Gets Audience Smoking," *Public Affairs: Your Online Newsletter*, November 2005, http://www.publicaffairs.ca/newsletter-files/nov05.htm.

49. Ontario, Office of the Integrity Commissioner, "Interpretation Bulletin #8: Grass-Roots Communication Registration Requirements" (Toronto: Office of the Integrity Commissioner, July 3, 2012), http://www.oico.on.ca/home/lobbyists-registration/interpretation-bulletins/grass-roots-lobbying.

50. "US: How Grassroots Organizing Has Been Co-Opted."

51. Greene and Shugarman, *Honest Politics* (1997), 128.

52. "Yukon Too Small for Lobbyist Registry: Premier Pasloski," *CBC News*, April 28, 2015, http://www.cbc.ca/news/canada/north/yukon-too-small-for-lobbyist-registry-premier-pasloski-1.3051600.

53. Greene and Shugarman, *Honest Politics* (1997), 128.

54. Three convictions were made under the federal *Lobbying Act*. The first was made in June 2014 regarding the case of Mr. Andrew Skaling who failed to register as a consultant lobbyist for a nonprofit organization (Canadian Network of Respiratory Care), which resulted in a fine of $7,500 imposed by a judge after a finding of guilt resulting from charges laid by the RCMP, and a prohibition of lobbying for four months imposed by the Commissioner. The second involved Mr. James Carroll, who was fined $20,000 in May 2016 following his conviction in the Ontario Court of Justice for failing to register in 2013. The third involved Mr. Bruce Carson who was fined $50,000 on three counts for violating principally the five-year prohibition requirements. See Canadian Press, "Bruce Carson, Former Harper Aide, Fined $50,000 for Illegal Lobbying," *Globe and Mail*, November 4, 2016, http://www.theglobeandmail.com/news/politics/bruce-carson-former-harper-aide-fined-50000-for-illegal-lobbying/article32675373/.

55. Adrian Morrow, "Ontario Politics: An Inside Look at Cash-for-Access Ontario Liberal Fundraisers," *Globe and Mail*, July 6, 2016, http://www.theglobeandmail.com/news/national/investigation-reveals-likely-guests-for-ontario-liberal-cash-for-access-fundraisers/article30783097/.

56. Canada, Office of the Commissioner of Lobbying, "Applicability of the *Lobbying Act* to Grass-Roots Communications," last modified May 16, 2016, https://lobbycanada.gc.ca/eic/site/012.nsf/eng/00874.html.

57. "US: How Grassroots Organizing Has Been Co-Opted."

# CHAPTER 8

1. We would like to acknowledge the research support of Ian Bron, PhD candidate in the

School of Public Policy and Administration, Carleton University. His research into the cases was an important contribution to the chapter.

2.  Vandekerckhove and Commers, "Whistle Blowing and Rational Loyalty."

3.  Miceli and Near, "Organizational Dissonance," 4.

4.  Devine & Massarani, *Corporate Whistleblowers Survival Guide*, 4.

5.  Council of Europe, Parliamentary Assembly, Committee on Legal Affairs and Human Rights, "Protection of Whistle-Blowers," accessed February 11, 2017, http://assembly. coe.int/nw/xml/XRef/Xref-XML2HTML-en.asp?fileid=17851&lang=en.

6.  A. Osterhaus and C. Fagan, "Alternative to Silence: Whistleblower Protection in 10 European Countries," Report for Transparency International (15 November 2009), https://issuu.com/transparencyinternational/docs/2009_alternativetosilence_en.

7.  Vickers, "Whistling in the Wind?" 428–30.

8.  Public Concern at Work, *The Whistleblowing Commission: Report on the Effectiveness of Existing Arrangements for Workplace Whistleblowing in the UK*, (London: Public Concern at Work, 2013), 7, www.pcaw.org.uk/files/WBC%20Report%20Final.pdf.

9.  Vandckerckhove, "European Whistleblower Protection."

10. Mendelsohn, "Calling the Boss or Calling the Press."

11. See British Columbia, Office of the Attorney General, *BC v. BCGEU*, BCCAAA no. 9, 1176 (WL), Carswell, BC, 1981.

12. *Fraser v. P.S.S.R.B.*, [1985] 2 S.C.R. 455, 1985.

13. Ibid., para. 46.

14. Canada, Public Servants Disclosure Protection Tribunal, *The Basics of Whistleblowing and Reprisal*, (Public Servants Disclosure Protection Tribunal, 2012), www.psdpt-tpfd. gc.ca/ResourceCentre/ArticlesAnalyses/BasicsWhistleblowing-eng.html.

15. Gomery, *Phase II Report*, 186.

16. Ibid., s. 8.

17. *Ottawa Citizen*, "Public Service Integrity Watchdog Mario Dion Steps Down," August 28, 2014, http://ottawacitizen.com/news/politics/public-service-integrity-watchdog-steps-down.

18. Canadians for Accountability, "About Accountability & Whistleblowing," last modified September 11, 2008, http://canadians4accountability.org/accountability-and-whistleblowing/.

19. Abott Martin, "Four Traits of Leading Compliance and Ethics Programs," Compliance and Ethics Leadership Council, 2013, https://degreed.com/articles/four-traits-of-leading-compliance-and-ethics-programs?d=527290.

20. CSA Group, *Whistleblowing Systems: A Guide* (Toronto: CSA Group, 2016), EXP01–16: 10–12.

21. In addition to the three cases discussed in this chapter, the ORNGE scandal in Ontario, the lobbying implications of which are analyzed in Chapter 7, also provides an example of whistleblowing. If Jacob Blum, a former senior employee at ORNGE, had not provided information to the *Toronto Star* about questionable financial practices in ORNGE, the maladministration in ORNGE, which endangered the lives of Ontarians,

may never have come to light. See Kevin Donovan, *ORNGE*, 11 ff. It is unfortunate that there was no official whistle-blowing mechanism in place that covered nonprofits such as ORNGE.

22.    E. Schmidt, personal communication, May 8, 2015.

23.    *Department of Justice Act*, R.S.C., c. J-2, 1985.

24.    Bill Curry, "Judge Raps Justice Officials for Treatment of Whistle-Blower," *Globe and Mail*, January 16, 2013, http://www.theglobeandmail.com/news/politics/judge-raps-justice-officials-for-treatment-of-whistle-blower/article7394559/?cmpid=rss1.

25.    Mario Dion, Public Sector Integrity Commissioner, "Re: Request for Legal Advice, File No. 2012-LAR-0132," Letter to Edgar Schmidt, September 12, 2012, http://charterdefence.ca/uploads/3/4/5/1/34515720/affidavit-of-john-mark-keyes-exhibits-3to10.pdf.

26.    Federal Court of Canada, "Statement of Claim (Edgar Schmidt)," File T-2225-12, (Ottawa: CharterDefence.ca, 2012), 12, http://charterdefence.ca/uploads/3/4/5/1/34515720/statement_of_claim_2012-12-14.pdf.

27.    Ibid., 9–11.

28.    Voices-Voix, "Edgar Schmidt," last modified October 25, 2016, http://voices-voix.ca/en/facts/profile/edgar-schmidt.

29.    Roderick Macdonell, "The Whistleblower," *Canadian Bar Association National*, November–December 2013, http://www.nationalmagazine.ca/Articles/November/The-whistleblower.aspx.

30.    Canadian Civil Liberties Association, "Federal Court Case Challenges Government's Respect for *Charter of Rights and Freedoms*," [Press release], September 30, 2015, www.ccla.org/federal-court-case-challenges-governments-respect-for-charter-of-rights-and-freedoms/.

31.    Voices-Voix, "Edgar Schmidt."

32.    Leslie MacKinnon, "Whistleblower Edgar Schmidt Loses *Charter* Suit Against His Former Department," *iPolitics*, March 22, 2016, http://ipolitics.ca/2016/03/02/whistleblower-edgar-schmidt-loses-charter-suit-against-his-former-department/.

33.    Voices-Voix, "Edgar Schmidt."

34.    Federal Court of Canada, *Edgar Schmidt and The Attorney General of Canada and Canadian Civil Liberties Association*, 2016 FC 269, March 2, 2016, http://cas-cdc-www02.cas-satj.gc.ca/rss/T-2225-12_20160302_JR_E_O_OTT_20160302095445_NSI_2016_FC_269.pdf.

35.    Ibid.

36.    Ibid., 131.

37.    Ibid., 122, 132.

38.    Kirk Makin, "Justice Department Whistleblower on a Crusade to Sustain the Rule of Law," *Globe and Mail*, February 23, 2013, http://www.theglobeandmail.com/news/national/justice-department-whistleblower-on-a-crusade-to-sustain-the-rule-of-law/article9001991/?cmpid=rss1.

39.    Court Challenges Program of Canada, "About CCP," accessed February 17, 2017, http://www.ccppcj.ca/en/about.php.

40. Helen Burnett, "Tories Chop Two Legal Programs," *Law Times News*, October 2, 2006, www.lawtimesnews.com/200610021298/headline-news/tories-chop-two-legal-programs.

41. Court Challenges Program of Canada, "Reinstatement News," accessed February 2, 2017, http://www.ccppcj.ca/en/news.php.

42. MacDonell, "The Whistleblower."

43. Makin, "Justice Department Whistleblower."

44. Omar Sabry, *Torture of Afghan Detainees: Canada's Alleged Complicity and the Need for a Public Inquiry* (Ottawa: The Rideau Institute, 2015), 70, http://www.rideauinstitute.ca/2015/09/23/torture-and-afghan-detainees-the-need-for-a-public-inquiry/.

45. Mitch Potter, "PMO Issued Instructions on Denying Abuse in '07," *Toronto Star*, November 22, 2009, http://www.thestar.com/news/canada/2009/11/22/pmo_issued_instructions_on_denying_abuse_in_07.html.

46. Steve Chase, "Canada Complicit in Torture of Innocent Afghans, Diplomat Says," *Globe and Mail*, November 18, 2009, http://www.theglobeandmail.com/news/politics/canada-complicit-in-torture-of-innocent-afghans-diplomat-says/article1347481/.

47. Sabry, *Torture of Afghan Detainees*, 24; and Voices-Voix, "Richard Colvin," accessed February 17, 2017, http://voices-voix.ca/en/facts/profile/richard-colvin.

48. Ibid.

49. Peter Goffin, "Canada and Torture in Afghanistan: The Truth is Still Waiting to Be Heard," *Rabble.ca*, January 24, 2013, http://rabble.ca/news/2013/01/canada-and-torture-afghanistan-truth-still-waiting-be-heard.

50. Affidavit of Richard James Colvin in the matter of a hearing before the Military Police Complaints Commission pursuant to subsection 2503. 8 (1) of the National Defence Act, R.S.C. 1985, c .N -5, http://www3.thestar.com/static/PDF/Colvin_Affidavit.pdf.

51. Voices-Voix, "Richard Colvin."

52. Sabry, *Torture of Afghan Detainees*, 18.

53. Steve Chase, "Canada Complicit in Torture of Innocent Afghans, Diplomat Says," *Globe and Mail*, November 18, 2009, http://www.theglobeandmail.com/news/politics/canada-complicit-in-torture-of-innocent-afghans-diplomat-says/article1347481/.

54. Richard Colvin, "Memo to David Mulroney: Afghan Detainees," October 24, 2007. This memo was described in detail in: Murray Brewster, Canadian Press, "Canada Defended Afghan 'Human-Rights Abuser,' Memos Allege," *Toronto Star*, December 13, 2009, https://www.thestar.com/news/canada/2009/12/13/canada_defended_afghan_humanrights_abuser_memos_allege.html. Seven previous memoranda were sent to Ottawa between May 26, 2006, and April 20, 2007, each outlining issues related to the transfer of prisoners, treatment, and procedural issues such as notification of Afghan authorities. See Aaron Wherry, "What Do We Know for Now?" *MacLean's*, November 27, 2009, http://www.macleans.ca/politics/ottawa/what-do-we-know-for-now/.

55. Colvin, Ibid., 1–2, and 4–5 of memo.

56. Voices-Voix, "Richard Colvin."

57. Richard Colvin, "Military Police Complaints Commission: Affidavit."

58. Peter A. Tinsley, *Chairperson's Final Report Concerning the Afghan Detainee Complaint by*

*Dr. Attaran, MPCC 2007-003* (Ottawa: Military Police Complaints Commission, 2009), 14, para. 37, http://www.mpcc-cppm.gc.ca/alt_format/300/3700/2007-003/2007-003-eng-rev.pdf.

59. *Sabry, Torture of Afghan Detainees,* 50-51; and Ibid., 64, para. 202.

60. Sabry, *Torture of Afghan Detainees,* 71.

61. "Tories Reject Call for Afghan Torture Inquiry," *CBC News,* November 19, 2009, http://www.cbc.ca/news/politics/tories-reject-call-for-afghan-torture-inquiry-1.801848.

62. "Ex-Diplomats Decry Government's Attack on Colvin," *CBC News,* December 8, 2009, http://www.cbc.ca/news/canada/ex-diplomats-decry-government-s-attack-on-colvin-1.796375.

63. Tonda MacCharles, "Whistleblower under Attack," *Toronto Star,* November 20, 2009, https://www.thestar.com/news/canada/2009/11/20/whistleblower_under_attack.html.

64. "Tories Reject Call for Afghan Torture Inquiry," *CBC News.*

65. "Colvin Fears Retaliation for Torture Testimony," *CBC News,* January 25, 2010, http://www.cbc.ca/news/politics/colvin-fears-retaliation-for-torture-testimony-1.900145.

66. Tonda MacCharles, "Diplomat Fires Back on Afghan Prisoner Abuse," *Toronto Star,* December 16, 2009, https://www.thestar.com/news/canada/2009/12/16/diplomat_fires_back_on_afghan_prisoner_abuse.html.

67. "Tories Reject Call for Afghan Torture Inquiry," *CBC News;* and Ibid.

68. Guillaume Bourgault-Côté, "Assurance-Emploi — Les Fonctionnaires Ont des Quotas de Prestations à Couper," *Le Devoir,* February 1, 2013, http://www.ledevoir.com/politique/canada/369853/les-fonctionnaires-ont-des-quotas-de-prestations-a-couper.

69. Guillaume Bourgault-Côté, "Assurance-Emploi — Quotas : Finley a Menti," *Le Devoir,* February 25, 2013, http://www.ledevoir.com/politique/canada/371788/quotas-finley-a-menti.

70. Guillaume Bourgault-Côté, "Assurance-Emploi — Ottawa Part à la Chasse aux Taupes," *Le Devoir,* March 21, 2013, http://www.ledevoir.com/politique/canada/373778/ottawa-part-a-la-chasse-aux-taupes.

71. Donovan Vincent, "EI Fraud Investigator Axed for Leaking "Quota" Details," *Toronto Star,* October 24, 2013, https://www.thestar.com/news/canada/2013/10/24/ei_fraud_investigator_axed_for_leaking_quota_details.html.

72. Guillaume Bourgault-Côté, "Assurance-Emploi — Pas de Quotas, Mais des Objectifs, Dit Finley," *Le Devoir,* February 26, 2013, http://www.ledevoir.com/politique/canada/371882/assurance-emploi-pas-de-quotas-mais-des-objectifs-dit-Finley; and Ibid.

73. Bourgault-Côté, "Assurance-Emploi — Les Fonctionnaires Ont des Quotas de Prestations à Couper."

74. James Gilbert, "Departmental Statement on Sylvie Therrien," October 21, 2013, accessed Feb. 17, 2017, http://www.esdc.gc.ca/eng/news/departmental_statement.sthml.

75. Bourgault-Côté, "Assurance-Emploi — Ottawa Part à la Chasse Aux Taupes."

76. Donavan Vincent. "EI Fraud Investigator Axed."

77. Guillaume Bourgault-Côté, "Réforme de l'Assurance-Emploi — Service Canada

Espionne," *LeDevoir*, March 5, 2013, http://www.ledevoir.com/politique/canada/372486/service-canada-espionne.

78. Bourgault-Côté, "Assurance-Emploi — Pas de Quotas."

79. Lee Berthiaume, "Feds Report Dramatic Increase in 'Fraudulent' EI Claims to $160 Million," *Ottawa Citizen*, October 31, 2013, http://o.canada.com/news/feds-report-dramatic-increase-in-fraudulent-ei-claims-to-160-million.

80. Bourgault-Côté, "Assurance-Emploi — Quotas : Finley a Menti."

81. "Tories Set 'Targets,' Not Quotas for EI Fraud," *CBC News*, February 25, 2013, http://www.cbc.ca/news/politics/tories-set-targets-not-quotas-for-ei-fraud-1.1330294.

82. Donovan Vincent, "Employment Insurance Whistleblower Still Seeking Justice Three Years Later," *Toronto Star*, January 31, 2016, http://www.thestar.com/news/insight/2016/01/31/employment-insurance-whistleblower-still-seeking-justice-three-years-later.html.

83. Guillaume Bourgault-Côté, "Ça a Détruit Ma Carrière, et Ma Vie," *Le Devoir*, October 24, 2013, http://www.ledevoir.com/politique/canada/390798/ca-a-detruit-ma-carriere-et-ma-vie.

84. Bourgault-Côté, "Assurance-Emploi — Pas de Quotas."

85. Bourgault-Côté, "Ça a Détruit Ma Carrière, et Ma Vie."

86. Vincent, "EI Fraud Investigator Axed."

87. Vincent, "Employment Insurance Whistleblower Still Seeking Justice."

88. Canada, Office of the Auditor General of Canada, *Report of the Auditor General of Canada, Chapter 7: Human Resources Development Canada and the Canada Employment Insurance Commission — Measuring and Reporting the Performance of the Employment Insurance Income Benefits Program* (Ottawa: Ministry of Supply and Services, 2003), 16.

89. "EI Whistleblower Sylvie Therrien Deserves Protection: Editorial," *Toronto Star*, July 25, 2013, https://www.thestar.com/opinion/editorials/2013/07/25/ei_whistleblower_sylvie_therrien_deserves_protection_editorial.html.

90. Bourgault-Côté, "Ça a Détruit Ma Carrière, et Ma Vie."

91. *Sylvie Therrien v. Canada (Attorney General), 2015*, 2015 FC 1351 (CanLII), http://tinyurl.com/k6sybjq.

92. *Sylvie Therrien v. Canada (Attorney General), 2017*, 2017 FCA 14 (CanLII). https://www.canlii.org/en/ca/fca/doc/2017/2017fca14/2017fca14.html?resultIndex=1.

93. David Yazbeck, "Sylvie Therrien — File No.: PSIC-2013-R-0288," Letter to Nathalie Thériault, February 14, 2017.

94. Vincent, "Employment Insurance Whistleblower Still Seeking Justice."

95. Vandekerckhove and Commers, "Whistle Blowing and Rational Loyalty," 226–27.

96. Donkin, Smith and Brown, "How Do Officials Report?" 83–106.

97. *Public Servants Disclosure Protection Act*, S.C. 2005, c. 46, s. 25.1. Normally, the maximum account that the commissioner may approve to cover the cost of legal advice incurred by a whistle-blower or potential whistle-blower is $1,500, although up to $3,000 may be approved in "exceptional circumstances."

## CHAPTER 9

1.    See Slayton, *Lawyers Gone Bad.*

2.    This chapter does not deal with the rise of the ombudsman movement at the local level or the jurisdiction of provincial ombudsmen over municipalities in some places. It also does not focus on election finance law, which is of growing importance at the local level.

3.    *Criminal Code* RSC 1985, c. C-46, s.123.

4.    France Charbonneau and Renaud LaChance, *Rapport Final de la Commission d'Enquete sur l'Octroi et la Gestion des Contrats Publics dans l'Industrie de la Construction,* November 2015; and Lawrence John Cannon, *Commission d'Enquete sur la Corruption dans l'Administration de Montreal 1909–10.*

5.    *R v. Gyles* 2005 Carswell, Ont 7422 (Ont.C.A.).

6.    Levine, *Law of Government Ethics,* 9.

7.    Ibid., 9, 10. See also Chapters 4 and 5 above.

8.    E.g. see *Municipal Conflict of Interest Act* R.S.O. 1990, c. M.50, s. 5; *Community Charter* S.B.C. 2002, c.26, s. 100 – note that the focus is on pecuniary interest but there is also reference to other interests as well; *Municipalities Act* S.S. 2205, c. M-36.1 ss. 141.1, 143, 144(1).

9.    E.g. see *Members' Integrity Act* S.O. 1994, c.38, s.2; *Members' Conflict of Interest Act* R.S.B.C 1996 c. 287, s.2.

10.    E.g. see City of Kitchener, *Code of Conduct for Members of Council, Local Boards and Advisory Committees (Kitchener Code),* October 2008; and see City of Ottawa, "Preamble Statement of Principles," *Code of Conduct for Members of Council,* ss.1, 5, 10.

11.    Cunningham, *Report of the City of Mississauga Judicial Inquiry;* and Barclay, *Final Report of the Inspection and Inquiry.*

12.    *Community Charter* (B.C.), Part 4, Division 6; *Municipal Ethics and Good Conduct Act* CQLR, c. E-15.1.0.1, Division 2; *Municipal Act,* 2001 S.O. 2001, c.25, 223.2(1).

13.    E.g. see *Kitchener Code,* Part 3.

14.    See *Kitchener Code,* Part 3 section on influence of office; *Community Charter* (B.C.), ss. 102, 103.

15.    *Gage Canadian Dictionary* (1997), 786.

16.    For a discussion of different types of lobbying systems and the purposes of those systems see Levine, *Law of Government Ethics,* chap. 4 and Levine, *Municipal Ethics Regimes,* chap. 3.

17.    *Municipal Act* (Ont.), s. 223.9(2).

18.    City of Surrey, Lobbyist Registration Policy, City Policy No. R-24.

19.    *Municipal Act,* (Ont.), ss.223.1, 223.9(2).

20.    City of Toronto, *Municipal Code,* Chapter 140. Note that the *Code* is in Article 6.

21.    *Lobbying and Transparency Ethics Act* CQLR c. T-11.011.

22.    Ibid., ss. 26, 28, 29.

23.    *Municipal Conflict of Interest Act* (Ont.), s.8; *Community Charter* (B.C.), s.111; *Lobbying*

*and Transparency Ethics Act* (Que.), ss. 60 to 65 – although note that the commissioner may also take disciplinary measures.

24.    *Municipal Conflict of Interest Act* (Ont.), s. 9.

25.    *Community Charter* (B.C.), s. 111.

26.    E.g. see City of Hamilton, *By-Law to Establish an Integrity Commissioner,* Bylaw 08-154, s. 20.

27.    *Municipal Ethics and Good Conduct Act* (Que.), s. 23.

28.    See the website of the Commission Municipale, ethics section, http://www.cmq.gouv. qc.ca/.

29.    *Municipal Ethics and Good Conduct Act* (Que.), ss. 20 to 22

30.    *Municipalities Act,* SS 2005, c. M-36.1 s.402(1); Cities Act SS 2002, c. C-11.1, s. 358.1(1).

31.    *Municipal Act* (Ont.), s. 223.4.

32.    Ibid. s. 223.4(5).

33.    E.g. see City of Hamilton, *By-Law to Establish an Integrity Commissioner,* s. 7(c) and (d).

34.    E.g. see City of Waterloo, *Code of Conduct for Members of Council,* November 2009, s. 19.1.

35.    At the federal and provincial level, ethics officers are protected from lawsuit if they act in good faith — no proceedings may be taken against them. Typically as well they may only be reviewed for lack of jurisdiction and they cannot be compelled in court to testify about their work. These protections insulate them and allow them some security to do their work. The municipal officers in Ontario have some confidentiality protection, but they have no statutory security of tenure or statutory indemnification, or alternatively, a requirement that municipalities insure them in the event of lawsuit. This lack of protection weakens their positions considerably.

36.    For an analysis of Ford's behaviour and survival as a politician despite what would have typically been seen as dishonourable conduct see Ogata et al., "Rob Ford and the End of Honour." Also, see Towhey and Schneller, *Mayor Rob Ford.*

37.    Integrity Commissioner, *Report on a Violation of the Code of Conduct* (Toronto: Office of the Integrity Commissioner, August 12, 2010), 9.

38.    Ibid., 4.

39.    Ibid., 8.

40.    Ibid., 12, 13.

41.    Ibid., 1, 2; and City Council, City of Toronto, CC.52.1 Action respecting Violation of the Code of Conduct, 2012.

42.    For more details, see Ogata et al., "Rob Ford and the End of Honour."

43.    Integrity Commissioner, *Report on Compliance with Council Decision CC 52.1* (Toronto: Office of the Integrity Commissioner, January 30, 2012).

44.    City Council, City of Toronto, *CC 16.6 Action Respecting Report on Compliance with Council Decision CC 52.1,* February 6 and 7, 2012.

45.    *Magder v Ford* 2012 ONSC 5615 (Ont.S.C.J.) reversed by *Magder v Ford* 2013 ONSC 263 (Ont.S.C.J. – Div. Ct.).

46.    *Municipal Act* (Ont.) s. 223.4(5).

47.    Guy Giorno "Municipal Conflict of Interest — What's New?" (Presentation to Ontario Bar Association's Institution, 2013, 2). Giorno prudently asks, "Is it acceptable to be conflicted (that is, to hold divided loyalties) or fail to disclose a conflict (divided loyalties) on a matter that subsequently turns out to be moot?"

48.    Ontario, Ministry of Municipal Affairs, "Modernizing Ontario's *Municipal Legislation Act*: What's Being Proposed," last modified November 16, 2016, http://www.mah.gov.on.ca/Page15155.aspx#.

49.    Cunningham, *Report of the City of Mississauge Judicial Inquiry.*

50.    Ibid., 69, 76.

51.    Ibid., 78.

52.    Ibid.,  82, 90, 91.

53.    Ibid.

54.    Ibid., 153, 154.

55.    David Rider, "McCallion — A Real and Apparent Conflict of Interest," *Toronto Star,* Octover 3, 2011.

56.    Note that in Saskatchewan a member of council including the mayor may be dismissed from office by the Lieutenant Governor in Council when it is in the public interest to do so — *Municipalities Act*, SS 2005, c. M-36.1 s. 402(1); *Cities Act* SS 2002, c. C-11.1, s. 358.1(1).

57.    E.g. see "Saskatchewan Reeve in Conflict of Interest on Land Deal That Could Have Made Him $57 Million, Probe Finds" *Postmedia*, February 5, 2015, http://news.nationalpost.com/news/canada/saskatchewan-reeve-in-conflict-of-interest-on-land-deal-that-could-have-made-him-57m-probe-finds; and "RM of Sherwood Removed for Conflict of Interest," *Global News,* February 5, 2015, http://globalnews.ca/news/1813615/rm-of-sherwood-reeve-kevin-eberle-removed-for-conflict-of-interest/.

58.    Barclay, *Final Report of the Inspection and Inquiry.*

59.    "Reeve of RM Sherwood Tossed From Office over Land Deal Conflicts," *CBC News,* February 5, 2015, http://www.cbc.ca/news/canada/saskatchewan/reeve-of-rm-sherwood-tossed-from-office-over-land-deal-conflicts-1.2946319.

60.    Barcla, *Final Report of the Inspection and Inquiry,* 38, 39.

61.    Ibid., 42.

62.    Ibid., 42, 43.

63.    Ibid., 43.

64.    Ibid.,  43, 44.

65.    Ibid., 44.

66.    Ibid. For a discussion of the various agreements and the Wascana Estates plan see 56 to 63.

67.    Ibid., 65, 66.

68.    Ibid., 67 to 78.

69. Ibid., 80. Note that the rural municipality's solicitor was also acting for the developer and would have been aware of the complexity of the reeve's interest in the matter.

70. Ibid. Pages 84 to 92 detail the reeve's involvement with the official plan — meetings in and out of council — and as well consider whether or not the reeve was in a "community of interest," i.e. one land owner among many.

71. Ibid., 95.

72. Ibid., 137, 138.

73. Ibid.

74. Ibid., 149, 150.

75. Bellamy, *Report of the Toronto Computer Leasing Inquiry / Toronto External Contracts Inquiry.*

76. Ibid., vol. 1, 34.

77. Ibid., vol.1, 35.

78. Ibid., vol. 2, 8. Lana Viinamae was Director, Computer Operations, City of Toronto, at the time.

79. Ibid., vol. 3, 33 ff.

80. Ibid., vol. 1.

81. Ibid., vol. 4, 6.

82. Ibid., vol. 4, 6.

83. Machiavelli, *The Prince*, chap. 18, 53.

84. Andre Marin, "Accountability Finally Coming to Ontario Cities," *Toronto Star*, July 10, 2014, https://www.thestar.com/opinion/commentary/2014/07/10/accountability_finally_coming_to_ontarios_cities_ombudsman.html.

85. E.g. see City of Vaughan, *Code of Ethical Conduct for Members of Council,* September 2009; City of Mississauga, *Council Code of Conduct,* December 2013.

# CHAPTER 10

1. O'Connor, *Commission of Inquiry*, 59.

2. Ibid., 270.

3. Ibid., 45.

4. Ibid., 260.

5. "Harper's Apology 'Means the World': Arar," *CBC News*, January 26, 2007, http://www.cbc.ca/news/canada/harper-s-apology-means-the-world-arar-1.646481.

6. Machiavelli, *The Prince*, chap. 18, 53.

7. Ibid., chap. 15, 48.

8. Ibid., chap. 18, 55.

9. Ibid.

10. The term Machiavellian is often used to refer to personalities, attitudes, styles, and

actions that are dismissive of the place of morality or codes of conduct in politics. Indeed, at times in his writings Machiavelli himself seemed to exemplify this cynical, *realpolitik* view of the nature of public life, whereby everything is about the struggle for power and morality has no function except as a ruse. But as we have tried to stress, there is another side to a Machiavellian approach to leadership, one that argues the need to do unsavoury things for the sake of the public good.

11.   Sartre, "Dirty Hands," 223.

12.   Weber, *Essays on Sociology*, 121.

13.   Trotsky, *Their Morals and Ours*, 37.

14.   White, *The Making of the President, 1964*, 261.

15.   Halberstram, *Best and the Brightest*, 496.

16.   Walzer, "Political Action," 164.

17.   Hobbes, *Leviathan*, book 1 chap. 13.

18.   For further elaboration of our argument here see Shugarman, "Use and Abuse of Politics."

19.   Bok, *Lying*, 182.

20.   *Toronto Star,* June 20, 1996.

21.   Jamieson, *Dirty Politics.*

22.   Jennifer Pagliaro, Bruce Campion-Smith, and Vjosa Isai, "Nick Kouvalis Resigns From Kellie Leitch Campaign," *Toronto Star*, February 2, 2017, https://www.thestar.com/news/gta/2017/02/02/nick-kouvalis-resigns-from-kellie-leitch-campaign.html.

23.   *Toronto Star,* May 18, 1993.

24.   McDonald, *Report of the Commission of Inquiry.*

25.   *Toronto Star,* January 12, 1978.

26.   *R. v. Ormerod* [1969] 2 *Ontario Reports* (C.A.), 230.

27.   Toronto *Star,* July 24, 1980.

28.   Alison Crawford, "CSIS Repeatedly Obtained Confidential Taxpayers Data Without Warrants, Watchdog Says," *CBC News*, January 28, 2016, http://www.cbc.ca/news/politics/sirc-cra-warrant-taxpayer-info-1.3423666.

29.   Colin Freeze, "Spy Agency Accidentally Shared Canadians' Data With Allies for Years," *Globe and Mail,* June 1, 2016, http://www.theglobeandmail.com/news/national/spy-agency-accidentally-shared-canadians-data-with-allies-for-years/article30243491/.

30.   These quotes are taken from the transcript of congressional committees of inquiry into Iran-Contra. They are cited by David Nacht in an excellent analysis of the conspiracy and its unravelling. We have relied heavily on Nacht for our own account, see Nacht, "Iran-Contra Affair," 56.

31.   Nacht, "Iran-Contra Affair."

32.   Dahl, *Democracy and Its Critics*, 338.

33.   Walkom, *Rae Days*, 236.

34.   Martin, *Iron Man*, 359.

35.  Ibid.

36.  Democracy Watch, "Stop Muzzling Scientists," accessed February 14, 2017, http://democracywatch.ca/campaigns/tell-harper-to-stop-muzzling-scientists/.

37.  "Frozen Out," *Nature* 483 no. 6 (2012), http://www.nature.com/nature/journal/v483/n7387/full/483006a.html.

38.  More precisely, the motion called upon "the Minister of Energy as well as the Ministry of Energy and Ontario Power Authority to produce, within a fortnight, all correspondence, in any form, electronic or otherwise, that occurred between September 1, 2010, and December 31, 2011, related to the cancellation of the Oakville power plant as well as all correspondence, in any form, electronic or otherwise, that occurred between August 1, 2011, and December 31, 2011, related to the cancellation of the Mississauga power plant." Legislative Assembly of Ontario, "Committee Documents: Standing Committee on Estimates - 2012-May-15 - Ministry of Energy," May 15, 2012, http://www.ontla.on.ca/web/committee-proceedings/committee_transcripts_details.do?locale=en&Date=2012-05-15&ParlCommID=8956&BillID=&Business=Ministry+of+Energy&DocumentID=26330.

39.  Ann Cavoukian, Information and Privacy Commissioner of Ontario, *Deleting Accountability: Record Management Practices of Political Staff — A Special Investigation Report* (Toronto: Office of the Information and Privacy Commissioner, 2013), https://www.ipc.on.ca/wp-content/uploads/2016/08/2013-06-05-Deleting-Accountability-1.pdf.

40.  Peter Tabuns, "Information Commissioner Should Investigate Liberal Document Destruction," *Peter Tabuns Toronto-Danforth*, April 12, 2013, http://petertabuns.ca/information-commissioner-should-investigate-liberal-document-destruction.

41.  Information and Privacy Commissioner of Ontario, *Deleting Accountability*.

42.  Ibid., 1.

43.  Not to mention that the research and expertise in question is paid for by the public through taxes.

44.  For an important comment on the nature of trust in government see Cox, "Ethics in Government."

45.  Smith 1942, quoted in Benjamin, *Splitting the Difference*, 172.

46.  Elshtain, *Democracy on Trial*, 60.

47.  Kuflik, "Morality and Compromise," 51–52.

48.  Ibid.

49.  Mill, *Utilitarianism*, 21.

50.  For philosophical arguments about dirty hands, both pro and con, see Rynard and Shugarman, *Cruelty and Deception*; and Coady, *Problem of Dirty Hands*.

# CHAPTER 11

1.  The first two paragraphs in this section are based on the report of Justice Peter Richard, *The Westray Story: A Predictable Path to Disaster* (Halifax: Report of the Westray Mine Public Inquiry. Vol. 2, 1997). Hereafter, *Westray Inquiry*. Part of the summary is also from Shugarman 2003. The quotation is from the Preface to Westray Inquiry.

2.    *Westray Inquiry*, Ibid. p.491.

3.    Chris MacDonald, Peter Loewen and Daniel Rubenson, "Public Perceptions of the Ethics of Canada's Political Leaders" (module of the Local Parliament Project 2015 Survey, Ted Rogers Leadership Centre, Ryerson University, 2015), http://www.ryerson.ca/content/dam/trlc/pdf/ethicssurvey2015.pdf.

4.    Fournier, "Talk is Cheap," 11.

5.    See Grayling, *Towards the Lights*.

6.    See Greene, *Charter of Rights and Freedoms*.

7.    See Bibby, *Bibby Report*.

8.    In 2015, the Prime Minister Justin Trudeau's Office released a document entitled "Open and Accountable Government," which could be considered a code of ethics for cabinet ministers. However, this document is not a code of ethics for the Liberal Party. It applies only to cabinet ministers, has no enforcement mechanism, and is top-down rather than bottom-up. The arbiter of whether the code has been adhered to is the prime minister himself, rather than an independent official. As a result, the prime minister was criticized for failing to adhere to his own code of conduct, especially with regard to "cash for access" fundraisers. Perhaps this document will become a forerunner for a genuine and effective code of conduct for the Liberal Party. Accessed December 14, 2016, http://pm.gc.ca/eng/news/2015/11/27/open-and-accountable-government.

9.    Michael Oliveira, Canadian Press, "Tory Staffer Sentenced to Nine Months in Robocall Scandal," *Globe and Mail*, November 19, 2014, http://www.theglobeandmail.com/news/politics/michael-sona-convicted-in-robocalls-voter-fraud-scandal-faces-sentencing-today/article21646553/; and Diana Mehta, Canadian Press, "Ex-Tory Staffer Michael Sona's Sentence Upheld in Robocalls Case," June 9, 2016, https://www.thestar.com/news/canada/2016/06/09/ex-tory-staffer-michael-sonas-sentence-upheld-in-robocalls-case.html.

10.    Hiebert, "A Code of Ethics for Political Parties."

11.    Kornberg, *Canadian Legislative Behavior*.

12.    Mancuso, *Ethical World of British MPs*, 51.

13.    Office of the Auditor General of Canada, "Chapter 2: Accountability and Ethics in Government," in *Report of the Auditor General of Canada to the House of Commons* (Ottawa: Office of the Auditor General, November 2003).

14.    *Canada, Report of the Auditor General of Canada to the House of Commons*. Office of the Auditor General of Canada (Ottawa, Vol 1, May 1995).

15.    Manitoba, Office of the Auditor General, *Manitoba's Framework for an Ethical Environment*, (Office of the Auditor General, March 2014), http://www.oag.mb.ca/wp-content/uploads/2014/03/Chapter-7-MB-Framework-for-an-Ethical-Environment-Web.pdf.

16.    We announce here a potential conflict of interest: several of us are members of York University's Collegium for Practical Ethics.

17.    Dewey, "Philosophy and Education," 297.

18.    Thompson, *Practical Ethics and Public Office*, 40 ff.

19.    Health Canada, "Commission of Inquiry on the Blood System in Canada (Krever

Commission)," last modified November 26, 2008, http://www.hc-sc.gc.ca/ahc-asc/activit/krever-eng.php.

20. Kernaghan and Langford, *Responsible Public Servant*, 215.

21. Greene and Shugarman, *Honest Politics* (1997), 209–10; MacDonald, "Referendums and Federal General Elections in Canada"; and McCormick, "Provision for the Recall of Elected Officials."

22. Gwyn, "Endless Enquiries Smother Common Sense with Legalisms." For a comprehensive look at the pros and cons of commissions of inquiry see Manson and Mullan, op.cit.

23. Langford and Tupper, *Corruption, Character and Confuct*, 16, 17. The case for adding institutionalized checks on our governors does not depend on choosing between a larger or a smaller state. It calls for re-orienting the structures and processes of government to make them more democratic. In this regard more generally, see Albo, Langille, and Panitch, eds., *A Different Kind of State?*

24. *Globe and Mail*, August 21, 1996, A1.

25. As work was underway on this edition, we learned of the passing of Warren Allmand on December 7, 2016.

26. *Toronto Star*, September 19, 1995, A19.

27. Christ Cobb, "Harper's Former Legal Adviser 'Taken Aback' When PM Rejected Advice on Duffy's Residency Qualifications," *Postmedia News*, August 20, 2015, http://news.nationalpost.com/news/canada/canadian-politics/harpers-former-legal-adviser-taken-aback-when-pm-rejected-advice-on-duffys-residency-qualifications; Cameron MacIntosh, "Mike Duffy Trial: Who is Benjamin Perrin?" *CBC News*, August 20, 2015, http://www.cbc.ca/news/politics/mike-duffy-trial-who-is-benjamin-perrin-1.3198633; Canadian Press, "Ben Perrin, Ex-PMO Lawyer, Says Tories Have Lost Moral Authority to Govern," *CBC News*, October 18, 2015, http://www.cbc.ca/news/politics/canada-election-2015-perrin-conservatives-govern-1.3277130.

28. Steven Chase and Tavia Grant, "Statistics Canada Chief Falls on Sword over Census," *Globe and Mail*, July 21, 2010, http://www.theglobeandmail.com/news/politics/statistics-canada-chief-falls-on-sword-over-census/article1320915/.

29. On democratic character see Putnam, *Making Democracy Work*; Putnam, "Bowling Alone"; Kateb, "Moral Distinctiveness of Representative Democracy"; and Rainer Knopff, "Courts and Character" (presented at the annual meeting of the Canadian Political Science Association, Brock University, June 2–4, 1996).

30. Held, "Mothering versus Contract."

31. From the perspective of Jean Piaget's study of child psychology, an acceptance of mutual respect tends to occur between the ages of eight and twelve. David Richards describes this age as a time when "there evolves mutual respect between equals: respect based on the feelings that others are equally competent in the exercise of their moral capacities of judging and acting in terms of 'the norm of reciprocity and objective discussion'" (Richards, *Theory of Reasons for Action*, quoting Piaget, *Moral Judgment of the Child*).

32. Sniderman, *Personality and Democratic Politics*.

33. Pateman, *Participation and Democratic Theory*.

34. Zussman and Jabes, *Vertical Solitude* 1989.

# SELECTED REFERENCES

Adorno, Theodore, et al. *The Authoritarian Personality.* New York: Norton, 1969.

Albo, Greg, David Langille, and Leo Panitch, eds. *A Different Kind of State? Popular Power and Democratic Administration.* Toronto: Oxford University Press, 1993.

Aucoin, Peter. *The New Public Management: Canada in Comparative Perspective.* Montreal: Institute for Research on Public Policy, 1995.

Auditor General of Canada. "Chapter 3 – The Sponsorship Program," and "Chapter 4 – Advertising Activities, in November Report of the Auditor General of Canada." Office of the Auditor General of Canada, November 2003. http://www.oag-bvg.gc.ca/internet/English/parl_oag_200311_e_1126.html.

Auditor General of Canada. "Ethics and Fraud Awareness in Government." Chap. 1 in *Report of the Auditor General of Canada to the House of Commons.* Ottawa: Ministry of Supply and Services, 1995.

Barclay, Hon. R.L. *Final Report of the Inspection and Inquiry into the R.M. of Sherwood No. 159.* Regina: Ministry of Government Relations, 2014. www.publications.gov.sk.ca/details.cfm?p=79357.

Bashevkin, Sylvia B. *Toeing the Lines: Women and Party Politics in English Canada.* Toronto: University of Toronto Press, 1985.

Bayefsky, Anne. "Defining Equality Rights." In *Equality Rights and the Canadian Charter of Rights and Freedoms,* edited by Anne F. Bayefsky and Mary Eberts. Toronto: Carswell, 1985.

Benjamin, Martin. *Splitting the Difference: Compromise and Integrity in Ethics and Politics.* Lawrence, Kansas: University Press of Kansas, 1990.

Bellamy, Denise E. *Toronto Computer Leasing Inquiry/Toronto External Contracts Inquiry Report.* Toronto: City of Toronto, 2005. www1.toronto.ca/inquiry/inquiry_site/report/index.html.

Bibby, Reginald W. *Beyond the Gods and Back: The Demise and Rise of Religion in Canada.* Lethbridge: Project Canada Books, 2011. .

———. *The Bibby Report.* Toronto: Stoddart, 1995

Black, Conrad. "Over-reaction to Problems Discriminatory." *Financial Post.* March 24, 1988. 16.

Bok, Sisella. *Lying: Moral Choice in Public and Private Life.* New York: Pantheon, 1978.

Brock, David M. and Harold J. Jansen. "Raising, Spending and Regulating Party Finances in the Provinces." *Canadian Political Science Review* 9, no. 1 (2015): 55–74.

Buckler, Steven. *Dirty Hands: The Problem of Political Morality.* Brookfield, Vermont: Avebury, Ashgate, 1993.

Caiden, Gerald E. and Judith A. Tuelson. "Whistle Blower Protection in the USA: Lessons Learned and to be Learned." *Australian Journal of Public Administration,* June 1988, 121.

Callahan, Joan C. ed. *Ethical Issues In Professional Life.* New York: Oxford University Press, 1988.

Cameron, Stevie. *On the Take: Crime, Corruption and Greed in the Mulroney Years.* Toronto: Macfarlane Walter & Ross, 1994.

Campbell, Kim. *Time and Chance.* Toronto: Doubleday, 1996.

Canada. Ethics Counsellor. *Conflict of Interest and Post-Employment Code for Public Office Holders.* Ottawa, 1994.

Canada. Industry Canada. Lobbyists Registration Branch. *Annual Report (Annual Report of the Lobbyist Registration Act).* Ottawa: Ministry of Supply and Services, 1996.

Canada. Senate. *Report of the Special Senate Committee on the Pearson Airport Agreements.* 1st sess., 35th Parliament, 1995.

Carter, Stephen L. "The Insufficiency of Honesty." *Atlantic Monthly* 227 no. 2 (February 1996): 74–76.

Cassidy, Michael, ed. *Democratic Rights and Electoral Reform in Canada.* Vol. 10 of *Research Studies of the Royal Commission on Electoral Reform and Party Financing.* Toronto: Dundurn, 1991.

Cheney, Peter and Dale Brazao. "Moores King of Movers, Shakers," *Toronto Star.* December 3, 1995. A18.

Coady, C.A.J. "The Problem of Dirty Hands." In *Stanford Encyclopedia of Philosophy,* edited by Edward N. Zalta, et al. Stanford University Press, 2009. https://plato.stanford.edu/entries/dirty-hands/.

Cox, Archibald. "Ethics In Government: The Cornerstone of Public Trust." *West Virginia Law Review* 94 no. 2 (Winter 1991–2): 281–300.

Cunningham, Hon. J. Douglas. *Report of the City of Mississauga Judicial Inquiry: Updating the Ethical Infrastructure.* Toronto: City of Mississauga, 2011. www.mississaugainquiry.ca/report/index_pdf.html.

Dahl, Robert, A. *Democracy and Its Critics.* New Haven, Conn.: Yale University Press, 1989.

Devine, Tom and Tarek F. Maassarani. *The Corporate Whistleblower's Survival Guide.* San Francisco: Berrett-Koehler, 2011.

Dewey, John. "Philosophy and Education." In *The Later Works, 1925–1953. Vol. 5, 1929–1930,* edited by Jo Ann Boydston. Carbon-dale, Ill.: Southern Illinois University Press, 1988. 289–298.

Dicey, A.V. *Introduction to the Study of the Law of the Constitution.* London: Macmillan, 1902.

Dimock, Susan, Mohamad Al-Hakim, Anthony Antonacci, Garrett MacSweeney, and Alessandro Manduca-Barone. *Ethics and the Public Service: Trust, Integrity, and Democracy.* Toronto: Nelson, 2013.

Donkin, Marika, Rodney Smith and A.J. Brown. "How Do Officials Report? Internal and External Whistleblowing." In *Whistleblowing in the Australian Public Sector: Enhancing the Theory and Practice of Internal Witness Management in Public Sector Organisations,* edited by A.J. Brown. Canberra: ANU E-Press, 2008. 83–106.

Donovan, Kevin. *ORNGE: The Star Investigation That Broke the Story.* StarDispatches. Toronto: Toronto Star, 2012. http://www.stardispatches.com/2012/10/ornge.pdf

Dworkin, Ronald. *Taking Rights Seriously.* Cambridge: Harvard University Press, 1978.

Elshtain, Jean Bethke. *Democracy on Trial.* Toronto: Anansi, Massey Lecture Series, 1993.

Ellis, Ron. *Unjust By Design.* Vancouver: UBC Press, 2013.

Evans, Hon. Gregory T. *Annual Report 1991–2.* Legislative Assembly of Ontario, Commission on Conflict of Interest, 1992.

———. *Annual Report 1993–4.* Legislative Assembly of Ontario, Commission on Conflict of Interest, 1994.

———. *Annual Report 1994–5.* Legislative Assembly of Ontario, Commission on Conflict of Interest, 1995.

Flanagan, Tom. "Reform's Culture of Concealment." *Globe and Mail.* September 28, 1996. D2.

Fallows, James. "Why Americans Hate the Media." *Atlantic Monthly* 277 no. 2 (February 1996): 45–64.

Fournier, Jean T. "Strengthening Parliamentary Ethics: A Canadian Perspective." Remarks by Jean T. Fournier Senate Ethics Officer, Senate of Canada, to the Australian Public Sector Anti-Corruption Conference. Brisbane, Australia, July 29, 2009. http://sen.parl.gc.ca/

seo-cse/PDF/BrisbaneSpeech-e.pdf.

———. "Talk is Cheap, Time to Fix Senate's Rules." *Hill Times.* June 13, 2016. 12.

Gomery, John H. *Phase I Report: Who is Responsible?* Ottawa: Commission of Inquiry into the Sponsorship Program and Advertising Activities, 2005. http://epe.lac-bac. gc.ca/100/206/301/pco-bcp/commissions/sponsorship-ef/06-02-10/www.gomery.ca/ en/phase1report/default.htm.

———. *Phase II Report: Restoring Accountability: Recommendations.* Ottawa: Commission of Inquiry into the Sponsorship Program and Advertising Activities. 2006. http:// epe.lac-bac.gc.ca/100/206/301/pco-bcp/commissions/sponsorship-ef/06-02-10/www. gomery.ca/en/phase2report/default.htm.

Grayling, A.C. *Towards the Light: The Story of the Struggles for Liberty and Rights That Made the Modern West.* London: Bloomsbury, 2007.

Greene, Ian. "On the Brink of a Crisis?" *Globe and Mail.* February 12, 1988. A7.

———. "Conflict of Interest and the Canadian Constitution: An Analysis of Conflict of Interest Rules for Canadian Cabinet Ministers." *Canadian Journal of Political Science* 23 (1990): 233–56.

———. "Allegations of Undue Influence in Canadian Politics." In *Political Ethics: A Canadian Perspective,* edited by Janet Hiebert. Toronto: Dundurn Press, 1991.

———. *The Courts.* Canadian Democratic Audit. Vancouver: UBC Press, 2006.

———. "The Evolution of the Office of Ethics Commissioner in Canada." Presented at the Annual Meeting of the Canadian Political Science Association. Ottawa, May 29, 2009. http://www.cpsa-acsp.ca/papers-2009/Greene.pdf.

———. "A Case for Personal Meetings with the Federal Ethics Commissioner." *Journal of Public Policy, Administration and Law* 2 no. 1 (2011): 5–18.

———. *The Charter of Rights and Freedoms: 30+ Years of Decisions That Shape Canadian Life.* Toronto: Lorimer, 2014.

Greene, Ian and David P. Shugarman. *Honest Politics: Seeking Integrity in Canadian Public Life.* Toronto: Lorimer, 1997.

———. "Commission of Inquiry into the Sponsorship Program and Advertising Activities, Phase I Report and Phase II Report." *Canadian Public Administration* 49 no. 2 (Summer 2006): 220–32.

Gutmann, Amy and Dennis Thompson. *Democracy and Disagreement.* Cambridge: Belknap Press, 1996.

Gwyn, Richard. "Endless Enquiries Smother Common Sense with Legalisms." *Toronto Star.* September 6, 1996. A21.

Halberstam, David. *The Best and the Brightest.* Greenwich: Fawcett Crest, 1972.

Hampden-Turner, Charles. *Radical Man: The Process of Psycho-social Development.* Garden City, New York: Anchor Books, 1971.

Heintzman, Ralph. "Public Service Values and Ethics: Dead End or Strong Foundation?" *Canadian Public Administration* 50 no. 4 (2007): 573–602.

Held, David. *Models of Democracy.* Stanford: Stanford University Press, 1987.

Held, Virginia. "Mothering versus Contract." In *Beyond Self-Interest,* edited by Jane Mansbridge. Chicago: University of Chicago Press, 1990. 287–304.

Hiebert, Janet. "A Code of Ethics for Political Parties." In *Political Ethics: A Canadian Perspective.* edited by Jane Hiebert. Toronto: Dundurn Press, 1991.

Hobbes, Thomas. *Leviathan.* Edited by C.B. Macpherson. Markham, Ont.: Penguin Books, 1968.

Hutchinson, Allan C. and Patrick Monahan, eds. *The Rule of Law: Ideal or Ideology.* Toronto:

Carswell, 1987. Hughes, Hon. E. N. (Ted). *Annual Report of the Commissioner of Conflict of Interest 1993–4.* Legislative Assembly of British Columbia, Commission of Conflict of Interest. 1994.

———. *Report of the Commissioner of Conflict of Interest 1995–6.* Legislative Assembly of British Columbia, Commission of Conflict of Interest, 1996.

Ignatieff, Michael. *The Rights Revolution.* Toronto: House of Anansi Press, 2000.

Jamieson, Kathleen Hall. *Dirty Politics: Deception, Distraction, and Democracy.* New York: Oxford University Press, 1992.

Jennings, Ivor. *The Law and the Constitution.* 5th ed. London: University of London Press, 1959.

Jones, David P. and Anne S. de Villars. *Principles of Administrative Law.* 6th ed. Toronto: Carswell, 2014.

Juillet, Luc and Ken Rasmussen. *Defending a Contested Deal: Merit and the Public Service Commission, 1908–2008.* Ottawa: University of Ottawa Press, 2008.

Kateb, George. "The Moral Distinctiveness of Representative Democracy." *Ethics* 91 no.3 (1981): 357–74.

Kernaghan, Kenneth. "The Ethical Conduct of Canadian Public Servants." *Optimum* 4 no. 3 (1973).

———. "Codes of Ethics and Administrative Responsibility." *Canadian Public Administration* 17 no. 4 (Winter 1974): 537–41.

———. "Codes of Ethics and Public Administration," *Public Administration* 58 no. 2 (1980): 207–23.

Kernaghan, Kenneth and John W. Langford. *The Responsible Public Servant.* 2nd ed. Toronto: Institute of Public Administration of Canada, 2014.

Kornberg, Allan. *Canadian Legislative Behavior: A Study of the 25th Parliament.* Toronto: Holt, Rinehart & Winston, 1967.

Kuflik, Arthur. "Morality and Compromise." In *Compromise in Ethics, Law and Politics,* edited by J. Roland Pennock and John W. Chapman. New York: New York University Press, 1979.

Laframboise, H.L. "Vile Wretches and Public Heroes: The Ethics of Whistleblowing in Government." In *Do Unto Others: Proceedings of a Conference on Ethics in Government and Business,* edited by Kenneth Kernaghan. Toronto: The Institute of Public Administration of Canada, 1991.

Langford, John. "Acting on Values: An Ethical Dead End for Public Servants." *Canadian Public Administration* 47 no. 4 (2004): 429–50.

Langford, John and Allan Tupper, eds. *Corruption, Character and Conduct: Essays on Canadian Government Ethics.* Toronto: Oxford University Press, 1993.

Law Reform Commission of Canada. *A Consultative Document — The Determination of Refugee Status in Canada: A Review of the Procedure.* Law Reform Commission of Canada, February 1991.

Levine, Gregory J. *The Law of Government Ethics: Federal, Ontario and British Columbia.* 2nd ed. Aurora, Ont.: Canada Law Book, 2015.

———. *Municipal Ethics Regimes.* St. Thomas: Municipal World, 2009.

Liberal Party of Canada. *Creating Opportunity: The Liberal Plan for Canada.* Ottawa: The Liberal Party of Canada, 1993.

Lightbody, James. 1993. "Cities: The Dilemmas on Our Doorsteps." In *Corruption, Character and Conduct: Essays on Canadian Government Ethics,* edited by John Langford and Allan Tupper. Toronto: Oxford University Press, 1993.

Locke, John. *The Second Treatise of Government.* c. 1689. Edited by C.B. Macpherson.

Indianapolis: Hackett Publishing, 1980.

Long, J. Anthony and Menno Boldt eds., with Leroy Little Bear. *The Quest for Justice: Aboriginal Peoples and Aboriginal Rights.* Toronto: University of Toronto Press, 1985.

MacDonald, David. 1991. "Referendums and Federal General Elections in Canada." In *Democratic Rights and Electoral Reform in Canada,* edited by Michael Cassidy. Toronto: Dundurn, 1991. 301–42.

MacEachen, Hon. Allan J. *Members of Parliament and Conflict of Interest.* Ottawa: Information Canada, 1973.

Machiavelli, Niccolo. *The Prince.* Edited and translated by David Wooton. Indianapolis: Hackett Publishing, 1995.

Macpherson, C. B. *The Real World of Democracy.* Montreal: C.B.C. Enterprises, 1965.

Malszechi, Gregory M. "He Shoots He Scores: Metaphors of War in Sport and the Political Linguistics of Virility." PhD diss., York University, 1995.

Mancuso, Maureen. *The Ethical World of British MPs.* Montreal: McGill-Queen's University Press, 1995.

Mancuso, Maureen, Michael Atkinson, André Blais, Ian Greene and Neil Nevitte. *A Question of Ethics: Canadians Speak Out About Their Politicians.* Oxford University Press Canada, 2006.

Marchak, Patricia. *Ideological Perspectives on Canada.* Toronto: McGraw-Hill, 1981.

Martin, Lawrence. *Iron Man, The Defiant Reign of Jean Chrétien.* Toronto: Viking, 2003.

McCormick, Peter. "Provision for the Recall of Elected Officials: Parameters and Prospects." In *Democratic Rights and Electoral Reform in Canada,* edited by Michael Cassidy. Toronto: Dundurn, 1991.

McDonald, David C. *Report of the Commission of Inquiry Concerning Certain Activities of the Royal Canadian Mounted Police.* Ottawa: Ministry of Supply and Services, 1981.

McLeod, D. G. *Annual Report 1994.* Saskatchewan, Conflict of Interest Commissioner, 1995.

McQuaig, Linda. *The Wealthy Banker's Wife: The Assault on Equality in Canada.* Toronto: Penguin Books, 1993.

———. *Shooting the Hippo: Death By Deficit and Other Canadian Myths.* Toronto: Penguin Books, 1996.

Mendelsohn, Jenny. "Calling the Boss or Calling the Press: A Comparison of British and American Responses to Internal and External Whistleblowing." *Washington University Global Studies Law Review* 8 no. 4 (2009): 723–45.

Miceli, Janet P. and Maria P. Near. "Organizational Dissonance: The Case of Whistle-Blowing." *Journal of Business Ethics* 4 no. 1 (1985): 1–16.

Mill, John Stuart. *Utilitarianism, On Liberty and Considerations On Representative Government.* Toronto: J. M. Dent and Sons Ltd, 1972.

Mittelstaedt, Martin. "Gigantes Resigns as Housing Minister." *Globe and Mail.* August 19, 1994. A1.

Montesquieu, Baron de. *The Spirit of the Laws.* Rev. ed. New York: Colonial Press, 1990.

Nacht, David. "The Iran-Contra Affair." In *Ethics and Politics: Cases and Comments,* 2nd ed. edited by Amy Gutmann and Dennis Thompson. Chicago: Nielson-Hall Publishers, 1990.

Nielsen, Eric. *The House Is Not a Home.* Toronto: Macmillan, 1989.

Newfoundland and Labrador, House of Assembly. *Annual Report of the Commissioner of Members' Interests, 1993–4.* 1994.

Newfoundland and Labrador, House of Assembly. *Annual Report of the Commissioner of Members' Interests, 1994–5.* 1995.

O'Connor, Dennis R. *Report of the Events Relating to Maher Arar: Analysis and Recommendations*. Ottawa: Commission of Inquiry Into the Actions of Canadian Officials in Relation to Maher Arar, 2006. www.publications.gc.ca/site/eng/9.688875/publication.html.

Ogata, Ken, Naomi Couto, and Ian Greene. "Rob Ford and the End of Honour." *The Innovation Journal: The Public Sector Innovation Journal* 19 no. 3 (2014): article 4. http://www.innovation.cc/discussion-papers/19_3_5_ogata_ford-manuscript499i.pdf.

Oliphant, Jeffrey J. *Report of the Commission of Inquiry into Certain Allegations Respecting Business and Financial Dealings Between Karlheinz Schreiber and the Right Honourable Brian Mulroney*. Ottawa: Government of Canada Publications, 2010. http://publications.gc.ca/site/archivee-archived.html?url=http://publications.gc.ca/collections/collection_2010/bcp-pco/CP32-92-3-2010-eng.pdf.

Organization for Economic Cooperation and Development. *Implementing the OECD Principles for Transparency and Integrity in Lobbying*. Vol. 3 of *Lobbyists, Governments and Public Trust*. Paris: OECD Publishing, 2014. http://www.oecd-ilibrary.org/governance/lobbyists-governments-and-public-trust-volume-3_9789264214224-en.

Osborne, David and Ted Gaebler. *Reinventing Government: How the Entrepreneurial Spirit is Transforming the Public Sector*. Reading, Mass.: Addison-Wesley, 1992.

Parker, William D. *Commission of Inquiry into the Facts of Allegations of Conflict of Interest Concerning the Honourable Sinclair M. Stevens*. Ottawa: Ministry of Supply and Services, 1987.

Pateman, Carole. *Participation and Democratic Theory*. Cambridge: Cambridge University Press, 1970.

Piaget, Jean. *Moral Judgement of the Child*. Translated by M. Gabian. New York: Collier, 1932.

Polyviou, Ployvios G. *The Equal Protection of the Laws*. London: Duckworth, 1980.

Pross, A. Paul. "Law and Innovation: The Incremental Development of Canadian Lobby Regulation." In *The Evolving Physiology of Government: Canadian Public Administration in Transition*, edited by O.P. Dwivedi, Timothy Mau, and Byron Sheldrick. Ottawa: Carleton University Press, 2009.

Pross, A. Paul and Robert Shepherd. "Something Borrowed, Something New: Lobby Legislation and Regulation at the Provincial Level." *Canadian Public Administration*. 60 no. 2 (forthcoming).

Putnam, Robert. "Bowling Alone: America's Declining Social Capital." *Journal of Democracy* 6 (1995): 65–78.

———. *Making Democracy Work*. Princeton: Princeton University Press, 1993.

Rand, Ayn. *Philosophy, Who Needs It*. Indianapolis: Bobbs-Merril, 1982.

Rawls, John. *A Theory of Justice*. Cambridge: Harvard University Press, 1971.

Richards, David J. A *Theory of Reasons for Action*. Oxford: Oxford University Press, 1971.

Russell, Peter H. and Jacob S. Ziegel. "Federal Judicial Appointments: An Empirical Test of the First Mulroney Governments Appointments and the New Judicial Advisory Committees." University Toronto Law Journal 41 no. 1 (1991): 4–37.

Rynard, Paul and David Shugarman, eds. *Cruelty and Deception: The Controversy Over Dirty Hands*. Broadview Press, 2000.

Sartre, Jean-Paul. "Dirty Hands." In *No Exit and Three Other Plays*, translated by Lionel Abel. New York: Vintage Books, 1955.

Savoie, Donald J. *What is Government Good At? A Canadian Answer*. Montreal and Kingston: McGill-Queen's University Press, 2015.

Sawatsky, John. *The Insiders*. Toronto: McClelland & Stewart, 1987.

Sheppard, Robert. "Why Fault Politicians for Trying to Mediate?" *Globe and Mail.* August 11, 1994. A23.

Shugarman, David P. "Commentary." In *Commissions of Inquiry: Praise or Reappraise?,* edited by Allan Manson and David Mullan. Toronto: Irwin Law Inc., 2003. 127–43.

———. "Ideology and the Charter." In *Federalism and Political Community: Essays In Honour of Donald Smiley,* edited by David P. Shugarman and Reg Whitaker. Peterborough: Broadview Press, 1989. 307–26.

———. "The Use and Abuse of Politics." In *Moral Expertise: Studies In Practical and Professional Ethics,* edited by Don MacNiven. London: Routledge, 1990.

Simpson, Jeffrey. *The Spoils of Power: The Politics of Patronage.* Toronto: W. Collins, 1988.

Slayton, Philip. *Lawyers Gone Bad: Money, Sex and Madness in Canada's Legal Profession.* Toronto : Penguin Canada, 2008.

———. *Mayors Gone Bad.* Toronto: Viking/Penguin, 2015.

Smith, David E. "Patronage in Britain and Canada: An Historical Perspective." *Journal of Canadian Studies* 22 no. 2 (Summer 1987): 34–54.

Smith, T.V. "Compromise: Its Context and Limits." *Ethics* 53 no. 1 (1942) 1–13.

Sniderman, Paul. *Personality and Democratic Politics.* Berkeley: University of California Press, 1975.

Sniderman, Paul, Peter Russell, Joseph Fletcher, Philip Tetlock, and D.A. Northrup. "The Psychological Foundations of Prejudice: The Case of Anti-Semitism in Quebec." *Canadian Review of Sociology and Anthropology* 30 no. 2 (May 1993): 242–70.

Sniderman, Paul, Peter Russell, Joseph Fletcher and Philip Tetlock. *The Clash of Rights.* New Haven: Yale University Press, 1996.

Stanbury, W. T. *Money In Politics: Financing Federal Parties and Candidates in Canada.* Vol. 1 of *Research Studies of the Royal Commission on Electoral Reform and Party Financing.* Toronto: Dundurn Press, 1991.

Stark, Andrew. "A 'Political-Discourse' Analysis and the Debate Over Canada's Lobbying Legislation." *Canadian Journal of Political Science* 25 no. 3 (September 1992): 513–34.

Starr, Michael and Mitchell Sharp, Co-Chairmen. *Ethical Conduct in the Public Sector.* Task Force on Conflict of Interest. Ottawa: Ministry of Supply and Services, 1984.

Stenning, Philip C. *Accountability for Criminal Justice.* Toronto: University of Toronto Press, 1995.

Sutherland, S.L. "The Problem of Dirty Hands in Politics: Peace in the Vegetable Trade." *Canadian Journal of Political Science* 28 no. 3 (September 1993): 479–507.

Tabuns, Peter. 2013. "Information Commissioner Should Investigate Liberal Document Destruction." *Peter Tabuns Toronto - Danforth.* Last modified April 12, 2013. http://petertabuns.ca/information-commissioner-should-investigate-liberal-document-destruction/.

Thompson, Dennis. "Mediated Corruption, The Case of the Keating Five." *American Political Science Review* 87 (June 1993): 369–81.

Thompson, Dennis. *Political Ethics and Public Office.* Cambridge: Harvard University Press, 1987.

Towhey, Mark and Johanna Schneller. *Mayor Rob Ford: Uncontrollable.* New York: Skyhorse, 2015.

Trotsky, Leon. *Their Morals and Ours: Marxist Versus Liberal Views On Morality. Four Essays by Leon Trotsky, John Dewey and George Novack.* New York: Merit Publishers, 1969.

Vandekerckhove, Wim. "European Whistleblower Protection: Tiers or Tears?" In *A Global Approach to Public Interest Disclosure,* edited by David B. Lewis. Cheltenham, UK: Edward Elgar, 2010.

Vandekerckhove, Wim and M.S. Ronald Commers. "Whistle Blowing and Rational Loyalty." *Journal of Business Ethics* 53 (2004): 225–33.

Vickers, Lucy. "Whistling in the Wind? The Public Interest Disclosure Act 1998." *Legal Studies* 20 no. 3 (2000): 428–44.

Walkom, Thomas. *Rae Days: The Rise and Follies of the NDP*. Toronto: Key Porter Books, 1994.

Walzer, Michael. "Political Action: The Problem of Dirty Hands." *Philosophy and Public Affairs* 2 (1973): 160–80.

Weber, Max. *From Max Weber: Essays in Sociology*. Edited and translated by H. Gerth and C. Wright Mills. New York: Oxford University Press, 1958.

Whitaker, Reg. "Between Patronage and Bureaucracy: Democratic Politics in Transition." *Journal of Canadian Studies* 22 no. 2 (Summer 1987): 55–71.

———. "The 'Bristow Affair': A Crisis of Accountability in Canadian Security Intelligence." *Intelligence and National Security* 11 no. 2 (April 1996): 279–305.

White, Theodore H. *The Making of the President 1964*. Toronto: The New American Library of Canada Ltd., Signet Books, 1965.

Williams, Sandra. "Conflict of Interest: The Experience of the American Congress." *The Parliamentarian* 64 no. 3 (July 1983): 138–45.

Wilson, J.O. *A Book for Judges*. Ottawa: Ministry of Supply and Services Canada, 1980.

Worth, Mark. *Whistleblowing in Europe: Legal Protections for Whistleblowers in the EU*. Berlin: Transparency International, 2013. www.transparency.org/whatwedo/pub/whistleblowing_in_europe_legal_protections_for_whistelblowers_in_the_eu.

Young, Lisa and Harold J. Jansen, eds. *Money, Politics and Democracy: Canada's Party Finance Reforms*. Vancouver: UBC Press, 2011.

Zussman, David and Jak Jabes. *Vertical Solitude*. Halifax: The Institute for Research on Public Policy, 1989.

# INDEX

## A

Abbott, Jim, 224
abuse of trust, 20-21, 40-41, 119-123, 190-198, 239, 300, 316
access to information, 31-33, 112-113, 218, 226, 300-306, 320, 327
*Access to Information Act*, 223
accountability
and responsible government, 44-45
and whistle-blowing, 211-212, 216-217, 224-225
line accountability, 44
methods of holding politicians to, 326-328
ministerial accountability, 44
personal accountability, 328-331
*Act Respecting the National Assembly* (Quebec), 144
*Act to Amend the Conflict of Interest (Members and Ministers) Act* (Yukon), 143
administrative monetary penalties (AMPs), 149
administrative tribunals
appointments to, 66-69
as enforcement mechanisms for breaches of ethics, 243-244, 265
AdScam affair. *See* sponsorship scandal
Afghan detainee issue, 32, 45, 219-226
agencies, boards, and commissions. *See* administrative tribunals
Air Canada, 16, 88, 180
Airbus affair, 16-18, 88, 180
Airbus Industrie, 16-18, 88, 180
Aird, John Black, 129-130
Alberta
and tobacco lawsuit, 112-114
conflict of interest legislation in, 137
election financing in, 87, 160-163
ethics commissioners for, 112, 137
whistle-blower legislation in, 209-210
Alberta Ethics Commissioner, 112-113
Allmand, Warren, 329
Appelbaum, Michael, 100
Apps, Alfred, 194-198
Arar, Maher, 267-270
*Archives and Recordkeeping Act*, 303
Assistant Deputy Registrar General (ADRG), 75, 77-78, 97-98
astroturfing, 199-203
Atcon Holdings, 106-108
Attaran, Amir, 219-220

## B

Baird, John, 105
Balkissoon, Bas, 260-262, 264
Barclay, Ron, 256-260
Barrow, Irvine, 103
Bayne, Donald, 171-172, 174
Begin, Monique, 326, 328-329
Bellamy Report, 260, 262-264
Bellamy, Denise, 262-264
Bentley, Chris, 33
Berntson, Eric, 16
Bienvenue, Judge Jean, 42
Bill of Rights, 213-214
Blencoe, Robin, 109-110
blind trusts, 75-77, 98, 149
Blouin, Pierre, 103
Bok, Sissela, 280
Bonner, Michael, 116-118
Bourgon, Jocelyne, 79
Brazeau, Patrick, 63, 167-168
bribery, 73, 83, 156-158, 168-173, 239, 309
British Columbia
conflict of interest legislation in, 111, 136-137
election financing in, 85-87, 160, 162-163
ethics commissioners for, 136, 153
recall legislation in, 44
bureaucracy, 61-62
Bush, George H.W., 282
Butts, Gerald, 91

## C

cabinet solidarity, 45, 291
Cameron, Donald, 326
Cameron, Stevie, 64, 77, 104, 180
Camp, Robin, 42
Campbell, Kim, 64, 67
Canadian Bar Association, 290
*Canadian Bill of Rights*, 25-26, 29, 213-214
*Canadian Charter of Rights and Freedoms*
and privacy, 275
consistency of new legislation with, 213-216
freedom of expression in, 155
human rights in, 316
impartiality in, 41-42
minority rights in, 29-30
restrictions on third-party advertising in, 82-83
rule of law in, 46-48
social equality in, 24-26,
Canadian Civil Liberties Association, 214-215
Canadian Doctors for Refugee Care, 54-55
Canadian Security Intelligence Service (CSIS), 293-295
Canadian Tobacco Manufacturers' Council, 200
Caplan, Elinor, 128-129
Caplan, Wilfred, 128-129
"cash for access" fundraisers, 159

Charbonneau Commission, 99-100
Chrétien, Jean
and conflict of interest rules, 78-79
and election financing, 84, 157
and ethics legislation, 146
and patronage appointments, 63-64
and Sponsorship Scandal, 100-101, 299-300
City of Toronto, 89, 204, 242-243, 260-263
Clark, Christie, 163
Clark, Joe, 75
Clayton, Diedra, 85
Clinton, Hilary, 89, 283
Code of Conduct (Mississauga), 255
Code of Conduct and Ethics for the Public Service of Alberta, 137
Code of Conduct for Members of Council (Toronto), 246-251
Code of Ethics and Conduct of the Members of the National Assembly (Quebec), 145
codes of conduct and ethics
for cabinet ministers, 146
for journalists, 35
for lobbyists, 182-183, 187-189, 242, 319
for members of parliament, 34, 77-78, 146
for municipalities, 240-243, 246-249, 265-266
for political parties, 38, 87, 124-125, 321-323, 327
for the Senate, 34, 77-78, 146, 169
codes of ethics. See codes of conduct and ethics
Collenette, Penny, 64
Colvin, Richard, 32, 45, 219-226
Commers, M.S. Ronald, 232
Commissioner for

Legislative Standards (Newfoundland), 137
Commission of Inquiry on the Awarding and Management of Public Contracts in the Construction Industry. See Charbonneau Commission
commissions of inquiry, 327-328
Commission municipale du Québec, 244
common law, 48-49, 209, 254-255, 258-260
Communications Security Establishment (CSE), 293-294
Community Charter (British Columbia), 243
conflict of interest commissioners. See ethics commissioners and conflict of interest commissioners,
Conflict of Interest Act (federal), 78, 105, 115-117, 137, 169
Conflict of Interest Act for public office holders (federal), 147-149
Conflict of Interest Act (New Brunswick), 141-142
Conflict of Interest Act (Newfoundland and Labrador), 137
Conflict of Interest Act (Nova Scotia), 144
Conflict of Interest Act (Prince Edward Island), 140
Conflict of Interest and Ethics Commissioner, 78, 105
Conflict of Interest and Post-Employment Code for Public Office Holders, 78. See also Conflict of Interest Act (federal)
Conflict of Interest Code for Members of the House of Commons, 72, 148
Conflict of Interest Code for Public Office Holders

(federal), 147-148. See also Conflict of Interest Act for public office holders
Conflict of Interest (Members and Ministers) Act (Yukon), 143
conflicts of interest
and blind trusts, 75-77, 98, 149
and disclosure of assets, 72, 98, 114-115, 127, 129-130, 132, 318
and disclosure of gifts, 131, 135
and recusal, 129-130, 132, 149,
apparent, 72, 95-96, 109-114, 123, 136
application of rules and guidelines to spouses and dependents, 75-76, 98, 128, 130-131
definition of, 70-71, 97-98, 109-111, 116-118
in municipal politics, 240-241
MacEachen green paper on, 74
potential, 72-73, 96-97
real, 71-73, 95-98, 104-109, 114, 118
types of, 71-73, 95-96
rules, guidelines, and legislation governing 49-50, 71-80, 94, 97-98, 109-111, 114-116, 124-153, 314, 318
Conflicts of Interest Act (Alberta), 112-113, 137
Cormie, Don, 85
consequentialism, 57-58, 270-273, 290-291
constitutional conventions. See parliamentary conventions
Convention Refugee Determination Division (CRDD), 64
Copps, Sheila, 281
Corriveau, Jacques, 19, 100-103
Cosgrove, Paul, 42

Court Challenges Program, 217
Criminal Code, 71-73, 95, 99, 157-158, 239
Cross, James, 287
Cunningham, Douglas, 252-255

**D**

Dahl, Robert, 297
Daigneault, Nancy, 200-201
Davis, William, 127-128
Dawson, Mary, 105-106, 115-118, 147-148
Del Mastro, Dean, 158-159
democracy
    and compromise, 306-306
    and "dirty-handed" politics, 21, 37, 271-272, 276, 310-311
    and election campaign promises, 280
    and rule of law, 46-47
    and social equality, 24-28
    and transparency, 305-306
    citizens' role in, 313-314, 330-331
    compromise in, 307-309
    five principles of, 24-38, 40, 55
    mutual respect and, 21-22, 306, 315-316
    public trust and, 263, 300, 305-306
    representative democracy, 23
Democracy Watch, 301
Denyes, Martin, 195-196
Department of Justice, 213-218, 222
*Department of Justice Act*, 213-216
Department of National Defence (DND), 221-222
Devine, Grant, 16
Dewey, John, 324-325
Dingwall, David, 91-92
"dirty-handed" politics
    and consequentialism, 270-273, 290-291
    and democracy, 21, 37, 271-272, 276, 310-
311
    and election campaign advertising, 282-284, 321
    and election campaign promises, 279-282
    and integrity, 37, 270, 321
    and morality, 272-274, 276
    and power, 271-273
    and surveillance, 275, 284-285, 284-295
    and war, 276-279, 280
    definition of, 21
disinformation, 268-269
document leaks. *See* media leaks
Dodek, Adam, 218
*Dominion Elections Act*, 81-82
Donahue, Gerry, 172
due process violations, 225-227
Duffy, Mike, 33, 63, 156, 167-177, 329-330
Dukakis, Michael, 282
Dworkin, Ronald, 31

**E**

Eberle, Kevin, 256-260
*Election Expenses Act*, 82-83
election campaign promises, 37-38, 279-282
election campaign advertising, 282-284, 321
election financing
    contribution limits, 158, 318-319
    corporate contributions, 157, 160, 162-163, 318
    donations, 156-158
    expense reimbursements, 156-157
    fundraising events, 159, 161, 204-205, 218-219
    individual contributions, 83-87, 157, 160-163
    regulation of, 81-84, 154-155
    spending limits, 158, 160, 162-163
    third-party advertising, 82-83
    transparency of, 158-159, 165-166
    union contributions, 157, 160, 162-163, 318
Ellis, Ron, 68
Ellsberg, Daniel, 285
Emerson, David, 19-20, 327
Employment and Social Development Canada. *See* Human Resources and Skills Development Canada (HRSDC)
Employment Insurance quotas documents leak, 227-234
entitlement of public officials, 119-123, 246-260, 314
Environment Canada, 300-301
Environmental Law Clinic at the University of Victoria, 301
ethics
    and journalism, 35-37
    and making ethical judgements, 53-58
    audits, 324
    cultural adoption of, 203-204, 211-212, 226, 234-236, 265-266, 314, 320-321
    education, 324-325
    in municipal politics, 237-266, 320
    legislation, 51-52, 314, 321
    rules-based approach, 177-178
    supports, 58-59
    values-based approach, 177-178
Ethics and Conflict of Interest Code for Senators, 149-150
ethics commissioners and conflict of interest commissioners,
    duties and powers of, 124-126, 135-136, 150-152, 318, 320
    federal, 78, 146-147
    in Alberta, 137

in British Columbia,
136-137
in Manitoba, 143
in New Brunswick, 141-
142
in Northwest Territories,
139
in Nova Scotia, 144
in Ontario, 98, 130-132,
134-135, 125-126
in Saskatchewan, 138-139
in Yukon, 143
selection of, 152
Ethics Counsellor, 77-78
Evans, Gregory, 34, 109, 132,
134, 164
expense claim abuse and
regulation, 89-92, 119-
120, 134-135, 156, 319.
*See also* Senate

**F**

Faist, Peter, 304
Fallows, James, 35-36
Fasken Martineau, 194-198
*Federal Accountability Act*,
147-149
Finley, Diane, 50, 104-106,
228-229
Fontaine, René, 129
Fontana, Joe, 121-122
Ford, Rob, 246-252
formal equality, 24-25
Fournier, Jean, 147, 149-150, 176
Fraser, John, 180
Fraser, Paul, 113
fraud, 16-19, 99-104, 119-
123, 138, 168-174
freedom of expression, 31-36,
155, 209
*Freedom of Information and
Protection of Privacy Act*
(Ontario), 303
freedom of information and
privacy laws, 33, 303
Front de Liberation du
Quebec (FLQ), 287

**G**

Gagliano, Alfonso, 19, 101
Galati, Rocco, 67, 294
Gallant, Cheryl, 224
gender equality, 27-28

Geneva Conventions, 220,
222, 224,
Getty, Don, 84, 137
Geurgis, Helena, 114-115
Gigantes, Evelyn, 133
Gillespie, Allistair, 75
Glémaud, Patrick, 183-190
Goldwater, Barry, 274-275
Gomery, John, 18-19, 101-
102
Gomery Commission, 18-19,
101-102, 210
Goodale, Ralph, 101
Goodyear, Gary, 184
Graham, Alan, 106-108
Graham, Shawn, 106-108
Graves, Frank, 88, 180
Green Power Generation,
183-190
Greene, Ian, 34, 35
Griffiths, Jeff, 261-262
GST election-promise
reversal, 37, 279-281
Guité, Charles, 101-103

**H**

Ha, Tu Thanh, 54
Hackland, Charles, 250
Halberstram, David, 274
Harb, Mac, 167-168
Harper, Stephen
and appointment of ethics
commissioner, 147
and cuts to refugee health
care, 54-55
and David Emerson
affair, 20
and election spending
limits, 158-159
and Maher Arar apology,
269-270
and muzzling of
federal government
scientists, 300-302
and patronage
appointments, 43,
63-67
and Senate expenses
scandal, 33, 167-170,
329-330
Harris, Mike, 68, 83, 161,
163-164
Hawkes, Robert, 112-114

Hees, George, 53
Heintzman, Ralph, 178
Hiebert, Janet, 322
Hillier, Rick, 219
Hobbes, Thomas, 276
Holland, Mark, 184
honesty. *See* integrity
Hughes, E.N. (Ted), 51-52,
108-110, 136, 143
Human Resources and Skills
Development Canada
(HRSDC), 227-234
human rights, 23-24, 29-30,
219-220, 225, 316, 325, 330

**I**

Iacobucci, Frank, 113
impartiality
definition of, 41-42
and duty of fairness,
48-49
and ideological
preference, 66-68
in journalism, 35
and judicial process, 42,
46-48, 315
and patronage, 42-43, 62-
63, 317-318
and responsible
government, 47-48
and term positions, 68
Information and Privacy
Commissioner of Ontario
(IPC), 303-304
integrity, 37-38, 211-212, 236,
307-310
*Integrity Act* (Nunavut), 142
integrity commissioners. *See*
ethics commissioners
and conflict of interest
commissioners
Intentionalist ethics, 57-58
Iran-Contra scandal, 295-297

**J**

Jaffer, Rahim, 115, 183-190
Jean, Brian, 184
Jennings, Marlene, 184
Johnson, Lyndon, 279-280
Joint Committee of the
Senate and House of
Commons on a Code of
Conduct, 34

Jones, David P., 49, 139, 143
JSS Barristers of Calgary, 112-113

**K**

Kant, Immanuel, 22
Kateb, George, 330-331
Keable Inquiry, 292
Kennedy-Glans, Donna, 45
Kenney, Jason, 116, 229
Kent, Peter, 105
Kernaghan, Kenneth, 44, 53-54, 74, 177
kickbacks, 18-19, 102-103, 172-176, 193
Klees, Frank, 196-197
Klein, Ralph, 114
Kornberg, Allan, 322
Kouvalis, Nick, 283-284
Kuflik, Arthur, 307-308

**L**

Lam, David, 84
Langford, John W., 44, 53-54, 177-178, 328
Laporte, Pierre, 287
Laskin, Bora, 289-290
Lavigne, Raymond, 63, 119-120
Law Reform Commission of Canada, 64
Le Hir, Richard, 50
leaked documents. *See* media leaks
LeBreton, Marjorie, 174
legal agents, federal, 65-66
Legislative Assembly and Executive Council *Conflict of Interest Act* (Manitoba), 143
Leitch, Kellie, 282-283
Liberal Party of Canada
    GST election promise reversal, 279-280
    Sponsorship scandal, 18-19, 78, 100-103
liberalism, 22-24
Livingston, David, 304
*Lobbying Act*, 115, 185, 187-189, 204
lobbying
    astroturfing, 199-203
    definition of, 179

ethics of, 182, 189-190
grassroots, 199-203
indirect lobbying, 199-203
in municipal politics, 241-242
legislation, 180-183, 199, 201-203
regulation of, 87-89, 179-180, 199, 201-204, 319
solicitor-client privilege and, 197-198
transparency in, 180-183, 188-190, 197-203, 205-206
*See also* lobbyists
*Lobbying and Transparency Ethics Act* (Quebec), 242-243
lobbyists
    categories of, 181, 187
    codes of conduct and ethics for, 182-183, 187-189, 242, 319
    increase in, 88-89
    registration of, 88-89, 134, 181, 185-189, 196-198, 241-242, 319
    post-employment rules for, 183, 190
    *See also* lobbying
*Lobbyist Act* (Saskatchewan), 139
*Lobbyists Act* (Alberta), 137
Lobbyists' Code of Conduct, 187-189
*Lobbyists Registration Act* (federal), 88
*Lobbyists Registration Act* (Ontario), 196-198
Locke, John, 47
Lyons, Jeffery, 261-262

**M**

Macdonald, John A., 81
MacKay, Peter, 45, 224
MacEachen, Allan, 74-75
MacFadden, Charles, 103
Machiavelli, Niccolo, 270-275
Mackenzie, Alexander, 81
Mactavish, Anne, 54-55
Magder, Paul, 249-250
Mancuso, Maureen, 322

Manitoba
    conflict of interest commissioners for, 142-143
    conflict of interest legislation in, 142-143
    election financing in, 87, 160, 162-163
    whistle-blower legislation in, 209-210
Maple Ridge Media, 172, 174
Martin, Paul, 32, 43, 101, 146
Martel, Shelly, 297-299
Mason, Gary, 87
Matthews, Deb, 191-193
Mazza, Chris, 191-194
McCallion, Hazel, 252-255
McCallion, Peter, 252-254
McDonald Royal Commission. *See* Royal Commission of Inquiry into Certain Activities of the RCMP
McDougall, Barbara
McGuinty, Dalton, 33, 90, 161, 194-195, 197, 302-304
McLaren, Lorne, 16
media leaks, 113, 229-234, 268-269, 284-285
media's role in politics, 35-36
*Members' Conflict of Interest Act* (British Columbia), 136
*Members' Conflict of Interest Act* (New Brunswick), 106-108
*Members' Conflict of Interest Act* (Ontario), 130-133
*Members' Integrity Act* (Ontario), 132-134
Mendes, Errol, 220
Mercer, Rick, 301-302
merit-based appointments, 61-62, 66-70, 175
Military Police Complaints Commission (MPPC), 32, 220, 222-223, 225
Mill, John Stuart, 31, 57, 310
Miller, Laura, 304
Minister of Public Safety and Emergency Preparedness, 293-294
minority rights, 29-30, 308

Montesquieu, Baronde de, 48
Moores, Frank, 88, 180
Morneau, Bill, 159
Morrison, Lynn, 195-197
Mulroney, Brian
    and Airbus affair, 16-18,
        88, 180
    and conflict of interest
        guidelines, 76-77
    and free trade, 279-280
    and lobbyists registration,
        88
    and patronage
        appointments, 63-64
Mulroney, David, 221
*Municipal Act* (Ontario),
    126-127, 242, 251-252,
    258, 260
Municipal Code (Toronto),
    243
*Municipal Conflict of Interest
    Act* (Ontario), 127-128,
    243, 249-255
mutual respect, 21-38, 46-48,
    51-55, 314
muzzling of federal
    government scientists,
    300-302
Myers, Steven, 141
MyChoice, 200-202

**N**

Nader, Ralph, 92
Nadon, Marc, 66-67
National Citizens' Coalition,
    82-83
National Directorate of
    Security (NDS), 219-220
New Democratic Party of
    Ontario, 280, 297-298
New Brunswick
    and Atcon Holdings loan,
        106-108
    conflict of interest
        commissioners for,
        141-142
    conflict of interest
        legislation in, 141-
        142
    election financing in, 87,
        160, 162-163
    whistle-blower legislation
        in, 209-210

Newfoundland and Labrador
    conflict of interest
        legislation in, 125,
        137
    ethics commissioners for,
        137-138
    election financing in, 86,
        162-163
    news leaks. *See* media
        leaks
1994 Program Review, 79
Nixon, Richard, 284-285
Noël, Simon, 215-216, 218
North, Oliver, 295-297
Northern Ontario Natural
    Gas (NONG) scandal,
    126
Northwest Territories
    conflict of interest
        commissioners for, 139
    conflict of interest
        legislation in, 139-140
    lobbying legislation in, 203
Notley, Rachel, 113
Nova Scotia
    conflict of interest
        commissioners for,
        144
    conflict of interest
        legislation in, 144
    election financing in, 87,
        162-163
    Westray Mine tragedy,
        312-313, 325-326
    whistle-blower
        legislation, 209-210
Nunavut
    conflict of interest
        legislation in, 142
    integrity commissioners
        for, 142
*Nunavut Elections Act*, 142

**O**

Obama, Barak, 282-283
O'Connor, Dennis, 268-269
Oda, Beverley Joan "Bev," 91
Oerlikon, 85
Office of the Communications
    Security Establishment
    Commissioner (OCSEC),
    293-294
Office of the Integrity

Commissioner (federal),
    231-232
Office of the Integrity
    Commissioner (Ontario),
    90, 198, 243, 245
Office of Public Sector Ethics,
    76
Office of the Public Sector
    Integrity Commissioner
    (federal), 116, 214, 216,
    230-231
Old Port project, 85
Oliphant inquiry, 16-17
Olive, David, 36
Ombudsmen, 59, 210, 245
Ontario
    and ORNGE scandal,
        190-198
    and power plant scandal,
        302-305
    conflict of interest
        legislation in, 125-
        136
    election financing in, 83-
        84, 87, 161-163
    ethics commissioners for,
        130-132, 134-135
    municipal ethics
        legislation in, 242-244
    municipal integrity
        commissioners for,
        90, 198, 243, 245
    regulation of expense
        claims in, 89-90
    whistle-blower legislation
        in, 209-210
Ontario Air Ambulance
    Services Company
    (OAASC). *See* ORNGE
    scandal
Ontario Ministry of Health
    and Long-Term Care,
    191-193, 195
Ontario power plant scandal,
    33-34, 302-305
order-in-council positions,
    69-70
ORNGE scandal, 190-198

**P**

Paradis, Christian, 115-116
Parker, William, 72-73, 76,
    96-98, 109

*Parliament of Canada Act*, 147, 149
parliamentary conventions, 134, 140
Parti Québécois, 18, 287
party financing. *See* election financing
Pateman, Carole, 31
patronage
    and government advertising, 43
    and partisan appointments, 42-43, 62-66, 175, 317-318
    and responsible government, 60-61
    and social class, 61-62
    appointments of federal legal agents, 42-43
    appointments to administrative tribunals, 43, 66-69
    appointments to order-in-council positions, 69-70
    in rewarding of contracts, 42-43
Pearson Airport affair, 42
Pearson, Lester B., 74
penalties for breaches of ethics, 142, 149, 204, 250-252, 320
Pentagon Papers, 284-285
Perrin, Benjamin, 170, 329-330
Peterson, David, 128-130
Philpott, Jane, 90-91
Poindexter, John, 295-296
Poirier, Robert, 99
Porter, Arthur, 295
power, 51, 60-62, 116, 239, 241, 271-273
Powers, Vic, 137-138
Praxis, 288
Prime Minister's Code. *See* Conflict of Interest and Post-Employment Code for Public Office Holders
Prince Edward Island
    and Provincial Nominee Program (PNP), 140-141

conflict of interest legislation in, 140-141
election financing in, 86, 162-163
ethics commissioners for, 140-141
Principal Group, 84-85
privacy, 234, 275, 286-295, 297-298
*Privacy Act* (Ontario), 298
Privy Council Office, 79, 213, 301
public debates, 31-36
public disclosure. *See* disclosure
*Public Inquiries Act* (Ontario), 130-131
*Public Interest Disclosure Act* 1998 (PIDA) (United Kingdom), 205-206
Public Prosecution Service of Canada (PPSC), 65-66
Public Sector Expenses Review Act, 90
*Public Servants Disclosure Protection Act* (PSDPA), 210-211, 230-232
*Public Servants Labour Relations Act* (PSLRA), 231
Public Service Labour Relations and Employment Board (PSLREB), 230-231, 234
Putnam, Robert, 330-331

**Q**
Quebec
    and jurisconsult, 144-146
    conflict of interest legislation in, 144-146
    election financing in, 83, 87, 160, 162-163
    ethics commissioners for, 145-146
    municipal ethics legislation in, 242-244
    nationalism, 18, 287
    tribunals in, 244
    whistle-blower legislation in, 209-210
Quebec Provincial Police, 287

**R**
Rae, Bob, 132, 280
Rawls, John, 52
RCMP "dirty tricks" campaign, 20-21, 286-295
RCMP Security Service, 286-295
Reagan, Ronald, 295-296
recall elections, 327
recall legislation, 44, 327
recusal, 129-130, 132, 149, Redford, Alison, 111-114, 120-121
referendums, 327
Regulation respecting the rules applicable to the Ethics Commissioner concerning conflicts of interest and a Regulation respecting conflicts of interest involving the jurisconsult (Quebec), 145
Renzella, Maria, 192
responsible government, 47-48, 60-61
Ricard, Lyse, 149
Robarts, John P., 126
Rob Ford Football Foundation, 246-250
Robinson, Neil, 141
robocalls scandal, 322
Rock, Allan, 65
Roland, Floyd, 140
Rousseau, Jean-Jacques, 31
Rowe, Malcolm, 67
Royal Commission of Inquiry into Certain Activities of the RCMP , 20, 289-295
Royal Commission on Electoral Reform and Party Financing, 83-87, 165, 321
rule of law, 46-48, 60-61, 226, 233, 289-290, 316
Rural Municipality of Sherwood, 256-260
Ryan, Patrick, 107-108

**S**
salary supplements for party leaders, 163-165
Sartre, Jean-Paul, 273-275

Saskatchewan
and communications
fraud, 138
and election financing,
86, 162-163
conflict of interest
legislation in, 138-
139
ethics commissioners for,
138-139
municipal ethics
enforcement
mechanisms in, 244-
245
whistle-blower legislation
in, 209-210
Savage, John, 64-65
Schmidt, Edgar, 213-218, 224
Schreiber, Karl-Heinz, 16-
18, 180
security, 268-270, 275, 286-
295
Security Intelligence Review
Committee (SIRC), 293-
294
Senate
and expense claim abuse
and regulation, 90,
156, 165-166, 168,
171, 173-176. See
also Senate expenses
scandal
and primary residence
claims, 166-170, 173,
176
and use of public funds
for third party
contracting, 166, 169,
172, 174-176
appointments to, 63, 68,
175
code of conduct for, 34,
77-78, 146, 169
conflict of interest code
for, 149-150
ethics officers for, 78,
146-147, 149-150
Senate expenses scandal, 33,
90, 156, 167-177, 329-330
Shapiro, Bernard, 146-147, 149
Sharp, Mitchell, 75
Sheikh, Munir, 330
Sherman, Barry, 159

Sherman, Raj, 112
Shugarman, David P., 35
Simpson, J.G., 103
Simpson, Jeffrey, 64
Slayton, Philip, 122-123
Smith, Danielle, 112
Smith, David, 48
Snarby, Ulf, 180
social equality, 24-28, 308
socialism, 286-287
solicitor-client privilege, 197-
198, 214, 216, 218, 294
Somalia Affair, 31-32
Sona, Michael, 322
sponsorgate. See sponsorship
scandal
sponsorship scandal, 18-19,
45, 78, 100-103, 210,
299-200
Stanbury, W.T., 81
Standing Committee
on Public Accounts
(Ontario), 193
Starr, Michael, 75
Starr-Sharp Report. See Task
Force on Conflict of
Interest
Stevens, Sinclair, 72, 76, 96-
97, 109
Stewart, Jane, 281
Strahl, Chuck, 294-295
Supreme Court of Canada,
appointments to, 66-67
surveillance, 228, 275, 284-
285

T

tainted blood inquiry, 326,
328-329
Tait, John, 79
Tait Report, 79
Task Force on Conflict of
Interest, 75-76
Telford, Katie, 91
Therrien, Sylvie, 227-234
Thomas, Bruce, 122
Tinsley, Peter, 222
Toronto Computer Leasing
Inquiry, 260-264
Toronto External Contracts
Inquiry, 260-264
torture of Afghan detainees.
See Afghan detainee issue

Treasury Board, 110
tribunals. See administrative
tribunals
Trotsky, Leon, 274-275
Trudeau, Justin
and "cash for access"
fundraisers, 159
and electoral reform, 282
and merit-based
appointments, 67-68,
175
and patronage
appointments, 43, 63
and social equality, 27-28
Trudeau, Pierre
and conflict of interest
guidelines, 75-76
and merit-based
appointments, 66
and patronage
appointments, 63
and wage and price
controls, 279-280
Trump, Donald, 36, 282-283
Trussler, Marguerite, 113
Tupper, Allan, 328
Turner, John, 63

U

undue influence
and election financing,
81-87, 154-159, 163-
165, 218-219, 323
and lobbying, 81, 87-89,
203
and Rob Ford conflict of
interest case, 247-249
and Senate expenses
scandal, 166
definition of, 80-81
Unité permanente
anticorruption (UPAC),
99-100, 103
United States of America
and election campaign
advertising, 282-283
and tribunals, 243-244
Cold War foreign policy
in, 274-275
influence on Canada,
277, 286, 289
patronage in, 43
Utilitarianism, 57-58

## V

Vaillancourt, Charles, 172-177

Vaillancourt, Gilles, 100

Valeriote, Francis, 184

Vandekerckhove, Wim, 232

VanderZalm, Bill, 49, 108-109, 136

Vanerply, 107-108

Viinamae, Lana, 261

Villars, Anne de, 49

voting rights, 23, 24

## W

Waffle, the, 286-287

Walkom, Thomas, 132

Wallin, Pamela, 167-168

Walzer, Michael, 275-276

Wascana Village, 256-260

Watergate scandal, 284-285

Weatherill, Ted, 92

Weber, Max, 61, 274-275

Western Guard, 289

Westland, Augusta, 193

Westray Mine, 312-313, 325-326

whistle-blowing
   and accountability, 211-212, 216-217, 224-225
   and employee loyalty, 212, 225, 232, 234-235
   and "speak-up" culture, 211-212, 218, 229, 235, 320
   and the media, 232-233
   definition of, 92-93, 207-208
   internal protective mechanisms for, 211-212, 231-235
   legislation in Canada, 104, 207, 209-212, 233
   legislation in the United Kingdom, 208-209
   legislation in the United States, 208
   and personal costs to whistle-blowers, 212, 217, 229, 235-236
   types of legislation, 209-210

Whitaker, Reg, 61-62

Wilkinson, Neil, 112-113

Williams, Claude, 107

Wilson, Howard, 78

World Class Development (WCD), 252-254

Wright, Jim, 115

Wright, Nigel, 33, 105, 156, 167-170, 173, 329

Wynne, Kathleen, 161

## Y

Yukon
   conflict of interest commissioners for, 143
   conflict of interest legislation in, 143
   lobbying regulation in, 203
   whistle-blower legislation in, 209-210

## Z

Zambito, Lino, 99-100, 104